Contract Law in Changing Times

This collection of essays provides a rich and contemporary discussion of the principle of *pacta sunt servanda*. This principle, which requires that valid agreements are to be honoured, is a cornerstone of contract law. Focusing on contributions from Asia, this book shows that, despite its natural and universal appeal, the *pacta sunt servanda* principle is neither absolute nor immutable. Exceptions to the binding force of contract must be available in limited circumstances to avoid hardship and unfairness.

This book offers readers new comparative perspectives on the appropriate balance between contractual certainty and flexibility in an era of social instability. Expert authors, mostly from East and Southeast Asia, explore when their domestic legal systems allow exceptions from the binding force of contracts. Doctrines discussed include impossibility, frustration, change of circumstance, force majeure, illegality as well as rights of withdrawal. Other chapters consider the importance of the pacta principle in international law. The challenges posed by the COVID-19 pandemic feature strongly in the majority of contributions.

Normann Witzleb is an associate professor at The Chinese University of Hong Kong, Faculty of Law, where he chairs the Obligations Lab Asia in the Centre for Comparative and Transnational Law. He is also an adjunct associate professor at Monash University Australia, Faculty of Law.

Professor Witzleb has published widely on private law, in particular torts and remedies, as well as on privacy and data protection law.

Markets and the Law

Markets and the Law is concerned with the way the law interacts with the market through regulation, self-regulation and the impact of private law regimes. It looks at the impact of regional and international organizations (e.g. EC and WTO) and many of the works adopt a comparative approach and/or appeal to an international audience. Examples of subjects covered include trade laws, intellectual property, sales law, insurance, consumer law, banking, financial markets, labour law, environmental law and social regulation affecting the market as well as competition law. The series includes texts covering a broad area, monographs on focused issues, and collections of essays dealing with particular themes.

Contract Law in Changing Times
Asian Perspectives on *Pacta Sunt Servanda*
Normann Witzleb
ISBN 978-1-032-39788-7

www.routledge.com/Markets-and-the-Law/book-series/ASHSER1252

Contract Law in Changing Times

Asian Perspectives on *Pacta Sunt Servanda*

Edited by Normann Witzleb

Routledge
Taylor & Francis Group
LONDON AND NEW YORK

Cover image: © Getty Images

First published 2023
by Routledge
4 Park Square, Milton Park, Abingdon, Oxon OX14 4RN

and by Routledge
605 Third Avenue, New York, NY 10158

Routledge is an imprint of the Taylor & Francis Group, an informa business

British Library Cataloguing-in-Publication Data
A catalogue record for this book is available from the British Library

ISBN: 978-1-032-39788-7 (hbk)
ISBN: 978-1-032-41486-7 (pbk)
ISBN: 978-1-003-35830-5 (ebk)

DOI: 10.4324/9781003358305

Typeset in Times New Roman
by Apex CoVantage, LLC

Access the [companion website/Support Material]: [insert comp website/ Support Material URL]

Contents

Contributors

Monica Chan
Ms. Monica Chan is a PhD student at the Faculty of Law, University of Macau. She earned her JM from Tsinghua University, LL.M (Arb&DR) from University of Hong Kong, JD from City University of Hong Kong and BA (Hons) in Accountancy from Hong Kong Polytechnic University. Her research interests include technology law and dispute resolution.

Boeun Chang
Professor Boeun Chang is an associate professor at the Law School, Hankuk University of Foreign Studies in Korea. Before joining the Law School in 2017, she had worked as a corporate lawyer for more than 11 years at Kim & Chang. She received her PhD from Seoul National University, her LL.M. from Harvard Law School, and her BA in Law from Seoul National University. She admitted to the Korean Bar, and the New York Bar as well. Professor Chang is a board member (director) of the Korean Association of Civil Law, the Korean Consumer Law Society and the Korea Personal Information Protection Law Association. Her areas of research and teaching interest are contract law, consumer law and privacy law.

Wayne Courtney
Wayne Courtney is a professor and the Vice Dean (Academic Affairs) at the Faculty of Law, National University of Singapore. Wayne specialises in contract law and has broader interests in commercial law and private law. He is the author of two books, *Contractual Indemnities* and *The Modern Contract of Guarantee* (now in its fourth edition), and co-editor of *Punishment and Private Law*. His work has been cited by the apex courts of Australia, Canada, New Zealand, Singapore and the United Kingdom, by the Hong Kong Court of Appeal, and by various other courts. He is a member of the editorial board of the *Journal of Contract Law*, section co-editor (SE Asia) for the *Journal of Banking and Finance Law and Practice*, and a past member of the editorial board of the *Sydney Law Review*.

Wayne is a Senior Fellow at Melbourne Law School, where he teaches regularly. He has been a visiting scholar at Osgoode Hall, York University, the Herbert

Smith Freehills Visitor at the Faculty of Law, University of Cambridge and the Cheng Yu Tung Visiting Professor at the University of Hong Kong.

Stephen Hall
Stephen Hall, LLB (Qld), LLM (Hons) (UTS), DPhil (Oxon) joined the Faculty of Law of The Chinese University of Hong Kong as a founding member and Professor in 2005, after having served as an Associate Professor in law at City University of Hong Kong for three years and as a senior lecturer in law at the University of New South Wales for six years. Professor Hall has been admitted as a barrister and solicitor in Australia, and practised law with the Australian Attorney-General's Department for nine years. His areas of research and teaching interest are contract law, international law, the traditions of the natural law and the common law and European and Roman legal history. Professor Hall's publications include *Ho & Hall's Hong Kong Contract Law* (6th ed, 2022), *Foundations of Contract Law in Hong Kong* (8th ed, 2023), and *Principles of International Law* (7th ed, 2022).

Geraint Howells
Geraint Howells is the executive dean of business, public policy and law and visiting professor of commercial law at the University of Manchester. He was previously the chair professor of commercial law and Dean of the Law School at City University of Hong Kong. He is a former president of the International Association of Consumer Law. He previously held chairs at Sheffield, Lancaster and Manchester and has been head of law schools at Lancaster, Manchester and City University of Hong Kong. He has been a barrister at Gough Square Chambers, London (though not currently practising). His books include *Comparative Product Liability*, *Consumer Product Safety*, *Consumer Protection Law*, *EC Consumer Law*, *Product Liability*, *European Fair Trading Law*, *Handbook of Research on International Consumer Law*, *The Tobacco Challenge* and *Rethinking EU Consumer Law*. He has undertaken extensive consultancy work for the EU and UK government as well as for NGOs.

Siyi Lin
Siyi Lin is currently a lawyer at Fangda Partners. Her practice mainly focuses on M&A, foreign direct investment, private equity and venture capital. She holds an LLB degree from China University of Political Science and Law (2014), an LLM in Chinese Business Law and PhD degree from the Chinese University of Hong Kong (respectively 2015 and 2019). Dr Lin's major research interests are unjust enrichment, trust law, Chinese contract law and tort law. She has published several in-depth research articles in international law journals.

Noble Po-kan Lo
Noble Po-kan Lo holds a Juris Doctor from CUHK. He completed his postgraduate degrees in English literature at HKU and the University of Oxford. He also obtained a Cambridge Certificate in Teaching English to Speakers of Other Languages and a Harvard Certificate in Advanced Education Leadership. He served

as a member of the Senate at OUHK. He is presently a fellow of the Royal Society of Arts, a chartered linguist of the Chartered Institute of Linguists and an ambassador of the Harvard Graduate School of Education. He currently teaches at PolyU College of Professional and Continuing Education.

His interest lies in comparative law. He presented his paper and wrote a column about EU and HK laws at the CUHK LAW's Centre for Financial Regulation and Economic Development. His essay about the law on intoxication was published by the Law Reform Commission of Hong Kong in 2021.

Jianbo Lou

Jianbo Lou is a professor of law, the co-director of the Centre for Real Estate Law, and the coordinator of the Commercial Law Section at Peking University Law School. He earned both bachelor's and master's in law from Peking University Law School and a PhD in law from the University of London. He taught five years at University of Cambridge and has been teaching and doing research on commercial law, property law and financial law at Peking University Law School since 2003. He has published extensively in both Chinese and English.

Célia F. Matias

Célia F. Matias is an assistant professor with the Department of Global Legal Studies of the Faculty of Law, University of Macau. Previously, she was a UM Macao Fellow with the same institution. She holds a PhD from the University of Hong Kong (2021), with a thesis titled 'Rethinking the Limits of Private Justice in the Information Age' and an LLM on Information Technology and Intellectual Property Law (2015) from the same institution. Her prior experience was focused on private legal practice, in both Portugal and Macau, where she has been living for more than a decade. She also holds a bachelor's degree in law (2006) from the Faculty of Law of the University of Lisbon and a postgraduate certificate in business law (2009) from the University of Coimbra.

Kingsley Ong

Kingsley Ong is a partner at CMS Cameron McKenna Nabarro Olswang LLP and an adjunct associate professor at the Law Faculty of The University of Hong Kong. He is a Hong Kong notary public, and is admitted to practise law in Hong Kong, England, and Singapore. Legal directories consistently rank Mr Ong as a leading lawyer in banking law, derivatives, structured finance, securitisation, restructuring & insolvency – the only lawyer in Asia to be ranked in all these categories. He has been described as '*brilliant strategic mind . . . predictions are impressively accurate*' (Chambers, 2022), '*pre-eminent practitioner for unwinding complex structured products in the context of insolvency proceedings*' (Legal 500, 2020), '*revered for his ability to advise on complex financial structures*' (Chambers, 2017). He also actively takes appointments as an arbitrator in arbitrations conducted in English and Chinese, and has particular expertise in resolving disputes related to financial and investment contracts. Connect with him on LinkedIn: www.linkedin.com/in/kingsleyong.

Hanh Hong Pham

Dr Hanh Hong Pham is a lecturer at the Public International Law Department, International Law Faculty, Hanoi Law University, Viet Nam. She graduated with a PhD from Hanoi Law University in 2019. She has over ten years' experience teaching and researching in international law. Her main research areas include the international law of treaties, international criminal law and the international law of the sea. She is the co-author of 'International Law Textbook' published by Viet Nam Education Publisher (2012) and participated in many projects and papers related to international treaties and international law.

Huong Thi Thu Phung

Ms Huong Thi Thu Phung is currently a lecturer at the Faculty of Finance and Banking, University of Economics Business, Vietnam National University. She obtained finance and business administration bachelor's degrees (2014) and master's degrees (2015) from the University of Bedfordshire, UK. She also holds a second degree in law from the School of Law, Vietnam National University (2019). Her major research areas are banking and finance, personal finance and business law.

Joel Slawotsky

Joel Slawotsky is a former law clerk to the Hon. Charles H. Tenney, (U.S.D.J., S.D.N.Y.) and AV peer-review rated (pre-eminent rating) litigator at Dentons. Joel teaches at Reichman University (IDC Herzliya, Israel), where his primary areas of research and teaching focus on corporate and economic governance, international economic law, national security and global governance. He has taught, lectured, and presented at conferences in Asia, Europe, and both North and South America. Publication venues include the Asia Pacific Law Review, Chinese Journal of Comparative Law, Chinese Journal of International Law, Delaware Journal of Corporate Law, Fordham International Law Journal, Georgetown Journal of International Law, Hong Kong Law Journal, Journal of World Trade, Review of Banking and Financial Law, Tsinghua China Law Review, UPenn. Business Law Journal, Virginia Journal of International Law and Virginia Law and Business Review. He may be reached at jslawotsky@idc.ac.il.

Normann Witzleb

Normann Witzleb is an associate professor at The Chinese University of Hong Kong, Faculty of Law, where he chairs the Obligations Lab Asia in the Centre for Comparative and Transnational Law. He is also an adjunct associate professor at Monash University, Faculty of Law, where he convenes the Privacy and Access to Information Group of the Castan Centre for Human Rights Law. He is admitted to practice in the Australian Capital Territory, a barrister of the High Court of Australia and a fully qualified German lawyer.

Professor Witzleb has published widely on private law, in particular torts and remedies, as well as privacy and data protection law. His recent book publications include *Remedies: Commentary and Materials*, 7th ed (Thomson Reuters, 2020), with Elise Bant, Simone Degeling, Kit Barker; and *Big Data, Political Campaigning and the Law: Democracy and Privacy in the Age of Micro-Targeting* (Routledge, 2020), with M Paterson & J Richardson (eds).

Chao Xi

Chao Xi is a professor and outstanding fellow of the Faculty of Law, The Chinese University of Hong Kong (CUHK). He is concurrently the associate dean (Research) and chair of the CCTL Corporate Law and Governance Cluster of the Law Faculty. He also heads the Chinese Law Programme, CUHK's Hong Kong Institute of Asia-Pacific Studies. He specialises in comparative corporate law, securities regulation, financial regulation and empirical legal studies. His research has received significant funding support from the Hong Kong SAR Research Grants Council, among others. He is a Member of the Assessment Panel, Public Policy Research Funding Scheme & Strategic Public Policy Research Funding Scheme of the Hong Kong SAR Government.

Yimeng Ye

Ye Yimeng is a PhD candidate in law at Peking University. Her research interest lies in property law and property theory. Currently she is working on property management from a doctrinal, theoretical and empirical perspective. She earned her bachelor's in law from China University of Political Science and Law, and a master's in law from Peking University Law School.

Yalun Yen

Yalun Yen is an associate professor of law at the National Cheng Kung University. Yalun Yen received a PhD from the College of Law, National Taiwan University and an LL.M. degree from the University of Michigan Law School. She joined National Cheng Kung University in 2014. Her main academic interests involve antitrust law, intellectual property law and financial regulations. She was a research scholar at the University of Michigan Law School from 2011 to 2012. Before embarking on an academic track, she was a partner in Infoshare Tech Law Office in Taipei, who have worked with and represented large corporate clients in Taiwan since 2001. She has also been a member of the New York State Bar since 2012.

Tomohiro Yoshimasa

Tomohiro Yoshimasa has been a professor of law at Kyoto University since 2017. Before that, he was a professor (2016–2017) and an associate professor (2005–2016) at Nagoya University. He teaches civil law at Kyoto University and his research specialisations include contract law as well as the basic theory of private law. His book publications include Jijō Henkō Hōri to Keiyaku Kihan [Change of Circumstances and lex contractus] (Yūhikaku, 2014) (in Japanese).

His latest English publications include 'The Effects of the Corona Crisis on Contractual Obligations under Japanese Law' (2021) 51 Journal of Japanese Law/Zeitschrift für Japanisches Recht 21. His German publications include 'Der Erfüllungsanspruch und seine Grenzen', in: Keizo Yamamoto und Gabriele Koziol (eds), Das reformierte japanische Schuldrecht: Erläuterungen und Text (Mohr Siebeck, 2021) 61.

Part A

Pacta sunt servanda in changing times

1 *Pacta sunt servanda*, the common law and Hong Kong

Stephen Hall

Pacta sunt servanda is one of those pocket-sized maxims to which all lawyers are exposed at the very earliest stages of their academic and professional lives. It expresses what may be characterised as a general legal principle of 'simple consensualism'; i.e. an agreement must be performed in good faith, and any agreement that is not inherently unlawful or impossible is enforceable as a cause of action without need of formalities, or performance by any of the parties.

This understanding of the *pacta* maxim, and the maxim itself, are a legacy of efforts by jurists of the European Enlightenment, building on foundations in the *ius commune* and the medieval canon law who understood simple consensualism to be a manifestation of the general principle of good faith. The goal of the Enlightenment jurists was to preserve the peace by identifying a legal basis for observing international agreements in a new system of sovereign states that accepted no higher institutional authority than themselves. Simple consensualism was absorbed into modern international law and the civil code traditions, but has never been embraced by the common law. Rather, the common law maintains a general requirement of formality for enforceable agreements; in order to be enforceable as a cause of action, the common law contract must observe either the written formality of a deed (evidenced by a seal), or the unwritten formality of a bargain (evidenced by consideration).

Consequently, the *pacta* maxim is not part of the common law. On the rare occasions it is employed by common law courts it serves as an exotic brocade, adorning with a patina of Latin learning the modest point that the common law will enforce some agreements. However, the essentially customary character of the common law makes it adaptive to simple consensualism on a piecemeal basis as the community's sense of justice demands. The recent adaptation in Hong Kong of the defensive equity of promissory estoppel to serve, in certain circumstances, as a *de facto* cause of action is a case in point.

I Origins of *pacta sunt servanda*

The *pacta* maxim is of course expressed in the language of the only ancient civilisation, and the first civilisation in history, that can plausibly claim to have been built on a foundation of law. The same civilisation's juristic accomplishments

DOI: 10.4324/9781003358305-2

have also furnished the modern world with most of its basic legal principles and concepts. Whatever our various genetic ancestries might be, as lawyers we are all descendants of the Romans.

Lawyers are marinaded in a culture that venerates the citation of authority. It is, therefore, somewhat surprising that the source of the *pacta* maxim is never cited. Were a lawyer to focus attention on this gap, he could be forgiven for assuming that the maxim's origins can be traced back to the celebrated *Corpus Iuris Civilis* of the emperor Justinian, that hugely important but highly selective compilation of Rome's juristic works assembled in the early sixth century AD and encompassing the labours of the previous 700 years. Such an assumption would certainly be justified in the case of a few Latin maxims to which modern lawyers are frequently exposed in their education and practice; e.g. *nemo dat quod non habet.*[1] However, as with most of our memorable maxims, the famous three-word *pacta* formulation is nowhere to be found in the Institutes, the Constitutions, or the 50 books of the Digest that make up the *Corpus Iuris Civilis*.

Of course, this is not to say that the Romans did not recognise and apply in practice some version of the principle expressed in the *pacta* maxim. On the contrary, 'Roman law is most highly regarded for its contract law even though the Romans did not develop a theory of contract but only individual types of contracts'.[2]

This absence of a general theory of contract reflected the Romans' aversion to abstract theorising and adventurous speculation, activities they were content to leave to the Greeks. In most of the arts and sciences, the Roman elites were Hellenophiles. Law was a conspicuous exception (along with military practice and engineering). Roman juristic culture was conservative, matter-of-fact and casuistic. Most fundamental legal concepts were taken for granted as being manifested in, evolved from, and satisfactorily justified by the *mos maiorem*, the (real or imagined) customary practices of the great ancestors. In this sense, the Roman jurists were archetypal pragmatists; if it works, it's true, and no further justification is necessary.

In its characteristically atheoretical fashion, the Digest contains numerous passages which employ language that simply takes for granted a highly qualified version of the idea encapsulated in our familiar *pacta* maxim, while focusing pragmatically on exceptional circumstances that preclude enforcement. Probably the passage that most closely resembles our maxim is Ulpian's report of the Praetor's edict in the Chapter *De Pactis* (On Pacts):

> Ait praetor: Pacta conuenta, quae neque dolo malo, neque aduersus leges plebis scita senatus consulta decreta edicta principum, neque quo fraus cui eorum fiat facta erunt, seruabo. (The Praetor says: I will enforce agreements in the form of a pact which have been made neither maliciously, nor in contravention of a statute, plebiscite, decree of the senate or edict of the emperor, nor as a fraud on any of these.)[3]

1 Digest, 50.17.54: No one can give what he does not have.
2 Alan Watson, *The Spirit of Roman Law* (University of Georgia Press, 1995) 22.
3 Digest, 2.14.7.7.

Clearly, this formulation lacks the brevity and elegance of the shorter *pacta* maxim, and is encumbered by contingent features of the Roman imperial legal system. It is hardly surprising that Ulpian's version does not feature in modern legal education or practice. Nevertheless, embedded within it is a recognition that certain agreements (*pacta*) are obligatory, if only because they will in fact be legally enforced.

For the Romans of the Digest, however, a *pactum* was an agreement that did not qualify as a contract. This disqualification arose either because the agreement (i) was made without certain ritualistic formalities; or (ii) did not fall within one of the numerous recognised types of contracts that dealt with certain common transactions, each of which was governed by its own distinct set of rules. There was no Roman 'law of contract', but laws for different types of contracts, just as the common law has no unified 'law of tort' but laws for different classes of torts.

The most common and important formality was *stipulatio*, which allowed a contract to be made where the parties precisely performed, in each other's presence and simultaneously in one continuous proceeding,[4] a ritual spoken formula (e.g. 'will you do [*x*]?', 'I will do'; 'do you pledge [*y*]?', 'I pledge'; 'do you promise [*z*]?', 'I promise').[5] *Stipulatio* was not content-specific, and could create a binding obligation to observe any promise that was not inherently illegal or impossible. It was not the product of simple consensualism because of the requirement of ritual formality.

There was also a host of contracts that dealt with recognised common types of transactions, each of which was governed by its own distinct set of rules. It is possible to consider these recognised types of contract as either *in re* (real) or *consensu* (consensual).

A recognised content-specific contract could be classified as *in re* when, as a matter of contract formation, the law required *datio* or *traditio* (giving or delivery) of a *res* (thing) that was part of the agreement's subject matter. Without *datio* or *traditio*, there was no binding obligation.[6] An important example of a contract *in re* was *mutuum*, which was a loan agreement that was not binding until the lender had delivered the agreed money or fungible thing to the borrower. A contract *in re* was not the product of simple consensualism because of the requirement of *datio* or *traditio*, i.e. performance by one of the parties.

A recognised content-specific contract could be classified as *consensu* when the contract was formed by the parties' agreement, without the need for *datio* or *traditio*. Probably the most common instance of a contract *consensu* was *emptio venditio*, which was an agreement to sell goods in exchange for a real (i.e. genuine or adequate) price in money. Superficially, all that was needed to establish a contract *consensu* was agreement, there being no requirement of either ritual formality or *datio*/*traditio*. However, one should resist the obvious temptation to embrace the contract *consensu* as a product of simple consensualism. As we shall see, at

4 Digest, 45.1.137pr.
5 Gaius, *Institutiones*, 3.92.
6 Digest, 2.14.17pr.

common law the doctrine of consideration establishes a formal requirement of contract formation in the absence of the formality of a deed. Although the Romans did not think and speak in terms of consideration, the various recognised types of contract *consensu* were defined in such a way that consideration/price was built into the agreement's very structure.[7] For instance, an agreement could not be recognised as *emptio venditio* where a vendor had not promised to sell goods or the purchaser had not promised to pay a real price in money. Unless the claimant could bring the defective agreement within another recognised content-specific contract or *stipulatio*, it could not ground a cause of action. Therefore, a contract *consensu* was not the product of simple consensualism because of the structural requirement of formal elements extending beyond mere consensus.

A formal or recognised type of contract could be enforced as a cause of action. By contrast, and subject to some qualifications and exceptions, a *pactum* was 'enforceable' only in the sense that it could sometimes be raised as a defence.[8] Indeed from about the middle of the fifth century BC, *pactum* and related words originally denoted a compromise agreement, i.e. an agreement not to sue. Subsequently, the idea of a defensive *pactum* broadened to include other informal or non-recognised agreements. Generally speaking, therefore, a *pactum* could serve as a shield but not as a sword.

In the seventh century AD, following the loss of the empire's western provinces, the *Corpus Iuris Civilis* sank into obscurity in the former imperial domains. With the qualified exception of Charlemagne's short-lived empire, most of Europe experienced conditions of chronic political, economic and social distress.

It was not until the proto-renaissance of the late eleventh and early twelfth centuries, that the *Corpus Iuris Civilis* was rediscovered in stages from fragmentary copies lurking in various Italian libraries. The Digest's reassembly, a revival of western scholarship, the church reforms of Pope Gregory VII, the gradual strengthening of central political authorities, and the return of urban and commercial life, laid the groundwork for centuries of juristic study. Almost all this work was undertaken by churchmen and/or through the lens of medieval Christianity in monastic, abbey and cathedral schools, and in the emerging universities.

With the restoration of conditions of relative stability and prosperity, the *Corpus Iuris Civilis* became a quarry of materials for the construction of more sophisticated administrations and legal orders in Christendom's numerous post-imperial realms. These included territories that had never or only briefly been part of the Roman empire, and the church itself which was now the only pan-European authority. The church established, or assisted in establishing, universities on the basis that they included at least one of four higher faculties, two of which were dedicated to the study of civil (Roman) law and canon (church) law respectively; the other two were faculties of theology and medicine.

7 WW Buckland, Arnold J McNair and FH Lawson, *Roman Law and Common Law* (2nd ed, CUP, 1965) 221–223.
8 Digest, 2.14. 7.4–5.

First the glossators, and then the commentators and canonists got to work processing the *Corpus Iuris Civilis*, and especially the Digest, in an attempt to understand its texts and identify an ideal law that could serve the needs of high-medieval civil and ecclesiastical life. They approached their task in the prevailing spirit of scholasticism, a method that sought the harmonisation of authoritative texts by the dialectical resolution of apparent textual contradictions, within the framework of Christian theology and philosophy.

In contrast to their humanist successors of the Renaissance in the fifteenth and sixteenth centuries, the scholastics rarely attempted to understand ancient documents in their historical context. This was partly because historical knowledge of the distant past was extremely limited and unreliable, partly because all ancient texts and artefacts were regarded with reverence simply by virtue of their antiquity, and partly because many ancient authors were pagans. The Digest must have appeared especially suited to the methods of scholasticism because of the decree and guarantee, issued by the Christian emperor Justinian himself, that any apparent contradictions in the vast and seemingly inconsistent compilation could be resolved by diligent textual study.[9]

There was no watertight seal separating the labours of the civilian jurist from those of his canonical cousin, each of whom curated a different wing of the *utrumque ius* (the one and the other law). Indeed, in the fourteenth century Baldus de Ubaldis was highly influential both as a civilian jurist and as a canonist. Civilian jurists provided insights for the canonists, and vice versa.

Although the canonists worked primarily with non-Justinianic sources, they were usually acquainted with the civil law and drew upon the Digest and other Roman materials where it seemed appropriate or convenient to do so. Canon law grew into a system distinct from theology largely by exposure of the canonists to Roman civil law.[10] Indeed, the transnational and hierarchical system of ecclesiastical courts that administered canon law were a principal vector for the spread of Roman law throughout western Europe.

By the fourteenth century, the interplay of the civil law and the canon law had resulted in a blend of learned jurisprudence. Many jurists were qualified *in utroque iure* (in both laws), and the blend came to be known as the *ius commune* (common law),[11] being an ideal law theoretically applicable to the whole of western Christendom and influencing the application and development of the *ius proprium* (proper or local law) in particular jurisdictions. In very general terms, and allowing for the inevitability of exceptions, Randall Lesaffer has concisely summarised the distinct contributions brought by the civilians and the canonists to the new common framework:[12]

> Roman law contributed legal technique and sophistication and canon law the general principles. From the rich casuistry of the Justinian collection, the

9 Justinian, *Constitutio Tanta*, 15.
10 John H Baker, *Introduction to English Legal History* (5th ed, OUP, 2019) 135.
11 Peter Stein, *Roman Law in European History* (CUP, 1999) 52.
12 Randall Lesaffer, *European Legal History* (CUP, 2009) 268.

> medieval jurists distilled thousands of concepts, institutions, rules and procedures. The moral/theological foundations of canon law rendered it a less formalistic or technical kind of law and placed the requirements of justice more in the forefront. The great principles of private law that to this day form the common foundation of the great continental law systems were in most cases first formulated in canon law.

It is, indeed, to the medieval canonists that we owe recognition of the modern general principle that all agreements – formal or informal, partly executed or fully executory, and with any lawful object – are to be complied with in good faith.[13]

As we have seen, the Romans of the Digest were not simple consensualists. Initially, this was also the stance of the medieval civilian jurists whose mission was to rediscover, understand, and explain Roman law.

The canonists approached agreements from a different angle. The ecclesiastical courts asserted jurisdiction *ratione materiae* over a range of conduct that fell under the broad rubric of morals and sin:

> Whereas civil normative systems were conceived of and directed toward founding and guaranteeing the commonweal and the terrestrial existence of structures and persons, canon law was charged with creating the best conditions, in this world, for man to avoid losing his soul.[14]

Among the sources of authority for canonical jurists were biblical and theological texts, of which the patristic works of the Church fathers were prominent. A contract involves promises, and it is immoral or sinful to break one's promise whether made formally (e.g. under oath) or informally. This resulted in the canonical declaration that a person who does not adhere to his formal or informal agreement will be 'disciplined by the church', and *pax servetur, pacta custodiantur* (peace must be observed, agreements must be kept).[15]

Before long, the civilians absorbed the canonists' simple consensualism into their own understanding of an idealised Justinianic law for a reconditioned Christian civilisation. A *pactum* could give rise to enforceable obligations provided it was supported by *causa* (cause). This denoted an object that is physically possible and not legally impermissible (e.g. by reason of being harmful to morals or other aspects of the common good): '*Causa* as a legal concept . . . appears to be a sophisticated medieval attempt to generalise the various reasons which led the Roman law to recognise as binding various types of agreement'.[16] Having been

13 Paul Collinet, 'The Evolution of Contract as Illustrating the General Evolution of Roman Law' (1932) 48 Law Quarterly Review 488–494.

14 Manlio Bellomo, *The Common Legal Past of Europe 1000–1800* (Catholic University of America Press, 1995) 75.

15 Pope Gregory IX, *Liber decretalium Extra decretum vagantium*, 1.35.1. The Digest (2.14.1) says that the word *pactum* derives from *pax* (peace).

16 Buckland, McNair and Lawson (n 7) 227.

embraced by both canonists and civilians, simple consensualism figured prominently as a general principle in the *ius commune* of the late-medieval Latin west.

With the rise of sovereign, centralised, ambitious and dangerously powerful States in the sixteenth century, juristic attention increasingly focused on developing a juridical framework to regulate international relations. The question of the bindingness of agreements became acutely important in the context of pacts between State sovereigns who could, after the protestant Reformation and the end of church unity, less frequently appeal to a higher institutional authority in the event of a dispute. This required a new international framework based on, but distinct from, the *ius commune.*

The absence of a generally recognised institutional authority above temporal sovereigns meant that the new framework would emphasise elements of the *ius naturale* (natural law) that had been in the toolkits of the Romans and, to a much greater extent, the medieval canonists and civilians. In the hands of mainly protestant jurists of the Enlightenment, the broad and deep *ius naturale* of the middle ages, that had been steeped in classical philosophy and patristic theology, was narrowed and deracinated into a substantially secularised 'law of nature' or 'law of reason'. The new juristic focus on international relations was significantly intensified during the devastating Thirty Years War and in the wake of the peace of Westphalia, which crystallised the modern State system.

Our familiar *pacta* maxim, or a grammatically identical version of it, made its first appearance in 1672 with the publication of Samuel von Pufendorf's *De jure naturae et gentium* (On the law of nature and nations). '*Pacta servanda sunt*' is the second section heading in the fourth chapter (*De servanda fide*, On maintaining trust) in the third of eight volumes. Pufendorf employs the *pacta* maxim as a signpost to the explanatory declaration that, 'Whenever men enter into agreements with each other, human sociability demands that they be observed as sacred'.[17] Pufendorf goes on to clarify that even entirely informal undertakings must be honoured.[18] Pufendorf's influence on the early development of international law was immense, and his work on agreements substantially strengthened the foundations of the international law of treaties. Indeed, his *pacta* maxim became so familiar that it has been codified as the heading of the provision in the Vienna Convention on the Law of Treaties that requires performance of treaties in good faith.[19]

Pufendorf's pithy maxim represented the culmination of a millennium of juristic evolution from the Digest to the Enlightenment, from a conception of contract limited by formality or subject-matter and part performance, to one requiring only the concurrence of wills to be bound.

17 Samuel von Pufendorf, *De jure naturae et gentium libri octo*, 3.4.2.

18 ibid, 3.5.9.

19 Convention on the Law of Treaties (Vienna, 23 May 1969) 1155 UNTS 331, entered into force 27 January 1980, art 26; see also Hanh Hong Pham and Huong Thi Thu Phung, 'Invoking COVID-19 to suspend or terminate the operation of a treaty', ch 12 (in this volume). See further Vienna Convention on the Law of Treaties between States and International Organizations or between International Organizations, Doc A/CONF129/15 (not yet in force) art 26.

II *Pacta sunt servanda* and the common law

The simple notion of legally binding agreements captured by Pufendorf's *pacta* maxim permeated not only the development of international treaty law, but also domestic systems of contract law. Indeed, Pufendorf's main contribution to treaty law was to transpose developments that had already occurred in the *ius commune* into the emerging realm of international law; he adopted the child and gave it a memorable name.

In the nineteenth century, inspired by the scientism of the Victorian era and the residue of Enlightenment rationalism, movements towards legal codification began to bear fruit on the European continent. The *ius commune*'s streamlined conception of contractual obligation was, subject to some content-specific exceptions, carried over into the new national codes. Indeed, the process of simplification was in some jurisdictions carried further by either dispensing with or eventually abolishing the general requirement of showing *causa*.

The law in England evolved along different lines. While the *utrumque ius* and the *ius commune* were developing on the continent in medieval conditions of relative legal and political fragmentation, England was consolidating as the most unified and centralised realm in Europe. England experienced an early and increasing solidity and confidence of national law and legal institutions, underwritten by a strong centralised government. This cramped the capacity of the learned law of both the civilians and the canonists to exert influence, and the emergent English common law bore fewer marks of Roman law and canon law than any other legal order in western Christendom.

The direct influence of canon law, the mother of simple consensualism, was particularly weak. The common law's borrowings from canon law were few and detached from their doctrinal context. Canon law was, furthermore, confined to the universities and not taught in the common law's own schools: 'To judges, serjeants, and barristers it was "their law" (*lour ley*) – a clerical preserve, remote from the secular world of Westminster Hall'.[20] The limited influence of canon law was further diminished after 1534 when the Church of England was severed from Rome's authority, and the teaching of canon law in England's universities was suppressed.

Political unification came first with the country's conquest by the Normans in 1066, at about the same time that the *Corpus Iuris Civilis* was being rediscovered in Italy. The Normans had come to Normandy from their Scandinavian homeland only a century and a half earlier and had never been subject to Roman rule. The first Norman king of England quickly strengthened and consolidated what was already, by the standards of the time, a highly centralised government. This was done within a framework of Anglo-Saxon and Norman customary laws.

Legal unification began in earnest about a century later with the establishment of a professionalised system of royal law courts that initially co-existed with, but eventually displaced, the non-professional communal courts administering local laws. The royal courts gradually developed, one case at a time, a body of law

20 Baker (n 10) 140.

common to the entire realm, a common law of England. The process was gradual but by no means glacial; the 'common law' was already known by that name in the late twelfth century, and had emerged as a 'fully fledged juristic entity, with its own specialist practitioners, its own technical language and literature, and its own law school' by the middle of the thirteenth century.[21]

Whereas the medieval civil law, canon law, and *ius commune* were essentially learned systems based on theoretical or putatively scientific understandings of authoritative texts, the common law was (and remains) an essentially customary system. A full treatment of the common law's essentially customary character is beyond the scope of this chapter, but for present purposes it is worth noting that an impressive consensus has long subscribed to a vision of the common law as customary or essentially customary in character. As Sir Frederick Pollock observed, 'the Common Law is a customary law if, in the course of about six centuries, the undoubting belief and uniform language of everybody who had occasion to consider the matter were able to make it so'.[22]

Rather than being court-made, the development of common law rules and principles is better understood as court-recognised. This reality has been acknowledged in Hong Kong's Court of Final Appeal:[23]

> Judges develop the common law . . . against a background of the social, moral, economic and political values and assumptions of the societies in which they work. Inevitably, these values and assumptions influence the development of the common law . . . But the values and assumptions of societies are not necessarily the same. This is the reason why the courts of former United Kingdom colonies have legitimately developed the common law of their countries so that it no longer retains its unity with the common law of the United Kingdom.

The common law has evolved over many centuries – first in England and later on every inhabited continent – and finds reflection in decisions of courts determining disputes between litigants. Instead of applying a theoretically postulated or codified rule to a dispute, courts seek to apply the law as derived from the customs, traditions and reasonable expectations of the various communities the common law serves, as reflected primarily in previous judgments. When judicial precedent no longer reflects the changed expectations of those communities, it tends to lose its persuasive force, and the common law rule is judicially qualified, refined, or reformulated (but almost never rejected) better to reflect the new realities.

Much the same is true of the application of common law rules and principles to particular disputes. The civil law tradition as manifested in the *ius commune* and

21 ibid, 34–35.

22 Sir Frederick Pollock, *A First Book of Jurisprudence for Students of the Common Law* (6th ed, McMillan, 1929) 254.

23 *Kensland Realty Ltd v Tai, Tang and Chong* [2008] HKCFA 13, (2008) 11 HKCFAR 237, [2008] 3 HKC 90, [168] (Sir Gerard Brennan NPJ).

its successor code systems employs primarily a process of deductive reasoning, deducing solutions downward from theoretically postulated or codified rules and principles. By contrast, the common law tradition embraces primarily a process of inductive reasoning, inducing solutions upward from the facts of the present case, and the facts and reasoning in earlier cases. Hence the ubiquity in common law reasoning of the reasonable person, whose assessments may vary according to time and place.

For most of the twelfth and thirteenth centuries, the principal means by which the royal law courts could enforce agreements lay in the actions of debt and, to a lesser extent, covenant. An action of debt (as either debt *sur obligation* or debt *sur contract*) lay where the claim was for restitution of a fixed sum or chattels ascertained at the time of contract.

A claimant could bring an action of debt *sur obligation* where the agreement was embodied in a bond. This sealed instrument committed an obligor to pay an obligee a penalty, usually in the form of a fixed sum of money. The simplest case was where a borrower executed a bond specifying his obligation to a creditor. If the creditor brought an action of debt on the bond, and if the debtor could not produce a sealed acquittance or establish a recognised vitiating factor, the debtor would be bound to pay by virtue of the bond itself. There was no need to try the underlying transaction. Indeed, even if the borrower had repaid the money but could not produce a sealed acquittance he would be obliged to pay again. Debt *sur obligation* was capable of serving transactions somewhat more sophisticated than simple loans. The parties to an agreed transaction might deposit parallel bonds with a stakeholder, who would then deliver both bonds to the non-breaching party in the event of the agreement's non-performance. At a slightly higher level of sophistication, and dispensing with the need of a stakeholder, there was the 'conditioned' or 'conditional' bond. Such a bond would state that the obligor was bound to pay the obligee a specified sum unless a condition was satisfied.[24]

In circumstances where the formality of a sealed bond was absent, the claimant might commence an action of debt *sur contract*. Similar to the recognised types of contracts in the Digest, the unsealed debt could arise in an array of commonplace transactions such as loans, sales, leases, hire, and services.[25] By the early fourteenth century,[26] and in echo of *datio* or *traditio* in the Digest's contracts *in re*, the absence of a requirement for sealing in an action of debt *sur contract* led to the alternative requirement that the claimant needed to prove that the defendant had received *quid pro quo*, i.e. a given (and not merely promised) thing or benefit (*quid*) in exchange for the amount of the claim (*pro quo*).[27] As John Cokayne

24 SFC Milsom, *Historical Foundations of the Common Law* (2nd ed, Butterworths, 1981) 250–251.
25 KO Shatwell, 'The Doctrine of Consideration in Modern Law' (1954) 1 Sydney Law Review 289–331, 295–296.
26 *Anon* (1338) 11 & 12 E 3 (Rolls Series) 587.
27 Baker (n 10) 322–323; John Barton, 'The Medieval Contract' in John Barton (ed), *Towards a General Law of Contract* (Duncker and Humblot, 1990) 15–37, 23–37; AWB Simpson, *A History of the Common Law of Contract* (Clarendon, 1975) 153–169, 193–196, 424–426; Kevin M Teeven,

judicially remarked, '*ex nudo pacto nulla oritur actio*' (no action arises from a bare pact).[28]

The alternative action of covenant emerged in the thirteenth century. It existed for the enforcement of obligations in the form of executory promises of future performance, initially in respect of leases of land but soon extending to executory promises more generally.[29] On its face it applied to all consensual agreements, and 'No more could be desired of a contractual remedy'.[30]

The ability of covenant to serve as a basis for simple consensuality in the common law was, however, thwarted by two developments in the early fourteenth century. First, access to the action of covenant was narrowed by a rule that where an action of debt lay it was to provide the exclusive remedy.[31] Second, and more importantly, there arose a rule in the royal courts that an action of covenant could not succeed unless the agreement had been embodied in a deed.[32] This insistence on formality was probably originally intended not as a change in the law, but as a practical means of managing the workload of the royal courts.[33] Provided the claim was for less than 40 shillings, an informal covenant could still be enforced by communal courts. However, the combined effects of monetary inflation and the decline of non-royal courts meant, by the later Middle Ages, that formality was in practice always required in order to bring an action of covenant.

In the early fifteenth century, covenant was encumbered with additional restrictions that made the action even less attractive. It became unavailable where the claim was for non-payment of money, non-delivery of goods, or performance that was either late or imperfect.[34] However, these additional curbs were justified and ameliorated by the introduction, in the late fourteenth century, of new actions for the enforcement of informal executory agreements. In order to navigate around the roadblock of formality in covenant, the royal courts adapted the action of trespass which granted relief for a wide and imprecisely defined range of civil wrongs going well beyond our current use of 'trespass' in tort. Indeed, Frederic Maitland referred to medieval trespass as 'that fertile mother of actions'.[35] Breach of certain informal agreements or undertakings was brought (or smuggled) within the ambit of actions of trespass as 'trespass on the case' or 'special trespass'.

A History of the Anglo-American Common Law of Contract (Greenwood Press, 1990) 11–13; David Ibbetson, *Historical Foundations of the Common Law* (2nd ed, Butterworths, 1981) 80–83; Milsom (n 23) 260–262.

28 (1421) Y.B. Mich. 9 Hen. V, fo. 14, pl. 23.

29 Ibbetson (n 27) 250–251; Simpson (n 27) 9; CHS Fifoot, *History and Sources of the Common Law: Tort and Contract* (Stevens, 1949) 255–256.

30 Baker (n 10) 339.

31 Fifoot (n 29) 258–259.

32 Baker (n 10) 340; RC Palmer, 'Covenant, Justices Writs, and Reasonable Showings' (1987) 31 American Journal of Legal History 97–117; DJ Ibbetson, 'Words and Deeds: The Action of Covenant in the Reign of Edward I' (1986) 4 Law and History Review 71–94.

33 Baker (n 10) 341.

34 ibid, 342; Teeven (n 27) 7.

35 FW Maitland, *The Forms of Action at Common Law: A Course of Lectures* (CUP, 1936) 48.

This species of trespass eventually came to be known as 'assumpsit' because the writ, in recounting the defendant's undertakings, employed the formula *assumpsit super se* (took upon himself). The requirement of formality was dispensed with but, in contrast to covenant, assumpsit was not available to enforce a promise without an equivalent of *quid pro quo*.[36] As late as 1505, the Chief Justice of the Court of Common Pleas remarked in connection with an unsealed agreement by which the defendant had undertaken, but failed, to deliver goods in return for a payment to be made by the plaintiff upon delivery:[37]

> if I covenant with a carpenter to make me a house, and pay him £20 to make the house by a certain day, and he does not make the house by the day, I shall have an action on my case [i.e. trespass on the case, assumpsit] because of the payment of my money; and yet it sounds only in covenant, and without payment of the money in this case there is no remedy.

Furthermore, and reflecting the still theoretically tortious character of assumpsit (*née* special trespass) in the early sixteenth century, the objective of an action of assumpsit was the restoration of the claimant to the position he would have been in had the defendant not made the undertaking or promise, rather than the modern contractual objective of compensating the claimant for his lost expectations.[38]

As England's early modern economic development gained momentum in the sixteenth century and the customs of her communities adapted to a post-feudal order, the common law needed to provide a law of contract in which a defendant's breach of an informal bargain could be actionable without the feudal strictures of written formality or performance on the claimant's side.

Whereas covenant was the progenitor of the modern gratuitous undertaking effected as a deed, assumpsit eventually developed into the modern common law of simple contract. However, before assumpsit's transformation could occur the requirement that the claimant must have given payment for the defendant's undertaking had to be removed.

By the late 1520s, the proper plea by a defendant seeking to resist a claim in assumpsit for non-performance was 'non assumpsit', rather than the trespassory plea of 'not guilty', thereby indicating that the real issue was the existence or performance of an agreed undertaking or promise as distinct from a breach of tortious duty. At about the same time, it became increasingly usual for the measure of an award in an action of assumpsit to resemble modern expectation or performance loss,[39] rather than the restorative relief awarded by reason of a breach of tortious obligation.

From the 1550s, it became possible to say in the Court of King's Bench that 'Every contract executory is an assumpsit in itself',[40] and that 'a promise against a

36 Milsom (n 24) 357; Teeven (n 27) 39.

37 *Orwell v Mortoft* (1505) B & M 407, 410 (Sir Thomas Frowyk CJ).

38 KCT Sutton, *Consideration Reconsidered* (University of Queensland Press, 1974) 6.

39 Ibbetson (n 27) 131–132.

40 *Norwood v Read* (1557) 1 Plowd 180, (1557) 75 ER 277.

promise will maintain an action on the case'.[41] In embracing the idea that an executory promise can support a contractual bargain, the Court of King's Bench was in effect developing or transforming the medieval requirement of *quid pro quo*. This transformed version of *quid pro quo* was increasingly referred to as 'consideration',[42] which implied something conceptually broader than *quid pro quo* in actions of debt. The emergence of consideration marked the transition from semi-feudal assumpsit to early-modern assumpsit and the modern common law of contract.

While early modern assumpsit thrived in the Court of King's Bench, it remained unwelcome in the Court of Common Pleas whose jurisdiction over actions of debt was exclusive. This led to an 'unseemly difference of practice'[43] between the two leading common law courts. It was not until 1602, with a watershed decision in the appellate Court of Exchequer Chamber, that the rift was finally closed in favour of the more pioneering position of King's Bench and the primacy of assumpsit over debt was established.[44]

In making the adjustment to consideration, and remaining true to its essentially customary character, the common law was reflecting rather than imposing changing patterns of English commercial life in the early modern period.

Although consideration was an important advance on *quid pro quo*, it did not represent a radical break. Both *quid pro quo* and consideration reflected the same basic understanding, running deep in England's commercial life, of legally enforceable promissory obligation. The law would not enforce mere promises or undertakings. Nor would it enforce mere agreements. In order to succeed, the claimant was required to show either that the breached promise or undertaking was made under seal, or that it was part of a bargain. A bargain is, by definition, an agreed exchange of something of value. The thing of value can be given or executed (medieval *quid pro quo* and modern consideration), or it can be merely promised or executory (modern consideration).

That the required bargain is not a substantive requirement but a mere formality is recognised by the principle that consideration does not need to be adequate (i.e. a reasonable, fair, or market price), provided it is sufficient (i.e. worth more than nothing): 'A peppercorn does not cease to be good consideration if it is established that the promisee does not like pepper and will throw away the corn'.[45] This principle has been part of the common law of contracts since at least 1586, at which time it was held that 'when a thing is to be done by the plaintiff, be it never so small, this is a sufficient consideration to ground an action'.[46] The unsealed undertaking need not be a real bargain, but it must be in the form of a bargain.

41 *Strangborough v Warner* (1589) 4 Leon 3, (1589) 74 ER 686.
42 The earliest reported use of 'consideration' as a substitute for, or development of, *quid pro quo* is in *Joscelin v Shelton* (1557) 3 Leon 4, (1557) Benl 57, (1557) Moore KB 51, (1557) 74 ER 503.
43 Sutton (n 38) 6.
44 *Slade's Case (Slade v Morley)* (1602) 4 Co Rep 91a, (1602) 76 ER 1072, (1602) Yelv 21, (1602) Moore KB 433, 667, (1602) 80 ER 15.
45 *Chappell & Co Ltd v The Nestlé Co Ltd* [1960] AC 87, 114, [1959] 2 All ER 701, 712, [1959] 3 WLR 168, 185 (Lord Somervell).
46 *Sturlyn v Albany* (1586) Cro Eliz 67, 68, (1586) 78 ER 327, 328.

The common law therefore knows nothing of simple consensuality. In this respect, the common law stands in contrast to the *ius commune*, the civil code tradition, and international law. It does not accept that an undertaking, unsupported by formalities of any kind, can be enforced as a claim. In order to ground a claim in contract at common law, the undertaking must be supported either by a written formality (a deed, of which signing and sealing are necessary evidence) or by an unwritten formality (a bargain, of which consideration is necessary evidence). For Justinian, similarly, a contract claim could be made only where the undertaking was made with ritual formality or as part of a recognised type of content-specific contract supported by performance (*in re*) or a price built into the contract's structure (*consensu*). Thus, the common law stance against simple consensuality is ironically closer in spirit to Justinian's Digest than the other, more Roman-inspired, medieval and modern legal traditions.

The explanation for the contrast between the common law and the other medieval and modern systems lies in a combination of historical contingency and some basic facts of English life.

The most important contingency was the early-fourteenth century jurisdictional requirement of written formality in an action of covenant before the royal courts. Had this not occurred, the common law might conceivably have remained on the path of simple consensuality.

The most important social fact was the early commercialisation of English life in the context of relative political stability and internal peace. England was the first large country to emerge from feudalism, develop a national commercial economy, and a substantial, prosperous, and powerful commercial class and urban population. Under the interwoven and mutually reinforcing influences of the Reformation and the Enlightenment, secularism was perhaps more influential in England than elsewhere in Europe. England would go on to lead the world in the agricultural, industrial and scientific revolutions, and establish the largest commercial empire in world history. In all this, deal-making supported by the King's justice was critical. In England, it was bargains – more than promises or agreements – that were sacred. By scrutinising promises through a more commercial than moral lens, the common law provided further evidence that England was the world's first modern country.

The common law courts very seldom invoke the familiar *pacta* maxim, and when they do it is little more than a rhetorical flourish in support of the anodyne proposition that parties should be held to their bargains. There is certainly no analysis of the maxim's sources, justification, or implications as to formalities. Indeed, the first reported deployment of the maxim in an English court does not occur until 1937, and then only in the briefest possible way to emphasise 'the paramount policy of the law that people should keep faith and fulfil their promises'.[47] The maxim makes no reported appearance in a Hong Kong judgment until 1991, in a similarly brief and inessential cameo.[48]

47 *Fender v St John-Mildmay* [1938] AC 1, 37–38, [1937] 3 All ER 402, 424 (Lord Wright).
48 *Ho Wing-cheong (t/a Hong Leong Securities) v Margot* [1991] 1 HKLR 245, 247 (HC, HK).

Pacta sunt servanda, as that maxim was formulated and published in the seventeenth century as an expression of simple consensuality, is not part of the common law.

III *Pacta sunt servanda* and Hong Kong

Since the United Kingdom transferred sovereignty functions over Hong Kong to the regime in Peking, the former Crown Colony has so far retained its common law legal system. Under the terms of Hong Kong's Basic Law, this is supposed to remain unchanged until at least 2047. As the *pacta* maxim has never been part of the common law, it is not part of Hong Kong's law.

Of course, this does not mean that the common law in Hong Kong and elsewhere lacks a principle supporting the legal enforceability of undertakings. A promise or undertaking is legally enforceable, in the sense that it can give rise to a cause of action, if it complies with the formality of a deed or a bargain. This is similar to the Digest's position that a promise or undertaking was legally enforceable as a claim if it complied with ritual formality (*stipulatio*) or if it involved an executed (*in re*) or executory (*consensu*) price.

However, the famous maxim expressly refers not to a contract, but to a *pactum*. To continental jurists of the Enlightenment and subsequently, there is effectively no difference between a contract and a pact. As we have seen, to the Romans of the Digest a *pactum* was an undertaking distinct from a contract. As a general rule, a *pactum* was enforceable only in the sense that it could be raised as a defence. In this respect, too, the common law is closer in spirit to the Romans' Digest than other, more Roman-inspired, legal traditions.

Where a contracting party makes an informal and gratuitous promise not to insist upon the performance of his counterparty's obligations, the position at common law is that such a promise is *nudum pactum* and contractually void. As we have seen, since the early fourteenth century an unsealed undertaking would not be legally enforceable by a claimant unless supported by *quid pro quo*. This bargain-based understanding of contractual obligation was still very much alive in the mid-nineteenth century when the Privy Council held that a promise not to enforce a bond to secure repayment of a loan could not, absent formality evidenced by a seal or consideration, be raised as a defence against enforcement.[49]

As an essentially customary system, the common law does not stand still. It gradually adapts its rules and principles, and the mode of applying those rules and principles, to comport more closely with the changing customs, traditions and reasonable expectations of the various communities it serves. By the middle of the twentieth century, the earlier refusal to recognise an informal promise *not to enforce* an extant contractual obligation had fallen out of step with these yardsticks. After the socially and economically traumatic experience of urban bombing campaigns in the Second World War, an issue arose as to the juridical effect of

49 *Jorden v Money* (1854) 5 HL Cas 185, (1854) 10 ER 868 (PC).

a landlord's informal promise not to insist on payment of full rent on residential properties that could not be easily sub-let. The earlier rule that would have prevented the effectiveness of such a promise was modified to permit, in principle and subject to conditions, the promise to be raised as an equitable defence to the landlord's claim.[50] However, it was made reasonably clear, and soon reaffirmed,[51] that an informal promise could not provide the promisee with a cause of action. This defence would soon come to be known as promissory estoppel. As with the Roman *pactum*, a promisee could raise the estoppel only 'as a shield and not as a sword'.[52] This limitation remains firmly part of the law in England.[53]

The common law's process of adaptation to social change is continuous, and usually subtle. Where an established rule or principle collides with the community's sense of justice, one of those judicial acts of refinement that causes a case to be regarded as a juridical milestone cannot be far away.

The principle that an informal promise (i.e. a promise not in the form of a deed or a bargain) cannot ground a cause of action was put under pressure in a case before Hong Kong's Court of Final Appeal.[54] The promisor and promisee had been a cohabiting couple for about four years when the promisee accepted the promisor's proposal of marriage. The promisee's infant daughter by an earlier union lived with them. The couple moved into a flat owned by a company in which the promisor owned a majority of the shares. The promisor undertook to give the promisee a 35% interest in the flat as financial security in anticipation of their marriage, and he gratuitously transferred 35% of the company's shares to her. The promisee altered her position in reliance on the promise by continuing to cohabit with him, not pursuing employment opportunities, and paying a mortgage instalment on the flat. Before the couple could marry, the promisor died intestate. The promisee was not aware that the company legally owned the flat until after the promisor's death, and she believed that the promisor had given her a 35% beneficial interest in the flat. The promisor's estate, through the company, gave the promisee notice of intention to terminate the licence by which she occupied the flat and instituted proceedings against her for possession of the flat and mesne profits. The promisee claimed, on the basis of promissory estoppel, an entitlement to a 35% share in the proceeds of the flat's eventual sale and in the meantime that she be allowed to live in the flat as her home. Had the promisor been the legal owner of the flat, the promisee would have had a claim in proprietary estoppel against the promisor's estate. As things stood, however, she was the addressee of a merely informal promise by her deceased fiancé that he would not exercise his powers of control over a third party (the company) in a way that would prevent it from transferring to her a 35% interest in the flat and a right to remain in residence until it was sold.

50 *Central London Property Trust Ltd v High Trees House Ltd* [1947] KB 130, [1956] 1 All ER 256 (Denning J); On similar facts, see *Chan Wing v Chow Lee Wah* [2004] 1 HKLRD 1051 (CFI, HK).

51 *Combe v Combe* [1951] 2 KB 215, [1951] 1 All ER 767 (CA).

52 *Combe v Combe* [1951] 2 KB 215, 224, [1951] 1 All ER 767, 772 (Birkett LJ).

53 e.g. *Thorner v Major* [2009] UKHL 18, [2009] 1 WLR 776, [2009] 3 All ER 945, [61].

54 *Luo Xing Juan Angela v Estate of Hui Shui See, Willy Deceased* [2008] HKCFA 48, (2009) 12 HKCFAR 1.

The Court accepted the promisee's claim in promissory estoppel, ordered that the flat be sold, and that she be given 35% of the sale proceeds with a right of residence in the meantime. There was no extant contractual or other legal relationship between the parties imposing obligations or duties on the promisee that the promisor undertook not to enforce.

Promissory estoppel was thus deployed as a functional substitute for proprietary estoppel where the latter was foreclosed because the promisor did not legally own the property. Although couched in terms of promissory estoppel, the promisee was in substance enforcing the promise as a claimant. This is, in effect, a new species of promissory estoppel that may be used as a sword.[55] It would not be inappropriate to refer to this doctrine of the common law in Hong Kong as 'Hong Kong estoppel'.[56]

IV Coda

Simple consensualism, of which *pacta sunt servanda* is the Enlightenment's apothegmatic expression, was conceived by the medieval canonists as a manifestation of the general moral principle of good faith. This understanding, or a secularised version of it, came to be shared by jurists of the medieval civil law, the *ius commune*, the Enlightenment, the modern civil codes, and international law. The common law of contract has been less receptive to a general principle of good faith:[57]

> In many civil law systems, and perhaps in most legal systems outside the common law world, the law of obligations recognises and enforces an overriding principle that in making and carrying out contracts parties should act in good faith. . . . English law has, characteristically, committed itself to no such overriding principle but has developed piecemeal solutions in response to demonstrated problems of unfairness.

Although the common law has never fully embraced the principle of *pacta sunt servanda*, its essentially customary character makes it adaptive to simple consensualism on a piecemeal basis as the community's sense of justice demands. The common law does this not by staging doctrinal revolutions, but by patching together solutions that are reflective of the community's customs and reasonable expectations, and with the juridical materials that lie at hand. This is as true of Hong Kong as of any other common law jurisdiction.

55 Followed in *Hong Kong Hua Qiao Co Ltd v Cham Ka Tai* [2015] HKCA 104, [2015] 4 HKC 167.

56 In imitation of the late Professor Guenter Treitel who referred to a new variety of estoppel recognised by the High Court of Australia (*Waltons Stores (Interstate) Ltd v Maher* (1988) 164 CLR 387, (1988) 76 ALR 513, (1988) 62 ALJR 110) as 'Australian estoppel', but which is known in Australia as 'equitable estoppel': GH Treitel, 'Consideration' in H Beale (ed), *Chitty on Contracts* (33rd ed, Sweet & Maxwell, 2018) 4–107.

57 *Interfoto Picture Library Ltd v Stiletto Visual Programmes Ltd* [1989] QB 433, 439, [1988] 2 WLR 615, 620–621, [1988] 1 All ER 348, 352–353 (Bingham LJ).

2 Exceptions to *pacta sunt servanda* in the Chinese Civil Code

Siyi Lin

I Introduction

The principle of *pacta sunt servanda* ('agreements must be honoured') is the most sacred principle in the modern contract law regime, implying that parties are bound by their promises and expected to fulfil their obligations in a contractual relationship.[1] Nonetheless, as it is normal for contracts concluded to be performed in the future, the strict application of this cardinal principle may be impossible or lead to significant unfairness due to interruption of unforeseen events. The outbreak of the coronavirus disease 2019 (COVID-19) is one such unexpected event that has drastically disturbed the performance of various kinds of contracts globally. A consensus has been reached in different legal systems that parties should be excused from the *pacta sunt servanda* principle on exceptional grounds.[2] Under the legal system of the People's Republic of China ('China' or the 'PRC'), the tools for dealing with the impact of unexpected future events on contracts are *force majeure* and changed circumstances. *Force majeure* refers to unforeseeable, inevitable and insurmountable objective events.[3] Typical *force majeure* events are natural disasters, such as floods, fires, droughts and earthquakes, and social events, such as civil riots and strikes.[4] Changed circumstances relate to situations where material changes occur to conditions contemplated by parties at the time of contracting,[5] of which repre-

1 Reinhard Zimmermann, *The Law of Obligations: Roman Foundations of the Civilian Tradition* (OUP, 1996) 577.

2 See Klaus Peter Berger and Daniel Behn, '*Force Majeure* and Hardship in the Age of Corona: A Historical and Comparative Study' (2019–2020) 6 McGill Journal of Dispute Resolution 78.

3 Zhonghua Renmin Gongheguo Minfa Dian (中华人民共和国民法典) [Civil Code of the People's Republic of China] (promulgated by the NPC on 28 May 2020, effective since 1 January 2021) ('PRC Civil Code'), art 180.

4 Liu Qingsheng and Chen Weibin, 'The Distinction and Application of *Force Majeure* and Changed Circumstances Rules in the *PRC Civil Code*' (《民法典》不可抗力与情势变更规则的界分与适用) (2021) 23 Journal of South China University of Technology (Social Science Edition) 78, 79; Jacques Henri Herbots, 'Covid-19 and Contracts in China and Europe' (2021) China-EU Law Journal <https://doi.org/10.1007/s12689-021-00091-5>, section 2.

5 *PRC Civil Code*, art 533.

DOI: 10.4324/9781003358305-3

sentative examples agreed in academia are the change of government policies as well as the surge or slump of goods prices.[6]

The unprecedented effects generated by COVID-19 have given rise to a significant increase in contractual disputes. The Supreme People's Court of the PRC ('SPC') issued a series of judicial interpretations concerning adjudicating civil and commercial cases in relation to the COVID-19 pandemic, providing more specific guidance on the parties' entitlement to be excused from contractual obligations.[7] Considering that the impact of the COVID-19 crisis will continue for years, if not decades, litigation and arbitration focusing on the application of the *force majeure* and changed circumstances doctrines are likely to keep cascading and rippling. Given the progressively important role assumed by these two exceptional grounds against this backdrop, this chapter intends to provide an assessment of the *force majeure* and changed circumstances doctrines in Chinese law and how they are applied in the context of the pandemic and other constellations. In particular, this chapter aims to identify problems existing in the current doctrines that hinder their effective operation and raise proposals for improvement.

Towards that end, this chapter is divided into five parts. Following this Introduction, Part II embarks on a journey through time, exploring the historic origins of the *force majeure* and changed circumstances doctrines in China. Part III then looks at how the *force majeure* and changed circumstances doctrines are formulated in the current Chinese legal system and examines the distinction and relationship between these two doctrines. Part IV explores existing problems in the operation of these two exceptional grounds and provides suggestions regarding the perfection of current doctrines. Finally, Part V concludes.

II A historical review

In China's long history, the *force majeure* notion can be traced back to *Tang Lv Shu Yi*, the code of Tang dynasty.[8] Later, the *Draft Civil Code of the Great Qing* and the *Civil Law of the Republic of China* also contained the notion of *force*

6 Liu and Chen (n 4) 79.

7 *Notice by the Supreme People's Court of Issuing the Guiding Opinions (Part I) on Several Issues of Properly Hearing Civil Cases concerning the COVID-19 Pandemic (最高人民法院印发《关于依法妥善审理涉新冠肺炎疫情民事案件若干问题的指导意见（一）》的通知)* (issued by SPC on 16 April 2020, effective since the same date) ('*Guiding Opinions I*'); *Notice by the Supreme People's Court of Issuing the Guiding Opinions (Part II) on Several Issues of Properly Hearing Civil Cases concerning the COVID-19 Pandemic (最高人民法院印发《关于依法妥善审理涉新冠肺炎疫情民事案件若干问题的指导意见（二）》的通知)* (issued by SPC on 15 May 2020, effective since the same date) ('*Guiding Opinions II*'); *Notice by the Supreme People's Court of Issuing the Guiding Opinions (Part III) on Several Issues of Properly Hearing Civil Cases concerning the COVID-19 Pandemic (最高人民法院印发《关于依法妥善审理涉新冠肺炎疫情民事案件若干问题的指导意见（三）》的通知)* (issued by SPC on 8 June 2020, effective since the same date) ('*Guiding Opinions III*').

8 Chapter 10 of *Tang Lv Shu Yi*, 'Miscellaneous Articles (*Za Lv*)' contained provisions, stating 'liability shall be exempted if there is too much rain abnormally beyond control', 'where a ship runs into a storm, no compensation is required for property loss or damage to personal interests'. See details in Li Zhimin, *Civil Law in Ancient China*（中国古代民法） (Law Press, 1988) 194.

majeure.[9] After the inception of the PRC in 1949, the Communist Party abolished all old Kuomintang laws and started establishing the socialist system.[10] Nevertheless, the modern development of the Chinese legal system started only after the implementation of the reform and opening-up policy in the late 1970s, prior to which not much attention had been paid to the role of law in Chinese society.[11] Hundreds of statutes concerning civil matters were enacted in support of its way to an open market economy.[12] This Part traces the evolution of *force majeure* and change of circumstances in China since the modernisation of the PRC legal system. The historical exploration is of significance for a better understanding of the current status and application of *force majeure* and changed circumstances doctrines and lays a foundation for later discussion.

A Force majeure

1 Prior to the enactment of CCL

Before the enactment of *Contract Law of the People's Republic of China* ('CCL') in 1999,[13] three separate laws regulated contractual matters in China, i.e. the *Economic Contract Law of the People's Republic of China* ('ECL'),[14] the *Law of the People's Republic of China on Foreign-Related Economic Contracts* ('FECL')[15] and the *Law of the People's Republic of China on Technology Contracts* ('TCL').[16] All the three contract laws contained provisions in relation to *force majeure*. Additionally, the concept of *force majeure* can also be found in the *General Principles of Civil Law of the People's Republic of China* ('GPCL'),

9 Yu Zheng, 'Reflection on the Improvement of the Changed Circumstances Principle in Our Country' (对完善我国情势变更原则的思考) (2017) 37 Journal of Xi'an Jiaotong University (Social Science) 108, 110.

10 See generally 'Order on the Abolition of Six Laws System of the Nationalist Party and Establishing the Judicial Principles in the Liberated Areas' (中共中央关于废除国民党的六法全书与确定解放区的司法原则的指示) (promulgated by CCP Central Comm., 28 February 1949) <www.dffyw.com/sifashijian/jj/200809/20080921204129.htm> last accessed on 14 February 2022.

11 Volker Behr, 'Development of a New Legal System in the People's Republic of China' (2007) 67 Louisiana Law Review 1161.

12 Jianfu Chen, *Chinese Law: Context and Transformation* (rev. ed., Brill Nijhoff, 2015) 335.

13 Zhonghua Renmin Gongheguo Hetong Fa (中华人民共和国合同法) [Contract Law of the People's Republic of China] (promulgated by the National People's Congress ('NPC') on 15 March 1999, effective since 1 October 1999, expired on 1 January 2021).

14 Zhonghua Renmin Gongheguo Jinji Hetong Fa (中华人民共和国经济合同法) [Economic Contract Law of the People's Republic of China] (promulgated by the NPC on 13 December 1981, effective since 1 July 1982, expired on 1 October 1999).

15 Zhonghua Renmin Gongheguo Shewai Jinji Hetong Fa (中华人民共和国涉外经济合同法) [Law of the People's Republic of China on Foreign-Related Economic Contracts] (promulgated by the NPC on 21 March 1985, effective since 1 July 1985, expired on 1 October 1999).

16 Zhonghua Renmin Gongheguo Jishu Hetong Fa (中华人民共和国技术合同法) [Law of the People's Republic of China on Technology Contracts] (promulgated by the Standing Committee of the NPC ('NPCSC') on 23 June 1987, effective since 1 November 1987, expired on 1 October 1999).

which were enacted in 1986 and provided general principles and rules of civil and commercial law.[17]

The *FECL* and the *GPCL* defined *force majeure* events as events that were unforeseeable by the parties at the time of contracting and the occurrence and consequence of which were inevitable and insurmountable.[18] The *FECL* also stated that the scope of *force majeure* events may be specified in the contracts.[19] All three contract laws and the *GPCL* specified that where a party was unable to perform a contract in full, in part or on time due to a *force majeure* event, the party shall bear no liability for non-performance.[20] The party had a right to rescind the contract if it is impossible or unnecessary to perform all contractual obligations due to a *force majeure* event.[21] The *ECL* also allowed parties to modify economic contracts in such circumstances.[22] Article 25 of the *FECL* imposed the obligation on the party unable to perform to promptly notify the other side of the *force majeure* event to mitigate the possible loss, and such party shall provide a certificate issued by relevant authority within a reasonable period. According to the *GPCL*, the limitation of action is suspended if the right of claim cannot be exercised in the last six months of the limitation period because of *force majeure*.[23]

2 Force majeure *in the CCL*

In 1999, the *CCL* was promulgated, invalidating the *FECL*, *ECL* and *TCL* simultaneously,[24] while the *GPCL* continued to be in effect. The regulation of *force majeure* in the *CCL* generally remained the same with some non-core provisions being deleted. Article 117 of the *CCL* stated:

> Where a contract is unable to be performed due to *force majeure*, the liabilities shall be exempted in part or wholly depending on the effects of *force majeure*, except as otherwise stipulated by law. If the *force majeure* occurs after one party has delayed in performance, the liability shall not be exempted.
>
> *Force majeure* stated in this law refers to objective events that are unforeseeable, unavoidable and insurmountable.

Article 94 of the *CCL* listed *force majeure* as a ground to rescind the contract if it was impossible for parties to 'realise the purpose of the contract' therefore.

17 Zhonghua Renmin Gongheguo Minfa Tongze (中华人民共和国民法通则) [General Principles of the Civil Law of the People's Republic of China] (promulgated by the NPC on 12 April 1986, effective since 1 January 1987, last amended on 27 August 2009, expired on 1 January 2021).
18 FECL (n 15) art 24 (3); *GPCL* (n 17) art 153.
19 *FECL* (n 15) art 24 (4).
20 *FECL* (n 15) art 24 (1) and (2); *ECL* (n 14) art 34; *TCL* (n 16) art 20; *GPCL* (n 17) art 107.
21 *FECL* (n 15) art 29; *ECL* (n 14) art 26; *TCL* (n 16) art 24.
22 *ECL* (n 14) art 27.
23 *GPCL* (n 17) art 139.
24 *CCL* (n 13) art 428.

Article 118 of the *CCL* preserved the obligation to notify as required in Article 25 of the *FECL* previously. The non-performing party should promptly notify the other party to mitigate possible loss with proof being provided within a reasonable period.

B Changed circumstances

1 The changed circumstances doctrines in judicial practice

The doctrine of changed circumstances in China originated from judicial policies and practice. Before the *CCL* was enacted, the changed circumstances doctrine was mentioned in judicial policy documents. The SPC opined in its reply concerning the case of *Wuhan Gas Co. v Chongqing Detection Instrument Plant* issued in 1992 ('*1992 Reply*') that if the performance of a contract resulted in obvious fairness due to changed circumstances that were unforeseeable and unpreventable during the performance of the contract, the contract could be modified or discharged by reference to Article 27 (1)(4) the *ECL*.[25] Article 27(1)(4) of the *ECL* allowed modification or rescission of economic contracts where it was impossible to perform due to a *force majeure* event or an unpreventable external cause with neither party being at fault. The SPC's reference to this article triggered doubts as to whether it meant the *force majeure* rule should apply to address changed circumstances. In 1993, the SPC formulated the doctrine of changed circumstances in the *Summary Proceedings of the National Symposium on the Work on Economic Adjudication*:

> If, due to causes for which neither party is responsible, there occur fundamental changes, unforeseeable to the parties, in the objective circumstances that are the foundation of the contract, thereby making it evidently unfair to perform the original contract, the contract may upon application by the parties be modified or terminated according to the principle of change of circumstances.[26]

However, even though the changed circumstances notion had already been settled in judicial practice, the *CCL* does not acknowledge this doctrine. A few reasons

25 *The SPC's Letter on the Question of Application of Law in the Case on the Disputes over the Contract for the Transfer of Technology on Assembly Lines for Gas Meters and the Contract for the Sale of Spare Parts for Gas Meters between Wuhan Gas Company and Chongqing Detection Instrument Plant (Fa Han [1992] No. 27) (最高人民法院关于武汉市煤气公司诉重庆检测仪表厂煤气表装配线技术转让合同购销煤气表散件合同纠纷一案适用法律问题的函)* (Fa Han [1992] No. 27) (issued by SPC, on 6 March 1992). See details of this case in Herbots (n 4) section 3.

26 *Summary Proceedings of the National Symposium on the Work on Economic Adjudication (全国经济审判工作座谈会纪要)* (issued by SPC on 6 May 1993, effective since the same date). The English translation is adopted from Bin Ling, *Contract Law in China* (Sweet & Maxwell Asia, 2002), 293.

were proposed to justify the rejection. The main concern was the uncertainty of the changed circumstances doctrine.[27] The determination of whether circumstances had changed relied on judges' discretion, which may undermine the *pacta* principle and the stability and security of transactions.[28] Besides, the legislators deemed the doctrine as unnecessary and were of the view that issues involving changed circumstances could be covered by *force majeure* in general.[29] However, the legislative inaction did not prevent the grant of relief in situations where adverse changes happened subsequent to contract formation. As an alternative approach, Chinese courts directly invoked a basic principle of civil law, i.e. the principle of fairness, to excuse non-performance of contracts in cases where insistence on performance would be evidently unfair on one party due to changed circumstances.[30]

2 Formal recognition

In 2008, the global financial meltdown and the Great Wenchuan earthquake led to a surge in contractual disputes, where parties sought to modify or terminate their contracts claiming material adverse changes had occurred after the contract formation.[31] To avoid judicial inconsistency due to lack of regulation, the SPC issued the *Interpretation II of the Supreme People's Court of Several Issues Concerning the Application of the Contract Law of People's Republic of China* ('*Interpretation II on Contract Law*') on 24 April 2009, which formally recognised the changed circumstances doctrine for the first time.[32] Article 26 of the *Interpretation II on Contract Law* stated:

27 Cao Shouye, 'The Understanding and Application of Changed Circumstances Issues in Interpretation II of the Supreme People's Court of Several Issues Concerning the Application of the Contract Law of People's Republic of China' (最高人民法院《关于适用<中华人民 共和国合同法>若干问题的解释（二）之情势变更问题的理解与适用》) (2009) 8 Journal of Law Application 44, 48.

28 Liang Huixing, *Minfa Xueshuo Panli Yu Lifa Yanjiu Er (民法学说判例与立法研究（二）)*, (National School of Administration, 1999) 191; Yu (n 9) 112; Shuqi Li, Peng Nai, Guang Yang and Tao Yu, 'Force Majeure and Changed Circumstances During the COVID-19 Pandemic: The Cases of Sports Service Contracts and Judicial Responses in China' (2021) The International Sports Law Journal <https://doi.org/10.1007/s40318-021-00206-x>, section 4.1.

29 Yu (n 9) 112; Ling (n 26) 293; Li and others (n 28), section 4.1.

30 For instance, during the outbreak of SARS pandemic, the SPC issued the *Notice of the SPC on Legally Carrying out Relevant Trials and Enforcement Work During the Prevention and Treatment of SARS* on 11 June 2003, specifying that contractual disputes where the SARS pandemic significantly affected the performance of the original contract shall be dealt with by reference to the principle of fairness. *Notice of the SPC on Legally Carrying out Relevant Trials and Enforcement Work During the Prevention and Treatment of SARS* (最高人民法院关于在防治传染性非典型肺炎期间依法做好人民法院相关审判、执行工作的通知) (issued by the SPC on 11 June 2003, effective on the same date, expired on 18 February 2013), art 3(3). See also Li and others (n 28) section 4.2.

31 Yao Hui and Que Zhibing, 'A Discussion on the Integration and Distinction between Changed Circumstances and *Force Majeure:* Taking the Prevention and Control of COVID-19 Pandemic and the Reestablishment Post Pandemic as An Opportunity' (论情势变更与不可抗力的交融与界分 – 以新型肺炎疫情防控与疫后重建为契机) (2020) 3 Journal of CUPL 137, 140.

32 *Interpretation II of the Supreme People's Court of Several Issues Concerning the Application of the Contract Law of People's Republic of China (最高人民法院《关于适用〈中华人民共和国合同*

> Where any material change in the objective circumstances that is unforeseeable by the parties at the time of contracting and is not caused by *force majeure* and falls outside the scope of commercial risk occurs after the formation of a contract, if the continuous performance of the contract is obviously unfair to one of the parties or cannot realise the purposes of the contract, and a party files a request for the modification or rescission of the contract with a people's court, the people's court shall decide whether to modify or rescind the contract under the principle of fairness and in light of the actualities of the case.

Accordingly, only unforeseeable changes in objective circumstances that are material, not caused by *force majeure* nor commercial risks could constitute changed circumstances. The two legal concepts are explicitly distinguished from each other. Soon after the *Interpretation II on Contract Law* was promulgated, the SPC issued one notification[33] and one guiding opinion,[34] requiring courts at all levels to apply the changed circumstance doctrine cautiously and to report to superior courts or even the SPC for review when applying the doctrine. The guiding opinion also provides more detailed rules for applying this doctrine, including the determination of unforeseen events, the distinction between changed circumstances and commercial risks and the encouragement of renegotiation between parties.[35] These requirements reflect the SPC's cautious attitude and intention to ensure that the changed circumstances doctrine is applied with a high degree of uniformity.

C Reflections on the historical review

Both *force majeure* and changed circumstances provide excuses when unforeseen events occur after contract formation. The historical review above reflects that the development of the *force majeure* and changed circumstances doctrines is intertwined with each other and are not properly distinguished in the Chinese legal system.

The *force majeure* doctrine has been accepted far earlier than that of changed circumstances in Chinese contract law. When the concept of changed circumstance

---

法〉若干问题的解释（二）》 (issued by SPC on 24 April 2009, effective since 13 May 2009, expired on 1 January 2021).

33 *Notice of the Supreme People's Court on Correctly Applying the Interpretation II of Several Issues Concerning the Application of the Contract Law of People's Republic of China So as to Serve the Primary Objectives of the Party and the State (最高人民法院关于正确适用《中华人民共和国合同法》若干问题的解释(二)服务党和国家的工作大局的通知)* (issued by SPC on 27 April 2009, effective since the same date).

34 *Guiding Opinions on Several Issues Concerning the Trial of Cases of Disputes over Civil and Commercial Contracts under the Current Situation (关于当前形势下审理民商事合同纠纷案件若干问题的指导意见)* (issued by SPC on 7 July 2009, effective since the same date).

35 ibid.

was first mentioned in the *1992 Reply*, the SPC stated that a dispute arising from a changed circumstance should be addressed by referring to the *force majeure* rule. In the process of drafting the *CCL*, the changed circumstances rule was considered unnecessary because those situations were already covered by the *force majeure* doctrine. However, when the changed circumstances doctrine was at last formally recognised, Article 26 of the *Interpretation II on Contract Law* excluded events caused by *force majeure* from the sphere of changed circumstances. The separation of these two notions is termed the 'dualistic approach' by Chinese scholars.[36] Whether an event happening after the formation of contract constitutes a *force majeure* event or a changed circumstance depends on the factual situations *per se*. The original intention was to distinguish the concepts of *force majeure* and changed circumstances from each other, with each performing its own function in different situations.[37] However, in practice it is difficult, if not impossible, to draw a clear line between the two concepts. Where a *force majeure* event occurred, the performance of contract may still be possible but obviously unfair to one party. According to Article 26 of the *Interpretation II on Contract Law,* the changed circumstances doctrine could not apply to redress the unfairness. As the party only has the right to rescind the contract on the ground of *force majeure* when it is impossible to realise the purpose of the contract, the party is not entitled to claim rescission or modification of the contract. However, judges in some cases still applied the changed circumstances doctrine to address factual situations recognised as *force majeure* in other cases.[38] The judicial inconsistencies and confusion arising from the inappropriate distinction between the two doctrines have been noticed and criticised by Chinese scholars for a long time.[39]

36 See Wan Fang, 'Reflections on the Constitutive Elements and Positioning Mode of Changed Circumstances in Our Country' (我国情势变更制度要件及定位模式之反思) (2018) 6 Law Review 57, 65; Zhang Pinghua and Wang Hui, 'The Integrated Response Mechanism to *Force Majeure* and Changed Circumstances in the Context of COVID-19 Pandemic' (新冠疫情背景下的'不可抗力/情势变更'一体化应对机制) (2020) 13 National Judges College Law Journal 100, 100–101; Han Shiyuan, 'Research on Issues of the Changed Circumstances Doctrine' (情势变更若干问题研究) (2014) 3 Peking University Law Journal 657, 659.

37 Cao (n 27) 48–49.

38 See Yao and Que (n 31) 138–139. For instance, in the case *People's Government of Yongxiu County of Jiangxi Province and the Office of Poyang Lake Sand Mining Management Leading Group of Yongxiu County v. Chengdu Pengwei Industrial Co., Ltd*, the SPC held the view that as the non-performance by Chendu Pengwei Industrial Co., Ltd ('Pengwei') was due to the rarely seen low water level of Poyang Lake, continuously performing the contract pursuant to the original contract terms would be unfair to Pengwei. The SPC supported Pengwei's request for modifying the contract. *People's Government of Yongxiu County of Jiangxi Province and the Office of Poyang Lake Sand Mining Management Leading Group of Yongxiu County v. Chengdu Pengwei Industrial Co., Ltd*, Zui Gao Renmin Fayuan (2011) Min Zai Zi No. 2. In this case, the rarely seen low water level of Poyang Lake was objectively unforeseeable, inevitable and insurmountable, which was a *force majeure* event. However, the SPC still modified the contract terms to avoid unfairness.

39 A few examples are: Cui Jianyuan, 'The Exploration of the Change of Circumstances Doctrine' [情事变更原则探微] (2021) 3 Contemporary Law Review 3, 5; Wan (n 36) 58; Zhang and Wang (n 36) 101–102.

III Current doctrines of *force majeure* and changed circumstances

In May 2020, China promulgated its first-ever civil code, the *Civil Code of the People's Republic of China* ('*PRC Civil Code*'). Those separate statutes covering various dimensions of civil society were repealed simultaneously when the *PRC Civil Code* took effect, including the *GPCL*, the *CCL*, the *Real Rights Law of the People's Republic of China*,[40] etc. The previous doctrines of *force majeure* and changed circumstances have been incorporated into the *PRC Civil Code*, albeit with minor revisions. Besides, when COVID-19 first ravaged China, the PRC's Legislative Affairs Commission of the NPCSC announced that the pandemic and measures taken by the government to combat the pandemic constitute *force majeure* for parties unable to perform contracts.[41] The SPC then issued a series of judicial interpretations before the *PRC Civil Code* went into effect, providing guidance on properly adjudicating civil cases involving the COVID-19 pandemic. Those judicial interpretations provide detailed rules in relation to the application of *force majeure* and changed circumstances doctrines, which are currently effective. This Part considers the doctrines both in the *PRC Civil Code* and the judicial interpretations to systematically present the current *force majeure* and changed circumstances rules in the Chinese legal system.

A The PRC Civil Code

1 Force majeure

The *force majeure* rules in the *PRC Civil Code* remain nearly the same as those in the *GPCL* and *CCL*. Article 180 of the *PRC Civil Code* provides the basic legal concept, stating:

> Where the non-performance of civil obligations is caused by *force majeure*, no civil liability shall arise therefrom, unless otherwise provided for by any law. *Force majeure* means unforeseeable, inevitable and insurmountable objective circumstances.

40 Zhonghua Renmin Gongheguo Wuquan Fa (中华人民共和国物权法) [Real Rights Law of the People's Republic of China] (promulgated by the NPC on 16 March 2007, effective since 1 October 2007, expired on 1 January 2021).

41 Zhang Mianmian (ed), *What To Do If Enterprises Cannot Perform Contracts Due to Pandemic? – The Spokesman of PRC's Legislative Affairs Commission of the National People's Congress Standing Committee, Zang Tiewei, Stated the Law Has Relevant Regulations* (企业因疫情不能正常履行合同怎么办？全国人大常委会法工委发言人臧铁伟说法律有相应规定) (Official Website of National People's Congress of China, 2020) <www.npc.gov.cn/npc/c30834/202002/b9a56ce780f44c3b9f6da28a4373d6c3.shtml> last accessed on 15 February 2022.

Article 563 (1) of the *PRC Civil Code* also sets forth *force majeure* as a statutory reason to rescind a contract if it is impossible to realise the purpose of contract. Article 590 of the *PRC Civil Code* partly repeats Article 180, specifying:

> Where a party is unable to perform the contract due to *force majeure*, the party shall be exempt from liability in part or in whole depending on the impact of *force majeure*, except as otherwise provided by the law. In such a case, the party shall, in a timely manner, notify the other party, to mitigate the loss possibly caused to the other party, and provide proof within a reasonable period.
>
> If *force majeure* occurs after a party delays performance, the party shall not be exempt from liability for breach.

2 Changed circumstances

Article 533 of the *PRC Civil Code* provides the changed circumstances doctrine, stating:

> After the formation of contract, where a material change in the basic conditions of a contract occurs which is unforeseeable by the parties at the time of contracting and falls outside the realm of commercial risk, rendering the continuation of the performance of the contract obviously unfair for either party, the adversely affected party may renegotiate with the other party; and if the renegotiation fails within a reasonable time limit, the party may request the people's court or an arbitration institution to modify or rescind the contract.
>
> The people's court or arbitration institution shall change or rescind the contract under the principle of fairness and in light of the actualities of the case.

In comparison to Article 26 of the *Interpretation II on Contract Law*, Article 533 of the *PRC Civil Code* makes the following changes. First, previously, material changes to objective circumstances after the formation of a contract may constitute changed circumstances, while pursuant to Article 533, the material changes must affect the basic conditions of a contract, emphasising the impact of the change on the contract. However, no laws or regulations have further clarified the definition or scope of 'basic conditions of a contract'. Second, Article 533 deletes the exclusion of material changes caused by *force majeure* from changed circumstances. Third, Article 533 narrows down the application of the changed circumstances rule only to situations where the continuous performance of contract will lead to evident unfairness to one party and excludes situations where the purpose of contract cannot realised. Where a party would like to rescind the contract on the ground of impossibility to realise the purpose of contract, the party can only rely on *force majeure*. This revision emphasises the different rationales underlying the *force majeure* and the changed circumstances doctrines, one based on impossibility and the other on unfairness as a result of continuous performance, and thereby avoids potential confusion arising therefrom. This revision is made considering that *force majeure* events are no longer excluded from events causing changed circumstances.[42] Lastly, Article 533 imposes an 'unreal' obligation to renegotiate on the adversely affected party before the court can be requested to modify or rescind the contract. The requirement on renegotiation is an 'unreal' obligation because it is not compulsory and the obligee cannot require enforced performance, which reflects respect to the parties' autonomy and aims to reduce courts' intervention in the market economy and the number of disputes going to courts.[43]

B The Supreme People's Court's interpretations

On 16 April 2020, the SPC issued the *Guiding Opinions I*, providing guidance on adjudicating cases involving COVID-19 pandemic.[44] By and large, the *Guiding Opinions I* confirm that where the pandemic or preventive measures directly lead to impossibility to perform the contract, the *force majeure* rules shall apply to exempt the parties' liability wholly or in part depending on the impact of pandemic or preventive measures.[45] However, if it is only difficult to perform the contract, the parties should renegotiate and the courts shall strengthen efforts in mediation to guide the parties to continue the performance where it is possible.[46] The courts shall not support the parties' claim for recission of contract on the grounds of difficulty in performing the contract.[47] However, if the continuous performance makes it obviously unfair to one party, the court shall consider whether to support the party's request to modify the performance period, performance method or price of the contract based on actual circumstances of the case.[48]

The SPC issued the 'Guiding Opinions II' on 15 May 2020.[49] The *Guiding Opinions II* provide specific rules regarding exemptions from continuous performance of different types of contracts, e.g. sales contract and leasing contract, in the context of the pandemic. The basic rationale remains the same. In brief, first, claims for recission of contracts shall only be supported where continuous performance cannot realise the purpose of the contract. For instance, it is stated that

42 See Liu and Chen (n 4) 86.

43 Gu Xiwei, 'The Preapplication of the Renegotiation of Changed Circumstances' (情势变更中重新协商的前置适用) (2020) 10 The People's Judicature 40, 42–43.

44 Guiding Opinions I (n 7).

45 ibid, art 3 (1).

46 ibid, art 3 (2).

47 ibid.

48 ibid.

49 Guiding Opinions II (n 7). *Guiding Opinions III* are not discussed in this chapter, as these opinions do not contain provisions concerning exceptions to the *pacta* principle.

for sales contract, where the pandemic or pandemic preventive measures only lead to an increase in the cost of performance or to delay in performance, but the purpose of contract can still be realised, the courts should not support claims for rescinding the contract.[50] Where the seller fails to complete the order or deliver goods and the continuous performance cannot realise the purpose of contract, the courts should support the buyer's claim for rescission and return of any advance payment or deposit, while the court should not support the buyer's request for the seller to bear liability for breach of contract.[51] Second, where the contract can still be performed but the performance will lead to obvious unfairness to one party due to the pandemic or pandemic prevention measures, the court should modify, at the adversely affected party's request, the contract based on the principle of fairness. For example, it is stated that if the sales contract can continue to be performed while it will be obviously unfair to one party because of increased costs of performance, e.g. labour, raw materials and logistics costs, or of significant price reduction, the courts should modify the contract price according to the principle of fairness.[52] Third, courts should not support a party's claim for breach of contract no matter whether the contract is rescinded where the purpose of contract cannot be realised or the contract is modified where the continuous performance will lead to obvious unfairness.[53]

When the COVID-19 pandemic first broke out, the *PRC Civil Code* had not been promulgated. The *Interpretation II on Contract Law* was still in force, under which only material changes not incurred by *force majeure* may constitute changed circumstances. Therefore, when the spokesmen of NPCSC first announced the pandemic as *force majeure*, some high people's courts issued guidelines stating that the rules of changed circumstances should not apply to contractual disputes arising from the pandemic.[54] However, at that time, the draft of the *PRC Civil Code* had been published, indicating the new legislative direction.[55] Due to this reason, the *Guiding Opinions I* and *Guiding Opinions II* do not mention the term 'change of circumstances', but state that courts should support parties' claims for modifying the contract if the continuous performance of contract is possible but evidently unfair. In substance, these judicial interpretations acknowledged the application of the changed circumstances doctrine where the material change is caused by *force majeure* even before the *PRC Civil Code* was promulgated.

50 ibid, art 1 (2).
51 ibid, art 1 (2).
52 ibid.
53 ibid, art 1 (1) to (5), and (7).
54 See *Guidelines of the High People's Court of The Inner Mongolia Autonomous Region on Issues in relation to the Trial of Civil and Commercial Cases Involving COVID-19* (*内蒙古自治区高级人民法院关于审理涉新冠肺炎疫情民商事案件相关问题的指引*) (issued by High People's Court of the Inner Mongolia Autonomous Region on 14 February 2020, effective since the same date).
55 The draft of the *PRC Civil Code* was published on 23 December 2019. See Wu Yongling (ed), 'Combined! The 'Complete' Draft of China's Civil Code is Published for the First Time' (合体！'完整版' 中国民法典草案首次亮相) (Xinhua Website, 23 December 2019) <www.xinhuanet.com/politics/2019-12/23/c_1125379323.htm> last accessed on 17 December 2022.

C *The relationship between* **force majeure** *and changed circumstances*

1 Differences in functionality and legal effect

As indicated in the above discussion of their historical development, the distinction between the *force majeure* and changed circumstances doctrines is often unclear due to their similarity in tackling unforeseeable events.[56] However, the two doctrines are different in nature and have different legal effects under current Chinese law.

Force majeure is a defence, providing an exemption of liability for non-performance. The party unable to perform its contractual obligations due to *force majeure* is not liable for the non-performance to the corresponding extent if the notification obligations are properly fulfilled.[57] Meanwhile, *force majeure* can also lead to rescission of contract where the purpose of contract can no longer be achieved.[58] The right to rescind the contract arising from *force majeure* is a statutory one. The party can exercise the right either by unilaterally notifying the other party or requesting the court to rescind the contract.[59]

In contrast, the doctrine of changed circumstances aims to provide an exception to the binding force of contracts. It neither gives rise to an exemption from liability nor does it generate a statutory right to rescind the contract. The adversely affected party is only entitled to request the court to modify or rescind the contract.[60] The different functionality and legal effects reflect that these two doctrines are based on different rationales. *Force majeure* chiefly concerns the impossibility to perform. The contract should be rescinded since it is impossible to achieve its purpose anymore. However, the changed circumstances doctrine focuses on redressing evident unfairness that may arise due to continuous performance of contract.

2 The scope of application of force majeure *and changed circumstances*

Under the *PRC Civil Code*, *force majeure* and changed circumstances are no longer mutually exclusive. As concluded above, although these two doctrines both address unforeseeable subsequent events, they are based on different rationales, one on impossibility to perform the contract and the other on redressing unfairness.[61] A factual situation may at the same time be considered as a case of

56 See II. above.

57 *PRC Civil Code*, arts 180 and 590.

58 ibid, art 563 (1).

59 Li Junye, 'Analysis of Cases of *Force Majeure* and Changed Circumstances of Obstacles of Performance of Contracts Caused by Pandemic' (疫情引发合同履行障碍之不可抗力与情势变更类案辨析) (2020) 6 Journal of Law Application 65, 68.

60 *PRC Civil Code*, art 533.

61 See III. C. 1. above.

changed circumstances and of *force majeure*. The impact of the unforeseeable event on the contract, rather than the factual event *per se*, should be the decisive factor determining which rule should apply. The amendment of the changed circumstances doctrine in the *PRC Civil Code* is a response to the long-standing criticism of the exclusion of *force majeure* events from changed circumstances in Article 26 of the *Interpretation II on Contract Law*.[62]

The *PRC Civil Code* requires *force majeure* events to be 'unforeseeable, inevitable and insurmountable', while changed circumstances are only 'unforeseeable'.[63] Logically, there exist unforeseeable events that are evitable and surmountable. With the two doctrines being no longer mutually exclusive, the two doctrines should be applied in the following ways. First, when an unforeseeable but evitable and surmountable event happens, only the changed circumstance doctrine may apply. Second, where a *force majeure* event occurs but the contract can still be performed, the changed circumstances doctrine should apply if the continuous performance is obviously unfair. Third, where it is impossible to perform the contract due to *force majeure*, the *force majeure* notion should apply to exempt the parties' liability for non-performance while the contract can only be rescinded if the purpose of contract cannot be achieved.

IV Remaining issues and proposals for future development

Since the COVID-19 pandemic affected China and the world from the beginning of the year 2020, the pandemic and measures implemented to combat the virus have generated a large number of disputes involving *force majeure* and changed circumstances. Based on the search on China Judgments Online, the official database run by SPC basically containing judgment documents delivered by all Chinese courts,[64] the numbers of civil cases involving *force majeure* claims arising out of the pandemic in 2020 and 2021 are 19,040 and 25,149 respectively. Meanwhile, there are 882 and 1,253 civil cases concerning the pandemic and the notion of changed circumstances. The COVID-19 pandemic provides a touchstone for the viability of the *force majeure* and changed circumstances doctrines. This section identifies existing problems in the application of the two doctrines in China and raises proposals for future improvements.

1 The application of the **force majeure** *and changed circumstances doctrines*

As discussed above,[65] under the *PRC Civil Code*, when an unforeseeable, inevitable and insurmountable event happens, whether the party is entitled to claim *force majeure* or invoke the changed circumstances doctrine is determined by

62 See II. C. above; Li and others (n 28), section 4.3.
63 *PRC Civil Code*, arts 180 and 533.
64 See the official website of China Judgements Online: <https://wenshu.court.gov.cn/>.
65 See III. C. 2. above.

the impact of the event on the performance of contract. In respect of contractual disputes arising from the pandemic or its preventative measures, the courts should first evaluate whether it is still possible to perform the contract. Although the distinction between these two doctrines appears rather straightforward in theory, their practical application remains chaotic.

In Chinese law, as reflected in the doctrinal analysis above, *force majeure* is a defence against liability for non-performance and provides a statutory reason for recission of contract where it is impossible to realise the purpose of contract.[66] No right to request for modification of contract arises from *force majeure*. When a *force majeure* event occurs, the party is only entitled to request modification if the situation constitutes a changed circumstance as well. Nevertheless, in practice, it is not rare for parties to claim for modification of contracts on the ground of *force majeure* instead of changed circumstances.[67] In some cases, courts decided to modify contract terms where the continuous performance would cause obviously unfairness due to *force majeure*, i.e. the COVID-19 pandemic, pursuant to the *Guiding Opinions I and II*.[68] The SPC's judicial interpretations affirm the pandemic as a potential *force majeure* event and allow parties to seek a judicial modification of contract without mentioning the changed circumstances notion where the continuous performance would result in obvious unfairness.[69] As discussed, this was because material changes caused by *force majeure* were excluded from the changed circumstance rule as it applied at that time.[70] However, the application of the changed circumstances doctrine in substance for modification on the ground of *force majeure* reflects the existing confusion and will continue to cause confusion in the functionality and distinction of the two concepts. It is suggested that the legislature should provide guidelines to further clarify the distinction between the two doctrines and how to determine which doctrine shall apply, such as factors to be considered when evaluating the impact on the performance of contract and the possibility to achieve the purpose of contract.

2 Exemption from liability

As introduced above, the *PRC Civil Code* sets forth *force majeure* as a ground for an exemption from liability.[71] In contrast, it does not state the doctrine of changed circumstances can exempt the adversely affected party from liability for non-performance or grant the right to withhold performance.[72] Controversy surrounds

66 See III. C. 1. above.

67 See Li (n 59) 69.

68 Two examples are *Ma Ying v Guan Jinying* (2021) Lu 15 Min Zhong No. 3335 and Longjin Comprehensive Development (Chengdu) Co., *Ltd v Gedeman* (Sichuan) Chemistry Co., Ltd (2021) Chuan 01 Min Zhong No. 26150.

69 See III. B. above.

70 ibid.

71 *PRC Civil Code*, arts 180 and 590.

72 *PRC Civil Code*, art 533.

the distribution of liabilities and losses where a change of circumstances occurs. A changed circumstance is often non-attributable to either party even though non-imputability is not a constitutive element of changed circumstances. Requiring the disadvantaged party to bear liability for breach of contract seems to be unfair.[73] A few scholars argue that parties should not be liable for non-performance due to change of circumstances,[74] while there are also voices of dissent. Some other scholars assert that a change of circumstances is not a legal basis for exempting a party from liability for non-performance.[75] Parties affected by *force majeure* bear no liability because they are objectively unable to perform the contract, while recission or modification of contracts pursuant to the changed circumstances doctrine is to adjust the imbalance between rights and obligations to avoid unfairness and, objectively, the contract can still be performed.[76]

Judicial interpretations also imply different answers to this issue. In 2016, the High People's Court of Tianjin Municipality issued the *Notice Concerning Properly Adjudicating Disputes over Real Estate Sales Contract* ('*Notice*'), stating that people's courts should allow modification or rescission of contract according to the actual conditions of the case where the contract cannot be performed owing to the issuance of regulatory policies restricting purchasing real estates.[77] This is an application of changed circumstances in substance. The *Notice* further stipulates that after rescission of contract, the seller shall return the received purchase price or deposit and the buyer should return the house. Any loss caused by the rescission of contract should be assumed reasonably by both parties based on the principle of fairness. If any party's fault results in serious imbalance of interests between parties, the party suffering a loss shall be entitled to require the other party to assume more losses and the courts should support such claim appropriately.[78] The *Notice* does not exempt the non-performing party from liability for damages but requires the liability to be distributed pursuant to the principle of fairness. The *Guiding Opinions II* also deal with the assumption of liabilities where the changed circumstances doctrine is applied substantially in disputes arising from the pandemic or preventative measures of the pandemic. The *Guiding Opinions II*'s position is that parties' breach of contract claims should not be supported, which acknowledges that the changed circumstance provides an exemption from liability.[79] The *Notice* and *Guiding Opinions II* are just two examples showing that different approaches

73 There are scholars holding the view that change of circumstances should be non-attributable to the parties of contract: see Cui (n 39) 8.

74 Yu (n 9) 110; Liang Huixing, *Civil Law (民法)* (Sichuan Renmin Press 1988) 424–425; Han (n 36) 660.

75 Li (n 59) 77; Zhang and Wang (n 36) 105.

76 Ibid.

77 *Notice Concerning Properly Adjudicating Disputes over Real Estate Sales Contract* (关于依法妥善审理房屋买卖合同纠纷案件的通知) (issued by High People's Court of Tianjin on 16 November 2016, effective since the same date), art 7.

78 ibid.

79 See III. B. above.

have been adopted in terms of the exemption of liability under the changed circumstances doctrine in different types of disputes.

The lack of unified guidance will lead to continuous inconsistencies in judicial practice and the situation calls for clear guidance provided by the legislature. As the aim of the changed circumstances doctrine is to redress unfairness caused by adverse changes happening after formation of contract,[80] the exemption of liability and the distribution of loss should be decided based on the principle of fairness as well. *Force majeure* is an exemption from liabilities because it is not only unforeseeable but also inevitable and insurmountable. The occurrence of *force majeure* is not attributable to the parties. However, a changed circumstance is only unforeseeable. Whether the changed circumstance is attributable to the parties should be the key factor when deciding whether a party should be exempted from liability for breach of contract and how to distribute the loss between the parties.

3 The courts' discretion

The above discussion points out the application procedure of *force majeure* and changed circumstances doctrines.[81] However, this does not mean that the judges can simply follow the procedure and apply legal rules. Factual situations in cases may be complex and diverse. Take the COVID-19 pandemic as an example. The pandemic is long-lasting and ever changing. The severity of the pandemic and measures taken to combat the virus vary in different areas. In each case, the impact of pandemic on the performance of contract should be carefully evaluated based on different case facts. Meanwhile, these two doctrines remain general and indefinite in many aspects. The law does not specify how to determine whether a subsequent event is 'unforeseeable', 'inevitable' and 'insurmountable'. The *force majeure* rules provide no guidance for determining whether performance of the contract remains 'possible' or whether the purpose of contract can still be realised. According to the changed circumstances doctrine, whether a contract should be modified or rescinded is decided by courts or arbiters in accordance with the principle of fairness. The application of *force majeure* and changed circumstances doctrines in specific cases unavoidably leaves courts a great deal of discretion, causing uncertainties and lack of uniformity in practice.

In fact, scattered provisions can be found in judicial interpretations addressing specific issues in the application of *force majeure* and changed circumstances doctrines to minimise uncertainties. For example, the *Guiding Opinions on Several Issues concerning the Trial of Cases of Disputes over Civil and Commercial Contracts under the Current Situation*, issued by the SPC in 2009, contains guidance on applying the changed circumstances doctrine, including how to evaluate the foreseeability of subsequent events and distinguish changed circumstances

80 See III. C. 1. above.
81 See III. C. 2. above.

and commercial risks.[82] The *Guiding Opinions I* and *Guiding Opinions II* instruct courts on the application of *force majeure* and changed circumstances doctrines in cases involving the COVID-19 pandemic. These two judicial interpretations specify factors to be considered when deciding the possibility to perform contracts, the modification of contract terms and exemption of liabilities in different types of contracts.[83] However, only a few issues have been addressed and most of the scattered provisions specifically focus on a certain type of contracts. Further clarification is required in order to provide systematic guidance for courts. Considering that sources of Chinese law are written statutes and legal documents are usually written at a high level of abstraction,[84] it is not possible and practical to create detailed provisions addressing various factual situations of *force majeure* and changed circumstances. The legislature can categorise different factual situations leading to a change of basic conditions of contract or difficulty in performing the contract based on the past judicial experience, and provide guidance on different categorisations of changed circumstances.

V Conclusion

The historical review shows that the *force majeure* and changed circumstances doctrines are not properly distinguished from each other in China even though these two exceptions to the *pacta* principle are rooted in different underlying rationales. The *PRC Civil Code* revises the changed circumstances doctrine, which is an improvement because it clarifies the relationship between these two doctrines. Whether the *force majeure* or changed circumstances rules should apply depends on the impact of the unforeseeable event on the parties' ability to perform the contract, rather than the facts of the event *per se*. A large number of contractual disputes arise out of the COVID-19 pandemic, offering a litmus test for the viability of *force majeure* and changed circumstances doctrines in the *PRC Civil Code* and SPC's judicial interpretations. Against this backdrop, this chapter points out that there are still numerous issues to be resolved and makes proposals for future development, including the provision of detailed rules clarifying the distinction between these two doctrines and the exemption from liability on the ground of changed circumstances, and reducing judicial inconsistencies.

82 See n 34.

83 See III. B. above.

84 Margaret Fordham, 'Comparative Legal Traditions – Introducing the Common Law to Civil Lawyers in Asia' (2006) 1 Asian Journal of Comparative Law 1, 2.

3 In a bubble by the sea

COVID-19, time and contract law in the Macau S.A.R.

Célia F. Matias and Monica Chan

1 Introduction

Every spring in Macau there is a day that signals the shift between cold and oppressively hot weather. Some locals call it 'the helmet', as mist and clouds descend upon the city, shrouding it in grey. The metaphor seems painfully adequate to the current times. With the onset of the COVID-19 pandemic, border restrictions were put in place that, until the present day (September 2022), prevent the generality of foreign nationals[1] from entering the region and require many of those permitted to enter to undergo a quarantine of 7 days – measures that have kept the virus at bay, but also left Macau largely closed to the outside world for more than two years.

With an economy that is dependent on the gaming industry and related tourism and commercial activities, Macau has been severely affected by the pandemic and these policies. Gaming operators saw their revenues shrink, as have business in the related entertainment, hospitality and retail sectors. In this scenario, many businesses as well as individuals are likely to face difficulties in meeting their contractual obligations: be it employers toward their employees, tenants toward landlords or retailers toward their suppliers.

The principle of *pacta sunt servanda* is one of the cornerstones of Macau's law of obligations and contract law in particular, with several mechanisms of protection available to the creditor in case of failure, delay and impossibility to comply. The law does, however, provide for certain exceptions, such as the mechanism of termination or modification of the contract based on change of circumstances.

Nevertheless, Macau courts are yet to apply this mechanism in the context of the pandemic. This may be due, in part, to its strict requirements, but also to informal contractual adjustments prompted by governmental intervention, in the form of subsidies and incentives. For now, it may be that these measures, as well as an effort to maintain 'harmony', is keeping these cases out of the courts. However, as the pandemic progresses and restrictive measures remain in place, the likelihood

1 Except for the nationals of 41 countries, as recently announced by the Macau government. Pierce Chan, 'Visitors from 41 countries allowed to enter Macau from Thursday' *Inside Asian Gaming* (31 August 2022) <https://www.asgam.com/index.php/2022/08/31/visitors-from-41-countries-allowed-to-enter-macau-from-thursday/> last accessed 14 September 2022.

DOI: 10.4324/9781003358305-4

of contractual defaults rise, while the successful use of mechanisms of exception turns into a mirage.

With the aim of better understanding these legal pathways and their possible applicability, this chapter begins with an overview of Macau contract law, from the perspective of *pacta sunt servanda*, and explores possible exceptions, with particular emphasis on the mechanism of change of circumstances. It then puts this framework to the test by focusing on the challenges faced by parties to long-term contracts in the local rental market.

2 Contract law in Macau

2.1 System overview and general principles

Following the transfer of sovereignty of Macau to the People's Republic of China on 20 December 1999 (known as the 'handover'), the Macau Special Administrative Region (S.A.R.) was granted, under the terms of the Basic Law,[2] a high degree of autonomy. It maintained its own legal system, composed of the laws already in force in the region, as well as those produced by the newly created legislative bodies of the S.A.R.[3]

The Macau Civil Code ('CC')[4] was enacted shortly before the handover with the purpose of modernising, consolidating and localising private law.[5] Its interpretation should, therefore, primarily consider the ongoing work of local courts and scholars, in view of the evolving reality of the Macau S.A.R., but, as the enactment largely follows the structure and content of the Portuguese Civil Code,[6] the Portuguese doctrinal *acquis* remains significant, especially in 'hard cases', which have not been previously decided by local courts.

Within the CC, Book II (Law of Obligations) sets out, under Title I (On Obligations in General) several sources of obligations – among which contracts – as well as several aspects of the life of an obligation, from its birth to its extinction. Title II (On Contracts in Particular) sets out specific rules for legally typified contracts, such as sale and purchase, loan or lease. Some contracts are also regulated in other laws, such as the Macau Commercial Code[7] or the Consumer Rights and Interests Protection Law.[8]

The overarching principles of Macau's contract law may be identified based on the above-mentioned body of rules, as well as the 'spirit' of the legal system, as

2 Basic Law of the Special Administrative Region of Macau of the People's Republic of China, adopted on 31 March 1993, by the First Session of the Eighth Legislature of the National People's Congress of the People's Republic of China (the 'Basic Law').

3 Basic Law (ibid) art 18.

4 Decree-Law No. 39/99/M, of 3 August 1999.

5 Jorge Noronha e Silveira, Deputy Secretary for Justice, 'Opening Note' in *Código Civil: Versão Portuguesa* (Imprensa Oficial, 2008).

6 Decree-Law no. 47344, of 25 November 1966.

7 Decree-Law no. 40/99/M.

8 Law no. 9/2021.

revealed by legal scholarship and court decisions.[9] Among them, private autonomy and good faith are seen as leading principles,[10] with their relative weight and interplay being determinant to the solutions offered by the legal system in several scenarios.

The individualist nature of the principle of private autonomy dictates that each the party shall have the ability to self-regulate their own interests,[11] namely by committing to any contractual clauses that they might see fit. In this context, the principle of *pacta sunt servanda* appears as another aspect of the principle of private autonomy, as once those clauses have been freely agreed to, the respective terms ought to be complied with.

These principles are, nevertheless, not absolute. In particular, the principle of good faith has been understood as an important counterweight to *pacta sunt servanda*, offering flexibility when it is called for.[12] Indeed, although it is not the subject of a general provision, the principle of good faith appears throughout the CC in multiple instances, namely as a general standard for the application of certain rules,[13] or as a criterion for the determination of abuse of right.[14]

A principle of contractual balance, which would limit the scope of *pacta sunt servanda*, has found modest support among legal scholars, despite multiple provisions that may be seen as instantiations thereof,[15] in particular, the termination or modification of a contract due to change of circumstances.

For a better understanding of how these principles translate into legal rules that can be directly applied to real-world contractual relationships, the next section offers a glimpse of the Macau CC rules on compliance, non-compliance, impossibility, modification and termination of contracts.

2.2 The life and death of obligations under the Macau Civil Code

As previously mentioned, Book II (Law of Obligations) of the CC is structured to mirror the different stages of the 'life' of an obligation – defined in article 391 of the CC as 'a legal bond by virtue of which a person is bound to perform something towards another person'.[16] An obligation does not necessarily carry any monetary

9 Aside from very limited exceptions, court decisions in Macau do not have the force of legal precedent, but only interpretative value in the decision of subsequent cases.
10 Mário Júlio de Almeida Costa, *Direito das Obrigações (Law of Obligations)* (9th ed, Almedina 2004), 95–106.
11 ibid, 97.
12 ibid, 104.
13 CC arts 431 to 433. An example of this is the formulation of the *rebus sic stantibus* clause in article 431 of the CC, which will be further discussed below.
14 CC art 326.
15 Rui Pinto Duarte, 'O Equilíbrio Contratual Como Princípio Jurídico' ('Contractual Balance as Legal Principle') in Maria João Antunes and Marta Cavaleira (eds), *Estudos em Homenagem do Conselheiro Artur Maurício* (Almedina, 2014), 1332–1345.
16 CC art 391.

value, but it must correspond to an interest of the creditor that is worthy of legal protection.[17]

In accordance with the principles of private autonomy and its corollary, freedom of contract, parties to a contract are bound by the agreed terms and conditions. Therefore, contractual performance is subject to a principle of 'punctuality', according to which the debtor is only discharged by performing what was agreed, in all relevant aspects, namely time, quantity, quality or place of performance.[18] Moreover, parties are expected to act in good faith in the course of contractual performance.[19]

Failure to perform is usually divided into the following categories: (i) permanent non-compliance; (ii) temporary non-compliance ('mora' or delay); (iii) permanent impossibility; (iv) temporary impossibility; and (v) defective compliance. Non-compliance and impossibility (both permanent and temporary) can also be classified as total or partial.

Failure to comply with the agreed terms in the contract or refusal to carry out the contractual obligations in accordance with the agreement is considered as an act of breach of contract or non-compliance. Hence, in a debtor-creditor relationship, if a debtor fails to carry out the contractual obligations, and as a result causes losses, such debtor shall be liable for the damage caused to the creditor pursuant to article 787 of the CC.[20]

In the case of a delay, where it is possible for the debtor to carry out the contractual obligations timely, yet they fail to do so and causes damage to the creditor, such debtor is liable[21] for compensation[22] subject to article 793 of the CC.[23] A delay in carrying out contractual obligations by the debtor may be converted into definitive non-compliance in case of loss of interest by the creditor or failure to perform within the period reasonably set by the creditor.[24]

An event with the gravity and impact of the COVID-19 pandemic is likely to have effects on the performance of contracts, but those effects are bound to differ from contract to contract. While some might be entirely unaffected (in which case any default will fall within the above-mentioned hypotheses of imputable non-compliance), others may be rendered impossible. In cases where

17 CC art 392(2).

18 CC art 752(1), as interpreted by legal scholars. It is often stated that compliance must be made 'point by point', perfectly matching the obligation to which the debtor is bound: João Paulo Rocha, 'Cumprimento e não cumprimento e outras causas de extinção das obrigações para além do cumprimento' ('Compliance and non-compliance and other causes of extinction of obligations beyond compliance') in Manuel Trigo and others (eds), *Repertório do Direito de Macau (Repertoire of Macau Law)* (Universidade de Macau – Centro de Estudos Jurídicos da Faculdade de Direito 2007), 463.

19 CC art 752(2).

20 CC art 787.

21 CC art 793(2).

22 CC art 793(1).

23 CC art 793.

24 CC art 797.

performance cannot happen (or cannot happen on time) due to circumstances outside the debtor's control, the law provides for a special framework, which is described below.

2.3 Non-imputable impossibility

Impossibility to perform may result from causes within or outside the debtor's control. It is the latter – known as 'non-imputable impossibility' – that is of particular interest in the context of the pandemic. In these cases, the debtor is released from the obligation,[25] which is deemed terminated.[26]

This is the case not only when the impossibility is objective (i.e. affects the obligation regardless of who was to perform it) but also when it is subjective (i.e. affects a specific debtor's ability to perform), provided that performance cannot be obtained from another person.[27] An example of this would be an obligation to paint a portrait that could only be discharged by a certain painter, who subsequently became permanently unable to paint. In these cases, the creditor is exempted from the corresponding payment and, if already made, is entitled to its restitution.[28]

Temporary impossibility to comply exempts the debtor from liability for the delay, but the impossibility shall only be deemed temporary for as long as the creditor remains interested in the performance.[29]

In case of partial impossibility, the debtor is released from the totality of the obligation by performing only the part which is possible, but the other party's obligation in a bilateral contract shall be proportionally reduced. The creditor may, however, terminate the contract if it does (justifiably) not have interest in the partial performance.[30]

Although the preceding paragraphs might suggest a spectrum of situations to which these rules apply, an important common denominator is that the performance of the obligation is truly impossible. Therefore, this framework does not apply to situations in which the performance has merely become more difficult or onerous. Such cases are governed by the principle of *pacta sunt servanda*. In other words, the debtor remains bound to the obligation even under more challenging conditions – unless one of the exceptions to this principle applies. The next sections analyse the general grounds for those exceptions as well as some of the relevant frameworks.

25 CC art 799/1.

26 This type of impossibility refers to causes that occurred subsequently to the entering into of the contract. Originary impossibility, on the other hand, occurs when performance was already impossible when the obligation came into being. According to CC art 395/1, this type of impossibility leads to nullity of the contract.

27 CC art 780.

28 CC art 784/1.

29 CC art 781.

30 CC art 782.

2.4 Difficulty in complying, contractual balance and good faith

Although Macau law does not include a general exception to *pacta sunt servanda* for situations where a party faces excessive difficulties in complying with their obligations, there are scattered provisions that provide flexibility in certain situations.

For instance, according to article 560/3 of the CC, compensation of a monetary sum may be fixed whenever restitution *in natura* (i.e. of what was originally due) is excessively onerous to the debtor. This shows the legislator was concerned with the reasonableness of the burden imposed on the debtor, establishing an exception to the principle of punctuality. In another example, article 326 of the CC states that 'the exercise of a right is illegitimate when the rightholder manifestly exceeds the limits imposed by good faith', in which case 'the debtor may legitimately fail to comply, [by virtue of] the creditor's abuse of right'.[31] In the context of contractual compliance[32] parties are also required to act in good faith.

Aside from good faith, some authors view contractual balance,[33] or 'substantive justice',[34] as a principle of contract law that may also justify deviations from the principle of *pacta sunt servanda*. In this realm, it is important to distinguish, following Pinto Duarte,[35] between contractual balance upon formation of the contract and during the performance of the contract. In the first case, one may ask if parties are bound to a certain balance of values within the contract. On this front, there is still a way to go before it can be said that parties are, in general, bound to a substantial balance of positions within a contract.[36] Therefore, unless the contract's purpose is contrary to the law, public order or common decency[37] and save for certain exceptions, the parties are free to agree to whatever they wish. As such, there is no obstacle to a friend selling a second-hand car to another for a price lower than its market value, or even, *ad absurdum*, to exchange a peanut for a gold ingot.[38]

A different issue is the maintenance of whatever balance was struck by the parties during the life of the contract. For instance, if as a result of abnormal circumstances, it became extremely onerous to mine the gold needed to produce the ingot (e.g. if an earthquake damaged the mine), the agreed balance of efforts is affected.

31 Paulo Rocha (n 18) 474.
32 CC art 752/2.
33 Pinto Duarte (n 15), 1332–1345.
34 José de Oliveira Ascenção, 'Alteração das circunstâncias e justiça contratual no novo código civil' (Change of circumstances and contractual justice in the new civil code') (2008) 13 Pensar – Revista de Ciências Jurídicas 7.
35 Pinto Duarte (n 15).
36 Article 399 of the CC subjects contractual freedom only to the 'limits of the law'. In Portugal, a corresponding provision has been interpreted as including values of substantive justice, security in trade and public order: Almeida Costa (n 10), 218.
37 CC art 274, pursuant to which such contracts are null and void. For example, a contract the purpose of which is fraud or money laundering.
38 Causes of invalidity, such as mistake, fraud or duress apply in the same way as they do to any other contracts, irrespective of the value of the consideration.

One may then ask if the parties are still bound to perform as agreed. The next section analyses one of the mechanisms that may provide a solution for these cases – the termination or modification of the contract for change of circumstances.

2.5 Change of circumstances

The legal framework for the modification or termination of the contract due to change of circumstances is set out in articles 431 to 433 of the CC. Article 431/1 states:

> If the circumstances upon which the parties based their decision to enter into a contract suffer an abnormal change, the injured party has the right to terminate the contract or to have it modified equitably, so long as the demand of compliance with the obligations taken up seriously affects the principle of good faith and is not covered by the contract's typical risks.[39]

Further, a party may oppose termination under this provision by accepting modification instead.[40] The injured party is, however, barred from using this mechanism if it was in a situation of default when the change of circumstances occurred.[41]

The key concept in this institute is expressed in article 431/1 as 'the circumstances upon which the parties based their decision to enter into a contract': the basis or foundation of the contract ('*base do negócio*'). A relevant event for purposes of termination and modification affects this nucleus. But how might it be interpreted?

In Portuguese law, the concept was introduced in the 1966 Civil Code but was not defined.[42] A relevant question in this regard is whose perspective should be adopted when determining what circumstances are fundamental to the decision to enter into the contract, given that parties may not have the same motives, and these might not be explicitly stated in the contract. Almeida Costa posits that one should adopt the perspective of the injured party requesting the termination or modification, provided the invoked circumstances appear as 'evident according to the contract's typical purpose' to both parties.[43]

The requirements for termination or modification are, then: (i) change of circumstances that affects the foundation of the contract; (ii) abnormality of such change; (iii) injury to one of the parties if the contract were to remain stable; (iv) such stability seriously affecting the principles of good faith; (iv) the fact that the change of circumstances is not included in the contract-typical risks; and (v) no default by the injured party.[44]

39 Translation from the Portuguese by the authors.
40 CC art 431/2.
41 CC art 432.
42 As explained by Almeida Costa (n 10) 293–302.
43 ibid, 303.
44 ibid, 302–308.

In Macau, few cases can be found that help to clarify the interpretation of these provisions. In a 2018 case[45] (with an appeal decided in 2019), the promissory buyer of a residential unit in a condominium sued the construction company based on change of circumstances, requesting the termination of the promissory sale and purchase contract, and restitution of all sums paid. The agreement, signed in 2012, stated that delivery of the unit was due 1,200 'good weather days' after the covering of the first floor. Despite the uncertainty as to the exact due date, the court estimated that this would amount to around five years in total. In 2016, the defendant's 25-year concession of the land expired without any construction being initiated by the defendant. As the extension of the concession was subject to the development of the land, which had not occurred at the time, the Government of the Macau S.A.R. declared the concession expired and prevented the defendant from carrying out any works on the land. That decision prompted the defendant to initiate several legal proceedings against the Macau S.A.R. Despite these attempts by the defendant to recover the land, the plaintiff considered that the Macau Government's decision amounted to an abnormal change of the circumstances upon which it based their decision to enter into the promissory contract. The court agreed that termination of the land concession was not within the typical risk of the contract and, therefore, could be considered an abnormal change of circumstances. Moreover, there was a high uncertainty as to the feasibility of the project, even if the defendant's legal actions against the Macau S.A.R. were to succeed. Therefore, termination of the contract, with restitution of all sums paid, was ordered by the first instance court.

Before the Second Instance Court, the defendant challenged this decision, arguing that the uncertainty as to the date of delivery of the unit was within contract-typical risk, as accepted by both parties. However, these arguments lost their relevance and were not further considered, in view of a final decision by the Court of Final Appeal confirming the termination of the concession.[46]

As far as we could ascertain, Macau courts are yet to decide any change of circumstances cases directly related to the COVID-19 pandemic, and literature on the topic has not gone beyond newspaper opinion pieces[47] and short articles published by law firms. This leads us to the question of whether recent work by Portuguese scholarship on the application of change of circumstances to the COVID-19 pandemic can be of any use in the decision of cases in Macau.

45 Decision of the Base Judicial Court of 23 January 2018, on case number CV1–16–0101-CAO.

46 Decision of the Second Instance Court of 7 March 2019, on case number 490/2018.

47 Cynthia Kou Ka, 'Alteração das circunstâncias à luz da pandemia de COVID-19 em Macau' ('Change of circumstances in light of the COVID-19 pandemic in Macau') *Plataforma* (5 November 2021) <https://plataformamedia.com/2021/11/05/alteracao-das-circunstancias-a-luz-da-pandemia-de-COVID-19-em-macau/>; on 10 May 2022.

The COVID-19 pandemic has, understandably, caused a 'large spectrum disturbance'[48] of social life, which may affect the 'identity of effort'[49] in a contract and make the applicability of the mechanism of change of circumstances plausible, albeit subject to a case-by-case analysis.

A question that has been discussed by authors in this context is the relevance of the requirement of no default of the party that is attempting to terminate or modify the contract. Whereas article 438 of the Portuguese Civil Code (corresponding to article 432 of the Macau CC) bars a party who is in default from terminating or modifying a contract based on change of circumstances, several scholars have expressed the opinion that this restriction is too broad. A position that has gathered some support distinguishes between situations in which default is a cause of the imbalance within the contract that the party invokes, and situations in which the imbalance would have occurred (due to exogenous causes) regardless of the situation of default.[50] According to these authors, termination or modification is only barred in the first hypothesis. As this solution goes against the letter of the law, some have labelled it a '*redução teleológica*'.[51]

Other authors place the emphasis on the issue of contractual risk.[52] From this perspective, the mechanism of change of circumstances is subordinate to the analysis of whether the imbalance in question (analysed on a case-by-case basis) is within the contract's normal spectrum of risk.

In this regard, Fonseca[53] argues that even a pandemic with the gravity and consequences of the current one may be within the spectrum of risk of certain contracts. The author starts by distinguishing between abnormality and unpredictability of the change of circumstances, noting that only the former is a requirement of the termination/modification mechanism set out in the CC, whereas the latter is irrelevant, as all risks are by nature unpredictable (whereas not all risks are by nature abnormal). As an example, Fonseca compares the closure of a childcare service during lockdown to the closure of the same business due to an infestation

48 Mariana Fontes da Costa, 'COVID-19 e Alteração Superveniente das Circunstâncias' ('COVID-19 and Subsequent Change of Circumstances') (2021) 81 Revista da Ordem dos Advogados 357, 358–359.

49 That is, the effort required of each of the parties in complying with their respective obligations under the agreement.

50 ibid, 369. Writing about the Brazilian Civil Code, but with references to the corresponding Portuguese provisions: Oliveira Ascenção (n 34) 7.

51 The restriction of a norm based on contradiction with its purpose. Manuel Carneiro da Frada, 'O COVID-19 e a Alteração das Circunstâncias' ('COVID-19 and Change of Circumstances') in Inês Fernandes Godinho and Miguel Osório de Castro (eds), *COVID 19 e o Direito (COVID 19 and the Law)* (Edições Universitárias Lusófonas 2020), 38.

52 Ana Taveira da Fonseca, 'Pandemia de COVID-19 e riscos próprios do contrato' (COVID-19 pandemic and contract-typical risks') in Gonçalo Malheiro and Luís Barreto Xavier (eds), *Contratos e Pandemia: Resolução, suspensão e modificação dos contratos em tempos de pandemia (Contracts and the Pandemic: Termination, suspension and modification of contracts in times of pandemic)* (Almedina, 2021), 13–36.

53 ibid, 33–35.

of cockroaches. In both cases there is an unpredictable event that affects the provision of the services, but are parents entitled, in either case, to a refund? Fonseca gives a *prima facie* positive answer to the question, considering that in both the infestation and the pandemic lockdown scenarios, the day care centre's inability to perform is within the normal contractual risk spectrum. Therefore, the centre's failure to comply would grant the parents the right to compensation (in the form of a refund). The author admits, however, that the risk of a pandemic-related lockdown might be considered atypical (or, in other words, outside the spectrum of normal contractual risk), in which case the contract could be modified based on change of circumstances (for instance, a reduction rather than full refund of the fees). One must, however, question if this partial acceptance of the mechanism of change of circumstances conforms with the law. Firstly, it must be noted that the abnormality of the change of circumstances (the law does not make any reference to predictability, which is irrelevant for the purpose at hand), and the determination of the normal contractual risk spectrum are two separate issues. Whereas it is generally accepted that the COVID-19 pandemic is an abnormal event (whereas a cockroach infestation is not), whether either one is comprised by the said risk spectrum depends on each contract and, therefore, calls for a case-by-case analysis. In this scenario, it is arbitrary to limit the functioning of the mechanism to only one of its possible outcomes. If all requirements are deemed fulfilled, then the injured party is entitled to terminate rather than only modify the affected contract.

Nevertheless, the determination of the contract's normal risk spectrum has been a decisive element in past change of circumstances cases. In Macau, a 2013 decision of the Second Instance Court seems aligned with this orientation. The case refers to a contract for temporary operation of a shop in a shopping centre, in which the owner of the shopping centre sued the shop operator for unpaid monthly fees and a contractual penalty. The defendant invoked, among other legal grounds, the termination of the contract based on change of circumstances, claiming that the shop was located on an intermediate floor, with a bad 'tenant mix' and low foot traffic. They blamed the shop's bad performance on these circumstances, which, according to them, constituted an abnormal change vis-à-vis the initial agreement between the parties. The court rejected these arguments, holding that the circumstances described by the defendant correspond to the normal risks of the commercial activity pursued by the defendant.[54] This decision leaves enough ground to admit that, faced with a clearer change of circumstances of abnormal nature, Macau courts might apply the mechanism, even if conservatively.

2.6 Force majeure

Macau law admits *force majeure* mechanisms of both statutory and contractual source. With regard to the former, whereas there is no general *force majeure* clause

54 Decision of the Second Instance Court of 25 June 2015, in case number 699/2013.

applicable to all contracts, the concept appears in some scattered provisions, such as article 117 of the Commercial Code, according to which a commercial tenant is under the obligation not to interrupt or cease the running of an enterprise unless a case of *force majeure* emerges.[55] Another important area of statutory application of *force majeure* is that of public work contracts, regulated by Decree-Law No. 74/99/M.[56] According to article 169(3) of this statute, *force majeure* would be deemed to arise in case of an unpredictable and irresistible natural event or situation, the effects of which occur regardless of the contractor's will or personal circumstances – for example, acts of war or subversion, epidemics, typhoons, earthquakes, lightning, floods, general or sectoral strikes. As this chapter does not focus on public works contracts, but on the more amorphous reality of private contracts, this statute is not further analysed.

As regards contractual *force majeure* clauses, anecdotal accounts seem to point – predictably – towards a common inclusion of epidemics as a cause of *force majeure*. However, these clauses are not present in all contracts, and, in many cases, parties can only rely on the law to obtain any relief from difficult contractual situations. This is of particular concern in long term contracts, such as rentals, in which parties may not experience an immediate impossibility to comply, but a gradual deterioration of their conditions.

3 The Macau rental market: a hypothetical case study

3.1 Overview

On 22 January 2020, Macau detected the first case of respiratory disease caused by a (then still unnamed) new coronavirus, which had, until that day, caused a total (reported) nine deaths in the city of Wuhan.[57] At the time, Macau was gearing up to Chinese New Year, a typically busy period of the year, which was just days away. As the news of the imported cases came one after the other, the city ground to a halt. Festivities were cancelled and streets – usually crowded even on normal working days – became deserted. However, this was not the result of a 'hard' lockdown enforced by the authorities, but governmental instructions and the citizens' own initiative.

55 Macao Commercial Code art 117, 'Obligation to Run Commercial Enterprise' <https://bo.io.gov.mo/bo/i/99/31/codcomen/codcom0501.asp> (unofficial English translation) (last accessed 13 May 2022).

56 Law Decree No. 74/99/M art 169, 'Force Majeure and Other Facts Not Attributable to the Contractor', promulgated on 3 November 1999 and published on 8 November 1999 <https://bo.io.gov.mo/bo/i/99/45/declei74_cn.asp> (in Chinese) (last accessed 13 May 2022).

57 Reuters Staff, 'Macau confirms first new coronavirus case – Xinhua', *Reuters* (22 January 2020) <www.reuters.com/article/china-health-macau-idUKL4N29Q04X> (last accessed on 13 May 2022).

The strongest of governmental measures came weeks later, on 5 February 2020, when the Chief Executive ordered a 14-day closure[58] of casinos[59] and 25-day closure for other premises offering leisure and entertainment services.[60] During this period, the focus of the authorities was to limit the entry of people coming from Hubei province and to track down those who had already entered the region, while keeping social interaction at a minimum and providing for the orderly supply of face masks, disinfectant and other goods of first necessity.

It was only when it became apparent that the epidemic had spread globally that the government began to implement measures aimed at limiting the entry of people infected with COVID-19 from outside Mainland China (while gradually easing restrictions on previously excluded areas). These measures are of two types: the prohibition of entry of foreign citizens (with some exceptions, including those who are residents of the Macau S.A.R.);[61] and the need to undergo a 14-day hotel quarantine[62] on entry by anyone coming from overseas, Hong Kong or Taiwan, as well as designated areas of Mainland China, based on a dynamic risk analysis. At the time of writing (September 2022), both measures remain in place, albeit with some adjustments,[63] and there is no set date for their expiry.

Thus, in comparison with western countries, Macau was deprived of the pre-pandemic way of life earlier on. However, after the initial stage, and during its long periods of no community outbreak, Macau regained a shrunken version of its social and business life – now limited to locals and individual travellers from low-risk areas of Mainland China: a bubble of normalcy that is, nevertheless, far

58 See Dispatch Order of the Chief Executive No. 27/2020, which came into effect on 4 February 2020 <https://bo.io.gov.mo/bo/i/2020/05/despce_cn.asp#27> (in Chinese and Portuguese). The special mandatory measures on the temporary closure for casinos were lifted on 20 February 2020 pursuant to Dispatch Order of the Chief Executive No. 39/2020 <https://bo.io.gov.mo/bo/i/2020/07/despce.asp#39> (in Chinese and Portuguese). Other premises offering leisure and entertainment services were able to reopen on 2 March 2020 pursuant to Dispatch Order of the Chief Executive No. 50/2020 <https://bo.io.gov.mo/bo/i/2020/08/despce.asp#50> (in Chinese and Portuguese). All last accessed on 13 May 2022.

59 Casinos are referred to as those premises which are authorised statutorily for gaming under Law No. 16/2001 art 2. See Dispatch Order of the Chief Executive No. 27/2020 (ibid).

60 These premises include venues such as cinemas, theatres, indoor amusement parks, amusement rooms and video games, Internet cafes, billiard and bowling rooms, sauna and massage establishments, beauty parlours, fitness centres, health club and karaoke establishments, bars, nightclubs, discos, dance rooms and cabaret pursuant to Decree-Law No. 47/98/M and Decree-Law No. 16/96/M. See Dispatch Order of the Chief Executive No. 27/2020 (n 58).

61 Government Information Bureau, 'Macao to ban overseas travellers in effort further to control COVID-19 locally' *Gov.mo* (17 March 2020) <www.gov.mo/en/news/123607/> (last accessed 13 May 2022).

62 Centre of Coordination of Contingency of New Type of Coronavirus, Health Bureau, Announcement (16 March 2020) <www.gov.mo/zh-hant/news/323430/> (in Chinese).

63 The hotel quarantine period has been lowered to 7 days, and the nationals of 41 countries have been allowed to enter Macau. Tony Lai, 'Macau to ease quarantine period for non-Mainland Chinese visitation to "7+3" from Aug 6' *Macau Business* (2 August 2022) < https://www.macaubusiness.com/macau-to-ease-quarantine-period-for-non-mainland-chinese-visitation-to-73-from-aug-6/ (last accessed 14 September 2022)>; Pierce Chan (n 1).

from the previous reality and at odds with the costs of living and doing business in the S.A.R.

In particular, the continued restrictions on entry of foreign citizens and the mentioned quarantine requirements have put a long-lasting strain on businesses and individuals that depend on international tourism, and which have seen their income significantly reduced, with no clear perspectives of improvement.[64]

In this scenario, rather than a sudden onset of a disturbance, to which *pacta sunt servanda* exceptions can be more clearly applicable,[65] it is the continuing effects of this 'bubble' on long-term contractual relationships – such as housing and commercial rentals – that seems more problematic, given the particular characteristics of the Macau property market.

3.2 Macau rental market

As of 2021, Macau had a total land area of 33km^2, a total population of 683,200, and a population density of 20,700/km^2,[66] making it one of the world's most densely populated territories. Concomitantly, since the early 2000s, Macau has seen a boom of its economy, brought about by the end of the monopoly over gaming licenses and the consequent opening of the sector to foreign investment.[67] This development has been seen to contribute to the problem of land scarcity in the territory, given that the manpower demands for new projects – such as large integrated resorts (combining hotel, leisure and gaming elements) – led to a higher demand for housing, but also considering the space granted to the construction of these resorts, namely in Cotai – a reclaimed area between the islands of Taipa and Coloane, which at an initial stage had been planned to house up to 150,000 people.[68]

In this context, real estate prices increased significantly, both in the purchase and the rental market, reaching record highs during the post-liberalisation boom and, reportedly, prompting residents to seek housing in neighbouring regions.[69]

In the rental market, during this period, despite legal provisions that granted housing tenants a minimum of two years before the landlord could terminate the

64 For a quantitative analysis of the impact of the pandemic on tourism and gambling in Macau, Weng Marc Lim and Wai-Ming To, 'The economic impact of a global pandemic on the tourism economy: the case of COVID-19 and Macao's destination-and gambling-dependent economy' (2022) 25 Current Issues in Tourism 1258.

65 E.g. a contract for a one-off supply of imported goods, the transportation of which became exponentially more onerous with the sudden onset of the pandemic.

66 Macau S.A.R. Government, Statistics and Census Service, Macao in Figures (2022), p 5 <www.dsec.gov.mo/getAttachment/8311b8c9-e835-4599-9975-3bacfd015102/E_MN_PUB_2022_Y.aspx> (last accessed 13 May 2022).

67 Mingjie Sheng and Chaolin Gu, 'Economic growth and development in Macau (1999–2016): The role of the booming gaming industry' (2018) 75 Cities 72.

68 ibid.

69 Yimou Lee and Farah Master, 'Casino riches fuel Macau property "bubble" forcing residents elsewhere' *Reuters* (7 April 2014) <www.reuters.com/article/macau-property-idINL4N0MM23Z20140406> (last accessed 13 May 2022).

contract,[70] the common practice was for tenants to be presented with one-year contracts, at the end of which landlords would either ask for a significant increase of the rent or simply terminate the contract and request tenants to vacate the unit. This situation was coupled with an unwillingness of landlords to rent out their properties for lower prices, even in periods of market downturns, preferring to leave their units empty. This was reportedly the case well into the COVID-19 pandemic, until it became evident that the downturn would not be reversed in the short term.[71]

In the commercial rental market, a similar evolution took place, with shop rentals in central areas of Taipa and Macau Peninsula reaching high values, which led many businesses to have to relocate or close shop due to rental hikes, making these prime areas prone to frequent rotation of tenants.[72]

In this scenario, difficulties in complying with contractual terms seem likely. However, as previously mentioned, this has not corresponded to an (as yet visible) increase in litigation based on the change of circumstances mechanism. Possible reasons for this – although further empirical studies would be necessary to ascertain it – are informal adjustments of contractual commitments, together with governmental measures aimed at supporting the local economy.

3.3 Governmental support and informal adjustments

In response to the unprecedented COVID-19 crisis, financial assistance measures were announced by the government on 13 February 2020,[73] 8 April 2020[74] and April 2022[75] to alleviate the financial hardship which negatively affected local businesses as well as local community, and aimed at reviving the tourism industry as soon as practicable.[76]

Soon after the pandemic commenced, a government subsidy scheme was introduced for eligible individuals as well as local companies to stimulate local

70 CC art 1038/2, which was subsequently amended by Law 13/2017, increasing the said guaranteed minimum period to three years.

71 Tony Lai, 'Tenant Market' *Macau Business* (21 September 2021) <www.macaubusiness.com/tenant-market/> (last accessed 13 May 2022).

72 Luciana Leitão, 'Shop 'till you drop' *Macau Business* (28 July 2014) <www.macaubusiness.com/shop-til-they-drop-2/> (last accessed 13 May 2022).

73 In the first round of economic relief measures, the Macao SAR Government spent a total of 46.2 billion patacas funding: Macao SAR Government, 'Policy Address for the Fiscal Year 2021' <www.gov.mo/en/wp-content/uploads/sites/2/2021/01/2021_policy_e.pdf> (last accessed 13 May 2022). (See also Macao Trade and Investment Promotion Institute, 'Government to spend MOP50 bln on spurring economic rebound', *Focus* Issue 76 (June 2020) <https://m.ipim.gov.mo/en/publication/issue-76-jun-2020/focus/government-to-spend-mop50-bln-on-spurring-economic-rebound/

74 Government Information Bureau, '10-billion-pataca fund aiming to bolster support for employees and businesses' *Gov.mo* (8 April 2020) <www.gov.mo/en/news/124630/> (last accessed 13 May 2022).

75 Government Information Bureau, 'Registration for electronic consumption benefits plan starts on 10 May' *Gov.mo* (29 April 2022) <www.gov.mo/en/news/267290/> (last accessed 13 May 2022).

76 Government Information Bureau (n 74).

consumption.[77] These financial assistance measures broadly included 'consumption subsidies,[[78]] tax waivers and deductions, water and electricity fee subsidies, a one-off cash allowance, waiver of business licence fees and a three-month rent waiver of government-owned properties, electronic vouchers for tourism incentive schemes, and subsidised local tours',[79] paid occupational training courses, subsidies for interest payment by self-employed individuals and SMEs,[80] tourism tax waiver and other tax benefits.[81]

There is, however, one governmental measure that more closely relates to the matter at hand: the introduction of tax benefits for landlords willing to reduce rents on their properties. According to the Macau Tax Department, from October 2021 to January 2022, more than 600 applications were received for this reduction of property tax.[82] This data is consistent with anecdotal accounts of extra-judicial rental reductions by landlords in both residential and commercial rental contracts. This points towards the informal adjustment of contractual relations, with the mentioned tax incentive, but also the local business culture, as probable causes (although, as mentioned, further empirical studies would be necessary to confirm these assertions). These informal adjustments, however, can only go so far, according to the representatives of local business associations, who have recently called for stronger measures from the government, namely as regards reduction of rents.[83]

As the crisis continues, and 'the borderline between the during- and post-crisis stages [is blurred]',[84] one must question the long-term sustainability of this situation. From a legal standpoint, this brings us back to the tension between *pacta sunt servanda* and contractual justice. How do these principles apply to long-term contracts whose internal balance is affected by a prolonged crisis that remains largely abnormal in both gravity and duration? The following subsection takes a

77 Macao SAR Government (n 73).

78 Staff Reporter, 'New round of electronic consumption cards to launch in May' *Macau News* (2 April 2022) <https://macaonews.org/economy/new-round-of-electronic-consumption-cards-to-launch-in-may/> (last accessed 13 May 2022). (Also see Staff Reporter, 'First round of MOP 10,000 cash handouts start today', Macau News (1 April 2022) https://macaonews.org/economy/first-round-of-mop-10000-cash-handouts-start-today/ (last accessed 13 May 2022)).

79 Macao SAR Government (n 73).

80 Government Information Bureau (n 74).

81 Macao Government Tourism Office, 'Measures get underway to help cushion the economic impact of COVID-19', *News* (February–May 2020) <https://mtt.macaotourism.gov.mo/2020/02/measures-get-underway-to-help-cushion-the-economic-impact-of-COVID-19/

82 Direcção dos Serviços de Finanças (DSF), 'Incentivos fiscais atribuídos aos proprietários para a redução das rendas foram eficazes, tendo-se registado 631 entradas na DSF' ('Tax incentives granted to land owners for the reduction of rents were effective, with 631 entries before DSF' (2022) Portal do Governo da RAEM <www.gov.mo/pt/noticias/580710/> (last accessed 15 May 2022).

83 Tony Lai, 'More, and more' *Macau Business* (14 May 2022) <www.macaubusiness.com/more-and-more/> (last accessed on 15 May 2022).

84 Jose C Alves and others, 'Crisis challenges of small firms in Macao during the COVID-19 pandemic' (2020) 14 Frontiers of Business Research in China 26.

practical approach to this query, by hypothesising three different scenarios involving commercial rental contracts.

3.4 Scenarios

For the purposes of this hypothetical analysis, the following scenarios concerning retail shop lots are considered:

a) A commercial rental contract entered into before January 2020, for a period of three years, with yearly rental increments.
b) A commercial rental contract entered into before January 2020, for a period of one year. In mid-2020, considering a seemingly positive evolution of the situation, the contract is renewed for another year at a higher rental.
c) A commercial rental contract entered into during the pandemic, for market price (lower than pre-pandemic levels), for a period of three years.

In all scenarios it is assumed that (i) the commercial activity of the tenant is dependent on tourism and foot traffic in a central area of Macau; (ii) the tenant has consequently suffered a significant reduction of their ability to comply with the terms of the contract as a result of the pandemic and related measures; and (iii) no default has taken place.

In all three scenarios, long-term commitments were accepted. However, while only the first tenant was unaware of the impending pandemic at the time of closing, this does not automatically make this tenant entitled to terminate or modify the contract based on change of circumstances (article 431 of the CC). As previously noted, a crucial step is to determine the contract's typical risk spectrum. As these scenarios all refer to commercial rentals for retail shops, there is, in that activity, an inherent risk of failure that may simply be the result of customer preferences or normal variations in visitation to the region (as was the case in the above-mentioned shopping centre case).[85] Some arguments may, however, point towards a different solution. For instance, if the business is well-established and of renown quality (and simply changing location) one might argue that if not for the pandemic, that tenant would not have suffered such a dramatic loss of business. Moreover, it is important to consider the timing of the request for termination or modification. During the initial stages of the epidemic in Macau (after the detection of the first case), and despite the absence of a 'hard' lockdown, tourism and local foot traffic were reduced to almost zero, as locals voluntarily isolated in their residences. Therefore, a request at this time would have had better odds of succeeding, as the link between the abnormal event and the tenant's loss of custom is readily established. At a later stage, the courts are likely to be more reluctant to use the mechanism, as that link weakens and the loss of business may plausibly be attributed to other factors, such as customer preference or normal market fluctuations.

85 Decision of the Second Instance Court of 25 June 2015, in case number 699/2013.

The other two cases differ in that the second tenant (b) was more confident in the economic outlook of the region and committed to a higher rental upon renewal, whereas the third (c) was able to negotiate a lower rent from the beginning. In the context of a change of circumstances, it may be said that tenant (b) accepted a higher risk, which means that the original contractual balance was arguably unequal in favour of the landlord. In this scenario, who has a broader spectrum of risk (and, consequently lower odds of successfully invoking the mechanism of change of circumstances)? Prima facie it would seem to be (b), as the contract is already imbalanced from the onset, but the contrary could also be argued.

Finally, tenant (c) entered into a contract under market conditions of the pandemic 'new normal'. In terms of contractual balance, one might say that this tenant was cautiously optimistic in their ability to operate a commercial venture in times of COVID-19. Under what circumstances could this tenant invoke the mechanism of change of circumstances? One possibility is the occurrence of an event within the pandemic that diverges from the overall evolution – for instance, a local outbreak that reduces to almost zero the modest demand that has characterised the current period. But what if no such event occurs, and instead restrictive measures are kept in place for much longer than expected?

Although this is a more far-fetched hypothesis, it is worth considering if a prolonged pandemic depression that depletes the resources of struggling business could, in itself, be seen as an abnormal event. Could we say that, following an initial period of disruption, the availability of vaccines and treatments would have led economic agents to expect that a recovery was in the horizon, and that the failure to lift restrictions in due time is susceptible of causing a supervening imbalance of contractual positions? It seems highly unlikely that such an argument might succeed in Macau courts. However, as the bubble remains unburst, the current stimulus and informal adjustment mechanisms may not meet the needs of local businesses, and the courts might finally be brought into the picture.

Within Roberto Unger's proposal of 'institutional imagination', dominant and subordinate principles could be manipulated by the interpreter to pursue social goals, such as social solidarity and the protection of the disadvantaged.[86] In the relationship between *pacta sunt servanda* and contractual justice, any innovative applications of the mechanism of change of circumstances along the lines of what is discussed above could be seen as a form of activism: taking from the rich to give to the poor. But would that be legitimate or necessary? Within the current circumstances of the region, going that far seems, at this stage, to be ill-advised. Instead, the interpreter ought to carefully weigh contractual burdens and strike a fair balance between *pacta sunt servanda* and contractual justice, having in mind the risks accepted and the reasonable expectations of the parties.

86 Roberto Mangabeira Unger, 'Legal Analysis as Institutional Imagination' (1996) 59 The Modern Law Review 1. Also see Scott Veitch, Emilios Christodoulidis and Marco Goldoni, *Jurisprudence: Themes and Concepts* (3rd ed, Routledge, 2018), 194–198.

4 Conclusion

Private autonomy and *pacta sunt servanda* are fundamental principles of Macau's law of obligations. However, good faith and, arguably, the principle of contractual balance (or justice) provide legal avenues for relief in case of abnormal changes of circumstances that affect the parties' ability to perform. Yet, doubts remain about the interpretation of such mechanisms in the context of a pandemic that has been largely controlled within the borders of Macau S.A.R. but which left it in a prolonged crisis without end in sight. Only time will tell when recovery comes, but in the meantime, it is up to the law and its practitioners to strike a fair balance of principles inside the bubble.

4 Contracts in the time of COVID-19

Common law and statutory solutions in Singapore

Wayne Courtney

I Introduction

The COVID-19 pandemic is the most significant world event in this century and, arguably, for some decades prior. It has affected almost every aspect of daily life. This Chapter addresses just a small part of the picture, namely, the impact of the pandemic on the performance of contracts under Singaporean law.

For contract lawyers in common law legal systems, frustration is the doctrine that is most obviously applicable to disruption caused by a global pandemic. The parties may also have sought to address matters themselves by way of a force majeure clause, whether such a clause covers events that would anyway constitute frustration or fall short of the stringent requirements of that doctrine. Aside from the common law, parliament may choose to intervene by passing legislation to address specific incidents of the pandemic as they affect the performance of contracts. This allows a far more nuanced adjustment of the parties' rights and obligations as compared to the guillotine effect of common law frustration. Indeed, one of the striking features of the COVID-19 pandemic is that it has provoked this kind of legislative response in so many jurisdictions. Few (if any) global events in the past half-century have had such an impact.

I am principally concerned with two matters: the common law doctrine of frustration, including statutory adjustment of the consequences of frustration;[1] and legislation enacted by the government in Singapore specifically to respond to the difficulties posed by the COVID-19 pandemic. I leave aside the application of force majeure clauses. This is not because such clauses are not important in practice: they are. Rather, they raise relatively few interesting issues of legal principle. Their application largely turns upon construction, informed by specific guidelines or presumptions about their effect.[2]

This Chapter is divided into three parts. I begin by outlining the general law on frustration in Singapore. After that, I turn to a significant Singaporean case that

1 Frustrated Contracts Act 1959 (2020 rev ed), which is based on the Law Reform (Frustrated Contracts) Act 1943 (UK).

2 *RDC Concrete Pte Ltd v Sato Kogyo (S) Pte Ltd* [2007] SGCA 39, [2007] 4 SLR(R) 413 [54]; *Holcim (Singapore) Pte Ltd v Precise Development Pte Ltd* [2011] SGCA 1, [2011] 2 SLR 106 [49].

DOI: 10.4324/9781003358305-5

considered whether the consequences of the COVID-19 pandemic led to arrangements being frustrated at common law. In the final part, I consider legislation introduced by the Singaporean government to ameliorate the impact of the pandemic upon certain types of agreement. This is the COVID-19 (Temporary Measures) Act 2020, accompanied by several sets of regulations.[3]

II Frustration of contract

A The frustration doctrine in Singapore

The common law doctrine of frustration of contract in Singapore is substantially the same as that in England. The starting point for the modern law in Singapore is the adoption of Lord Radcliffe's 'radical change in obligation' test from *Davis Contractors Ltd v Fareham Urban District Council* ('*Davis*').[4] On this account, frustration is a legal principle applied *ab extra* to the contract, albeit one which pays close regard to the parties' objective intentions and the context at the time of formation. So, in *Alliance Concrete Singapore Pte Ltd v Sato Kogyo (S) Pte Ltd* ('*Alliance*'),[5] the Court of Appeal referred to 'a supervening event that has occurred after the formation of the contract [which] renders a contractual obligation radically or fundamentally different from what has been agreed in the contract'. Under the *Davis* test, the event must occur without default of either party. Singaporean courts have also accepted[6] the methodological refinements introduced by the relatively recent English case of *The Sea Angel*.[7] There, Rix LJ advocated a 'multi-factorial' process of evaluation, which takes into account the terms of the contract, the factual matrix, the parties' knowledge and assumptions at the time of contract, particularly as to allocation of risks, and the nature of the supervening event.[8]

In *Alliance*, the Court of Appeal reasoned that the frustration doctrine embodied 'justice and fairness'.[9] I remain a sceptic on that score: at best, it is a peculiar kind of fairness.[10] The negative case, namely, that frustration is rarely established, might be grounded in the notion that it is only fair that parties be held to their

3 eg COVID-19 (Temporary Measures) (Temporary Relief for Inability to Perform Contracts) Regulations 2020; COVID-19 (Temporary Measures) (Rental and Related Measures) Regulations 2020; COVID-19 (Temporary Measures) (Part 8 Relief) Regulations 2020.
4 [1956] AC 696, 729.
5 [2014] SGCA 35, [2014] 3 SLR 857 [33].
6 *Davis* (n 4) [37].
7 *Edwinton Commercial Corp v Tsavliris Russ (Worldwide Salvage & Towage) Ltd (The Sea Angel)* [2007] EWCA Civ 547, [2007] 2 Lloyd's Rep 517.
8 ibid, 111.
9 *Alliance* (n 5) [38]. See also *Hirji Mulji v Cheong Yue Steamship Co Ltd* [1926] AC 497, 510 (Lord Sumner); *Denny, Mott & Dickson Ltd v James B Fraser & Co Ltd* [1944] AC 265, 275 (Lord Wright).
10 cf *Scanlan's New Neon Ltd v Tooheys Ltd* (1943) 67 CLR 169, 187–8 (Latham CJ); *National Carriers Ltd v Panalpina (Northern) Ltd* [1981] AC 675, 687 (Lord Hailsham).

bargains (*pacta sunt servanda*) or that parties ought to bear a risk that was previously allocated. But for the affirmative case, that parties ought to be discharged when the circumstances are radically different, 'fairness' merely begs the question.

The justification for the affirmative case may depend upon the theory of frustration chosen. If, for example, frustration simply reflects the true basis or limits of the parties' undertakings, it is fair in the sense that it holds the parties to their bargain and no more. But then it is hard to see it as having independent existence as a doctrine. So far as frustration rests upon impossibility or intervening illegality, it recognises that the contract simply cannot go on. It is debatable whether this is pragmatism or 'fairness' and, in any event, the application of the doctrine will depend upon whether it can be established that a party is 'at fault' for the obstruction. Fault excludes frustration but may establish a breach of contract. A situation where, for example, war makes trading with the enemy illegal is entirely different from one where a party fails to obtain a necessary export licence, in breach of an obligation to exercise reasonable efforts to do so. Moreover, one of the puzzling features of the fairness argument is that it pays little regard to the consequences of frustration. The common law remedies available to mop up the aftermath of a frustrating event do not operate in any systematically fair manner.[11] The same criticism has been levelled at the Law Reform (Frustrated Contracts) Act 1943 (UK).[12]

B The application of frustration to pandemics

A conclusion as to whether a contract has been frustrated is a matter of law[13] which depends upon the particular facts of a case. Conclusions reached in prior cases, even if involving the same event and similar kinds of contract, can only ever be indicative. Even so, the prevailing tests for frustration have come to be applied by reference to categories or types of frustrating event. A conventional taxonomy divides cases into impossibility of various kinds (e.g. destruction of the subject-matter, unavailability of the subject-matter, death or incapacity of persons), supervening illegality, impracticability or frustration of the commercial venture, frustration of purpose and so on. There is not, in practice, always a clear distinction between each category.

Pandemic, of itself, is no more a sufficient ground for frustration than is war alone. What matters is the way in which the event impacts upon the expected performance of the contract. We can conceive that a pandemic may impede the production of goods,[14] render specific goods or a source of supply unavailable, render persons unavailable or incapable of performing services, make performance

11 *Fibrosa Spolka Akcyjna v Fairbairn Lawson Combe Barbour Ltd* [1943] AC 32, 49 (Viscount Simon LC), 59 (Lord Macmillan), 76 (Lord Roche).

12 *Panalpina* (n 10), 707 (Lord Simon).

13 Or, perhaps, mixed fact and law: *Davis Contractors* (n 4), 718 (Lord Morton).

14 cf *Citrus Soap Co v Peet Bros Manufacturing Co* 50 Cal App 246 (1920) (turning upon an excuse clause akin to a force majeure provision).

impracticable so as to frustrate the commercial venture, or frustrate the purpose of the parties' agreement. Similarly, governments may legislate in response to pandemic conditions in a manner that renders performance of the contract illegal or impossible.

C Pre-COVID-19 common law decisions

Although epidemics and pandemics are not uncommon, I have not been able to find any reported cases in England or Singapore, prior to the arrival of COVID-19, that have considered whether the effects of a pandemic frustrate a contract. The absence of such cases before the 1860s is explicable by the state of the law.[15] Thereafter, it might have been thought that the Spanish flu in 1918, or SARS and avian flu epidemics in Asia during 2003 and 2004, would throw up one example. Apparently not so in England and Singapore.

Even in the United States, historical authority is slender. The waters are muddied by theories that attribute the effects of disease upon contractual performance to a principle of public policy rather than frustration. Isolated illustrations do exist, scattered across various categories. One famous instance is *Lakeman v Pollard*,[16] where a worker abandoned his job with a sawmill due to fears of contracting cholera. His non-performance was excused on the ground that cholera was sufficiently prevalent in the area to make a reasonable person flee in fear of his or her safety. Nowadays, such a case could be assigned to the category of frustration by death or incapacity.[17]

There is a line of decisions on school-teachers' claims to be paid for a period during which schools were closed due to pandemics.[18] In a similar vein are claims brought by providers of transportation for school students, servicing schools that were closed.[19] These decisions yield inconsistent results and are hard to square with the current Anglo-Singaporean understanding of the law of contract. A significant factor in the school-teacher cases seems to have been who made the decision to close the school and whether the closure occurred under legal compulsion. On that basis, these decisions might best be assigned to the category of frustration

15 *Taylor v Caldwell* (1863) 3 B & S 826, 122 ER 309 marked the start of the modern doctrine of frustration.

16 43 Me 463 (1857).

17 This is where it is mentioned in the *Restatement of the Law (2d) Contracts*, §262 Reporter's Note, com a.

18 *Dewey v Union School District of the City of Alpena* 43 Mich 480 (1880) (outbreak of smallpox – school not excused from obligation to pay); *School Town of Carthage v Gray* 10 Ind App 428 (1894) (outbreak of diphtheria – school not excused); *Libby v Douglas* 88 NE 808 (Mass, 1900) (outbreak of diphtheria – school not excused); *Gregg School Township v Hinshaw* 76 Ind App 503, 132 NE 586 (1921) (influenza epidemic – school excused); *Phelps v School District No 109* 302 Ill 193, 134 NE 312 (1922) (influenza epidemic – school not excused).

19 *Crane v School District No 14 of Tillamook County* 188 P 712 (Or, 1920) (influenza epidemic – school not excused from obligation to pay); *Sandry v Brooklyn School District No 78 of Williams County* 47 ND 444, 182 NW 689 (1921) (influenza epidemic – school excused).

by supervening illegality. There are, however, other features that conflict with modern contract doctrine. The decisions suppose that a radical change in circumstances can suspend, rather than discharge, a contract.[20] And they appear to accept that, where the defendant or an external event prevents performance, the plaintiff's readiness and willingness to perform services is sufficient to earn a salary[21] or the contract sum.

Hanford v Connecticut Fair Association[22] might nowadays be seen as an instance of frustration of the commercial venture or perhaps frustration of purpose. The plaintiffs agreed to promote and manage a baby show in Hartford in September 1916. The plaintiffs were to provide advertising material and 120 prizes; the defendant was to provide the rooms for the show and to pay the plaintiffs $600. In August and September 1916, the city of Hartford was struck by an epidemic of 'infantile paralysis', that is, polio. The defendant purported to cancel the contract and the show was never held.

In rejecting the plaintiff's claim for damages, the preferred ground for decision was that to assemble a group of babies in such circumstances would be dangerous to public health and therefore the contract became contrary to public policy. However, the decision might equally be explained in terms of frustration. The pandemic would cause a small (or no) patronage to the show and a lack of babies eligible for the 120 prizes. On that view, the commercial venture may have been frustrated. Or, it might be said that the parties had a common purpose, fundamental to the contract, in awarding prizes to babies and profiting from the attendance of eager parents. Shumway J remarked that the agreement was a 'joint undertaking . . . to furnish and to do such things as were deemed essential to attract a number of babies' to the show. If that is right, then the parties' purpose may have been frustrated by the pandemic.

I emphasise the element of common purpose because frustration of purpose must be kept within narrow bounds. It would be all too easy to say that the 'purpose' of the agreement has been defeated when pandemic conditions have substantially eroded one party's benefit under it. This is not sufficient to establish frustration. Vaughan Williams LJ issued a similar warning in *Herne Bay Steam Boat Co v Hutton*,[23] one of the coronation cases decided close together with the companion case of *Krell v Henry*.[24] The Court of Appeal held that the contract was not frustrated in *Herne Bay* and that it was frustrated in *Krell*.

20 This lends support to the view that these cases turned upon illegality or public policy simpliciter rather than frustration by illegality. See generally *Arab Bank Ltd v Barclays Bank (Dominion, Colonial and Overseas)* [1954] AC 495, 530 (Lord Reid); *Dyco Hotels Pty Ltd v Laundy Hotels (Quarry) Pty Ltd* [2021] NSWCA 332 [66]–[71] (Bathurst CJ).

21 Contrast *Automatic Fire Sprinklers Pty Ltd v Watson* (1946) 72 CLR 435, 450, 452 (Latham CJ), 461 (Starke J), 465 (Dixon J), 476 (Williams J).

22 92 Conn 621 (1918).

23 [1903] 2 KB 683 (CA).

24 [1903] 2 KB 740 (CA).

Readers may recall that in *Krell* Vaughan Williams LJ discussed the hypothetical example of a customer hiring a cab to go to Epsom to see the races. Contrasting that hypothetical with the facts in *Krell*, he explained that the cancellation of the races at Epsom would *not* have frustrated the contract for carriage. There was nothing special about the cab and the cab driver had no particular interest in the conduct of the races. Even if the races had been cancelled, the passenger could have insisted that the cab proceed to Epsom.[25] Vaughan Williams LJ touched on the same hypothetical in *Herne Bay*, this time perceiving an analogy between it and the facts in that case. He said:[26]

> I see nothing that makes this contract differ from a case where, for instance, a person has engaged a brake to take himself and a party to Epsom to see the races there, but for some reason or other, *such as the spread of an infectious disease*, the races are postponed. In such a case it could not be said that he could be relieved of his bargain.

D Singaporean decisions on the COVID-19 pandemic

Singaporean courts will continue to apply conventional principles governing frustration to new situations created by the COVID-19 pandemic. At the time of writing, there appears to be only one decision delivered by a superior court, *Dathena Science Pte Ltd v Justco (Singapore) Pte Ltd*.[27] The plaintiff was a Singaporean cybersecurity company with offices around the world. The defendant provided workspaces in offices and commercial buildings. The plaintiff was looking to relocate its operations in Singapore. In January 2020 it entered into a contract with the defendant, called a 'membership agreement', to rent premises for two years starting on 1 May 2020. The arrangement is described in the judgment as a lease though, strictly, it may have been only an agreement for lease or a licence.[28] An appendix to the agreement imposed obligations upon the defendant to perform certain fit-out renovations, including constructing meeting rooms and data ports. Before entering the agreement, the plaintiff had emphasised the importance of being able to relocate its data servers into the new premises before the starting date of 1 May 2020. This was because its existing lease was expiring on that same day.

On 7 April 2020, the Singaporean government activated what were known as 'circuit-breaker' measures, intended to contain the spread of COVID-19. Under those measures the supply of many non-essential services was to cease; most office workers switched to working from home. The defendant claimed that, due to the

25 ibid, 750–1.
26 [1903] 2 KB 683 (CA), 689 (emphasis added).
27 [2021] SGHC 219.
28 Nothing in the following analysis turns on whether the arrangement was a lease, an agreement for lease or only a licence.

circuit-breaker measures, it was unable to complete the fit-out in time for the start of the lease on 1 May 2020. The defendant initially proposed a revised schedule to complete the fit-out by 1 June and then, after the circuit-breaker was extended,[29] by 30 June. The concession offered was that the plaintiff's obligation to pay rent would be deferred to begin on 1 July. However, by 26 May the defendant admitted to the plaintiff that it was not certain when the premises would be ready.

On 29 May, the plaintiff sent a document titled 'Notice of Termination' to the defendant. In it, the plaintiff hedged its bets, asserting that the membership agreement was 'now terminated, or frustrated'. It demanded return of certain sums it had paid, including a substantial security deposit. The reason given in the notice for termination was, rather vaguely, that completion of the fit-out and giving possession had been delayed for a lengthy period and still no definite date was known. In its statement of claim the plaintiff put forward a blanket case, asserting a 'repudiatory breach' or a breach of a 'fundamental term' or a breach depriving it of substantially the whole benefit of the agreement, or a repudiation. As for frustration, the plaintiff's justification was that the COVID-19 pandemic and governmental response was unforeseen. And, since the government's response to the pandemic signalled that working from home would continue to be the norm for the foreseeable future, the plaintiff's 'original intended use of the [p]remises [was] no longer possible or viable'.

The trial judge upheld the plaintiff's claim on two grounds. On the breach ground, the court reasoned as follows. The expected delay in completing the fit-out and giving possession was, even on the defendant's case, about four months. This amounted to about 17% of the duration of the lease.[30] The option under clause 2(c) of the agreement, which allowed the defendant to switch the office space allocated to the plaintiff with office space of a comparable size in any of the defendant's other premises, had not properly been exercised. In any event, it was rendered ineffective by the Unfair Contract Terms Act.[31] The judge then considered whether there was a right to terminate for breach. The judge rejected the argument that there was no clause in the agreement that permitted the plaintiff to terminate. This, the judge said, 'cannot be right as a matter of contract law in a commercial context'.[32] The presence of an entire agreement clause did not prevent the court implying terms. In short, there was a right to terminate for breach, which the plaintiff had exercised.

The alternative ground was that the contract had been frustrated. Here, the court offered several reasons. It said that the expected four-month delay in completing the fit-out and giving possession frustrated the agreement.[33] It also said that the

29 The measures were originally intended to cease on 4 May but on 21 April they were extended into June 2020.

30 [2021] SGHC 219 [157].

31 ibid, 179. There was also some discussion of indemnity and exclusion clauses in the agreement, which is not relevant here.

32 ibid, 160.

33 ibid, 186–187.

defendant's contractual obligations were radically different from those originally agreed. In support of this, the court referred to the fact that the defendant had attempted to persuade the plaintiff to enter a fresh agreement for entirely different premises. This amounted to a 'fundamentally different contract than what the parties bargained for'.[34] Accordingly, under s 2(2) of the Frustrated Contracts Act, the sums paid by the plaintiff, including its security deposit, were to be returned.

The reasoning in the case raises many questions. I will begin with the claim based upon termination for breach. The court's emphasis on the plaintiff losing 17% of the term of the lease is puzzling. At no point, so far as I can tell, did the court reach a conclusion on the classification of the term to complete the fit-out and give possession. Under Singaporean law, timely performance of that term might have been essential (a condition) or inessential (a warranty).[35] In the former case, the extent of delay or its consequences were entirely irrelevant. Alternatively, if the court thought that the term was a warranty, then it ought to have gone on to apply the test for gravity of breach set out by Diplock LJ in *Hongkong Fir Shipping Co Ltd v Kawasaki Kisen Kaisha*,[36] which is accepted in Singaporean law.[37] That test requires that the breach – here, the delay – deprive the innocent party of substantially the whole benefit that it was intended that party should obtain from the contract. On that view, it is hard to see how a loss of 17% of the term of the lease reaches the threshold. So, if the term had been merely a warranty, the breach produced no right to terminate. The defendant's continuing equivocation *together* with the fact of breach might have been sufficient to establish repudiation, but this line of argument was not pursued by the court.

The discussion of clauses permitting the plaintiff to terminate is, likewise, surprising. The court's reasoning, as I understand it, was that the plaintiff's right to terminate for breach must have been sourced in an express or implied term to that effect. Since there was no express term, a term had to be implied. In that respect, the existence of an entire agreement clause was no obstacle. While I agree with the last proposition, the earlier steps in the argument are unnecessarily complicated. Contrary to what the court asserted, it is entirely plausible that a commercial agreement contains no express or implied term permitting the plaintiff to terminate for breach. The reason is that such a term is unnecessary. The law long ago abandoned the fiction of implied terms to explain the right to terminate for serious breach.[38] More recently, the Singaporean Court of Appeal moved away from the implied term theory as a basis for explaining discharge for repudiation.[39] Both developments are to be encouraged. A term of this nature implied into *all* contracts simply states a rule of the common law.[40] The more straightforward

34 ibid, 188.
35 *RDC Concrete* (n 2).
36 [1962] 2 QB 26 (CA), 70.
37 *RDC Concrete* (n 2) [99], [107].
38 See, e.g. *Hongkong Fir* (n 36) 71 (Diplock LJ) ('now unnecessary colophon').
39 *The STX Mumbai* [2015] SGCA 35, [2015] 5 SLR 1 [42]–[45], [51]–[53].
40 JW Carter, *Carter's Breach of Contract* (2nd ed, Hart Publishing 2018) [7–20].

analysis is this: the common law confers rights to terminate for wrongdoing by a contracting party in circumstances recognised as being sufficiently grave to warrant that response.

The second aspect of the judgment, regarding the application of the Unfair Contract Terms Act, can be put aside. It was moot in any event as the court found that the defendant never made an offer of alternative space which met the requirements of the clause.[41]

The third aspect of the judgment, concerning frustration, deserves close attention. The factual matters emphasised by the court – that the defendant had attempted to negotiate a fresh and very different kind of lease from that originally agreed – were in my view unhelpful to establish frustration. Frustration must rest upon the impact of supervening events upon the original contract; whatever else the parties may attempt to negotiate afterwards is entirely beside the point. The parties' arguments and the judgment reveal four different perspectives on frustration.

It may have been that the delay itself, shortening the effective term of the lease, rendered the contract something radically different. Although the court apparently endorsed that conclusion, it must be unlikely. I will assume that the doctrine of frustration in Singaporean law applies to leases.[42] Even so, the point is that the interruption was insufficiently prolonged and serious. *National Carriers Ltd v Panalpina (Northern) Ltd*[43] ('*Panalpina*') provides a benchmark for comparison. There, closure of an access road rendered the leased premises unusable as a warehouse. This was the sole purpose for which the premises were fitted out and for which, under the terms of the lease, use of the premises was permitted. The closure occurred a little over five years into a 10-year lease and was indefinite in duration when it commenced. As matters transpired, it was expected to last around 20 months, after which there would be about three years left on the lease. The House of Lords had little difficulty in concluding that the lease was not frustrated.

The interruption in *Paralpina* amounted to about 16% of the term of the lease, which is similar in proportion to the delay expected in *Dathena*. As in *Dathena*, the period of interruption was indefinite when it started. In each case, the parties contemplated a particular use for the premises, which was unachievable while the interruption persisted. In *Panalpina* the lessee remained liable to pay rent, in sharp contrast to *Dathena*, where the assumption seems to have been that rent would not start to run until after the original start date and perhaps not until possession was given. In short, *Dathena* was, if anything, a weaker case: if there was no frustration in *Panalpina* there should not have been in *Dathena*. A useful

41 *Dathena* (n 27) [164]–[165].

42 The same assumption was made in *Housing & Development Board v Microform Precision Industries Pte Ltd* [2003] SGHC 214. Note that the membership agreement in *Dathena* may have only created a licence: see above n 28.

43 [1981] AC 675.

cross-check is Diplock LJ's equation, in *Hongkong Fir*,[44] of the standard to be applied for frustration with that applied for breach of an intermediate term producing a right to terminate. As I said earlier, a delay of four months of itself did not deprive the plaintiff of substantially the whole benefit of the lease.

Another angle was that the circumstances rendered the defendant's obligation to fit-out the premises for 1 May radically different. The court appeared to endorse this ground.[45] Of course, the mere fact that labour shortages render a contract more cumbersome or expensive to perform, or lead to delays, does not of itself establish frustration. There may be some force in the view that the circuit-breaker measures, bringing with them the restrictions on non-essential services, did fundamentally change the nature of the obligation to fit-out the premises. However, this alone is not sufficient to establish frustration. Despite Lord Radcliffe's classic statement of the test for frustration in terms of a 'contractual obligation . . . incapable of being performed', the appropriate perspective is the whole contract and not merely one obligation within it. The importance of the fit-out as an aspect of a lease for two years must be weighed up. Nor was the fit-out obligation wholly incapable of being performed; rather, a delay in performance of about four months was anticipated.

A third angle might have been that frustration was established by the parties' inability to complete the fit-out and transfer possession at the time originally planned. In other words, the commercial venture was frustrated because a lease starting in September 2020 was fundamentally different from a lease starting on 1 May 2020.[46] One could point to the importance of the commencement date to the plaintiff, as its existing lease finished on the same day and it needed accommodation for its servers (and, in principle, its staff) for its business to continue to operate. This is, in my opinion, the most promising argument in favour of frustration, though not a surefire one.

Lastly, there was the plaintiff's assertion of inutility contained in its notice of termination. Its claim was that the circuit-breaker measures, and ongoing government policy for working from home, meant that the premises were no longer viable or to be used as originally intended. This argument was not addressed in the judgment. The fact that one party's benefits from a contract are diminished or undermined is not, of course, sufficient to establish frustration. The plaintiff would have to go further and set up a frustration-of-purpose-type argument. The argument would be that the fundamental purpose of the contract was to house the plaintiff's servers and staff, and that this was defeated by the circuit-breaker measures and government policy requiring staff to work from home.

The implications of this kind of argument provoke an instinctive wariness. It is easy to imagine lessees under various kinds of lease raising it for the Singaporean

44 *Hongkong Fir* (n 36) 66. See also *Canary Wharf (BP4) T1 Ltd v European Medicines Agency* [2019] EWHC 335 (Ch) [195], [199].

45 *Dathena* (n 27) [186]–[187].

46 cf *Jackson v Union Marine Insurance Co Ltd* (1874) 10 CP 125, 141.

circuit-breaker measures, as many non-essential retail businesses suffered a total or near-total loss of custom. Vaughan Williams LJ's Epsom races counterexample from *Herne Bay* draws a firm boundary. It is, then, unsurprising that English cases on leases of real property during the COVID-19 pandemic have so far eschewed a finding of frustration.[47]

The same logic applies to many chattel leases of income-producing assets. In *Salam Air SAOC v Latam Airlines Group SA*,[48] the claimant, an Omani carrier, acquired three aircraft under 'dry' leases for terms of six years each. It claimed that these leases were frustrated when, in response to the pandemic, the sultanate banned almost all flights to or from Omani airports. Foxton J dismissed that argument with little difficulty. He explained that, even though the carrier shared its business plans with the lessor, there was nothing to suggest that the (profitable) use of the aircraft was a shared objective of both lessor and carrier.[49] That conclusion was bolstered by the terms of the leases, which contained 'hell or highwater' clauses compelling the payment of rent in almost all circumstances.

Returning to the facts of *Dathena*, the argument for frustration of purpose is unconvincing. It is hard to say that the accommodation of staff was a fundamental purpose shared by both parties. The maximum capacity of the premises was known to both parties and was a factor in the plaintiff's selection of them, but the defendant had no real interest in the number of staff who actually attended each day. Further, frustration cuts both ways. To adopt the converse hypothesis raised by Vaughan Williams LJ in *Krell*,[50] it would be odd if the *defendant* could rely upon the same circumstances (viz, circuit-breaker measures and the government's work-from-home policy) to assert that the lease was frustrated, notwithstanding the plaintiff's desire to continue. Following the reasoning in *Herne Bay*, it could also be argued that the lease had the dual purpose of housing equipment and staff, and that the government's working-from-home policy only prevented the latter. In any event, unlike *Krell*, the plaintiff could enjoy the use of the premises for their intended purpose for a substantial part of the rental period.

A final puzzling aspect of *Dathena* concerns the relationship between breach and frustration as alternative grounds for discharge. Since the plaintiff only sought the return of certain sums paid before discharge, the distinction probably made no difference to the outcome. But the circumstances could easily have been different: for example, the plaintiff might also have claimed damages for loss of the bargain. The distinction between discharge for breach and frustration is also important in principle.

If breach was the basis for discharge, then discharge took effect on 29 May 2020 or shortly thereafter, when the notice of termination was communicated to the

47 *Bank of New York Mellon (International) Ltd v Cine-UK Ltd* [2021] EWHC 1013 (QB) [209]–[210]; *London Trocadero (2015) LLP v Picturehouse Cinemas Ltd* [2021] EWHC 2591 (Ch) [4].

48 [2020] EWHC 2414 (Comm).

49 ibid, 49–50.

50 *Krell* (n 24) 751.

defendant. If, however, the basis of discharge was frustration then, depending upon the particular perspective taken, the contract may well have been discharged earlier: upon the introduction of the circuit-breaker measures or, perhaps, when it became reasonably apparent that they would endure and prevent timely completion of the fit-out or full occupation of the premises. If that occurred before 1 May then there was no breach at all.[51] And if it occurred after 1 May but before 29 May, then there was no contract left alive to be terminated. Either way, the plaintiff would not have been entitled to damages for loss of the bargain for the full term.

III Legislative responses to the COVID-19 pandemic

Recognising that frustration is a blunt instrument, the Singaporean government passed the COVID-19 (Temporary Measures) Act 2020 (the 'COTMA'). The Act commenced on 7 April 2020, coinciding with the start of circuit-breaker measures, and has been amended on several occasions since. Several features of the Act stand out as being noteworthy for contract lawyers. The Act operates alongside, rather than displaces, the doctrine of frustration. Unlike the doctrine of frustration, it takes a highly targeted approach, dealing with particular problems in performance affecting particular classes of contract. The Act also offers distinct kinds of response to the COVID-19 pandemic. In some circumstances, the Act gives temporary relief, to a party adversely affected by the pandemic, from performance or enforcement of the contract. The Act goes further in select situations, encouraging parties to renegotiate the terms of their contract and facilitating that process of renegotiation. This is, perhaps, the most interesting innovation for contract lawyers versed in the common law. I will discuss three kinds of temporary relief and then the renegotiation procedure. The provisions of the Act are comprehensive and intricate, so what I offer below is only a brief summary of its full effect.

A Temporary relief from inability to perform in general

Part B of the Act provides temporary relief for inability to perform certain kinds of contract. The classes of contract include: secured loan contracts with licensed lenders,[52] performance bonds,[53] lease or hire-purchase agreements for plant, machinery and commercial vehicles,[54] leases or licences of non-residential property,[55] contracts between developers of housing or commercial property and

51 cf *Avery v Bowden* (1855) 5 El & Bl 714, 119 ER 647; (1856) 6 El & El 962, 119 ER 1122.
52 COTMA, sch 1, items 1(a), (b).
53 COTMA, sch 1, item 1(c).
54 COTMA, sch 1, items 1(d) and (da).
55 COTMA, sch 1, item (h).

new buyers,[56] event contracts,[57] tourism-related contracts,[58] construction contracts and supply contracts related to construction work.[59]

A party who is unable to perform a contractual obligation, such inability being caused to a material extent by a COVID-19 event, is able to invoke a protective procedure by issuing a notice.[60] Once the notice takes effect, the counterparty is generally barred from taking steps to enforce the contract directly or indirectly: for example, by an action against the contracting party or that party's guarantor, by enforcing security, by petitioning for bankruptcy or seeking to wind-up the party, by repossessing goods, by levying distress, or by exercising a right of termination or re-entry or forfeiture.[61] The window period for serving notices and the period of protection has varied depending upon the class of contract; some of these periods have been extended several times. At the time of writing, the notice and protection periods had already expired for most classes of contract; for those still outstanding, the latest deadline for notification was slated to be 28 February 2022.[62] Within the first six months of the Act, at least 7,400 applications for relief were lodged through the Ministry of Law's electronic system.

It will be noted that this protective procedure bars enforcement but does not alter the substance of the parties' agreement. There are supplementary provisions that *do* affect substantive rights and obligations. For construction and related supply contracts, for example, the period during which the party's inability to perform is caused by a COVID-19 event is disregarded in calculating liquidated or unliquidated damages for delay.[63] In some circumstances an inability to supply goods or services caused by a COVD-19 event even provides a defence to a claim for breach of contract.[64] For event and tourism-related contracts, the fact that the inability was caused by a COVID-19 event provides a defence to any claim for a cancellation fee[65] and the supplier's ability to forfeit a deposit is severely restricted.[66] And for a subset of contracts within Part B, if the COVID-19 event causes an inability to pay money, then any additional interest or late payment charges cannot exceed a prescribed maximum rate.[67]

56 COTMA, sch 1, items (i)–(l).
57 COTMA, sch 1, item (e). These are contracts to provide a venue, accommodation, transport, entertainment or catering for meetings, conferences, exhibitions, sales shows, concerts, weddings and so forth, or to provide the same to participants at such events.
58 COTMA, sch 1, item (f).
59 COTMA, sch 1, item (g).
60 COTMA, s 5(1). In the case of event or tourism-related contracts, an inability to hold the event, or to accept the goods or services under contract, counts as inability: s 5(1A).
61 COTMA, s 5(3).
62 See Singapore, Ministry of Law, 'Relief under Part 2 of the Act' <www.mlaw.gov.sg/covid19-relief/temporary-relief-from-inability-to-perform-contract> accessed 10 April 2022.
63 COTMA, s 6(5).
64 COTMA, s 6(6).
65 COTMA, s 7(4).
66 COTMA, ss 7(2), 7(3).
67 COTMA, s 7A. The maximum interest rate is set at 5% per annum: COVID-19 (Temporary Measures) (Temporary Relief from Inability to Perform Contracts) Regulations 2020, reg 3C(1).

Aside from waiting for the moratorium on enforcement to expire, the other route out of the protection provided by Part B is to refer the dispute to an assessor. The assessor determines whether the situation is one to which Part B applies and, if so, assessors are given considerable latitude to make orders to achieve an outcome that is 'just and equitable'.[68] The assessor process is free and is intended to be used without resort to lawyers.[69] Within the first six months of the Act, some 1,400 applications for assessment were lodged with the Ministry of Law.

B Rental relief and rental waiver

Parts 2A and 12 of the Act provided for rental relief and rental waiver during two distinct periods of the COVID-19 pandemic, one in 2020 and the other in 2021. The provisions are largely of historical interest and can be dealt with briefly. In broad terms, the lessees and licensees eligible for assistance were small-to-medium enterprises and non-profit organisations. It is notable that residential tenants and large commercial tenants were not covered. The first round of aid in 2020 was, in effect, to share the burden of rental obligations among the government, landlords and tenants for a period of two to four months, depending upon the type of property. The sharing was accomplished by a combination of government payments to landlords and rental waivers to tenants. The second round of aid in 2021 provided for a two-week rent waiver to eligible tenants, combined with a separate series of cash payments made by the government directly to eligible tenants.

C Contracts affected by delays in performance or breach of construction contracts or supply contracts

Part 8 of the Act addresses a specific set of circumstances, namely, where a contract between the parties is affected by defaults or delays under *another* contract, being a construction contract or supply contract related to a construction contract. The scope of Part 8 is narrowed by regulations, which limit the application of the Part to particular kinds of contracts affected in particular ways,[70] and to a period extending from to 1 February 2020 to 31 March 2021.[71]

In effect, Part 8 covered three situations. First, where a party hired goods to be used for construction work (e.g. scaffolding or heavy equipment) and, due to delays in that work, they had to extend the period of hire and incur extra rental charges.[72] Secondly, for leases or licences of real property where the lessor/licensor was unable to deliver possession due to delays or defaults in construction work on the property.[73] This may have covered the position of the defendant in

68 COTMA, ss 9(2), 13.
69 COTMA, s 14.
70 COTMA, s 36(1); COVID-19 (Temporary Measures) (Part 8 Relief) Regulations 2020 (the 'Part 8 Regulations'), regs 3 and 4.
71 Part 8 Regulations, reg 3A.
72 Part 8 Regulations, reg 3(c).
73 Part 8 Regulations, reg 3(a).

Dathena and the defendant mentioned the Part 8 procedure in some of its correspondence with the plaintiff. Yet, curiously, there was no evidence that it ever took steps to invoke it. Thirdly, for leases of real property where the tenant is unable to carry out renovations or fit-out within a discounted or rent-free period, due to delays in construction work on the property.[74]

The notification procedures and relief available for such contracts are broadly similar to those under Part B. The affected party may issue a notice seeking the appointment of an assessor.[75] Upon invoking that procedure, a moratorium comes into effect, preventing the counterparty from enforcing its rights under or in relation to the affected contract.[76] The assessor when appointed, must resolve the dispute in a just and equitable manner.[77] The assessor has the power to vary the relevant terms of the affected contract, for example, to extend the date for hirer to redeliver the hired goods or to alter the rent payable, or to extend the date for the landlord to deliver possession of the property or the rent-free period for the tenant to perform the fit-out. The assessor also has the power to discharge or release the affected party from certain obligations in the affected contract.

D Renegotiation of contracts

The aspect of the Act most novel for contract lawyers is Part 10, which facilitates the renegotiation of contracts affected by the COVID-19 pandemic. The Part is limited to certain classes of contract and requires a close connection between the contract and Singapore. The classes of contract include:[78] leases or licences of non-residential property, leases or hire-purchase agreements for commercial equipment, contracts to supply any goods, and contracts to supply any services. There are various exclusions from coverage, the most notable of which are: contracts with individuals not acting principally for business purposes,[79] employment contracts,[80] construction contracts[81] and contracts for financial services.[82] The contract must be governed by Singaporean law and at least one party must have a place of business in Singapore.[83]

Recognising that renegotiation is a sweeping power, eligibility is restricted to those parties who are thought to be more ‘deserving’. Applicants must have had an annual revenue not exceeding SGD 30 million in FY 2019 and must have

74 Part 8 Regulations, reg 3(b).
75 COTMA, s 37.
76 COTMA, s 37A.
77 COTMA, s 38(2)(b).
78 COTMA, s 42(1)(a) and sch 2 pt 1.
79 COTMA, sch 2 pt 1 item 2(a).
80 COTMA, sch 2 pt 1 item 2(b).
81 COTMA, sch 2 pt 1 item 2(c).
82 COTMA, sch 2 pt 1 item 2(h).
83 COTMA, s 42(1).

suffered a decline in revenue of at least 70% in July-December 2020 as compared to the same period in the previous year.[84]

If the contract and the affected party meet the eligibility criteria, the affected party can seek to negotiate an adjustment to the rights and obligations under the affected contract. The Act allowed a six-week period, from 15 January to 26 February 2021, to initiate the process.[85] If the renegotiation succeeds, then the parties proceed on the basis of the renegotiated contract. If the renegotiation fails, then the contract is terminated.[86] Notwithstanding whatever the contract may provide, the Act sets out a default adjustment of rights and obligations upon termination for some classes of contract.[87] *Either* party may also apply for an assessor to further adjust the parties' rights upon termination on a 'just and fair' basis.[88] Just over 400 such applications have been lodged.[89]

IV Conclusion

The doctrine of frustration is a crude, and often unpredictable, instrument to apply to contracts affected by the COVID-19 pandemic. Although one Singaporean High Court decision to date has been willing to reach a conclusion of frustration, in my view that conclusion was questionable. Given the high threshold needed to establish frustration, and the drastic consequences of its application, it is not surprising that the Singaporean government quickly enacted remedial legislation designed to address the impact of the pandemic upon contracts.

The legislation operates concurrently with the doctrine of frustration. It is highly targeted, in a way that recognises the unique social and economic interests at stake in Singapore. It is remarkably detailed and prescriptive in some respects about the effects of the pandemic upon contracts. Part 10, which deals with renegotiation, is both novel and forceful in its structure of incentives and consequences. The threat of termination – possibly on terms fixed by the legislature – appears to have forced many parties to the negotiating table. Most of the relief afforded by the Act has been designed to operate only for a relatively limited period. By the time this Chapter appears in print, the windows for the most significant kinds of relief under the Act will have closed. In sum, parties in Singapore had to adjust quickly to the changes wrought by the COVID-19 pandemic and it is now time to accept the 'new normal'.

84 COTMA, s 43(1)(a) and sch 2 pt 3. See also Singapore, Ministry of Law, 'Key Features of Re-Align Framework' <www.mlaw.gov.sg/realign/key-features#1eligiblity> accessed 10 April 2022.
85 COTMA, s 45(3).
86 COTMA, s 43(1)(d).
87 COTMA, s 43(2) and sch 2 pt 4.
88 COTMA, s 47(1).
89 Oral advice from Mr Edwin Tong SC, Second Minister for Law (24 January 2022).

5 The principle of *pacta sunt servanda* and its exceptions under Japanese contract law

Tomohiro Yoshimasa※

1 Introduction

The binding force of contracts is a foundation of our society. It is indispensable for any kind of interactive activities in a society to assure its members with safe exchange of money, goods, service, information, etc. While the opinions may vary among legal academics about whether the binding force of contracts is justified by the notions of promise, reliance, fairness, efficiency, or on other normative concepts, the principle of *pacta sunt servanda* is widely recognised as a general rule in jurisdictions throughout the world.

Japanese law is no exception. Although the Japanese Civil Code makes no explicit provision for the principle of *pacta sunt servanda*, the Code does provide a contracting party access to remedies if the opposing party does not fulfil its obligations under the contract. The existence of, and the rules on, remedies for breach of contract indicate that this principle is a basic tenet of contract law in Japan as well. The law of obligations in the Japanese Civil Code was significantly amended in 2017 and the revised Code has come into force as of 1 April 2020. Therefore, the next part of the chapter will begin with providing some general information on the reform (2.1). It will then explain the basic rules on formation of contract (2.2) before exploring the basic structure of the rules on remedies (2.3).

As fundamental as it may be, the principle of *pacta sunt servanda* has important exceptions. Not only are these exceptions important as a practical matter, they also draw academic attention because the limits on the binding force of contracts are embodied in the exceptions. The exceptions to the principle of *pacta sunt servanda* can be conceptualised at two different levels. First, there are cases in which the parties are allowed to invalidate a contract at their own will even when the conditions for formation of contract are met: the most prominent example being the withdrawal rights of the consumers. Second, with regard to remedies for breach of contract, the parties' non-observance of contractual duties may be excused in case certain events occur after the conclusion of a contract. The third

※ The author would like to thank Professors Normann Witzleb and Antonios Karaiskos for their comments and editorial assistance in English. The references in this chapter are basically limited to English literature. For further references in Japanese, see the citations therein.

DOI: 10.4324/9781003358305-6

part of this chapter will begin with some comments on legal consciousness in Japan (3.1), before discussing the rules in Japanese contract law which fall under these two categories of exceptions to the principle of *pacta sunt servanda* (3.2 and 3.3). The question of whether the pandemic of COVID-19, which has had a serious impact on our society, would in any way affect the contractual obligations of the parties is also discussed in the third part.

2 The principle of *pacta sunt servanda* and the Japanese Civil Code

2.1 The Japanese Civil Code and the 2017 reform

The Japanese Civil Code (*Minpō*)[1] is the basic legislation providing the general rules on contracts. The Code was promulgated in 1896 (first three parts, namely General Provisions, Property Law, and Law on Obligations) and in 1898 (parts four and five, namely Family Law and Succession Law); the Code came into force in July 1898.[2] As is evident from the fact that the Code adopts the *Pandekten* system, the style of codification which provides for general provisions before providing for specific rules, the Code is strongly influenced by German law. However, it is also important to point out that French law had as large an influence as German law, and that some important provisions of the Code derive from English case law. To quote a famous passage of one of the drafters of the Code, Nobushige Hozumi, '[t]he Japanese Civil Code may be said to be a *fruit of comparative jurisprudence*'.[3]

It is noteworthy here that the number of provisions contained in the Japanese Civil Code is small when compared with other civil codes in the civil law jurisdictions. The Japanese Civil Code had 1146 provisions when it was first enacted, whereas the French Civil Code (*Code civil*) and the German Civil Code (*Bürgerliches Gesetzbuch*; *BGB*) contain more than 2,300 provisions. This is a result of the

1 Law no. 89 of 1896 and no. 9 of 1898. A non-official English translation of the Code is available at <www.japaneselawtranslation.go.jp/?re=2> accessed 27 May 2022.

2 For English accounts of the history of the Japanese Civil Code, see Shusei Ono, 'Comparative Law and the Civil Code of Japan (1)' (1996) 24 Hitotsubashi Journal of Law and Politics 27; Hiroyasu Ishikawa, 'Codification, Decodification, and Recodification of the Japanese Civil Code' in Julio César Rivera (ed), *The Scope and Structure of Civil Codes* (Springer, 2013) 267; Antonios Karaiskos, 'Civil Code Reform in Japan: Is the New Regulation of Standard Contract Terms a Desirable One?' in Maren Heidemann and Joseph Lee (eds), *The Future of the Commercial Contract in Scholarship and Law Reform: European and Comparative Perspectives* (Springer, 2018) 73, 76–77; Masami Okino, 'The Interpretation of Contracts under Japanese Law' in Mindy Chen-Wishart and Stefan Vogenauer (eds), *Studies in the Contract Laws of Asia III: Contents of Contracts and Unfair Terms* (OUP, 2020) 161; Hiroshi Oda, *Japanese Law* (4th ed, OUP, 2021) 117–122.

3 Nobushige Hozumi, *The New Japanese Civil Code: As Material for the Study of Comparative Jurisprudence* (Tokyo, 1904) 11. This book is based on the lecture Hozumi gave at the International Congress of Arts and Science, at the Universal Exposition, Saint Louis 1904.

policy of the drafters of the Japanese Civil Code to make the Code plain and simple, and not to prescribe provisions on general definitions and basic principles of law. This approach has caused judges and legal academia to play a large role in the interpretation of the Japanese Civil Code. After the enactment of the Code, many important doctrines were therefore established by the courts to fill the lacuna left in the legislation. In this process, especially before the Second World War, German legal theory had a significant influence over Japanese lawyers.[4]

From the late 1990s, various important pieces of legislation have been enacted in the field of private law.[5] This period is sometimes referred to as a 'third legal reform era' in Japan; the first being the period of *meiji* restoration in the late nineteenth century, and the second being the period after the Second World War. As for the reform of the law on obligations,[6] the Working Group on the Reform of the Law on Obligations was established within the Legislative Council of the Ministry of Justice in November 2009. The Working Group agreed upon the final draft in February 2015, and the Japanese Civil Code was amended based on the draft in 2017.[7] This is the most wide-ranging reform of the Code since its enactment and the first time the law on obligation was modernised overall.[8]

The new law on obligations was drafted based on two guiding principles.[9] First, the reforms aimed to modernise the provisions of the Japanese Civil Code which had become obsolete due to the socio-economic changes after the enactment of the Code in the late nineteenth century. Second, it was considered important to

4 Even provisions that derive from French or English law were interpreted based on German legal theory, disregarding the origins of the provisions. Article 416 of the Code on scope of damages (see 2.3) is a prominent example. The provision was drafted based on the English case of *Hadley v Baxendale* (1854) 156 ER 145, 9 ExCh 341, but was interpreted as having provided for the German theory of adequate causality (*adäquater Kausalzusammenhang*). This phenomenon was formulated as a 'theory reception (*Theorienrezeption*)' by Zentaro Kitagawa in the 1960s. For an English summary of his argument, see Zentaro Kitagawa, 'Japanese Civil Law and German Law – From the Viewpoint of Comparative Law' in Zentaro Kitagawa and Karl Riesenhuber (eds), *The Identity of German and Japanese Civil Law in Comparative Perspectives* (De Gruyter, 2007) 11.

5 For an analysis of changes in various fields of law, see the contributions in Daniel H Foote (ed), *Law in Japan: A Turning Point* (University of Washington Press, 2007).

6 For English accounts of the process of the 2017 reform of the law on obligation, see Takashi Uchida, 'Contract Law Reform in Japan and the UNIDROIT Principles' (2011) Uniform Law Review 2011, 705; Naoko Kano, 'Reform of the Japanese Civil Code – The Interim Draft Proposal of 2013' (2013) 36 Journal of Japanese Law/Zeitschrift für Japanisches Recht 250; Karaiskos (n 2) 80–87; Tomohiro Yoshimasa, 'The Reform of Japanese Contract Law and the Principle of Self-responsibility' (2019) in Keizo Yamamoto, Yuko Nishitani and Harald Baum (eds), *Gegenwärtiger Stand und Aufgabe der Privatautonomie in Japan und Deutschland, Zeitschrift für Japanisches Recht* (Sonderheft, 2019) 14, 27.

7 Law no. 44 of 2017.

8 To be more precise, the 2017 reform amended the provisions which relate to contract law; namely the provisions on juristic acts (arts 90 to 137) and prescription (arts 144 to 169) in the general part, the general provisions of the law on obligations (arts 399 to 520–20), and the specific provisions on contracts (arts 521 to 696). The provisions on property (arts 175 to 398–22) and torts (arts 709 to 724–2), as well as on family law (arts 725 to 881) and succession law (arts 882 to 1050) were not, in principle, revised. The law on succession was subsequently amended in 2018 (Law no. 72 of 2018).

9 See Consultation No. 88 of the Minister of Justice.

make the Code more transparent and easier for the citizens to understand. Based on this idea, the new Code contains explicit provisions on basic principles of law and some important doctrines established by the courts. As will be discussed below, this includes new provisions in the Code that relate closely to the principle of *pacta sunt servanda*.

2.2 The basic rules on formation of contract[10]

Unless a valid contract is concluded, there is no room for the principle of *pacta sunt servanda* to have its effect. In this sense, the rules on formation of contract provide prerequisites for the principle to apply.

Just as in many other jurisdictions, the Japanese rules on formation of contract are based on the 'offer and acceptance model', according to which a contract is concluded when one person (offeror) makes an offer to another person (offeree) and the latter accepts the offer. Although this basic model has been acknowledged since the enactment of the Japanese Civil Code, there was no explicit provision on this model before the 2017 reform. The new Code, however, prescribes in article 522(1) that '[a] contract is formed when a party manifests the intention to offer to conclude a contract' 'and the other party accepts the offer'. This new provision was established based on the guiding principle to make the Code more understandable to the citizens.

The Japanese rules on formation of contract are based on the principle of freedom of contract. Article 521 of the new Civil Code, which is titled 'Freedom of Conclusion and Terms of Contract', prescribes in paragraph 1 that '[u]nless otherwise provided for in laws and regulations, any person may freely decide whether or not to conclude a contract'. Furthermore, in principle, no form is required for a valid formation of contract as article 522(2) of the Code provides that 'it is not required to satisfy any formalities such as preparation of a written document in order to form a contract'. Japanese contract law is said to show strong adherence to the principle of freedom of form in comparison to other jurisdictions. In practice, however, many Japanese lawyers would point out that it is difficult to prove formation of contract without any written documents and that documentary evidence actually plays a crucial role in litigation.[11]

The important exceptions to the principle of freedom of form include guarantee contracts. As provided in article 446(2) and (3) of the Japanese Civil Code, a guarantee contract is not effective unless it is concluded in writing or by electronic record. This restriction, which was introduced by the reform in 2004,[12] is to ensure

10 For details of the rules on formation of contract, see Hiroo Sono, Luke Nottage, Andrew Pardieck and Kenji Saigusa, *Contract Law in Japan* (Wolters Kluwer, 2019) paras 74–130.

11 See an interesting case study of sales of land in Shinichiro Michida (Veronica L Taylor tras.), 'Contract Societies: Japan and the United States Contrasted' (1993) 1 Pacific Rim Law and Policy Journal 199, 213.

12 Law no. 147 of 2004. In the 2017 reform, further regulations were introduced for guarantee contracts for obligations arising from business. According to the new art 465–6, such guarantee

that the guarantor is aware of their responsibility under the contract and to make the contract binding only when their intention is clearly expressed.

A second exception to the principle of freedom of form concerns loans for consumption, loans for use, and deposits (or bailments). Before the 2017 reform, the Japanese Civil Code treated these three types of contracts as 'real contracts', meaning that the object of the contract must be transferred to the receiving party for a contract to be concluded and that the only obligation under the contract is for the receiving party to return such object (article 587 of the Code on loans for consumption, article 593 of the old Code on loans for use, and article 657 of the old Code on deposits). In our society today, however, it is very difficult to stick to this rule, which has its roots in the Roman tradition, especially with regard to loans for consumption. The new Civil Code has thus adopted the position that loans for use and deposits are validly concluded when the parties have agreed to a contract (articles 593 and 657 of the new Civil Code) and that a loan for consumption is validly formed if it is made in writing even when its object is not yet transferred to the borrower (article 587-2 of the new Civil Code). Since more contracts would have the binding force under the new Civil Code, this (partial) abolition of formality may seem to have an affinity with the principle of *pacta sunt servanda*. At the same time, however, the new Code provides for occasions in which the parties to loans for consumption, loans for use, and deposits may terminate a contract at their will.[13]

While the 'offer and acceptance model' seems to assume that a contract is formed instantly by an agreement between the offeror and the offeree, many contracts are concluded only after long negotiations between the parties. The issues of when a binding contract is formed in these circumstances and whether a party can be liable for breaking off negotiations are controversial in Japan, as well.[14] Whereas freedom of contract generally includes the party's freedom to break off negotiations, it is widely accepted that the opposing party's legitimate reliance on the formation of a contract should be respected in certain situations. To prevent disputes on this issue, there are cases in which deal protection clauses are agreed upon, a topic which was discussed in Professor Hiroyuki Watanabe's presentation[15] in the conference out of which many contributions in this book originated. When such clauses do not provide solutions, however, the courts face the difficult

contracts are effective only if a guarantor manifests its intention to perform the obligation by means of a notarial instrument.

13 See below 3.2.

14 For an English overview of precontractual liability under Japanese law, see Shoji Kawakami, 'Japan' in Ewoud H Hondius (ed), *Precontractual Liability: Reports to the XIIIth Congress International Academy of Comparative Law Montreal, Canada, 18–24 August 1990* (Kluwer Law and Taxation Publishers, 1991) 205.

15 Hiroyuki Watanabe, 'Pacta sunt servanda in the context of Japanese M&A law: the Sumitomo vs. UFJ case'. For an English analysis of the Sumitomo vs. UFJ case, see Veronica L Taylor, 'Japanese Commercial Transactions and Sanctions Revisited: Sumitomo v. UFJ' (2009) 8 Washington University Global Studies Law Review 399.

question of under which conditions a party is held liable for not entering into a contract. The Working Group on the Reform of the Law on Obligations discussed whether an explicit provision on this issue of pre-contractual liability should be introduced into the Japanese Civil Code. The Working Group was, however, unable to come to consensus on the conditions for the liability, and the new Civil Code thus remains silent on the topic.

2.3 The basic structure of the rules on remedies for breach of contract[16]

The principle of *pacta sunt servanda* demands that in case of breach of contract the aggrieved party's interest should be protected in an appropriate manner. Under Japanese contract law, a party confronted with the non-performance of the opposing party can seek the following remedies; the specific performance, damages, termination of the contract, the right to demand cure, and the right to demand price reduction.

Just as in other civil law jurisdictions, the aggrieved party is entitled to ask for specific performance under Japanese contract law. Although this rule has been acknowledged as a basic principle of law on obligations since the enactment of the Japanese Civil Code, the Code did not explicitly provide before the 2017 reform that the creditor had the substantive right to specific performance. The Code only had a provision on 'Compelling Performance' (article 414), which authorises the creditor to enforce performance through compulsory execution process. In the course of the 2017 reform, the Working Group on the Reform of the Law on Obligations proposed establishing a new provision that would explicitly state the creditor's right to specific performance. The Ministry of Justice, however, came to the conclusion that such right is implicitly stipulated in the new provision on 'Impossibility of Performance' (article 414-2(1)).[17] The Ministry of Justice considered that providing for a ground of exclusion of the right to specific performance in the Civil Code implies that the right is acknowledged under the Code.

The second and most important remedy for breach of contract is damages. In case of non-performance, the aggrieved party may ask for compensation for loss or damage arising from the non-performance (article 415(1)). The non-performing party must compensate for loss or damage incurred by the opposing party that would ordinarily arise from the non-performance (article 416(1)), and if the damage has arisen from any special circumstances, the non-performing party

16 For details of the rules on remedies for breach of contract, see Sono and others (n 10) paras 452–509. For the right to specific performance and damages in particular, see Kunihiro Nakata, 'Performance and Monetary Remedies for Breach of Contract in Japan' in Mindy Chen-Wishart, Alexander Loke and Burton Ong (eds), *Studies in the Contract Laws of Asia I: Remedies for Breach of Contract* (OUP, 2016) 107. On the 2017 reform, see also Tomohiro Yoshimasa, 'The Reform of the Law on Remedies for Breach of Contract in Japan' in Alexander Bruns and Masabumi Suzuki (eds), *Reactive Instruments of Social Governance* (Mohr Siebeck, 2019) 29.

17 See below 3.3.3 on this provision.

is held liable for the damage if the party did foresee, or should have foreseen, the circumstances (article 416(2)). The non-performance is, however, excused if it is due to 'grounds not attributable to the obligor', a rule which will be discussed in the next Part as a ground for exemption from contractual liability.[18] Article 415(2) provides prerequisites for 'damages in lieu of the performance of the obligation', i.e. damages that are incompatible with the performance of the obligation; the aggrieved party may not ask for both specific performance and damages in lieu of the performance. The aggrieved party is entitled to damages in lieu of performance if (i) the performance of the obligation is impossible; (ii) the non-performing party manifests the intention to refuse performance of the obligation; or (iii) the aggrieved party acquires the right to terminate the contract due to the non-performance.

Third, whereas specific performance and damages intend to protect the interest the aggrieved party would have gained under the contract, termination is a remedy that enables the party to end the contractual relationship. Under Japanese contract law, an aggrieved party may, as a rule, terminate the contract if the party demands performance of the contractual obligation specifying a reasonable additional period for the performance and performance is not completed during that period. Termination is, however, not allowed if the non-performance is considered to be 'minor' in light of the contract and the common sense in the transaction (article 541). Furthermore, an aggrieved party may immediately terminate the contract without fixing an additional period (i) if the performance of the obligation is impossible; (ii) if the non-performing party manifests the intention to refuse performance of the obligation; (iii) if the performance of part of the obligation is impossible, or if the non-performing party manifests the intention to refuse performance of part of the obligation and the purpose of the contract cannot be achieved by the performance of the remaining part of the obligation; (iv) if, based on the content of the contract, the purpose of the contract cannot be achieved unless the obligation is performed at a specific time or within a certain period of time, and the party fails to perform the obligation at that time or before that period of time expires; or (v) if it is obvious that the non-performing party is unlikely to perform the obligation to the extent necessary to achieve the purpose of the contract even if the aggrieved party demands the performance (article 542 (1)). The basic idea of this provision is to allow an aggrieved party to terminate the contract immediately if it has become impossible for the party to achieve the purpose for which it has concluded the contract.

Under the Japanese Civil Code, the rules on the right to demand cure and the right to demand price reduction are prescribed in the section on sales contracts. The Code sets out specific provisions for thirteen types of contracts (Part III, Chapter II, Sections 2–14), and the provisions on sales contracts apply *mutatis mutandis* to contracts for value other than sales (see article 559). In the specific provisions for sales, it is provided that if the object delivered to the buyer is not

18 See below 3.3.1.

in conformity with the contract, the buyer may not only ask for damages or terminate the contract (see article 564), but also demand that the seller cure the non-conformity by repairing the object or delivering a substitute (article 562). While some jurisdictions grant the right to choose the method of the cure to the seller, under the article 562 (1) – a new provision established by the 2017 reform – the buyer may as a rule choose the method. However, the seller may cure the non-conformity by a method that is different from the one demanded by the buyer if it does not impose any undue burden on the buyer. It has been pointed out that the related provision in the proposed Common European Sales Law (CESL)[19] may have influenced the drafters of the new Japanese Civil Code in this respect (see article 111 of the CESL on 'Consumer's choice between repair and replacement'). Moreover, the buyer may demand a reduction of the price in proportion to the degree of non-conformity. Based on the assumption that reduction of the price is functionally equivalent to partial termination of the contract, article 563 – which is also a new provision – prescribes prerequisites similar to that of termination of the contract described in the previous paragraph.

3 The exceptions to the principle of *pacta sunt servanda* under Japanese law

3.1 Debate over 'legal consciousness' in Japan

Before discussing the exceptions to the principle of *pacta sunt servanda*, it is perhaps worth making a brief comment on the debate over 'legal consciousness' in Japanese society.

In 1967, Takeyoshi Kawashima, a prominent legal sociologist of the time, published the famous book titled 'The Japanese Legal Consciousness'[20]. In this book, Kawashima argued that in Japanese society contracts are drafted in a very simplistic manner, and that if the disputes were to arise, the contracting parties intend to come to a solution through flexible negotiations, not by enforcing the contract terms through litigation. Kawashima's argument was a part of his general observation that Japanese people are averse to law and are very reluctant to litigate even if the disputes were to arise in spite of the fact that modern legislation was implemented by the government. If this is the case, then it may be argued that whereas the principle of *pacta sunt servanda* is widely acknowledged as a legal rule in

19 European Commission, Proposal for a Regulation of the European Parliament and of the Council on a Common European Sales Law, 11.10.2011, COM (2011) 635 final.

20 Takeyoshi Kawashima, *Nihon-jin no Hō-ishiki* [The Japanese Legal Consciousness] (Iwanami Shoten 1967). For an English translation of the third chapter of this book on contracts, Takeyoshi Kawashima (Charles R Stevens tras.), 'The Legal Consciousness of Contract in Japan' (1974) 7 Law in Japan 1. See also Takeyoshi Kawashima, 'Dispute Resolution in Contemporary Japan' in Arthur Taylor von Mehren (ed), *Law in Japan: The Legal Order in a Changing Society* (Harvard University Press, 1963) 41.

Japan, the legal principle actually has only limited significance in the context of dispute resolution in Japanese society.

More recent scholars are, however, sceptical of Kawashima's argument.[21] An American Japanologist in the field of law has argued that the fact that the number of litigated cases in Japan is small is due to the limited access to the courts, not the reluctance of Japanese people to litigate.[22] There is also research based on broad multinational surveys finding that Japanese students are as litigious as students in other Western countries on contractual disputes.[23] Given the more recent research, it must be too hasty to conclude that the legal principle of *pacta sunt servanda* has less significance in Japanese society when compared to other mainly Western societies.

3.2 The limits on the binding force of contracts

Although the binding force of contracts is, as a rule, created by a legal agreement between an offeror and an offeree, there are cases in which a party may escape from the binding force at their own will. Such cases may be regarded as exceptions of, or limits on, the principle of *pacta sunt servanda.*

The first limit concerns gratuitous contracts. Under the Japanese Civil Code, contracts for gifts are also formed validly by an agreement between the parties without any formal requirements. In the late nineteenth century, the drafters of the Code believed that Japanese people were not familiar with the notarial system and that it is not appropriate to require notarial instruments for formation of contracts for gifts. Nonetheless, article 550 of the Code provides that contracts for gifts that are not concluded in writing may be terminated by either party at will except for a portion of the gift for which performance has already been completed. This provision is based on the idea that by requiring a written agreement, it is possible to provide the parties with an opportunity to deliberate on the conclusion of the gift contract and to prevent possible future disputes. The same rule is adopted for other gratuitous contracts, namely for loans for use (see article 593-2) and for gratuitous deposits (see article 657-2 (2)).

Second, as to contracts for work and mandate contracts, a party may terminate the contract at any time even if there is no breach of contract on the part of the opposing party. Regarding contracts for work, the party ordering work (client) may terminate the contract at any time whilst the contractor has not completed the work (article 641). Regarding mandate contracts, either party may terminate

21 For a survey, see Setsuo Miyazawa, 'Taking Kawashima Seriously: A Review of Japanese Research on Japanese Legal Consciousness and Disputing Behavior' (1987) 21 Law & Society Review 219. For a (partial) defence of Kawashima's argument, see Christian Wollschläger, 'Historical Trends of Civil Litigation in Japan, Arizona, Sweden, and Germany: Japanese Legal Culture in the Light of Judicial Statistics' in Harald Baum (ed), *Japan: Economic Success and Legal System* (De Gruyter, 1997) 89.

22 John Owen Haley, 'The Myth of the Reluctant Litigant' (1978) 4 Journal of Japanese Studies 359.

23 Michael K Young, Masanobu Kato and Akira Fujimoto, 'Japanese Attitudes towards Contracts: An Empirical Wrinkle in the Debate' (2003) 34 George Washington International Law Review 789.

the contract at any time (article 651(1)). In both cases, the party terminating the contract must pay compensation for loss or damage incurred by the opposing party. The same rule applies to deposits (bailments) (article 662(1)).[24] The termination at the party's will is justified on the ground that it is meaningless to bind the party receiving the service to the contract if that party has lost interest in the performance. In addition, for mandate contracts, it is often argued that it is inappropriate to bind a party to the contract if they have lost trust in the other party. In many jurisdictions throughout the world, similar rules are adopted for various service contracts and mandate contracts.[25]

Third, several special statutes provide for withdrawal rights, namely consumers' rights to revoke an offer or to terminate a contract during the 'cooling-off' period. Important examples include the Act on Specified Commercial Transactions[26] (see article 9 on door-to-door sales contracts, article 24 on telemarketing sales contracts, article 48 on continuous service contracts, and article 58-14 on door-to-door purchase contracts), the Instalment Sales Act[27] (see articles 35-3–10 and 35-3–11), and the Insurance Business Act[28] (see article 309 on insurance contracts). Strongly influenced by European,[29] mainly German, academia, prominent scholars argue that while some types of withdrawal rights are justified by the fact that consumers may be caught off-guard, others are explained by the complexity of the object of the contract. In both cases, the consumers are in need of a certain period of time to deliberate on the necessity of entering into the contract.

3.3 Exemption from contractual liability

As described in the previous Part, a contractual party confronted with the non-performance of the opposing party may resort to the remedies prescribed in the Japanese Civil Code. Under certain circumstances, however, the party is not allowed to seek the remedies. In this section, it will be discussed when a party's

24 For other types of contracts which were treated as 'real contracts' (see above 2.2), art 587-2(2) (the borrower's right to cancel the contract before the reception of the object in loans for consumption made in writing), art 591(2) (the burrower's right to return the object in loans for consumption in general), and art 598(3) (the borrower's right to cancel the contract in loans for use) provide similar rules.

25 For an overview of the rules on service contracts in the EU countries, see Maurits Barendrecht and others (eds), *Principles of European Law: Service Contracts* (OUP, 2007) 304–307. For an overview of the rules on mandate contracts in the EU countries, see Christian von Bar and Eric Clive (eds), *Principles, Definitions and Model Rules of European Private Law: Draft Common Frame of Reference (DCFR)*, vol 3 (OUP, 2010) 2222–2230.

26 Law no. 57 of 1976.

27 Law no. 159 of 1961.

28 Law no. 105 of 1995.

29 For a discussion regarding the rationale of withdrawal rights in EU legislation, see Geraint Howells, '*Pacta sunt servanda* and the consumer's right of withdrawal', ch 10 (in this volume).

non-performance is excused, and whether the pandemic of COVID-19 would provide a ground for exemption under Japanese contract law.[30]

3.3.1 Excuses for non-performance

Grounds of exemption from damages were the subject of heated debate in the 2017 reform of the law of obligations. Before the reform, article 415 of the Japanese Civil Code provided that a non-performing obligor was liable to pay damages when the non-performance was due to 'grounds attributable to the obligor'.[31] The traditional view saw the prerequisites for damages provided in the article 415 as a manifestation of the fault principle. Under this view, to hold the non-performing party liable for damages, not only the mere fact of non-performance but also the fact that the party was at fault is required. More recent authors, on the other hand, argue that the criterion should not be whether the non-performing party is at fault in a strict sense but whether it is in breach of an obligation arising from the contract.[32] These authors emphasise that the justification of contractual liability lies in the binding force of contracts, and their argument may be regarded as being more faithful to the principle of *pacta sunt servanda*. In the course of the 2017 reform, there was a harsh conflict of opinions among the members of the Working Group on the Reform of the Law on Obligations. As a result of an unsophisticated compromise, the revised article 415 (1) of the Japanese Civil Code provides that the non-performing party is not held liable for damages if the non-performance is due to 'grounds not attributable to the obligor in light of the contract or other sources of obligation and the common sense in the transaction'. The new provision refers to both 'the contract' and 'the common sense in the transaction' as criteria to determine whether the non-performing party is liable for damages; while the former criterion is advocated by recent authors, the latter has an affinity with the traditional view.

After the outbreak of COVID-19, it has been debated whether the instances of non-performance caused by the pandemic are excused under article 415 of the Japanese Civil Code. The answer to the question depends upon the content of the contract and the direct cause of the non-performance. For instance, in the case of a sales contract, even if the cost necessary for the material procurement has substantially increased because of the pandemic, in most cases the manufacturer (seller) is a superior risk-bearer compared to the demander (buyer), and the former is likely to have assumed the risk of the change in the market price of the material. On the other hand, if it has become impossible to perform a contractual obligation due to special measures taken by local governors based on the Act on

30 This section draws upon my previous article, Tomohiro Yoshimasa, 'The Effects of the Corona Crisis on Contractual Obligations under Japanese Law' (2021) 51 Journal of Japanese Law/Zeitschrift für Japanisches Recht 21.

31 On art 415 of the Japanese Civil Code before the 2017 reform and its interpretation, see Nakata (n 16) 112–115.

32 For an English account, see also Nakata (ibid) 113–115.

Special Measures concerning the New Influenza,[33] e.g. a request or order by a governor not to use public facilities (see article 24 (9), article 45, and article 31-6) or an expropriation of the necessary goods (see article 55), it is hard to imagine that either party had assumed the risk of such an impediment before the outbreak. In the latter case, therefore, the non-performance may be regarded as having been caused by 'grounds not attributable to the obligor', and the non-performing party may hence be exempted from liability.

3.3.2 Force majeure *clauses*

Japanese legislation does not adopt the concept of *force majeure* as a criterion to determine whether non-performance is excused. Many standard contract terms used in Japan nevertheless stipulate the notion of *force majeure* (*fuka kōryoku*) as a ground of exemption for contracting parties. While *force majeure* clauses are often used in practice, it is not always clear whether the parties intended to deviate from article 415 of the Japanese Civil Code. It is therefore necessary to determine by way of contractual interpretation whether the parties actually intended to opt out of article 415. From this perspective, exemption from non-performance under *force majeure* clauses is not an exception to the principle of *pacta sunt servanda*, but a consequence thereof.

Just as in many other jurisdictions, it is discussed whether the COVID-19 pandemic justifies an application of *force majeure* clauses under Japanese contract law. A very interesting reaction to the question can be observed in the field of construction contracts. One of the prominent standard contract terms used for construction contracts, the Standard Contract Terms for Construction prepared by the Central Council for Construction Business, an independent council within the Ministry of Land, Infrastructure, Transport and Tourism (MLIT), provide that, in a case of *force majeure*, the contractor may ask for postponement of the completion date and that the loss resulting from the *force majeure* is to be borne by the party ordering work (client).[34] In April 2020, the MLIT announced that if it has become impossible for a contractor to continue the construction due to the COVID-19 pandemic, it should be regarded as having been caused by *force majeure* as provided in the Standard Contract Terms for Construction.[35] Although the MLIT is not an authoritative body for contractual interpretation in any sense, its opinion should have a certain practical significance, and it is likely to affect

33 Law no. 31 of 2012. This Act was amended in March 2020 so as to be applied to the new Coronavirus diseases (Law no. 4 of 2020). The Act was further amended in February 2021 to reinforce the authority of the local governors (Law no. 5 of 2021).

34 See arts 21 and 30 of the Standard Contract Terms for Private Construction Contracts (1) *(Minkan kensetu kōji hyōjun ukeoi keiyaku yakkan* [*kō*]).

35 Announcement on 17 April 2020 from MLIT, Real Estate and Construction Economy Bureau, Real Estate Industry Division <www.mlit.go.jp/common/001341805.pdf> (in Japanese) accessed 27 May 2022.

parties' negotiations outside the courts and arbitration tribunals resolving the disputes on construction contracts.

3.3.3 The limits on the right to specific performance

Under the Japanese Civil Code, an aggrieved party's right to specific performance is limited only in case of impossibility. The non-performing party is not allowed to escape from its obligation to perform by paying compensation for loss and damage incurred by the aggrieved party.[36] Article 412-2(1) of the Code prescribes that the aggrieved party may not ask for performance of an obligation if the performance is 'impossible in light of the contract or other sources of claims and the common sense in the transaction'. Although this provision adopted a text similar to article 415 on damages,[37] most Japanese lawyers believe that the criteria prescribed in both provisions are not the same. As to article 412-2 on 'Impossibility of Performance', one prominent author, who was a member of the Working Group on the Reform of the Law on Obligations, asserts that the exclusion of the right to specific performance should be decided based on a comparison of the value of the performance for the receiving party (aggrieved party), on the one hand, and the cost that will be incurred by the counterparty (non-performing party) in performing the obligation, on the other. According to this view, which is explicitly influenced by the rules prescribed in article 275(2) of the German Civil Code and article 1221 of the French Civil Code, the exclusion of the right to specific performance is justified on the principle of abuse of rights.

3.3.4 'The principle of change of circumstances'

As a doctrine which allows parties to terminate or adapt a contract under a severe change of circumstances, 'the principle of change of circumstances (*jijō henkō no gensoku*)' has been established by the Japanese courts and academia.[38] While the doctrine is widely acknowledged by Japanese lawyers in general terms, the number of court judgments which have actually applied the doctrine is very limited. As far as the highest courts in Japan are concerned, only one old court decision is reported in which a party was allowed to terminate a contract by application of this doctrine.[39] This may be a reflection of a reluctance of Japanese courts to admit exceptions to the principle of *pacta sunt servanda*.

36 However, there is an interesting debate over the duty to mitigate; see Tomohiro Yoshimasa, 'Preventive Measures in Contract Law – Recent Debate over "Duty to Mitigate" in Japan' in Alexander Bruns and Masabumi Suzuki (eds), *Preventive Instruments of Social Governance* (Mohr Siebeck, 2017) 43.

37 See above 3.3.1.

38 For an English account of the doctrine, see Kiyoshi Igarashi and Luvern V Rieke, 'Impossibility and Frustration in Sales Contracts' (1967) 42 Washington Law Review 445, 451.

39 See Japanese Imperial Court, 6 December 1944, *Minshū* 23, 613.

Even under the corona crisis, no reported cases have applied the 'principle of change of circumstances'. This does not mean, however, that all contracts are enforced as it was originally agreed to before the pandemic. There must be many cases in which the parties have voluntarily agreed upon modification of contracts to deal with the pandemic outside the courts. Contract clauses that impose a duty to negotiate in good faith upon parties should play an important role in this context.

3.3.5 The special rules on lease contracts

It is also worth making a brief remark on the special rules on lease contracts.[40]

After the outbreak of COVID-19, disputes regarding rent for buildings were the focus of considerable public attention in Japan. Many lessees (tenants), mostly of retail shops and restaurants, who were unable to make profits in rented buildings due to the pandemic sought a reduction of the rent to which the parties had agreed in the lease contract. These lessees had the following potential avenues for such a reduction.

First, article 611(1) of the Japanese Civil Code provides that if it has become impossible to use the object of a lease, the rent is reduced in proportion to the value of the part that can no longer be used. This provision is based on the idea that a lessor is under an obligation to make the object of a lease available for the lessee to use, and that if the object is unavailable for use, the lessor is not entitled to ask for the rent. This means that as long as the object is available for use, the risk of not being able to make benefit by using the office or store is assumed by the tenant. According to the prevailing view, therefore, even if the profit of a tenant had decreased under the pandemic, the rent may not, in principle, be reduced by applying this provision. On the other hand, however, where the object of a lease is not available for use, e.g. due to the closure of a large commercial facility upon the request or order of a local governor (see articles 45 and 31-5 of the Act on Special Measures concerning the New Influenza), it is likely that the tenants may ask for reduction of the rent under article 611(1) of the Japanese Civil Code because in such a case the lessor is in breach of its obligation under the lease contract.

Second, a tenant could ask for a decrease in rent based on the Act on Land and Building Leases,[41] the special legislation providing for rules on leases of land and buildings. Article 32 (1) of the Act provides that if the rent of a building has become unreasonable due to the fluctuations in economic circumstances or in comparison to the rents for similar buildings in the vicinity, the parties may request future increases or decreases in the rent (article 11(1) of the Act provides the same rule for leases of land). Many authors consider this provision as an embodiment of the 'principle of change of circumstances' described above. The

40 For details of the rules on lease contracts, see Sono and others (n 10) paras 710–760.
41 Law no. 90 of 1991.

provision is mostly justified on the ground that law ensures long duration period for leases for land and buildings, and it is not improbable that economic fluctuations will occur during the course of the contract. In such long-term contracts, it is likely that neither party had fully assumed the risk of subsequent increase or decrease of market price of rent in the initial contract. Thus, if the economic deterioration caused by the corona pandemic results in a decline in market price of rent, the tenant may request the lessor to reduce the future rent to a reasonable amount based on this provision.

4 Concluding remarks

In this chapter, two fields of contract law which are closely related to the principle of *pacta sunt servanda* were discussed, namely the rules on formation of contract and remedies for breach of contract. As the Japanese Civil Code is said to be a 'fruit of comparative jurisprudence',[42] the basic framework of these rules in Japan is to a considerable extent similar to that of the Western jurisdictions. Comparative study with other East Asian jurisdictions is, however, still in its early stages. The valuable contributions in this volume should illuminate the characteristics of Japanese contract law from the perspective of East Asian jurisdictions.

42 See above 2.1.

6 Change of circumstances in Korean contract law

An exception to *pacta sunt servanda*

Boeun Chang

1 Introduction

Pacta sunt servanda is one of the most important and basic principles in Korean contract law.[1] Contracts should be kept. When a party fails to perform an obligation under a contract, and if non-performance is intentional or negligent, he or she is liable for damages for the default.[2] The other party may terminate the contract if the breach is material.[3] Following a breach of a contract, the compulsory performance procedure is also available to the obligor as a standard remedy, unless the nature of the obligation does not permit.[4] This is in contrast to common law jurisdictions, where specific performance is granted only if a monetary remedy will not adequately compensate the other party.[5]

In law and economics, the theory of efficient breach of contract posits that a party should be allowed to breach a contract and pay damages, if doing so would be more economically efficient than performing under the contract.[6] In Korean law, this legal theory of efficient breach is not generally accepted, because contracts have sanctity that goes beyond the economic interests of the parties.[7]

Is there any exception to the principle of *pacta sunt servanda*? The right of withdrawal under some special acts could be regarded as an exception. For example,

1 Seoul High Court Decision 2003Na37862, 16 January 2004; Supreme Court Decision 2004Da31302, 29 March 2007; Supreme Court en banc Decision 2012Da13637, 26 September 2013; Supreme Court Decision 2016Da249557, 8 June 2017, etc.

2 Article 390 of the Korean Civil Code (see Annex).

3 Articles 544 and 546 of the Korean Civil Code (see Annex). It is generally accepted that the contract may be terminated only when there is a material breach. If there is a mere breach of the contract, only a claim for damages is possible. Yun-Jik Kwak, *Obligations: Specific Part (Chaekwonkakron)* (6th ed, Parkyoungsa, 2003) 95 (in Korean)

4 Article 389 of the Korean Civil Code (see Annex).

5 Dan B Dobbs and Caprice L Roberts, *Law of Remedies, Damages-Equity-Restitution* (3rd ed, West Academic Publishing, 2017) 787–788.

6 Richard A Posner and Andrew M Rosenfeld, 'Impossibility and Related Doctrines in Contract Law: An Economic Analysis' (1977) 6 The Journal of Legal Studies 83, 89; see also the opinion of Judge Richard Posner in *Lake River Corp. v. Carborundum Co.*, 769 F.2d 1284 (7th Cir. 1985).

7 See the opinion of Justice Park Sang-ok and Justice Kim Jae-hyung in Supreme Court en banc Decision 2017Do4027 17 May 2018.

DOI: 10.4324/9781003358305-7

in multi-level sales or online transactions where consumers frequently enter into a contract without fully considering detailed contents of the contract, or financial transactions where it is difficult for a party to understand the contents or effects of the contract, the right of withdrawal is granted for a certain period of time even if there is no special reason.[8]

In addition, Korean courts have expressly stated that the doctrine of change of circumstances is an exception to the principle of compliance with the contract. Since the Supreme Court held in 2007 that the doctrine of change of circumstances was to be accepted,[9] similar rulings have followed.[10] Further, there have been some Supreme Court cases where termination of a contract was permitted by applying this doctrine since 2020,[11] and thus change of circumstances is assuming relevance in practice, rather than being a merely theoretical declaration.

In particular, the doctrine is expected to play a greater role, as society changes more rapidly and more unpredictably. This is already evident from some court cases that had to confront unprecedented situations due to COVID-19.[12] In addition, the newly amended Commercial Building Lease Protection Act provides that parties may claim revision of rent or security deposit if the amount is no longer fair in light of a material change in economic conditions by a Class 1 infectious disease,[13] and that a lessee may terminate the lease agreement when they close their business due to the material change of economic conditions caused by government measures for 3 months or more.[14] These articles may be understood as further expression of the doctrine, in particular for COVID-19 related cases. Therefore, the doctrine of change of circumstances will be a vehicle to understand the meaning of *pacta sunt servanda* in Korean contract law, especially in this changing era.

2 The change of circumstances doctrine

2.1 Overview

Change of circumstances under Korean contract law is defined as the doctrine that a party may alter or extinguish the effect of the contract so as to be consistent with the principle of good faith and justice, if it is unreasonable to maintain and enforce the contents of the original contract as it is, as the environment which existed at

8 Article 8 of the Door-to-Door Sales Act or article 46 of the Financial Consumer Protection Act (see Annex). See also Geraint Howells, '*Pacta sunt servanda* and the consumer's right of withdrawal', ch 10 (in this volume).

9 Supreme Court Decision 2004Da31302, 29 March 2007.

10 Supreme Court en banc Decision 2012Da13637, 26 September 2013; Supreme Court Decision 2016Da249557, 8 June 2017, etc.

11 Supreme Court Decision 2020Da254846, 10 December 2020.

12 Seoul Central District Court Decision 2020GaDan5261441, 25 May 2021.

13 Article 11(1) of Commercial Building Lease Protection Act (amended on 29 September 2020).

14 Article 11–2 of Commercial Building Lease Protection Act (amended on 4 January 2022).

the time of the execution of the contract or the circumstances under which the act was conducted are substantially changed thereafter.[15]

The law of contracts in Korea is in great part codified in the Korean Civil Code (the 'KCC'). However, there is no provision in the KCC which generally recognises the doctrine of change of circumstances. The Korean Ministry of Justice (the 'MOJ') initiated attempts to give legislative form to the doctrine, once in 2004 and again in 2013, but the amendments to the KCC were not achieved. In the absence of codification, there was disagreement, at least before the 2020 Supreme Court decision, on whether this doctrine should be accepted in Korean contract law.[16]

The main argument of the opponents of the doctrine was that recognising the change of circumstances would greatly threaten the binding force of contracts and the safety of transactions.[17] However, this position had become difficult to maintain after the Supreme Court decided in favour of the doctrine of change of circumstances in 2007.[18] The majority of legal scholars affirms the doctrine of change of circumstances now.

Without specific statutory backing, the grounds for the doctrine are generally found in article 2 of the KCC, which prescribes the principle of good faith. When a situation arises outside the contract that is beyond ordinary risks, it would be reasonable to solve the problem in accordance with the principle of good faith as a general norm of contract law.

2.2 Changes in judicial precedents

Korean courts' traditional view was to reject the doctrine of change of circumstances. In a series of decisions in the 1950s, contractual relationships were affected by severe market price fluctuations after the Korean War and currency reforms.[19] In one Supreme Court decision, a request for termination of a paper sales contract was filed for the reason that the market price of paper had increased by a factor of 25.[20] However, the court concluded:

> [T]he principle of so-called change of circumstances, which is the norm that in case where original benefit becomes markedly unfair to a party as a result of changes in the circumstances which became the basis of at the time of execution of the contract, and both parties were unable to predict and foresee

15 Kwak (n 3) 92 (*in Korean*).

16 As to the detailed legal theories on this issue, see Tuck-Soo Song, 'Beiträge zu aktuellen Fragen der Lehre von der Geschäftsgrundlage in dem koreanischen BGB' (2018) 23 Ewha Law Journal No. 1 (*in Korean*).

17 Kim Dae Jeong, 'A consideration on § 544–4 of the Draft of the Korean Civil Code (2001) which Provides the Principle of the Circumstances' (2011) 22 Chonbuk Law Review 254 (*in Korean*).

18 Supreme Court Decision 2004Da31302, 29 March 2007.

19 See also Supreme Court Decision 4298MinSang109, 10 February 1955; Supreme Court Decision 4288MinSang234, 235, 10 March 1956; Supreme Court Decision 63Da452, 12 September 1963.

20 Supreme Court Decision 4286MinSang231, 14 April 1955.

> to the changes, the affected party may suggest to the other party to modify the details of the benefit in a proper manner in accordance with the principle of good faith, and if it is refused by the other party, the party may terminate the contract, shall not be approved by the interpretation of the KCC.[21]

In the decades since then, the Supreme Court had not accepted the plaintiffs' request for termination of a contract for the reason of the change of circumstances. However, unlike the earlier precedents, it was difficult to know what the Supreme Court's position was on the doctrine itself, as it did not specifically consider whether the change of circumstances doctrine itself was recognised or not.

In 2007, the Korean Supreme Court finally recognised the doctrine itself as follows:

> A so-called termination of a contract due to a change in circumstances occurs when a significant change in circumstances happens that a party to the contract could not have foreseen at the time of contract formation and when such change in circumstances occurs due to a reason for which the party with the right to rescind is not responsible.[22] Where the binding power is recognised as stipulated in the contract, instances in which outcomes run significantly counter to the principle of good faith are recognised as an exception to the general rule of the observance of contracts.[23]

Despite accepting in principle that a contract may be terminated on grounds of change of circumstances, the court concluded that, on the facts of the case, the plaintiff was not entitled to terminate the contract based on a change of circumstances. In this case, the plaintiff intended to build a restaurant and purchased land from a local government, the defendant. The land was subsequently incorporated into public land, thereby making the purchaser's intended construction of a restaurant on the land impossible. The court denied the plaintiff's termination right on the basis of the change of circumstances doctrine if the specific circumstance in that case did not form the foundation of the contract. In such a case, even though an inability to achieve the goal of the contract as intended at the time of formation resulted in loss to one party, it was not deemed to contravene the principle of good faith in maintaining the contract.

Since then, similar decisions followed. While courts accepted the doctrine itself, they erected high hurdles for a termination of a contract based on the doctrine of change of circumstances. Applying a strict standard, courts were reluctant to hold

21 ibid (own translation).

22 In most court cases, plaintiffs requested termination of a contract not an adaptation. As to the relationship between the right to adapt a contract and the termination right as an effect of the change of circumstances doctrine, please see 3.5 below.

23 Supreme Court Decision 2004Da31302, 29 March 2007 (official translation, see <https://library.scourt.go.kr/SCLIB_data/decision/4-7%20Supreme%20Court%20Decision%20 2006Da50499%20%20March%2029.htm>).

that the relevant event was unforeseeable or that it was a significant change in circumstances, etc. For instance, in the famous so-called KIKO cases, the Supreme Court stated that the currency option contract could not be terminated for the reason of change of circumstances.[24] In the knock-in knock-out ('KIKO') currency option contracts in question, buyers would buy a certain amount of dollars at the agreed exchange rate if the won-dollar exchange rate was within a certain range. However, if the won-dollar exchange rate fell below the range, the contract would become void (the knock-out condition). In addition, if the won-dollar exchange rate rose above the range, banks would have a call option so that buyers would have to resell the dollars to banks at a price below market value, causing buyers a loss (the knock-in condition). From 2006 to 2008, since the won-dollar exchange rate fluctuation was not large for a while, many small and medium-sized enterprises were prompted to enter into KIKO currency option contracts with banks. After the Lehman Crisis, however, the global financial market began to become unstable, and as the exchange rate surged in a short period of time, the knock-out condition was met. The court viewed that exchange rate volatility was the premise or content of the contract, and both parties assumed the risk of exchange rate volatility that moved in the direction against expectation, and that expecting the exchange rate to stay within a certain range was not the basis of the contract.

In 2020, the Supreme Court finally made a decision allowing termination of a contract based on a change of circumstances.[25] In this case, the plaintiff entered into a lease for the land owned by the defendant for the purpose of constructing a model house for a housing construction project, with that purpose specified in the lease. Later, when the local government rejected the application for constructing a temporary building it became impossible to construct a model house on the land. The lessee gave notice of termination for the lease and sought the return of the deposit. The Supreme Court viewed that the construction of a model house constituted the basis for the lease contract. As achieving the objective of the contract had become impossible, maintaining the contract would have resulted in a significant imbalance between parties. Based on the change of circumstances, the Court held that the lease was duly terminated by the lessee, and the lessor was liable to returning the security deposit to the lessee.[26]

24 Supreme Court en banc Decision 2012Da1146, 1153, 26 September 2013 <https://library.scourt.go.kr/SCLIB_data/decision/20_2012Da1146%201153.htm>; Supreme Court en banc Decision 2013Da26746, 26 September 2013; Supreme Court en banc Decision 2012Da13637 26 September 2013 <https://library.scourt.go.kr/SCLIB_data/decision/21_2012Da13637.htm>.

25 Supreme Court Decision 2020Da254846, 10 December 2020.

26 I submit that this case should have been resolved by implying a term into the lease without need to resort to the doctrine of change of circumstances. The facts of the case make it doubtful whether the parties could indeed not anticipate at the time of the execution of the contract that the construction of a model house may become difficult or impossible. Given that the parties specified the constructing of the model house as the purpose of a contract, it would be reasonable to imply that they did not want to maintain the lease if it became impossible to achieve the purpose. This is a process of completive interpretation, which is to fill the gap in contents of a contract.

In a number of cases since then, courts accepted termination of contracts based upon the change of circumstances doctrine.[27] On that basis, it is cautiously submitted that the doctrine will be more actively applied and play a practical role in the future.

3 Change of circumstances: emerging issues

3.1 Contracts in unpredictable times

We are living in an era of rapid change. During the course of the Fourth Industrial Revolution, technologies such as artificial intelligence, genome editing, augmented reality, robotics and 3-D printing, are expected to change the way humans create, exchange, and distribute value. In addition, there is widespread discussion of the need to fundamentally change the economic, environmental and living patterns, including production and consumption, in the face of climate crisis. What if the paradigm of the relevant market has been completely changed due to the drastic development of technologies or climate change? What will the contract look like then? How should we cope with changes in circumstances that we have never foreseen? Could the change of circumstances doctrine be a useful tool in these situations?

Currently, we are witnessing another unprecedented situation, the COVID-19 pandemic. While the impact of, and the response to, the COVID-19 may differ from one society to another, it is clear that the pandemic has changed the daily lives of people all over the world, and that it has also affected countless contractual bargains. As in many other countries, Korea has had lively debates over how to resolve breaches of contract that can be attributed to the impact of COVID-19. At the centre of this discussion is the change of circumstances doctrine.

3.2 COVID-19 outbreak and change of circumstances

The COVID-19 pandemic has had a serious impact on the global economic cycle and has made it difficult to execute or perform many private contracts properly. Fear of unknown circumstances undermined people's activities, and many events were cancelled. People postponed planned trips and cut down nonessential consumption. Instead, the consumption of masks and other protective equipment surged, and online life has been strengthened. At first, people believed the situation was temporary but, unfortunately, it has turned out to continue much longer. Humanity has been developing vaccines and treatments at unprecedented speed, but at the time of writing we are still struggling with COVID-19.

As in many other countries, the Korean government has imposed social distancing requirements. To prevent the spread of the disease, it restricted the operation

27 Supreme Court Decision 2019Da276338, 30 June 2021; Seoul Central District Court Decision 2020GaDan5261441, 25 May 2021.

of specific types of business, such as gyms, public baths, restaurants, bars, etc. The number of persons who can visit hospitality venues, or their times of operation, were also limited. Other public health measures banned private meetings with more than a certain number of participants. Telecommuting has increased, and the customer frequency in the hospitality industry has decreased significantly.

Some manufacturers have failed to supply goods and services in a timely manner, and this has affected the next stage of production. Due to sometimes sudden changes in the government's public health policies, wedding hall or travel contracts have been entered while no one can guarantee whether the event is able to take place. Some commercial leases for operating a business have suffered from the situation where the business fall sharply or is closed by the governmental order. How should we treat non-performance or other contractual impediments in this situation?

If the contract has allocated the risks arising from the situation regarding pandemics, the risk should be borne by the person who accepted it according to the contents of the contract. For instance, many international contracts have a *force majeure* clause, although it is not very common in domestic contracts in Korea. If a pandemic or an order of an administrative authority is specified as a relevant event in such a *force majeure* provision, there is a good chance for the debtor to be discharged from contractual liability. What if it contains only '*force majeure* of a natural disaster, etc.' without further specification? It shall be determined whether COVID-19 falls under this provision after reviewing the totality of circumstances.[28]

The KCC does not provide any limit to liability if the breach of contracts is due to *force majeure*. The term *force majeure* is found in the KCC only for the case where a collateral is extinguished when the subject matter is destroyed or damaged without negligence,[29] or the lessee is responsible for damages without negligence when he or she subleases.[30] Courts often acknowledge the existence of the concept

28 According to article 79 of the United Nations Convention on Contracts for the International Sale of Goods ('CISG'), there are four elements for force majeure: a) there is an impediment that is beyond the party's control; b) the impediment is unforeseeable; c) the impediment and its consequences could not have been reasonably overcome or avoided; and d) the non-performing party has to show that the non-performance is due to the impediment. There is little doubt that the impediment caused by COVID-19 satisfies the requirements of a) externality and d) causality is not a major hurdle for COVID-19-related non-performance. In contrast, determining whether it is impossible to perform the contractual obligation is not a simple matter and must be assessed case by case. As to the further assessment of the possible attitudes of arbitral tribunals towards COVID-19 cases, see Ş Esra Kiraz and Esra Yıldız Üstün, 'COVID-19 and *force majeure* clauses: an examination of arbitral tribunal's awards' (2020) 25 Uniform Law Review 437 <doi:10.1093/ulr/unaa027>. In CIETAC, Arbitration Award, 5 March 2005, L-Lysine case, SARS was not considered a force majeure event and the non-performing party was not excused from performance under article 79 of the CISG because SARS had happened a few months before the contract was signed. The element of foreseeability depends on the specific circumstances, and the conclusion will depend on the timing of the contract and the specific reason for non-performance.

29 Article 314 and article 336 of the Korean Civil Code (see Annex).

30 Article 308 of the Korean Civil Code (see Annex).

of *force majeure*, but it is hard to find decisions excusing the non-performing party from performance due to *force majeure*. Therefore, if the governing law of a contract is Korean law, and the parties did not allocate the related risks from COVID-19 in advance, it would be a more natural approach to follow the general rules of Korean contract law, the impossibility of performance and the doctrine of change of circumstances.[31]

3.3 Boundary with impossibility of performance

If the contract can no longer be performed, performance has become impossible. If the cause for the impossibility is attributable to the debtor, he or she shall be liable for damages, and if not, the question remains as to who shall bear the risk under Korean contract law. For those cases, the doctrine of change of circumstances cannot be applied. Only when performance is still possible, but seems highly unreasonable, the change of circumstances doctrine may apply to the case.

The impossibility is generally understood in Korean contract law as meaning that the performance of the obligation cannot be expected from the debtor in view of the general notion of society.[32] In practice, various forms of impossibility are recognised. For instance, the performance is physically impossible when the obligation to return the leased premises cannot be fulfilled because it was burnt down by a fire. In addition, even if it is not physically impossible by the law of nature, sometimes the performance is prohibited by law or legally impossible. For example, if the exporting country has issued an order of embargo in a trade transaction, the obligations to deliver goods cannot be performed.[33]

Suppose that A entered into a travel contract with a travel agency B for overseas travel before COVID-19. If A's intended destination was thereafter designated as a travel-prohibited country due to the pandemic situation, the performance of B's obligations under the travel contract would become impossible for legal reasons. Neither A nor B is responsible for this event. In such a case, the risks shall be distributed according to article 537 of the KCC[34]: Unless otherwise stipulated, B shall be exempted from the obligations under the travel contract, and A shall be exempted from the obligation to pay the fee. No one may claim damages in

31 A recent lower court case held that a lessee under a commercial lease was entitled to terminate the lease based on a force majeure clause (Seoul Central District Court Decision 2020GaDan5261441, 25 May 2021). The lease agreement did not specifically mention 'epidemic' or 'pandemic' as an instance of force majeure, but provided more generally. The plaintiff established that its sales dropped by more than 90% due to the COVID-19 outbreak and the government measures that followed. The court held that a lessee under a commercial lease was entitled to terminate the lease in these circumstances but simultaneously reviewed the applicability of the doctrine of change of circumstances. It concluded that the lessee could have terminated the lease agreement based upon the doctrine even in the absence of a force majeure clause in the lease.

32 Yang, Chang-soo and Jae-Hyung Kim, *Civil Code (Minbup) I* (2nd ed., Parkyoungsa, 2020) 401 *(in Korean)*.

33 ibid, 403.

34 Article 537 of the Korean Civil Code (see Annex).

relation to the non-performance, since – without negligence of both parties – it became impossible to perform.[35]

How about economic hardship of the debtor? If it can be regarded as making performance impossible, the doctrine of change of circumstances will not be considered, because the doctrine is applicable only to the cases where the performance is possible. It is certain that impossibility of performance does not arise merely because the cost of performance has increased, but if an extraordinary hardship may result in actual economic ruin to the debtor, or requiring the performance in accordance with the original terms and conditions is different from the will of the contract parties, could it be deemed impossible?[36] However, it would not be fair to determine the impossibility based solely on the subjective circumstances of the debtor. Also, it is common that contracts are not to be performed immediately after the execution, the circumstance that the cost of performance has increased in the meantime shall be borne by the debtor. Korean contract law does not recognise the impossibility of performance for monetary payment. It is not appropriate to reach a different conclusion depending on whether the debt is a monetary one or not. In this regard, it would be reasonable that economic hardship cannot make the performance impossible.[37]

Let us assume that a wholesaler of medical supplies C entered into a contract before COVID-19 with hospital D for supplying medical masks, but the price of the mask has soared due to a shortage of masks after the outbreak. The obligation of C to supply medical masks cannot be deemed impossible solely on the ground that the price has risen. If the shortage of masks made it extremely difficult for C to obtain masks to supply to D, is it impossible to supply them? The totality of circumstances should be considered on a case-by-case basis: whether it is possible to secure the quantity with a higher price, whether there is another supplier in the market, how difficult it is in practice to find an alternative supplier, what efforts C has made or could have made, and what efforts have been made by other wholesalers, etc. Once it is indeed determined that the supply is impossible, the next issue to be examined is whether the impossibility is attributable to A. If there is a way to supply at an additional cost and effort, it shall not be easily recognised as impossible. If it is determined that the performance is not impossible, then it is necessary to consider whether to apply the doctrine of change of circumstances.

The question of how to deal with the temporary impossibility is another issue. In general, the impossibility to perform means permanent inability. The contractual

35 The issue of how to compensate for losses incurred by a travel agency due to the government order is beyond the scope of contract law. The Act on the Protection of and Support For Micro Enterprises was amended on 7 July 2021 to provide a basis of compensation for severe business losses due to preventive measures against infectious diseases under the Infectious Disease Control and Prevention Act.

36 As to the opinion that it is impossible to perform the contract in this case, see Yang and Kim (n 32) 404, 405; as to the opposing opinion, see Sangyong Kim, *Obligations: General Part (Chekwonchongron)* (Hwasan Media, 2003) 128 (in Korean).

37 Park Yeong-bok, 'Force Majeure and Hardship as Limits of Contract Liability' (2011) 35 HUFS Law Review 91, 94 (*in Korean*).

obligations are temporarily suspended until performance becomes possible again. If the debtor is not responsible for the temporary impossibility, the issue of compensation shall not arise. It would be fair that the other party's benefits in return shall be suspended while the obligation is suspended, since both obligations ordinarily should be performed in a concurrent matter.[38] This does not apply where a party is to bear the eventual risk. If the objectives of the transaction cannot be achieved for a prolonged period, the impossibility may no longer be said to be temporary, and it becomes permanent.

For example, if a factory owner F entered into a contract for manufacturing and supplying masks to trader E, and the factory has to be shut down for two weeks due to a confirmed case among workers, it could be said that the supply of masks becomes temporarily impossible. Of course, in order to determine whether it is indeed impossible to perform the obligation, additional issues should be examined, such as whether it is possible to produce in another factory during that period or whether it is necessary or possible to procure the same quality of masks on the market. Suppose that it is concluded that it is impossible to perform the obligation for some time, F must begin to perform its obligations as of the time when it becomes possible to resume production two weeks later. E's obligation to pay may be postponed accordingly. If there were further contracts in the distribution chain, they may be affected as well. In the event of even temporary delay to the supply, it needs to be established whether there has been any cause attributable to the parties to each contract. Otherwise, liability for damages shall not be imposed. If the closure of F's factory is prolonged, such as when additional confirmed cases are discovered, it shall be examined whether the supply becomes permanently impossible. It shall not be concluded easily that the performance is impossible for the reason only that the factory of F has to be closed for a longer time. It may be required for F to find an alternative production or procurement method proactively, because humans are capable of adapting to the changing environment.

3.4 Change of circumstances due to COVID-19

Let us get back to the supply contract for medical masks between wholesaler C and hospital D. Once we reach the conclusion that the performance of C is still possible, it is open for us to consider the applicability of the change of circumstances doctrine. If it is not a mere increase in the purchasing cost, but a marked change, it may be seen as too severe to enforce the contract as it is. If the price of the masks increases drastically after the execution and if the supply contract is for an enormous volume of masks, requiring C to perform the contract on its original terms may cause C to suffer enormous damage and possibly to go bankrupt. What about a lessee of a hospitality venue who is unable to open for business because of the government's administrative order? Even if the parties did not specify this

38 Chinwoo Kim, 'COVID-19-Pandemie und Leistungstoerungen' (2020) 27 The Journal of Comparative Private Law 308, 309 (*in Korean*).

in the lease, it is a fair assumption that a lessee is using the premises for his or her business. This assumption is no longer valid.

Taken together with the legal theories and court precedents discussed above, the requirements for the doctrine can be said generally to be as follows: a) the circumstances on which the contract was established have changed substantially; b) the parties were not able to foresee the change at the time of execution of the contract; c) maintaining the contract would result in a serious violation of good faith.

These three requirements are interrelated with each other, rather than independent. For instance, when determining a substantial change in circumstances, the question of how much change could be considered substantial is closely related to the question whether the parties could have expected the change, and further to the question of whether maintaining the contents of the contract as it is would lead to a result against the principle of good faith.

According to court decisions, circumstances in this context mean the underlying circumstances based on which the parties entered into the contract. It does not encompass circumstances on which the parties did not base their decision to enter into the contract or circumstances in which either party agreed to assume any disadvantage or risk emanating from a change thereof.[39] Additionally, even if a circumstance that did not form the foundation of the contract changes afterwards and resulted in damage to one party because he or she could not achieve the goal of the contract as intended at time of formation, it shall not be deemed to contravene the principle of good faith to maintain the effect of the content of the contract.[40]

It would be obvious that COVID-19 itself is a remarkable change in circumstances that the parties of a contract could not foresee at the time of execution of the contract. However, when it comes to applying the exception to the principle of compliance with the contract, it should be reviewed whether it is related to the premise of the contract. Not all contracts have been directly affected by COVID-19 and the anti-pandemic measures. There are contracts that are not significantly affected or where the contractual subject-matter can be easily substituted by finding alternatives. For example, some restaurants have had a hard time due to decreased customer flows, while others have received more orders through delivery business. Private teaching institutes could not open at first due to the government order but, after some time, they found alternative ways to teach classes online and could reach out to more students without limitation of distance. Hence, it must be examined on a case-by-case basis whether a substantial change of circumstances has occurred due to COVID-19.

If parties of a contract were able to foresee the change, they would have had the opportunity not to enter into the contract or to conclude the contract with different content so as to prepare for the change. In that case, the risk arising from the

39 Supreme Court Decision 2016Da249557, 8 June 2017 <https://library.scourt.go.kr/SCLIB_data/decision/14_2016Da249557.htm>.

40 Supreme Court Decision 2004Da31302, 29 March 2007 <https://library.scourt.go.kr/SCLIB_data/decision/4-5%20Supreme%20Court%20Decision%202004Da31302%20%20March%2029.htm>.

change should be allocated according to the original intent of the parties without intervening on the basis of the change of circumstances doctrine. To determine whether a change was unforeseeable, courts should consider the totality of circumstances in a specific case, including the type and contents of the contract, the status or transaction experience of the parties, recognisable risk, the size or specificity of the risk, etc.[41]

The timing of execution of the contract is also important to determine unforeseeability. In the early stages of the outbreak, COVID-19 was not well-known, and the epidemic was expected to end soon. Although it may not now even be said that we know and understand COVID-19 well, foreseeability has improved, compared with the early stage. We have been vaccinated sequentially and are able to manage the number of confirmed cases and other circumstances. So, if a contract is entered now, it can be generally expected to allocate the risks arising out of COVID-19 to the extent possible. It would be more difficult to apply the change of circumstances to such contracts, unlike those entered before COVID-19 or at the early stage of it.

The last requirement of the doctrine is that maintaining the contract as it is would result in a serious violation of good faith.[42] Courts have developed this element that maintaining the contract as it is would cause a material imbalance in the interests of the parties or make it impossible to achieve the objectives for which the contract is concluded.[43] Reflecting court decisions, the bill proposal suggested by the MOJ in 2013[44] tried to codify the requirement as follows:

> If circumstances forming the basis of the contract are significantly changed, the parties were unable to predict such change at the time of execution of the contract, and maintaining the contract as it is would cause a serious imbalance in the interests of the parties or make it impossible to achieve the purpose of the contract, the parties may request the revision of the contract or terminate the contract.[45]

41 Supreme Court Decision 2019Da276338, 30 June 2021.

42 Supreme Court Decision 2004Da31302, 29 March 2007. <https://library.scourt.go.kr/SCLIB_data/decision/4-5%20Supreme%20Court%20Decision%202004Da31302%20%20March%2029.htm>.

43 Supreme Court Decision 2016Da249557, 8 June 2017 <https://library.scourt.go.kr/SCLIB_data/decision/14_2016Da249557.htm>; Supreme Court Decision 2019Da276338, 30 June 2021.

44 The Special Subcommittee on the Civil Code Amendment under the MOJ prepared an amendment bill in 2004. However, the bill proposal was discarded due to the expiration of the session of the National Assembly without being properly deliberated. In February 2009, the Civil Code Amendment Committee under the MOJ was re-launched and prepared a new amendment bill for five years. This amendment was based on the bill proposal in 2004, but included more developed content and new amendments. Among them, provisions on behavioural ability, adult guardianship, guarantee debt, and travel contracts were passed, some other provisions were submitted to the National Assembly but passed, and most of them including the provision regarding the change of circumstances were not submitted to the National Assembly. It was mainly due to the schedule of the National Assembly, rather than any substantial legal issues on the provisions.

45 Korean Ministry of Justice, Draft Amendment to the Korean Civil Code (Proposal), 2013, art 538–2.

However, it is still hard to ascertain when a material imbalance arises and whether the achievement of the objectives has become impossible. Suppose that a producer rented a grand theatre for a musical performance, but the performance became completely prohibited due to COVID-19. It is not impossible for the producer to pay the rent fee, but it would be impossible to achieve the purpose of the contract. In contracts for the supply of goods, there has been no established precedent as to when a price fluctuation becomes material so as to amount to a change of circumstances. While this is likely to be a matter that is heavily influenced by the circumstances, it can also be expected that more guidance will emerge as the doctrine develops in practice and more cases are decided.

3.5 Effect of the change of circumstances doctrine

In most court cases where the change of circumstances was at issue, the debtor sought a termination of the contract. The right to terminate a contract is the major effect of the doctrine. According to the MOJ amendments, however, in the alternative to termination, parties may request modification of the contract when performance becomes excessively onerous because of changes in circumstances. Is the right to request adapting the contract a proper effect of the change of circumstances?

The change of circumstances doctrine is based on the principle of good faith. It applies when it is unjust to enforce performance of the contract as it is. Then is it always fair not to perform the contract as a whole when there is a significant change of circumstances that no one has anticipated. Is it the only way to reasonably allocate risks associated therewith? There could be intermediate solutions between termination of the contract and keeping the contents of the contract as originally agreed. In suitable cases, it may be desirable that the contract be maintained rather than terminated, when performance on the original terms becomes excessively onerous. A right to modification would prompt the parties to enter into negotiations on whether and, if so, how to adapt the contract, although it does not necessarily mean that they would be required to reach an agreement on modification of the contract.[46]

Let us consider the case where an investment was made based in the belief that there would be an ongoing contractual relationship between the parties. Terminating the contract, even after significant change of circumstances, may cause unnecessary harm to the parties or at least to one of them, and it may be also economically detrimental to society. In such cases, if the parties were unable to agree on an amendment, it would be necessary to further consider

46 Kim (n 38) 308.

whether to allow the judge to amend the contract. This may lead to a controversial debate over judicial activism, which shall here only be mentioned rather than resolved.[47]

Another issue may be the relationship between terminating a contract and requesting to amend a contract when the change of circumstances doctrine is applied. The question is whether these two rights can be selectively exercised, otherwise whether the party must try to amend the contract before exercising the termination right. Some scholars insist that parties' interests must be adjusted by adapting the contract first and, if they cannot reach an agreement or there is no possibility of adjustment, then termination of the contract can be considered.[48] This view is based on the fact that termination of a contract has the material effect of extinguishing the contractual relationship between parties. This is the case, for example, in the German Civil Code[49] or in the French Civil Code as amended in 2016.[50] However, sometimes it may become completely impossible to achieve the purpose of a contract, or continuation of a contract with modification is not favourable at all to the party who claims the change of circumstances. Therefore, it would be unreasonable to say that negotiations for adapting the contract should take precedence and termination can be claimed only after the failure. It is consistent with the position of the amendment proposal of the MOJ in 2013, which allowed the parties' request for the revision and termination of the contract as parallel effects on the doctrine. It is also in line with the court precedents so far that a party does not need to make an attempt to modify a contract prior to seeking termination. If a party requests to terminate the contract on the grounds of change

47 Jae-Hyung Kim, 'The Proposed Amendment to the Korean Civil Code on Rescission and Termination of the Contract, Risk of Loss, and Change of Circumstance' (2014) 55 Seoul Law Journal 54 (*in Korean*).

48 Hyung-Bae Kim, *Contract Law (Kyeyakbup) I* (Parkyoungsa, 2001) 74 (*in Korean*).

49 Section 313 (1) and (3) of the German Civil Code (Interference with the basis of the transaction): '(1) If circumstances which became the basis of a contract have significantly changed since the contract was entered into and if the parties would not have entered into the contract or would have entered into it with different contents if they had foreseen this change, adaptation of the contract may be demanded to the extent that, taking account of all the circumstances of the specific case, in particular the contractual or statutory distribution of risk, one of the parties cannot reasonably be expected to uphold the contract without alteration. (3) If adaptation of the contract is not possible or one party cannot reasonably be expected to accept it, the disadvantaged party may revoke the contract. In the case of continuing obligations, the right to terminate takes the place of the right to revoke.' <www.gesetze-im-internet.de/englisch_bgb/englisch_bgb.html#p1146>.

50 Article 1195 of the French Civil Code: 'If a change of circumstances that was unforeseeable at the time of the conclusion of the contract renders performance excessively onerous for a party who had not accepted the risk of such a change, that party may ask the other contracting party to renegotiate the contract. The first party must continue to perform his obligations during renegotiation. In the case of refusal or the failure of renegotiations, the parties may agree to terminate the contract from the date and on the conditions which they determine, or by a common agreement ask the court to set about its adaptation. In the absence of an agreement within a reasonable time, the court may, on the request of a party, revise the contract or put an end to it, from a date and subject to such conditions as it shall determine.' <www.trans-lex.org/601101/_/french-civil-code-2016/>.

of circumstances, the issue of termination of the contract is to be decided without consideration of modification or adaptation.[51]

4 Conclusion

Korean courts have explicitly acknowledged that the change of circumstances doctrine is an exception to *pacta sunt servanda*. In situations where the parties recognised and allocated the risk of an unforeseen event, the contract must be fulfilled even if there has been some material change, because that was the parties' intention. However, a different story emerges if significant change occurs that was unexpected and not covered in the contract. In the latter situation, we cannot predicate that the parties' intention was to require that the contract be complied with in its original form even when doing so has now become excessively onerous to one of the parties. In these exceptional circumstances, the change of circumstances doctrine will become relevant.

Courts traditionally tended to be prudent in granting the right to terminate a contract by recognising that compliance with the contract is one of the most important principles in Korean contract law. However, in recent years, courts have further elaborated the doctrine, and taken a more positive attitude toward applying it to actual cases and allowing the contract to be terminated.

The doctrine of change of circumstance may also allow more flexible and reasonable solutions in between either termination of the contract as a whole or maintenance of the original contract as it is. In our society where circumstances can change rapidly and unpredictably, the doctrine may play an important role in coordinating interests and addressing the risk of unfairness arising from bargains that, without knowledge and responsibility of the parties, have become harsh.

For instance, in the unprecedented situation due to COVID-19, the change of circumstances doctrine has been used as a tool to solve unexpected problems arising out of it. Courts are considering the doctrine as a fair basis for terminating a contract severely affected by COVID-19. The doctrine is being also reflected in laws and regulations such as the Commercial Building Lease Protection Act. Of course, COVID-19 itself is not sufficient for applying the change of circumstances, it is necessary to carefully analyse how the premised situations of the contract were affected by COVID-19 in each actual case.

To maximise the potential of the doctrine to respond appropriately to the rapidly changing environment in the future society, it is important that it maintains sufficient flexibility. Yet, it is also important for the court to further refine the doctrine so that its outcomes can be more easily predicted and so it can be effective in solving problems in practice.

51 Song (n 16) 109–112; Park (n 37) 446–447.

[Annex]

Korean Civil Code[52]

Article 308 (responsibility where of chonchonse, etc.)

In case the subject matter of *chonsegwon* becomes that of *chonchonse* having *chonsegwon* who has so leased or contracted for *chonchonse* shall be responsible for the damage arising from an act of God which would not have arisen if the contract for *chonchonse* or leases had not been entered.

Article 314 (loss by act of God)

(1) If the whole or part of the subject matter of *chonsegwon* is destroyed by an act of God over which the party has no control, the *chonsegwon* over the portion destroyed shall be extinguished. [. . .]

Article 336 (sub-pledge)

A pledgee may, within his own right, sub-pledge the pledged article on his own responsibility. In such case, he shall be responsible even for damage due to an act of God which would not have occurred if the article had not been sub-pledged.

Article 389 (compulsory performance of obligation)

(1) Where an obligor fails to perform his/her obligation at will, the obligee may apply for compulsory performance thereof to a court: *Provided*, that this shall not apply where the nature of an obligation does not so permit.
(2) Where the obligation referred to in the preceding paragraph has a juristic act for its subject, an application may be made to a court for a ruling which shall substitute for a declaration of intention by the obligor; if it has an act which is not entirely personal to the obligor for its subject, application may be made to a court to compel performance by a third person at the expenses of the obligor.
(3) Where the obligation has nonfeasance for its subject, and the obligor has violated it, an application may be made to a court to have that which has been violated by the obligor removed at the expenses of the obligor, and that reasonable precautionary steps be taken against future repetition.
(4) The preceding Paragraph (3) shall not affect a claim for compensation.

52 The English translation of the Civil Code can be found at <https://elaw.klri.re.kr/eng_service/lawView.do?hseq=55222&lang=ENG>.

Article 390 (non-performance of obligations and compensation for damages)

If an obligor fails to effect performance in accordance with the tenor and purport of the obligation, the obligee may claim damages: *Provided*, that this shall not apply to where performance has become impossible and where this is not due to the obligor's intention or negligence.

Article 537 (obligor's burden to bear risk)

If the performance of an obligation of one of the parties to a bilateral contract becomes impossible by any cause for which neither of the parties is responsible, the obligor may not be entitled to counter-performance.

Article 544 (delay of performance and termination)

If one of the parties does not perform his obligation, the other party may fix a reasonable period and give peremptory notice demanding its performance, and may terminate the contract, if no performance is effected within such period: *Provided*, that if the obligor declares in advance his intention that he will not effect such performance, no peremptory notice shall be required.

Article 546 (impossibility of performance and rescission)

If performance has become impossible for any cause for which the obligor is responsible, the obligee may rescind the contract.

Door-to-Door Sales Act[53]

Article 8 (withdrawal of subscription)

(1) A consumer who has signed a contract for purchase of goods or services through door-to-door sales or telemarketing (hereinafter referred to as "door-to-door sales, etc.") is entitled to withdrawal of subscription, etc. within the relevant period specified in the following subparagraphs (or the agreed-upon period, if the parties to a transaction have agreed on a period longer than the relevant period specified in the following subparagraphs).

[. . .]

53 The English translation of the Door-to-Door Sales Act can be found at <https://elaw.klri.re.kr/kor_service/lawView.do?hseq=57068&lang=ENG>.

Financial Consumer Protection Act[54]

Article 46 (withdrawal of offer)

(1) An ordinary financial consumer who has offered a contract for an indemnity product, an investment product, or a loan product specified by Presidential Decree or for advisory service on financial products with a financial product distributor or advisor may withdraw such offer within the relevant period specified in the following subparagraphs (if the parties to a transaction have agreed on a period longer than the period specified in the relevant subparagraph, such longer period).

[. . .]

54 The English translation of the Financial Consumer Protection Act can be found at <https://elaw.klri.re.kr/kor_service/lawView.do?hseq=54646&lang=ENG>.

Part B

Pacta sunt servanda in specific contexts

7 The property management service contract with Chinese characteristics

An exception to pacta sunt servanda?

Jianbo Lou and Yimeng Ye

I Introduction

The principle of *pacta sunt servanda* is incorporated into the Civil Code of the People's Republic of China (*'PRC Civil Code')*. According to articles 119 and 465 of *PRC Civil Code*, the parties shall keep their agreement. Logic dictates that the property management service contract (PMS contract), a newly introduced typical contract in the *PRC Civil Code*, binds the parties. However, articles 940 and 946 of *PRC Civil Code* grant homeowners the right to terminate the preliminary/ordinary PMS contracts, respectively, without cause. Homeowners appear to enjoy the privilege to escape from their contract with property management service companies (PMS companies), the major type of PMS providers in the Chinese mainland.

The tension between homeowners' rights in relation to the PMS contract and *pacta sunt servanda* exists not only at the rule level, but also in practice. Under PMS contracts, homeowners are obliged to pay property management fees (PM fees) and PMS providers must provide service as promised. However, both parties fail to perform their contractual obligations, as evidenced by the high rate of PM fees arrears[1] and poor service quality.[2] Furthermore, it appears that the Chinese mainland courts do not treat PMS contracts with enough respect: they often make 'discount' judgments at discretion in PM-fee-arrear-disputes, reducing the principal of PM fees that the homeowner is supposed to pay and lower, or even exempt from paying, outstanding interests or damages.[3]

1 The general collection rate of property management fees was less than 60% in 2018, and the long-term arrears led to the difficult collection. See WeiXiaoqu, 'Report on Property Management Fees Collection in 2018' <www.sohu.com/a/300978634_120106845> accessed 4 January 2022.

2 Yingying Zhao, 'Special Campaigns on Property Management Yields Good Results' Beijing Daily (Beijing, 1 May 2021) 5. For example, in Beijing's 12345 government service hot-line, one of the most frequently received complaints is about property management. The complaints include disorderly parking and poor sanitation of common areas inside residential communities, property management companies' inefficiency to deal with problems, sub-standard information disclosure and lack of community safety.

3 Shuqing Zhu, 'A Study on the Legal Protection of Claims for Property Management Fees' (LLM thesis, Peking University, 2011).

DOI: 10.4324/9781003358305-9

This chapter will investigate why PMS contracts in the Chinese mainland have 'softened' binding force, and whether this 'softening' contradicts the principle of *pacta sunt servanda* and the doctrine of rule of law.

This chapter has three parts. In the first part, we identify the scope and purpose of the *pacta sunt servanda* principle under the *PRC Civil Code*. This is followed, in the second part, by analysis of why PMS contracts in the Chinese mainland have softened binding force. The final part addresses the impact of the PMS contracts' soft binding force on the rule of law. We conclude that while the flexibility of PMS contracts harms the principle of *pacta sunt servanda*, it is nevertheless still in line with the rule of law generally, given that the flexibility and uncertainty are predictable to PMS companies in China.

II *Pacta sunt servanda* in the Chinese mainland

The principle of *pacta sunt servanda* is regarded as another facet of freedom of contract,[4] which is rooted in liberal legal thought in the 19th century.[5] The new PRC *Civil Code* has also embraced this principle but, unlike its foreign peers, places a more pragmatic value on this principle. This part will first define the principle of *pacta sunt servanda* under *PRC Civil Code* and then examine why the Chinese legislature varied in its use of the principle, and particularly look into its pragmatism from a historical perspective.

A **Pacta sunt servanda *in the* PRC Civil Code**

Articles 119, 136.2 and 465 of the *PRC Civil Code* are regarded as the legislative authorities of *pacta sunt servanda.*[6] They stipulate as follows:

> Article 119 A contract formed in accordance with law is legally binding on the parties to the contract.
> Article 136.2 A person that performs a civil juristic act may not change or revoke the act without authorisation, unless doing so is in compliance with law or as consented to by the other party.
> Article 465 A contract formed in accordance with law is protected by law.
> A contract formed in accordance with law is legally binding only on the parties thereto, unless otherwise provided by law.

The Legislative Affairs Commission of the Standing Committee of the National People's Congress (NPC, China's top legislature)[7] rightly points out that the

4 P S Atiyah, *An Introduction to the Law of Contract* (6th ed, Clarendon Press, 2005) 45–46.

5 Huaishi Xie, *Understanding Foreign Civil Law* (3rd ed, Law Press China, 2014) 204–205.

6 Shiyuan Han, *The Law of Contract* (6th ed, Law Press China, 2018) 64.

7 As a working organ of the NPC Standing Committee (NPCSC), the Legislative Affairs Commission assists the NPC and its Standing Committee to exercise legislative power. Its specific duties include: (1) to plan, organise, and coordinate the legislative work of the Standing Committee, as well as to provide relevant guidance and services; (2) to undertake the drafting, revision, research,

principle has four aspects: (1) the parties shall perform their contractual obligations; (2) the parties shall not arbitrarily terminate or modify the contract; (3) defaulting parties shall bear the liability for a breach of contract according to law; and (4) a contract established legally shall be protected by the state and no organisation or individual shall illegally interfere with the contract.[8]

Guangxin Zhu, a law professor of Chinese Academy of Social Science (CASS), further expounds the fourth aspect into four further points:

> (1) in case that a revocation cause exists, the parties shall try to modify the contract to maintain its validity prior to revocation; (2) partial invalidity of the contract does not necessary affect the validity of the contract as a whole; (3) the statutory termination of the contract shall be strictly defined; and (4) if the interpretation of a contract is in doubt, the one that maintains the validity of the contract shall be adopted.[9]

B Purposes of **pacta sunt servanda** *in the Chinese mainland*

The Chinese legislature considers the principle of *pacta sunt servanda* to be 'a necessary requirement'[10] of the principle of freedom of contract. *Pacta sunt servanda* is a 'logical corollary'[11] because the parties' freedom of contract would be meaningless if a contract they concluded was not legally binding and enforceable. Underneath the notion of freedom of contract lies people's 'need for stability, certainty and predictability',[12] which Lon Fuller defines as characteristics of the rule of law.[13] So we can argue syllogistically that the Chinese legislature adopts *pacta sunt servanda* to promote the rule of law through legal stability and predictability. This purpose is similar to that of legal traditions of other major jurisdictions.

Chinese legislators, however, have created pragmatic exceptions to *pacta sunt servanda* for 'social interests',[14] producing flexibility to the principle. These exceptions cover each of the four meanings of *pacta sunt servanda*, including:

---

and deliberation of bills; (3) to carry out legality examination of administrative regulations, rules as well as local decrees; and (4) to conduct concrete work of supervising Constitution implementation instructed by the Standing Committee. Introduction to the Legislative Commission of the Standing Committee of the National People's Congress <www.npc.gov.cn/npc/fgw001/202009/37a38fef089e499bb63b9d58ceda9ba4.shtml> accessed 12 March 2022.

8 Wei Huang (ed), *Interpretations on the Civil Code of the People's Republic of China*, vol 1 (Law Press China 2020) 235; Wei Huang (ed), *Interpretations on the Civil Code of the People's Republic of China*, vol. 2 (Law Press China, 2020) 891.

9 Guangxin Zhu, *Studies on the Contract Law*, vol. I (China Renmin University Press, 2018) 44.

10 Huang, *Interpretations on the Civil Code of the People's Republic of China,* vol 1 (n 8) 20, 235.

11 Zhu (n 9) 44.

12 S M Waddams, 'Unconscionability in Contracts' (1976) 39 The Modern Law Review 369.

13 Lon L Fuller, The Morality of Law (rev. ed, Yale University Press, 1969) 39.

14 Omri Ben-Shahar, David A Hoffman, Cathy Hwang, 'Nonparty Interests in Contract Law' (2022) University of Pennsylvania Carey Law School Research Paper 22–17, 49 <https://papers.ssrn.com/sol3/papers.cfm?abstract_id=4038584> (accessed 12 March 2022) define social interests as 'non-party interests' such as '"green", "fair trade", "local", or other humanitarian or cosmopolitan values'.

(1) the application of objectivism in interpreting contracts;[15] (2) the judicial discretion to modify contract terms in special circumstances such as frustration of contract,[16] adjustment of liquidated damages,[17] and the standard term rules;[18] (3) the parties' statutory power to terminate certain types of contracts without cause[19]; and (4) no specific performance when it is legally or practically impossible.[20] Legislators, judges and scholars in the Chinese mainland are also committed to a refined typological analysis in order to avoid prejudice to the parties' freedom of contract. For example, in terms of unilateral termination of contract, lawmakers distinguish between ordinary contracts and non-fixed-term contracts,[21] paid contracts of mandate and gratuitous contracts of mandate.[22]

Such pragmatism stemmed from the planned economy, when legislators used *pacta sunt servanda* to implement state plans rather than protecting freedom of contract. Chinese legislators have pragmatically manipulated the strength of contractual binding force to benefit society at large. In the planned economy, the binding force of contract varied according to contract parties and contract types.[23] Economic contracts closely related to state plans had stronger binding force. The parties to economic contracts performed their contractual obligations to 'ensure the fulfillment of state plans'.[24] The termination or modification of the

15 Civil Code of the People's Republic of China 2020 ('PRC Civil Code'), art 142.1.
16 PRC Civil Code, art 533.
17 PRC Civil Code, art 585.
18 PRC Civil Code, arts 496–498.
19 PRC Civil Code, art 563.2 provides: 'For a contract under which the debtor is required to continuously perform an obligation for an indefinite period of time, the parties thereto may rescind the contract at any time, provided that the other party shall be notified within a reasonable period of time'. Specifically, PRC Civil Code stipulates the right to terminate without cause in relation to non-fixed-term loan contracts (art 675), lease contracts (art 730), contracts for custody of property (art 899), warehousing contract (art 914), PMS contracts (art 948.2), partnership contracts (art 976.3) and contracts authorising the use of one's image (art 1022.1). Besides, there are other articles in the PRC Civil Code granting the following parties rights of termination without cause in typical contracts, such as art 787 (the client), art 816 (the passenger), art 829 (the consignor), art 899.1 (the custodian), art 933 (the principal or the agent), art 946 (homeowners). Special laws stipulating rights of termination without cause include art 65 of the PRC Tourism Law 2018 (the tourist), art 15 of the PRC Insurance Law 2015 (the insurance applicant), and art 37 of the PRC Labor Contract Law 2012 (the employees).
20 PRC Civil Code, art 580.
21 PRC Civil Code, art 563.
22 Hu Zhu, 'Commons and Differences: Discretionary Right to Terminate in the Civil Code' (2020) 32 Peking University Law Journal 1018, 1040. Moreover, the PRC Civil Code grants rights of termination without cause only to parties to some typical contracts.
23 Under the Economic Contract Law of People's Republic of China 1982 (PRC ECL (1982)), economic contracts and non-economic contracts were classified according to different contract subjects. Economic contracts could be further classified into two contract types: economic contracts related to state plans, and economic contracts (including foreign economic contracts) unrelated with state plans.]
24 PRC ECL (1982), art 1.

economic contract had to be approved by competent authorities[25]; the courts' function was to enforce economic contracts, with relevant authorities supervising their implementation;[26] and the specific performance was the principal remedy of economic contract because it could strengthen state plans.[27] The foreign economic contracts and non-economic contracts that were not subject to state plans had weakened binding force. Compared with the economic contract, their parties enjoy 'more autonomy' and 'less government interference with contract'.[28] For example, in terms of remedies, parties to non-economic contracts have more freedom to choose remedies because it is not tied to state plans.[29] In a market economy, contracts are no longer a mechanism to implement state plans and freedom of contract becomes a prerequisite for *pacta sunt servanda*. As a result, the parties enjoy greater autonomy in deviating from contract obligations, which leads to further weakening of the binding force. With such a pragmatic approach, it is no surprise that today's legislators embrace exceptions and flexibility against the rigid principle of *pacta sunt servanda* for broader social interests.

III The 'soft' binding force of PMS contracts in the Chinese mainland and its causes

As one of the 19 typical contracts in the *PRC Civil Code*, the PMS contract is subject to the *pacta sunt servanda* principle. However, the contract's binding force has been softened both at the rule level, i.e. homeowners' right to terminate without cause, and in practice, i.e. high rate of PM fee arrears. We investigate the causes of the softening in this section by conducting comparative studies on PMS in five jurisdictions: the Chinese mainland, the United Kingdom (UK), the United States of America (US), the Hong Kong Special Administrative Region (HK SAR) and Chinese Taiwan.

A Homeowners' right to terminate without cause

The termination of contracts, which frees the parties from their contractual obligations, is in tension with the principle of *pacta sunt servanda*, and has always been subject to rigorous restrictions. Given that termination with cause is subject to strict conditions and procedures, it is applied to all civil contracts, including PMS contracts.

25 PRC ECL (1982), art 29. (If the modification or rescission of an economic contract involves products or projects under a mandatory state plan, before the agreement is signed the parties shall report it for approval to the department in change of specialised work that issued the plan.)
26 PRC ECL (1982), chapter 6 (Administration of Economic Contracts). The chapter was abolished by the 1993 amendment.
27 PRC ECL (1982), art 35. (The breaching party must continue to perform the obligation if the injured party so demands, even after the payment of damages.)
28 Bing Ling, *Contract Law in China* (Sweet & Maxwell Asia, 2002) 13.
29 General Principles of the Civil Law of the People's Republic of China (1986 enacted, 2009 amended) art 111.

The right of termination without cause is not enjoyed by parties to all civil contracts, and it must be either stipulated by law or agreed to by the parties. The PMS contract is one of just a handful contracts in which the *PRC Civil Code* grants parties the right of termination without cause. The *PRC Civil Code* gives homeowners the right to terminate the preliminary PMS contract (Article 940) by entering into a new PMS contract,[30] and the right to terminate ordinary PMS contract (Article 946) without cause, in spite of voices opposing to grant homeowners the latter right before the *Civil Code* was promulgated.[31]

Though other jurisdictions such as Chinese Taiwan also permit homeowners to terminate the PMS contract at will, which is consistent with the general theory that parties to contracts based on the special trust relationship (such as contracts for mandate[32]) may terminate the contract once the trust-basis disappears, legislators in the Chinese mainland are more motivated to grant homeowners the right to terminate without cause. This is because the long-term nature of PMS contracts in the Chinese mainland necessitates homeowners' right to terminate without cause. PMS contracts in the other four foreign jurisdictions, namely, the US,[33] the UK,[34] HK SAR[35] and Chinese Taiwan[36] only last for one or two years with a renewal term. However, the period of PMS contracts in the Chinese mainland is much longer. Theoretically, the preliminary PMS contract is temporary and transitional.[37] But in practice, when a developer hires a PMS company, the contract period is

30 In the Chinese mainland, scholars hold different views on the nature of art 940 of PRC Civil Code. Most commentators argue that it grants homeowners a statutory right to terminate preliminary PMS contract by concluding a new PMS contract: see e.g. Liming Wang, 'Discussion on Several Issues of Property Service Contract Legislation' (2018) 3 Law and Economy 5, 13; Hui Zhao, 'On the Nature and Termination of Property Management Contract', (2010) 11 Legal Application 35). Others hold that the termination is automatic upon a new PMS contract taking effect: see e.g. Weiping Luo, 'Some Issues of Preliminary Property Management Contract', (2006) 5 Journal of South-Central Minzu University, 97). We adopt the majority view, which is also the position of the PRC Supreme People's Court: see PRC Supreme People's Court (ed), *Interpretation and Application of the PRC Civil Code (Contract)*, vol 4 (People's Court Press, 2020) 2571.

31 Wang (ibid) 13–14. Liming Wang supports homeowners' right to terminate preliminary PMS contract without cause because the homeowners did not participate in the conclusion of the preliminary PMS contract.

32 Jianghong Zhou, 'The Future of Service Contracts as Typical Contracts' (2020) 1 Wuhan University Journal (Philosophy & Social Science) 77; Jianghong Zhou, 'On the Orientation and Systematic Construction of Service Contracts in PRC Civil Code' (2008) 1 Law Science 76.

33 Samples of US PMS Agreement <www.adobe.com/sign/esignature-resources/property-management-agreement.html> accessed 30 December 2021.

34 UK Association of Residential Managing Agents (ARMA), Management Agency Agreement, art 1.8.

35 The Hong Kong Institute of Surveyors, Standard Property Management Agreement, art 1.

36 Chinese Taiwan Model Contract of Management and Maintenance Service for Apartment Building Management and Maintenance Company, art 4.

37 PRC Civil Code, art 940.

often stipulated as 'from the time of contract conclusion until the *owners' assembly*[38] sign a new contract with the PMS company or hires another PMS company'. Since only a small proportion of residential communities in the Chinese mainland manage to establish homeowners' associations,[39] the preliminary PMS contracts have become *de facto* long-term contracts. As for the ordinary PMS contracts in the Chinese mainland, the contract period is normally two to five years (often three years),[40] which is also longer than periods in other jurisdictions.

If the contract period is short, even if the homeowners do not enjoy the right to terminate without cause, contract will expire before very long. However, in the Chinese mainland where the PMS contract period is usually long, the homeowners would be at a significant disadvantage if they did not have the right to terminate without cause.

B High rate of PM fee arrears

The principle of *pacta sunt servanda* requires the parties to fully perform their contractual obligations, and the contractual obligations can be enforced in case of non-performance. The low collecting rate of PM fees implies a 'softening' of PMS contracts in the Chinese mainland, however. When predicting revenues, it is usual for PMS companies in the Chinese mainland to set the PM fees collection rate as 70%. Tongue-in-cheek, they also call an actual collection rate of 70% as 'adequate for survival', 80% as 'fairly well-off', and 90% as 'affluent pleasure'.[41]

Although there are problems with PM fees arrears in other jurisdictions, none have been found to be as severe as those in the Chinese mainland.[42] Four Chinese

38 In the US, the homeowners' self-governance body is called homeowner association (HOA), while other jurisdictions name the similar body differently: in the UK, it is called a 'residential management company' (in leasehold) or 'commonhold association' (in commonhold); in HK SAR, it is called a 'homeowners' corporation'; in Taiwan, it is a 'unit owner assembly (區分所有權人會議)'; in the Chinese mainland, it is called 'owner's assembly'. The PRC Civil Code and Chinese Taiwan Condominium Act use 'assembly' to indicate that a mere assembly is neither a legal person nor an unincorporated organisation. For the sake of clarity, coherence and consistency, we adopt the US term homeowners' association (HOA).

39 As of 2019, the percentage of residential communities with a homeowners' association in Beijing, Shenzhen, Jilin Province, Hangzhou and Gansu province were respectively 17.1%, 41%, 24.4%, 48.9% and less than 23.8%: China Property Management Association (ed), *China Property Management Industry Yearbook 2020*, vol 1 (China Architecture Publishing & Media Co Ltd 2020) 380, 487, 416, 430, 495.

40 Some cities, e.g. Dalian, require the PMS contract period to be 'at least three years in principle': Notice of the Dalian Municipality on Implementing the State Council's Regulation on Property Management and Promoting the Property Management in Dalian Municipality, art 3.

41 China Property Management Association (n 39) 202, 414. Compared with high-end residential communities, PM fee arrears are more severe in mid-end and old residential communities.

42 Fei Wang, 'Interview with Professor Patrick Gray on English Property Management: Clear Property Title Keeps English PMS Companies Away from Disputes' ['产权清晰，英国物企远离纠纷漩涡 – 与Gray教授谈英国物业管理'] (2016) 10 Housing and Real Estate 15. See also Lectures

characteristics can be extracted from comparative studies to explain the severely high PM fee arrears rate in the Chinese mainland.

Firstly, the *'one-to-many' PMS relationship* plus *weak HOAs* make the withholding of PM fees a convenient way for individual homeowners to express dissatisfaction. In the Chinese mainland, a PMS contract is concluded between a HOA and a PMS company, and the PMS company provides services for the benefit of homeowners as a whole as well as individual homeowners. While the PMS company provides services directly to homeowners and collects PM fees from them,[43] in the other four jurisdictions, PMS companies collect fees from HOAs. Therefore, HOAs have a strong incentive to use their power to dismiss unsatisfactory PMS companies. When the services provided are of poor quality, factually and legally speaking, individual homeowners must liaise with one another to reach an agreement to dismiss the PMS company.[44] Given how difficult and time-consuming it is to reach a consensus, a rational yet 'apathic'[45] homeowner is more willing to express dissatisfaction by not paying or underpaying PM fees rather than exercising the collective right of termination without cause. Furthermore, such a 'one-to-many' structure provides a misalignment of incentives: HOAs do not bear the costs of property maintenance and so may have weak incentives to ensure that individual homeowners receive good service and value for money.

Secondly, due to *the comprehensiveness of PMS* in the Chinese mainland, PMS companies are unable to discontinue service to the common area just because individual homeowners have not paid PM fees. In other jurisdictions, the scale of PMS zones is usually smaller, and HOAs typically hire PMS companies to provide special services. For example, in 2020, 22.5% of the US population lived in more than 355,000 community associations, with an average of 209 people per community.[46] Among the community associations, 6,000–9,000 are large-scale associations, i.e. those that meet at least two of the following three characteristics: a single, contiguous community with a general manager; a minimum of 1,000 lots and/or homes; and a minimum annual budget of $2 million. Self-managed community associations account for 30–40% of all community associations, which means they may hire professional help for specific projects, activities and services but do not hire a professional manager or management firm.[47] Only a few associa-

Series of Hong Kong Institute of Certified Property Managers <www.youtube.com/watch?v=dkiHNYTbxbQ&list=UUT3YAUyJLyYRUDlmEnHQwVA&ind%20ex=8> accessed 30 May 2021.

43 Exceptions might be the PMS companies' disclosure and report obligations in art 943 of PRC Civil Code.

44 In contrast, if the period of the PMS contract is short, homeowners dissatisfied with the PMS company would wait for the expiration of the contract and refuse to renew it.

45 Mancur Olson, *The Logic of Collective Action: Public Goods and the Theory of Groups* (Harvard Law Press, 1971).

46 See 2020–2021 U.S. National and State Statistical Review <https://foundation.caionline.org/wp-content/uploads/2021/07/2021StatsReview_Web.pdf> accessed 11 April 2022.

47 Home Affairs Department of Hong Kong SAR, Measures for Recovery of Outstanding Payments, <www.buildingmgt.gov.hk/en/Daily_Operation_of_Building_Management/5_1_3_2.html> accessed 30 May 2021.

Table 7.1 Statistics on urban population and residential property scale in some provinces and cities in the Chinese mainland as of 2019

Area	*Urban pop (10 K)*	*Rpmp* number*	*Rpmp area (100 mill m2)*	*Hoa number*
Beijing	1865	4017	4.87	1200
Tianjin	1304	2851	3.5	
Shanghai	2144		6.73	
Chongqing	2087	7913		
Wuhan	902.45	2123	2.64	
Shenzhen	1343.88	3861	3.13	
Shijiazhuang	469.55	4346	2.2	216
Inner Mongolia	1609	10534	5.6	5530
Jilin	1568	12068		3017
Heilongjiang	2284		5.9	
Anhui	3553	18429	11.60	3161
Fujian	2642	12946	8.45	2624
Jiangxi	2679	7335		
Shandong	6194	23037	19.36	2122
Hunan	3959	12145	12.8	4191
Gansu	1284	7743	4.52	1889
Xinjiang	1309	7158	3.36	2091

* RPMP is short for Residential Property Management Project. *Data source: China Statistical Yearbook 2020, China Property Management Industry Yearbook 2020* and *White Paper of Beijing Housing and Urban-Rural Construction Development (2020)*

tions are very large.[48] Therefore, if the collecting rate of PM fees is low, property managers in the US may decide to stop providing service.

By contrast, residential communities in the Chinese mainland are more densely populated and larger in size, and PMS companies are frequently entrusted with comprehensive management and services. Statistics show that, in 2019, the average construction area of residential property management projects (RPMP) is 69,300 square meters, with over 120,000 square meters in Beijing, Tianjin and Wuhan. The average number of households in residential property management projects is 2,725, with over 4,000 in Beijing, Tianjin and Wuhan.

Because of the large scale of common areas in the Chinese mainland, PMS companies usually provide comprehensive services involving almost every aspect of the residential communities, such as facility maintenance, security, parking, gardening and sanitation. So, they could not just stop taking care of common areas because some individual homeowners failed to pay PM fees.

Thirdly, the *quasi-public nature of PMS* in the Chinese mainland prevents PMS companies from dropping out of the contract due to the default of homeowners. In the other four jurisdictions, PMS companies are commercially entrusted by

48 Jeremy Shearmur, 'Living with a Marsupial Mouse' (2002) 18 Policy 19; Barbara Coyle McCabe, 'Homeowners Associations as Private Governments: What We Know, What We Don't Know, and Why It Matters' (2011) 71 Public Administration Review 536.

HOAs to provide services, and only bear limited and largely voluntary corporate social responsibilities. However, in the Chinese mainland, PMS is regarded a quasi-public product with ramifications for grassroots social governance. Local government regulations and decrees govern practically every area of community formation and operation. The government has recently increased its influence in grassroots governance by supporting 'administrative implementation in the residential community'.[49] The government also requires PMS companies to perform public service duties outside of PMS contracts for free or for lean remuneration. These extra-contractual obligations include stopping and reporting illegal activities, performing government tasks such as garbage sorting and maintaining social stability, and cooperating with the government during extraordinary periods, such as strong prevention and control tasks and responsibilities during COVID-19.[50]

Fourthly, PMS companies' *weak remedies for breach of contract* result in more PM fees arrears in the Chinese mainland. In the other four jurisdictions, PMS companies enjoy strong remedies against defaulting homeowners, including enforcing liens on the defaulting condominium in the US,[51] filing a default payment record with the Land Registry against the property concerned in HK SAR,[52] and petitioning the court to sell the defaulting homeowner's property in both Taiwan[53] and HK SAR.[54]

In the Chinese mainland, however, PMS companies are only allowed to demand that defaulting homeowners pay PM fees and outstanding interests. Worse still, in litigation, homeowners frequently request to reduce PM fees because of defective services. It can be difficult to assess PMS quality because it is a subjective, qualitative measurement rather than an objective, quantitative measurement. Therefore,

49 See Notice by the Ministry of Housing and Urban-rural Development, et al., of Strengthening and Improving the Administration of Residential Properties (住房和城乡建设部等部门关于加强和改进住宅物业管理工作的通知) (PRC) 2021.

50 Because the prevention and control tasks during the COVID-19 are not in the PMS contract, and the government authorisations are not always clear-cut, PMS companies undertaking relevant jobs are more vulnerable to homeowners' complaints: China Property Management Association & China Economic Information Co, Investigation Report on the Impact of the COVID-19 on the Property Management Industry, in China Property Management Association (ed) (n 39) 316–322.

51 Uniform Common Interest Ownership Act (US), s 3–116: Unless the declaration provides otherwise, fines, late charges and other fees are treated as assessments for lien purposes. Most importantly, the statutory lien also extends all assessments and charges, not just late charges.

52 In HK SAR, according to the Deed of Mutual Covenant (大厦公契), property management companies can request lawyers to file a default payment record against the property concerned at Land Registry (commonly known as 'imposing an encumbrance' (钉契) should the homeowners fail to pay the fees for more than 30 days. The defaulting homeowners must pay the management fees, interest and other legal fees before clearing the encumbrance and selling the property. HK SAR Home Affairs Department (n 47).

53 Condominium Administration Act (Chinese Taiwan), s 22(2). In practice, the officer (or board) in most lawsuits only requests evictions, not forced sales. Yunchien Chang, 'Condominium Law in Taiwan: Doctrinal Overview Under the Lens of Information-Cost Theory' (2015) 23 Asia Pacific Law Review 89.

54 Home Affairs Department of Hong Kong SAR (n 47).

courts may support the homeowner's defence and thereby make discretionary 'discount' judgments. Even if PMS companies obtain favourable judgments, they face additional challenges, such as difficulties to enforce the judgment, and deterioration of relationships with homeowners, etc.

As a result, 'free-rider' problems have been exacerbated in Chinese residential communities. The 'discount' judgments enable defaulting homeowners to take 'free ride' to enjoy the services paid for by other paying homeowners. Moreover, other homeowners may follow suit so that the property management companies eventually need to reduce or even stop maintaining the operation and use of the common areas, which in turn affects the interests of all homeowners and generates a problem similar to the tragedy of the commons.

Chinese mainland legislatures remain very cautious about introducing stricter measures, such as those found in other jurisdictions. For example, the *2007 Model Rules of Decision-Making Procedures for Homeowners' Association (Draft)* of Guangzhou and the *2010 Shanghai Residential Property Management Measures (Revised Draft)* attempted to adopt HK SAR rules, so as to restrict homeowners with PM fees arrears from transferring or mortgaging their property, but they were ultimately given up on due to fierce opposition.[55] The Chinese mainland courts are also reluctant to take harsh measures against the home concerned to pay off PM fees. According to our research, as of now, only one grassroots court in the Chinese mainland issued a five-day final repayment order to the defaulting homeowner, warning that if the payment was not made on time, the court would seal up and auction his second dwelling house. This order has stirred up heated debates online, and many netizens were against the decision.[56]

IV The softening of PMS contracts in Chinese mainland: A theoretical analysis

Stability and flexibility are two competing values of contract law.[57] While the principle of *pacta sunt servanda* seeks legal stability, it is never absolute and has exceptions. We argue in this part that although the binding force of the PMS contract in the Chinese mainland has been softened, it does not violate *pacta sunt servanda* as a whole. In current Chinese mainland laws, this principle has the following four meanings: (1) the parties shall perform their obligations and (2) shall not arbitrarily alter or terminate the contract, (3) otherwise the defaulting

55 '"No House Transfer with Unpaid Property Management Fees" Has No Legal Basis' <www.chinanews.com/cj/kong/news/2007/09-08/1021692.shtml> accessed 30 May 2021.

56 'Hot topic! Unoccupied Rough Housing with Property Fees to Pay, House to be Auctioned if Not Paid?' <https://baijiahao.baidu.com/s?id=1711402375474190567&wfr=spider&for=pc> accessed 1 January 2022.

57 Rosalie Jukier, 'Flexibility and Certainty as Competing Contract Values: A Civil Lawyer's Reaction to the Ontario Law Reform Commission's Recommendations on Amendments to the Law of Contract' (1988) 14 Canadian Business Law Journal 13, 14.

party shall be liable for breach of contract, and (4) the State shall ensure that the contract be enforced in accordance with law by the court.

Soft PMS contracts are exceptional to the second and fourth meanings of *pacta sunt servanda*: homeowners have the right to terminate without cause; and courts do not grant PMS companies strong remedies against defaulting homeowners. This anomaly may be explained by the theory of path dependence. Adopting a more nuanced definition of flexibility, we argue that the PMS contract is still in line with the doctrine of rule of law generally.

A Partial violation of **pacta sunt servanda**

Relating to the first meaning, PMS contracts in the Chinese mainland are legally binding because both the homeowners and the property management companies are obliged to fulfil their contractual obligations.[58] Relating to the third meaning, homeowners who are in arrears with PM fees 'shall bear corresponding liabilities for breach of contract',[59] including a duty to pay 'the property fees arrears and the corresponding outstanding interest, unless it is otherwise provided in the contract'.[60]

However, PMS contracts are exceptional in the second and fourth meaning. The second meaning of *pacta sunt servanda* stands in the way of parties terminating or modifying the contract without cause. Yet, the *PRC Civil Code* enables homeowners to escape from the binding force of the contract through providing a right of termination at any time without cause, which indeed constitutes an exception to *PSS*.

Pacta sunt servanda, in its fourth meaning, requires the courts to protect legally concluded contracts and to enforce their performance. Therefore, the courts' failure to provide adequate remedies to the parties in accordance with the contract shall be deemed a deviation from the principle. So, 'discount' judgments, which adjust the PM fees agreed in the contract[61] and the refusal to enforce the judgment against the home concerned are not consistent with the principle of *pacta sunt servanda*.

B Chinese legislators' pragmatic approach towards PSS: a path dependence

The theory of path dependence sheds light on why Chinese legislators and courts have softened the binding force of PMS contracts at the expense of legal stability. As Douglas North has commented, '[p]ath dependence means that history

58 PRC Civil Code, art 937.

59 PRC Civil Code, art 944.2.

60 Huang, *Interpretations on the Civil Code of the People's Republic of China*, vol 1 (n 8) 1698.

61 The more serious consequence of adjusting the property management fees through judgments is that it creates an imbalance of the abiding parties pay more but the defaulting parties pay less for homeowners who have paid the property fees as agreed.

matters'.[62] In terms of the *pacta sunt servanda* principle, lawmakers and courts in the Chinese mainland have been taking a pragmatic[63] approach ever since its *Economic Contract Law*. During the planned economy period, it was used to implement state plans. Legislators nowadays, motivated by pragmatism, might also follow or limit the principle of *pacta sunt servanda* in order to promote the public interest or meet social interests. The softening of PMS contracts illustrates legal pragmatism of lawmakers in the Chinese mainland.

Chinese legislators grant homeowners the right of termination without cause to offer a way out of the continuing long-term relationship, in line with the general theory that parties to long-term contracts based on the special trust relationship may terminate the contract once the trust-basis disappears. It is also worth noting that it is not unfair to PMS companies because they will be compensated for loss in accordance with the contract and the law.[64] Given the general theory that both parties to a contract based on special trust should have the right to terminate relationship without cause (such as an entrustment contract[65]), it might be sought that PMS companies, conversely, should also enjoy such a right to terminate their contract with the homeowners. However, the Civil Code does not contain a right for PMS companies to terminate without cause,[66] which is 'based on social considerations including the importance of property services to the homeowners'.[67] We believe that this importance stems from the fact that PMS companies in the Chinese mainland often provide services to communities of a big size and with a large population. Moreover, PMS companies do not only provide services in accordance with the contract, but also shoulder many public services in accordance with the law or instruction from the government.

C Assessment under a more nuanced conception of flexibility

Predictability is a cornerstone of rule of law. Flexibility, according to Lutz-Christian Wolff, is incompatible with rule of law, because it entails uncertainty, which in turn leads to unpredictability. To sharpen his analysis, Professor Wolff divides flexibility into three categories: rule-intrinsic flexibility (e.g. when the law grants judicial discretion), application flexibility (e.g. breach of contract) and

62 Douglas C North, *Institutions, Institutional Change and Economic Performance* (CUP, 1990) 100.

63 Under a pragmatic approach, lawmakers may define *pacta sunt servanda* differently depending on the contract in question, the parties concerned and the purposes pursued, see discussion in II. B. above. This has similarities to the concept of 'policy' in the common law.

64 PRC Civil Code, art 946.2.

65 PRC Civil Code, art 933.

66 Zhu (n 22) 1037.

67 cf First Civil Division of the Supreme People's Court (ed), *Interpretation and Application of the Judicial Interpretation of the Supreme People's Court on the Partitioned Ownership of Building Areas and Realty Services* (People's Court Press, 2009) 338. (Before the enactment of Civil Code, the PRC Supreme People's Court held that PMS companies shall enjoy the right to terminate without cause.)

form flexibility (e.g. the law incorporates vague concepts such as 'reasonableness'), and explains why each is incompatible with predictability.[68]

Though Professor Wolff's taxonomy is inspiring, his analysis contains a logical flaw: he uses the wrong equation for flexibility and unpredictability. Though he rightly states that 'legal certainty is a direct result of predictability',[69] the obverse does not follow: uncertainty does not always imply unpredictability, and flexibility implying uncertainty does not necessarily lead to unpredictability. Actually, a new type of flexibility that we discovered – rule-based flexibility, which refers to legal rules from which deviation is permissible within the framework – entails uncertainty while remaining predictable.[70]

Using the more nuanced conception of flexibility, we may resolve the tensions we have identified above with regard to the *pacta sunt servanda* principle in PMS contracts. And it might be safe for us to argue that, notwithstanding that a soft PMS contract brings uncertainty, it is nonetheless consistent with rule of law in general.

Firstly, flexibility brought on by homeowners' statutory right to terminate without cause is rule-based and hence does not result in unpredictability. For one thing, it is clearly stipulated in the *PRC Civil Code* and thus allows PMS companies to expect being dismissed without cause. For another, homeowners' right to terminate is not limitless. To balance the interests of PMS companies and homeowners, the *PRC Civil Code* imposes strict procedural requirements, including: the right shall not be exercised by any individual homeowner but the homeowners' association; the homeowners' association shall notify the other party in writing 60 days in advance.[71] In other words, if homeowners collectively decide to terminate the PMS contract, the PMS company shall give 60 days' written notice. Such termination notices are intended to assist PMS companies not only to make a smooth exit and handover, but also to prepare for the termination and make alternative plans as early as possible.

Secondly, 'discount' judgments are an example of form flexibility. The legal ground for 'discount' judgments is article 582 of *PRC Civil Code*, which creates the possibility of a 'decrease in price or remuneration' on PMS companies providing defective services. However, the courts may only support homeowners

68 Lutz-Christian Wolff, 'Law and Flexibility – Rule of Law Limits of a Rhetorical Silver Bullet' (2011) 11 The Journal Jurisprudence 549. During the conference on *Pacta Sunt Servanda in Changing Times* (June 2021), Professor Wolff stated that breach of contract is an example of application flexibility.

69 ibid, 553.

70 cf. rule-intrinsic flexibility, in Professor Wolff's analysis, brings both uncertainty and unpredictability.

71 According to PRC Civil Code art 278, the decision to dismiss a PMS company requires the consent of two-thirds or more of all the owners, provided that the area of private portions owned by such owners accounts for two-thirds or more of the total area. The decision shall be subject to the consent of over a half of the owners participating in the voting, provided that the area of private portions owned by such owners accounts for over a half of tshe total area.

who 'reasonably' request such remedy.[72] But it is not easy to predict when and by how much a court may find a 'decrease in remuneration' to be reasonable. This is because PMS cannot be quantified with certainty. The lack of uniform national or local standards for the quality of PMS is largely to blame for this uncertainty. Without standards, courts have to rely upon specific PMS contracts, many of which are sparsely detailed. It is therefore difficult for courts to determine if and to what extent PMS companies have provided services in compliance with the contract, whether or not PMS are defective, and whether or not there shall be corresponding reduction in PM fees, resulting in 'likes case not being treated alike'. Fortunately, the Chinese mainland is currently undertaking reforms promulgating uniform standards for PMS.[73] It is hoped that, with more objective standards, 'discount' judgments will become more predictable.

Finally, the hesitation of the Chinese mainland courts in enforcing into the homes of defaulting homeowners shows that the law is applied flexibly. The Chinese mainland law grants a claimant the ability to execute against a defendant's dwelling to realise a monetary claim, if the flat is not the only dwelling of the defendant.[74] However, in PMS cases, courts barely apply this rule to allow PMS companies to execute against the dwelling of the defaulting party, if it is not his/her only dwelling. Actually, we only find one reported case in 2021 that a court executed against a roughcast dwelling of a defaulting party, the court found that the owner had not made necessary fit-out of the dwelling and had never lived in it. The case stirred fierce discussion online, with many netizens opposing to the judgment, some saying that they 'have never heard of a possible execution for non-payment of PM fees'.[75]

However, the courts' refusal to allow enforcement against non-essential dwellings may not significantly harm the rule of law because policy makers are exploring reputation penalties as a substitute to enhance remedies for PMS companies. For example, in some cities of Jiangxi Province, if employees of administrative agencies, public institutions, state-owned enterprises refuse to pay PM fees, reputational punishment may be imposed against them, with their names being published in the list of defaulting debtors.[76]

72 Zhu (n 9) 54–56.

73 The PRC National Technical Committee of Property Service Standards of the Chinese mainland (全国物业服务标准化技术委员会) is currently drafting national standards for the PMS industry (Property Management Terminologies, Customer Satisfaction Evaluation of Property Management Services and Safety and Emergency Response of Property Management Services), with similar efforts at provincial or municipal level also being underway.

74 PRC Provisions of the Supreme People's Court on Several Issues concerning the Handling of Enforcement Opposition and Reconsideration Case, art 20.

75 'A man refuses to pay the PM fee for 7 years, his house may be auctioned' <https://baijiahao.baidu.com/s?id=1711390554647909916&wfr=spider&for=pc> accessed 12 March 2022.

76 'Jiangxi Province Property Management Industry Development Report', in China Property Management Association (ed) (n 39) 451.

V Conclusion

Pacta sunt servanda is currently a logical deduction of freedom of contract in Chinese mainland, and it has four meanings: (1) the parties must fully perform their contractual obligations; (2) arbitrary modification or termination of contracts is prohibited; (3) defaulting parties shall bear liability for breach of contract; and (4) the State shall enforce the execution of contracts through law and by court. *Pacta sunt servanda* is important because it provides stability, certainty and predictability.

However, *pacta sunt servanda* is not absolute in Chinese mainland. It must, after all, be subject to social interests, such as maintaining social stability and protecting the vulnerable. When social interests so require, the contract's binding force can be weakened, even if this flexibility results in legal uncertainty. The pragmatic approach of Chinese mainland legislators toward *pacta sunt servanda* has been evident throughout recent history: in the planned economy period, legislators relied on this principle to implement state plans; under the *PRC Civil Code*, the principle has been weakened in support of social interests for contracts such as PMS contracts, resulting in tensions between *pacta sunt servanda* and broad social interests, as well as between legal stability and flexibility.

The PMS contract is like Newton's triangle prism reflecting the above tensions. Comparatively speaking, the binding force of PMS contracts in Chinese mainland has been softened to protect homeowners' rights and interests. However, using a more nuanced conception of flexibility, we argue that soft PMS contracts are still compatible with the rule of law, because the flexibility and uncertainty are still predictable.

8 *Pacta sunt servanda* in the age of cryptocurrency

The case of China

Chao Xi[*]

Introduction

In modern contract law, the foundational principle of *pacta sunt servanda* can be limited by such doctrines as force majeure, impossibility and impracticability.[1] Illegality, another deviation from *pacta sunt servanda*, has largely escaped the attention of contract law scholarship,[2] although the COVID-19 pandemic has brought the illegality deviation to the forefront of contract law developments.[3]

This chapter, however, places the *pacta sunt servanda* doctrine in a different context, namely, the context of cryptocurrency.[4] In May 2021, the market capitalisation of crypto assets reached an all-time high of US$2.5 trillion.[5] Legislators and regulators around the globe have scrambled to respond to the challenges posed by the rise of cryptocurrencies and the broader crypto ecosystem.[6] National

* This research has been supported by a CUHK Direct Grant. The author would like to thank Professor Normann Witzleb and an anonymous reviewer for their useful comments. The usual disclaimers apply.

1 For a comparative overview in the context of the COVID-19 pandemic, see e.g. Franz T Schwarz, John A Trenor and Helmut Ortner, 'Introduction' in Franz T Schwarz, John A Trenor and Helmut Ortner (eds), *Contractual Performance and Covid-19: An In-Depth Comparative Law Analysis* (Kluwer Law International, 2020).

2 Illegality as a deviation from *pacta sunt servanda* has received some attention from international arbitration lawyers. See e.g. Richard Kreindler, 'Aspects of Illegality in the Formation and Performance of Contracts' in Albert Jan Van den Berg (ed), *International Commercial Arbitration: Important Contemporary Questions* (Kluwer 2003), 210.

3 See e.g. Quinn Emanuel Urquhart & Sullivan, 'COVID-19 – Issues Affecting Performance of Contractual Obligations In Construction Contracts Governed By English Law' <www.quinnemanuel.com/media/je2pl3td/client-alert-covid-19-issues-affecting-performance-of-con_.pdf> accessed 31 March 2022.

4 On the global rise of cryptocurrency, see e.g. Paul Vigna and Michael J Casey, *The Age of Cryptocurrency: How Bitcoin and Digital Money are Challenging the Global Economic Order* (Picador, 2018).

5 International Monetary Fund, *Global Financial Stability Report – COVID-19, Crypto, and Climate: Navigating Challenging Transitions* (October 2021) <www.imf.org/-/media/Files/Publications/GFSR/2021/October/English/text.ashx> accessed 31 March 2022.

6 For a review of the global regulatory landscape, see e.g. Apolline Blandin and others, *The Global Cryptoasset Regulatory Landscape Study* (Cambridge Centre for Alternative Finance, April 2019) <www.jbs.cam.ac.uk/wp-content/uploads/2020/08/2019-04-ccaf-global-cryptoasset-regulatory-landscape-study.pdf> accessed 31 March 2022.

DOI: 10.4324/9781003358305-10

regulatory approaches to crypto assets vary greatly, ranging from a 'wait-and-see' approach to a restrictive approach.[7] The People's Republic of China (PRC or China hereafter) has gradually tightened its crypto regulation to eventually become, in September 2021, the first major economy in the world to impose a blanket cryptocurrency ban.[8]

This chapter offers a descriptive and analytical account of how, under PRC law, the *pacta sunt servanda* doctrine has been thrust into a state of uncertainty amidst China's changing cryptocurrency regulatory landscape. The research in this chapter shows that in the face of the legal ambiguity sparked by China's changing regulatory stance, the PRC courts have diverged in their approaches to the validity and enforceability of crypto investments and transactions. In particular, some PRC courts and contract parties have invoked illegality to limit the *pacta sunt servanda* principle in the cryptocurrency age.

The remainder of the chapter is structured as follows. Part II depicts the dramatic shift in China's regulatory approach to cryptocurrencies within a relatively short period of time. This depiction sets the stage for the analysis in Part III, which analyses the legal uncertainty resulting from the country's changing crypto regulation, particularly the uncertainty over the basic question of whether cryptocurrency transactions and investments are legal *per se* under PRC law. Part III then proceeds to a demonstration of how *pacta sunt servanda* has survived the legal uncertainty in judicial proceedings before some PRC courts while falling victim to it in others. Part IV offers concluding remarks.

China's changing approach to cryptocurrency regulation: an overview

Defining China's shifting regulatory stance on cryptocurrencies over the past decade are three sets of regulatory rules enacted in 2013, 2017 and 2021. This part of the chapter provides an overview of these rules. As will be seen, the tone of PRC crypto regulation was largely tolerative under the 2013 regime. The regulatory developments unfolding in 2017 and 2021, however, marked a turn against crypto assets and transactions therein. In fact, with the enactment of the third set of regulatory rules in 2021, China became the world's first major economy to impose a blanket ban on all forms of cryptocurrency. Before proceeding to an examination of the three sets of rules, it is worth noting that the bulk of their provisions are concerned with what are essentially government administration matters, such as inter-agency coordination and information sharing, the surveillance

7 Global Future Council on Cryptocurrencies, *Navigating Cryptocurrency Regulation: An Industry Perspective on the Insights and Tools Needed to Shape Balanced Crypto Regulation* (September 2021) <https://www3.weforum.org/docs/WEF_Navigating_Cryptocurrency_Regulation_2021.pdf> accessed 31 March 2022.

8 Chao Xi, 'The End of the War or the Commencement of Battle? Cryptocurrency Regulation in China' (2022) 37 Banking & Finance Law Review 339. This chapter is drawn in part from the article.

and monitoring of cryptocurrency-related activities, as well as public awareness campaigns and investor education. Albeit important, these matters are not the central concern of the present research. Rather, the chapter focuses on the broader legal and regulatory approaches to cryptocurrencies in China.

2013 Notice

Promulgated in December 2013,[9] the 2013 Notice constituted one of China's first official attempts to exert a regulatory grip on crypto assets. To put the 2013 Notice in context, Bitcoin, then a four-year-old virtual currency, was starting to gain momentum around the world. Amateur investors, venture capitalists and technology enthusiasts were taking a growing interest in Bitcoin assets, pushing Bitcoin's price to record levels,[10] and Chinese demand for Bitcoin assets had reportedly helped to fuel the rise.[11] Although the Chinese regulatory authorities were concerned about the potential risks of amateur Chinese investors being drawn to Bitcoin assets, they were broadly tolerative. Indeed, the People's Bank of China (PBOC), China's central bank, attempted to walk a tightrope. On the one hand, the PBOC declared that it would not "recognize [the legality] of the Bitcoin".[12] On the other hand, investments in Bitcoin were permitted, access to Bitcoin exchanges was allowed, and Bitcoin investors were expected to bear the associated risks on their own.[13] The PBOC's position largely set the tone for the 2013 Notice, as it has long played the role of inter-agency coordinator on cryptocurrency regulation in China.

The 2013 Notice started with a categorical declaration that Bitcoin should not be recognised as currency 'in a real sense',[14] because it 'is not issued by a monetary authority, and it does not bear the necessary attributes of currency such as fiat money and mandated acceptance'.[15] The Notice further declared that Bitcoin 'does not enjoy the same legal status as fiat currencies'.[16] The verdict that Bitcoin is not legal tender predates but echoes the Basel Committee on Banking Supervision's

9 关于防范比特币风险的通知 [Notice on Preventing the Risks of Bitcoin] (jointly enacted on 3 December 2013 by the PBOC, Ministry of Industry and Information Technology, China Banking Regulatory Commission, China Securities Regulatory Commission and China Insurance Regulatory Commission) <www.csrc.gov.cn/pub/newsite/flb/flfg/bmgf/zh/gfxwjfxq/201401/t20140122_242972.html> accessed 31 March 2022.

10 Robin Sidel and Saabira Chaudhuri, 'Bitcoin Price Hits a New Record' *Wall Street Journal* (New York, 13 November 2013) <www.wsj.com/articles/bitcoin-price-hits-new-record-high-1384357897> accessed 31 March 2022.

11 Chao Deng, 'Bitcoin Market Gets a Lift From China' *Wall Street Journal* (New York, 4 December 2013) <www.wsj.com/articles/bitcoin-market-gets-a-lift-from-china-1386184737> accessed 31 March 2022.

12 Liyan Qi, 'Beijing Tolerates Bitcoin, for Now' *Wall Street Journal* (22 November 2012) <www.wsj.com/articles/BL-CJB-19712> accessed 31 March 2022.

13 ibid.

14 2013 Notice, Provision 1.

15 ibid.

16 ibid.

(BCBS) more recent position that '[c]rypto-assets are not legal tender, and are not backed by any government or public authority',[17] as well as the International Monetary Fund's recent caution against granting crypto assets legal tender status.[18] However, the 2013 Notice went further to declare that Bitcoin 'should not and cannot be used or circulated in the markets as currencies',[19] thereby denying Bitcoin a formal role in the Chinese economy. With the benefit of hindsight, China's approach differed significantly from the more permissive policy positions adopted by other national regulatory regimes and international standard setters.[20]

Although the 2013 Notice denied Bitcoin a formal role in China's real economy, it did not go so far as to ban transactions in Bitcoin assets altogether. Rather, it suggested that Bitcoin 'should be deemed a specific type of virtual commodity'.[21] This position was further elaborated in the official remarks accompanying the Notice:

> Transactions in Bitcoins are a form of sales and purchases in goods on the Internet. The general population shall enjoy the freedom to engage [in such transactions] while bearing the ensuing risks.[22]

Supplementing the 2013 Notice's characteristically permissive approach was its call to enhance investor education on virtual commodities and virtual currencies so as to 'guide the general population to form a correct understanding of currencies, as well as a correct investment philosophy'.[23]

The regulatory focus of the 2013 Notice was on insulating PRC financial institutions and payment agencies from risky exposure to Bitcoin assets. The Notice placed an outright ban on the provision of Bitcoin-related services by such institutions/agencies. More specifically, they were prohibited from providing pricing services, from acting in the capacity of a central counterparty, from providing

17 BCBS, 'Statement on Crypto-assets' (13 March 2019) <www.bis.org/publ/bcbs_nl21.htm> accessed 31 March 2022.

18 Tobias Adrian and Rhoda Weeks-Brown, 'Cryptoassets as National Currency? A Step Too Far' (26 July 2021) *IMF* (blog) <https://blogs.imf.org/2021/07/26/cryptoassets-as-national-currency-a-step-too-far> accessed 31 March 2022.

19 2013 Notice, Provision 1.

20 BCBS stated in its recently released consultative document that crypto assets 'are a digital representation of value, which can be used for payment or investment purposes or to access a good or service'. See BCBS, 'Consultative Document: Prudential Treatment of Cryptoasset Exposures' (June 2021) <www.bis.org/bcbs/publ/d519.pdf> accessed 31 March 2022. A similar approach can be found in the FATF's recently amended glossary wherein cryptocurrency is defined as 'a digital representation of value that can be digitally traded, or transferred, and can be used for payment or investment purposes'. See FATF, 'International Standards on Combating Money Laundering and the Financing of Terrorism & Proliferation: The FATF Recommendations' (updated June 2021) 130 <www.fatf-gafi.org/media/fatf/documents/recommendations/pdfs/FATF%20Recommendations%202012.pdf> accessed 31 March 2022.

21 2013 Notice, Provision 1.

22 人民银行等五部委发布关于防范比特币风险的通知 [Five Departments and Ministries, PBOC Included, Issued Notice on Preventing the Risks of Bitcoin] <www.gov.cn/gzdt/2013-12/05/content_2542751.htm> accessed 31 March 2022.

23 2013 Notice, Provision 5.

insurance coverage and from providing their clients with any services pertaining to Bitcoin.[24] Also targeted by the 2013 Notice were Bitcoin exchanges and platforms, which were required to register with the competent PRC regulatory authorities.[25] Those exchanges/platforms operating in violation of anti-money laundering and know-your-client rules could face closure.[26]

2017 Circular

Enacted in September 2017,[27] the 2017 Circular marked a dramatic shift away from the permissive approach to crypto asset transactions enshrined in the 2013 Notice. To place the 2017 Circular in context, there was a surge in the scale and scope of initial coin offerings (ICOs) in China amidst the sudden global rise of ICOs in 2017.[28] In the first half of that year, 65 ICOs were completed in China, raising RMB2.6 billion (US$398 million)[29] and attracting over 100,000 investors.[30] ICO fundraising increased sharply to RMB5 billion (US$747 million) in August 2017.[31] At the time, there was little regulatory scrutiny of ICO fundraising, making China a potentially 'free and wild place' for ICOs.[32] An investigation carried out by the PBOC that eventually led to the enactment of the 2017 Circular found 90% of the ICOs launched in China to be fraudulent.[33] With financial stability elevated to a top national policy priority in 2017, financial regulators

24 2013 Notice, Provision 2.

25 2013 Notice, Provisions 3 and 4.

26 2013 Notice, Provision 4.

27 关于防范代币发行融资风险的公告 [Circular on Preventing the Risks of Fundraising by Initial Coin Offerings], enacted on 4 September 2017 <www.csrc.gov.cn/pub/newsite/zjhxwfb/xwdd/201709/t20170904_323047.html> accessed 31 March 2022.

28 Nathaniel Popper, 'An Explanation of Initial Coin Offerings' *The New York Times* (27 October 2017) <www.nytimes.com/2017/10/27/technology/what-is-an-initial-coin-offering.html> accessed 31 March 2022 (noting that the funds raised by ICOs in 2017 were 3,000% more than those in 2016). For a review of the global regulatory response to ICOs, see eg Wulf A Kaal, 'Initial Coin Offerings: The Top 25 Jurisdictions and their Comparative Regulatory Responses (as of May 2018)' (2018) 1 Stanford Journal of Blockchain Law & Policy 41–63.

29 Lulu Yilun Chen and Justina Lee, 'Bitcoin Tumbles as PBOC Declares Initial Coin Offerings Illegal' *Bloomberg* (4 September 2017) <www.bloomberg.com/news/articles/2017-09-04/china-central-bank-says-initial-coin-offerings-are-illegal> accessed 31 March 2022.

30 Brenda Goh and Elias Glenn, 'Cryptocurrency Chaos as China Cracks Down on ICOs' *Reuters* (12 September 2017) <www.reuters.com/article/us-china-finance-digital-ico-analysis-idUSKCN1BN33R> accessed 31 March 2022.

31 Gabriel Wildau, 'China Targets Speculative Frenzy from "Initial Coin Offerings"' *Financial Times* (1 September 2017) <www.ft.com/content/dd5bbbc2-8e08-11e7-a352-e46f43c5825d> accessed 31 March 2022.

32 Sidney Leng, 'China "Mulls Crackdown on Digital Currency Fundraising Schemes"' *South China Morning Post* (29 August 2017) <www.scmp.com/news/china/article/2108786/china-mulls-crackdown-digital-currency-fundraising-schemes> accessed 31 March 2022.

33 Amanda Lee, 'China Virtual Currency Events Moved or Delayed as Central Bank Bans Digital Coin Fundraising' *South China Morning Post* (4 September 2017) <www.scmp.com/tech/china-tech/article/2109729/china-virtual-currency-events-moved-or-delayed-central-bank-bans> accessed 31 March 2022.

were at the time concerned that ICOs could become 'a magnet for scammers preying on the speculative fervour of Chinese investors'.[34]

Before proceeding to an examination of the 2017 Circular, it is worth noting that, in addition to the PBOC, the Circular counted an array of departmental-level governmental and regulatory bodies amongst its co-sponsors. These included the Cyberspace Administration of China, the Ministry of Industry and Information Technology and the State Administration for Market Regulation, as well as China's financial sector regulators (namely, the China Banking Regulatory Commission, the China Securities Regulatory Commission and the China Insurance Regulatory Commission), all of which are departments of national authorities.[35] The 2017 Circular thus constituted departmental-level agency legislation.

The 2017 Circular followed the 2013 Notice in declaring that cryptocurrencies of all sorts (including Bitcoin) 'do not enjoy the same legal status as fiat currencies' and 'should not and cannot be used or circulated in the markets as currencies'.[36] It maintained the same prohibitions as those of the 2013 Notice, barring PRC financial institutions and non-bank payment agencies from engaging in any crypto asset business.[37]

What sets the 2017 Circular apart from the 2013 Notice is that it effectively banned crypto asset exchanges and platforms, which were expressly prohibited from conducting virtually any type of crypto asset transaction. The prohibition covered exchange services between fiat currencies and cryptocurrencies, exchange services between one or more forms of cryptocurrency, trading cryptocurrencies in the capacity of a central counterparty, the provision of information intermediation and pricing services pertaining to trade in cryptocurrencies, and so on and so forth.[38] In the aftermath of the 2017 Circular's enactment, the major crypto asset exchanges shuttered their trading operations within the borders of mainland China.[39] Online platforms and mobile apps that offered exchange-like services also became targets of the regulatory clampdown on cryptocurrency trading.[40] As a consequence, commercial trading in crypto assets effectively came to an end in mainland China in late 2017. To put the significance of this development into context, Bitcoin trading in RMB accounted for 98% of all Bitcoin trading globally in 2016.[41]

34 Wildau (n 31).
35 These governmental and regulatory agencies are subordinate to and accountable to PRC national authorities, namely the State Council, China's cabinet, and the Communist Party of China Central Committee, as appropriate.
36 2017 Circular, Provision 1(2).
37 2017 Circular, Provision 4.
38 2017 Circular, Provision 3.
39 Reuters Staff, 'OkCoin, Huobi Shut Down Yuan-based Trading by Oct 31' *Reuters* (London, 15 September 2017) <www.reuters.com/article/bitcoin-china-exchanges-idINL4N1LW4KD> accessed 31 March 2022.
40 Bloomberg News, 'China Escalates Crackdown on Cryptocurrency Trading' *Bloomberg* (New York, 15 January 2018) <www.bloomberg.com/news/articles/2018-01-15/china-is-said-to-escalate-crackdown-on-cryptocurrency-trading> accessed 31 March 2022.
41 Paul Vigna and Chao Deng, 'Bitcoin Losses Worsen as Chinese Exchange Closes' *Wall Street Journal* (New York, 14 September 2017) <www.wsj.com/articles/bitcoin-losses-worsen-as-chinese-exchange-closes-1505404288> accessed 31 March 2022.

Despite its regulatory crackdown on crypto asset exchanges, the 2017 Circular fell short of categorically declaring crypto asset transactions *per se* illegal. Rather, it targeted, *prima facie*, only those ICO fundraising activities[42] and cryptocurrency platform businesses and services that violated PRC laws,[43] thereby appearing to imply that at least some crypto asset transactions could be regarded as lawful under the 2017 Circular. This view seems to be supported by a provision in the Circular cautioning that crypto asset financing and transactions carried multiple risks and that 'investors should bear their own investment risks'.[44] It thus seems clear that the 2017 Circular did not explicitly place a blanket ban on crypto asset transactions. We will discuss in detail in Part III how the ambiguity concerning the legality of crypto asset transactions thrust the *pacta sunt servanda* principle under PRC law into a state of uncertainty. However, that ambiguity was largely removed by the 2021 Notice, to which we now turn.

2021 Notice

Promulgated in September 2021,[45] the 2021 Notice marks the culmination of China's years-long war against cryptocurrencies. It is significant for the purposes of this research in two important respects. First, the Notice removes the previous ambiguity over the legality of crypto asset activities by declaring all crypto asset businesses and services unlawful. It makes the sweeping declaration that, as a matter of principle, 'cryptocurrency-related business activities are illicit financial activities'.[46] Hence, all crypto asset businesses and services are 'strictly' prohibited and will be 'resolutely cracked down on'. The 2021 Notice further makes it clear that crypto asset activities and services may constitute criminal offences, with those who conduct prohibited cryptocurrency activities or operations potentially being held criminally liable.

Second, and more importantly to the present research, the 2021 Notice offers some much-desired clarity as to whether cryptocurrency transactions *per se* are valid and effective under PRC law. Such transactions may involve the peer-to-peer, off-the-exchange sale and purchase of cryptocurrencies or take place between cryptocurrency traders and the crypto asset exchanges on which they trade. The Notice provides, as a matter of principle, that an entity or person's act

42 2017 Circular, Provision 1(1).

43 2017 Circular, Provision 3.

44 2017 Circular, Provision 5.

45 关于进一步防范和处置虚拟货币交易炒作风险的通知 [Notice on Further Preventing and Disposing of the Risk of Cryptocurrency Trading and Speculation], jointly enacted on 15 September 2021 by the PBOC, Cyberspace Administration of China, the Supreme People's Court, the Supreme People's Procuracy, Ministry of Industry and Information Technology, Ministry of Public Security, State Administration for Market Regulation, China Banking and Insurance Regulatory Commission, China Securities Regulatory Commission, and State Administration of Foreign Exchange <www.gov.cn/zhengce/zhengceku/2021-10/08/content_5641404.htm> accessed 31 March 2022. For a fuller treatment of the 2021 Notice, see Xi (n 8).

46 2021 Notice, Section 1(2).

of investing in cryptocurrencies and crypto-related derivatives shall be considered null and void where such act violates 'public order and good morals'. The entities and persons found in violation shall bear all losses resulting from their crypto investments.[47]

The principle of *pacta sunt servanda* in a state of uncertainty

As seen above, whilst the 2017 Circular sought to crack down on illegal crypto asset transactions, it fell short of specifying the precise parameters of the transactions deemed to be illegal.[48] Its lack of clarity gave rise to considerable uncertainty regarding the legality of crypto asset transactions, even for the PRC courts, as this part of the chapter will show. The question of legality has significant implications for *pacta sunt servanda*, as demonstrated below. Illegality is a substantive limitation on *pacta sunt servanda* under PRC law. Should a crypto asset transaction be treated as illegal or contrary to public policy, then contractual parties to the transaction would not be able to avail themselves of the *pacta sunt servanda* principle. Drawing on selected PRC court cases,[49] this part illustrates how the principle was thrust into a state of uncertainty by the 2017 Circular. Whilst some PRC courts have upheld *pacta sunt servanda* despite the legal ambiguity, others have allowed deviations from it on the ground of illegality.

Pacta sunt servanda *and illegality under PRC law: a synopsis*

Pacta sunt servanda is a well-recognised doctrine under PRC law.[50] Placing a substantive limitation upon it, however, is illegality. Illegality in PRC contract law can, to borrow Burrows' analytical framework,[51] be understood to involve two questions: first, what counts as an illegal contract or contract that is contrary to public policy and, second, what is the effect of illegality on a contract?

47 2021 Notice, Section 1(4).

48 See n 42–44 and the accompanying text.

49 The use of selected PRC court judgments raises methodological considerations. First, the PRC legal system falls broadly into the civil law tradition, and decided cases are not generally binding precedents, with the important caveat of 'guiding cases'. On guiding cases, see eg Björn Ahl, 'Retaining Judicial Professionalism: The New Guiding Cases Mechanism of the Supreme People's Court' *The China Quarterly* (March 2014) 217, 121–139. Second, although the accessibility of PRC court cases has been significantly improved thanks to the judicial transparency project China Judgements Online <https://wenshu.court.gov.cn/>, not all cases handed down by the PRC courts are publicly accessible. For a general overview of these matters, see e.g. Chao Xi, 'How the Chinese Judiciary Works: New Insights from Data-Driven Research' (2022) 22(3) *The China Review* 1.

50 See also Siyi Lin, 'Exceptions to Pacta sunt servanda in the Chinese Civil Code', ch 2 (in this volume), and Jianbo Lou and Yimeng Ye, 'Property Management Service Contract with Chinese Characteristics: An Exception to *Pacta Sunt Servanda*?', ch 3 (ibid).

51 Andrew Burrows, *A Restatement of the English Law of Contract* (2nd ed, Oxford University Press, 2020) 229.

Illegality

A contract is illegal under PRC law if it violates any mandatory provisions in national legislation.[52] National legislation in the context of PRC contract law has two sources. The first is primary national legislation enacted by the National People's Congress, China's top-level national legislature, and its Standing Committee. The second is 'administrative regulations' enacted by the State Council, China's cabinet. Laws enacted by other PRC legislative authorities do not qualify as national legislation under PRC contract law, which has significant bearing on the question of whether the 2017 Circular qualifies as national legislation. As noted, the Circular counts as co-sponsors a number of departmental-level national governmental or regulatory bodies under the State Council, albeit not the State Council itself.[53] Accordingly, it is not by nature a piece of national legislation under PRC contract law, but only departmental-level legislation. From this viewpoint, it could be argued that the 2017 Circular is incapable of rendering conduct illegal in the context of PRC contract law.

PRC contract law also recognises the doctrine of public policy,[54] although it remains unclear what public policy entails. A highly authoritative judicial document promulgated in late 2019 by the Supreme People's Court, China's highest court, provides that certain departmental-level legislation, although it does not qualify as national law under PRC contract law, can be regarded as manifesting public policy.[55] Such legislation typically involves inter-agency, coordinated departmental-level rulemaking and counts multiple ministries, departments and commissions under the State Council amongst its co-sponsors.[56] It differs from departmental-level legislation sponsored by a single State Council department.[57] In this light, the 2017 Circular can be regarded as embodying public policy, as it featured multiple departmental-level (financial) regulators and authorities as its co-sponsors. It follows that a breach of the Circular is arguably contrary to China's public policy.

Effect of illegality

As noted, a contract that is illegal or contrary to public policy is null and void under PRC contract law.[58] A void contract is void *ab initio*,[59] and is unenforceable.

52 PRC Contract Law, art 52(5). This provision has largely been replaced by Art 153 of the PRC Civil Code. The PRC Contract Law was applicable at the material time of the disputes in the cases discussed in this part.

53 See n 35 and the accompanying text.

54 PRC Contract Law, art 52(4).

55 全国法院民商事审判工作会议纪要 [Minutes of the National Judicial Civil and Commercial Adjudication Work Conference], promulgated on 8 November 2019 (hereinafter "2019 Conference Minutes").

56 SPC Second Civil Division (ed) 《全国法院民商事审判工作会议纪要》理解与适用 [Understanding and Application of the Minutes of the National Judicial Civil and Commercial Adjudication Work Conference] (People's Court Press 2019) 258. The treatise offers official annotations of the 2019 Conference Minutes.

57 ibid.

58 PRC Contract Law, art 52.

59 PRC Contract Law, art 54.

The effect of a void contract is broadly a matter of restitution under PRC contract law. Property should be restituted if acquired by way of a void contract. If property transferred under a void contract is unrecoverable, the transferor should be duly compensated by the transferee.[60] Also in operation is a fault-based doctrine in respect of any losses arising from the void contract. The contract party found to be at fault for voiding the contract is liable for compensating the innocent party for the losses incurred. If both parties are in the wrong, their responsibilities for the losses are determined by their respective shares of the fault in question.[61]

The illegality question: a split in judicial views

As noted above, the 2017 Circular left largely open the critical question of whether crypto asset transactions are illegal or contrary to public policy under PRC law (until the 2021 Notice offered greater clarity). Our research suggests that the PRC courts held divergent views on that question.

Crypto assets as legally recognised property

Some PRC courts saw little illegality in trading and investing in crypto assets, a position reflected in a court case heard in Beijing Municipality, *Hu Juntao v Wang Guijie*.[62] Wang had acted for the issuer of a lesser-known cryptocurrency, TBToken. Upon solicitation by Wang, Hu had invested in TBToken, only to subsequently find his investments in limbo. Hu initiated an action against Wang for the return of his principal. Although neither party brought up the issue of legality, the court commented on it extensively. It cited both the 2013 Notice and 2017 Circular at length, but opined that the investments in question did not violate any PRC laws or policies. The court laid out its three-limb reasoning. First, virtual property is protected under PRC law. The court noted:

> Virtual property exists in the form of data. It is of value, and can be produced, possessed and legally transacted. Owners of virtual property are entitled to transact and assign their rights over it, thereby reaping economic gains.

Second, cryptocurrencies should be categorised as a type of virtual property, as their creation meets the definition of virtual property. This view echoes the

60 PRC Contract Law, art 58. Several under-studied issues here are found at the intersection between PRC contract law and property law. They include the extent to which an innocent party is entitled to recover property that has subsequently been transferred to a bona fide third party and the extent to which the innocent party has a claim to any increase in the value of the property transferred under a void contract. For a general reflection on the matter, see e.g. Lutz-Christian Wolff, 'The Relationship between Contract Law and Property Law' (2020) 49 Common Law World Review 31.

61 PRC Contract Law, art 58.

62 胡均涛与王桂杰买卖合同纠纷案, 北京市通州区人民法院(2019)京0112民初37191号 [Hu Juntao v Wang Guijie Sales and Purchase Contract Dispute Case, the People's Court of Tongzhou District, Beijing Municipality, (2019) Jing 0112 Min Chu No. 37191].

position taken in the 2013 Notice.[63] Third, despite the 2017 Circular, cryptocurrencies are not categorically denied to possess a proprietary nature by PRC law, and as virtual property they should be tradable.

The foregoing view was echoed by another Beijing court in *Feng Yiran v Beijing LeKuDa Network Technology Co. Ltd.*[64] Feng possessed 38.748 Bitcoins in an account held with Beijing LeKuDa Network Technology (LeKuDa), the operator of OKCoin. LeKuDa had promised to give its account holders complimentary Bitcoin cash commensurate to the number of Bitcoins they owned and kept with LeKuDa. Feng brought an action claiming that LeKuDa had failed to deliver the Bitcoin cash promised. The first instance court ruled in favour of Feng. It opined that Bitcoins are 'objects of transaction' under PRC contract law and that Bitcoin ownership should thus be treated as a form of 'civil rights and interests' protected by Chinese law. The court further opined that anyone is entitled to legally possess virtual commodities such as Bitcoins and that the 2017 Circular prohibited only the exchange of cryptocurrencies for fiat currencies. The appellate court upheld the first instance court's ruling.[65] It is worth noting that the first instance court, the Haidian District Court in Beijing – widely known as a nationally leading court on law and technology – named *LeKuDa* as one of its 'classic' Internet-related cases.[66]

A similar position was adopted by the Internet Court of Hangzhou, China's – and arguably the world's – first Internet-based court,[67] in *Chen v A Communications Technology Company in Zhejiang Province*.[68] The court cited the 2017 Circular in affirming that Bitcoin is not a type of fiat currency. However, it also opined that PRC law did not (at the time) prohibit the production,[69] possession or lawful transfer of Bitcoin, which it held to be a commodity that could be

63 See *supra* note 21 and the accompanying text.

64 冯亦然与北京乐酷达网络科技有限公司合同纠纷案，北京市海淀区人民法院（2018）京0108民初24805号 [Feng Yiran v Beijing LeKuDa Network Technology Co. Ltd. Contract Dispute Case, the People's Court of Haidian District, Beijing Municipality (2018) Jing 0108 Min Chu No. 24805].

65 冯亦然与北京乐酷达网络科技有限公司合同纠纷案，北京市第一中级人民法院（2018）京01民终9579号 [Feng Yiran v Beijing LeKuDa Network Technology Co. Ltd. Contract Dispute Case, the First Intermediate People's Court, Beijing Municipality (2018) Jing 01 Min Zhong No. 9579].

66 比特币分叉，利益该归谁？涉互联网商事典型案例 [Bitcoin Forks: To Whom Should Yield Go – Classic Internet-Related Commercial Cases] <https://bjhdfy.chinacourt.gov.cn/article/detail/2019/04/id/4017371.shtml> accessed 31 March 2022.

67 For a review of China's Internet court initiative, see e.g. Huang-Chih Sung, 'Can Online Courts Promote Access to Justice? A Case Study of the Internet Courts in China' (2020) 39 *International Review of Law Computers & Technology* 105461; Meirong Guo, 'Internet Court's Challenges and Future in China' (2021) 40 International Review of Law Computers & Technology 105522.

68 陈某诉浙江某通信科技有限公司网络购物合同纠纷案，杭州互联网法院(2018)浙0192民初2641号. The identity of the parties was anonymised when released by the Hangzhou Internet Court.

69 Crypto mining was not banned until early 2021. See Alun John, Samuel Shen and Tom Wilson, 'China's Top Regulators Ban Crypto Trading and Mining, Sending Bitcoin Tumbling' *Reuters* (London, 25 September 2021) <www.reuters.com/world/china/china-central-bank-vows-crack-down-cryptocurrency-trading-2021-09-24/> accessed 31 March 2022.

purchased using fiat currencies. It is worth noting that the *Chen* case was selected by the Internet Court of Hangzhou as one of the ten 'model cases' released in 2019 to celebrate its two-year anniversary.[70]

Crypto assets are illegal

Other PRC courts rejected outright the legal validity of crypto asset transactions. In the widely noted case of *Jin Chen v Huobi Technology Co Ltd*,[71] Jin, a trader on Huobi, alleged that Huobi was liable for his loss of 123,424.78911 Tether USDT tokens, which took place in March 2018. Both the court of first instance and appellate court in Jiangsu Province rejected his claim. Citing the 2017 Circular, the two courts ruled that Jin's claimed loss was *not* a loss in 'lawful rights and interests deriving from lawful transactions' and that legal protection cannot be granted to 'illegal rights and interests'.[72] Investors in Tether USDTs therefore bear all of the risks associated with their investments, the courts held.

An appellate court in Anhui Province took a similar view in *Jinan Kaige Internet Technology Co Ltd v Sun Chenghao*.[73] In this case, Sun had purchased five Bitcoins from Jinan Kaige but had made only a partial payment of the agreed purchase price. Both the court of first instance and the appellate court ruled that the sale and purchase of Bitcoins were rendered illegal by the 2017 Circular. Accordingly, the sale and purchase agreement between the parties was null and void, the courts held, leaving Jinan Kaige with no legal right to claim for the purchase price due.

The principle of* pacta sunt servanda *standing firm

Illegality would have no bearing on the *pacta sunt servanda* principle were crypto asset transactions not considered illegal or contrary to public policy, in which case whatever had been agreed between the contract parties on the conduct of such transactions must be honoured. The promisor must therefore discharge the contractual obligations owed to the promisee as contracted.

70 杭州互联网法院成立两周年十大影响力案件之三 [Ten Impact Cases Featuring the Two-year Anniversary of the Internet Court of Hangzhou: Case No. 3] <www.pkulaw.com/pfnl/a6bdb3332ec0adc4c61c064fc5f9c23d313391743198335fbdfb.html> accessed 31 March 2022.

71 金晨与北京火币天下网络技术有限公司网络侵权责任纠纷案，江苏省徐州市中级人民法院(2019)苏03民终3461号 [Jin Chen v Huobi Technology Co Ltd Internet Tort Liability Dispute Case, the Intermediate People's Court of Xuzhou City, Jiangsu Province (2019) Su 03 Min Zhong No. 3461].

72 For linguistic analysis of the notion of 'illegal rights and interests' under PRC law, see e.g. Michele Mannoni and Deborah Cao, 'On the Meaning of *Feifa Quanyi* in Chinese Legal Language: A Semiotic and Corpus Analysis' (2018) 12 Linguistics and the Human Sciences 177.

73 济南凯歌网络科技有限公司、孙呈昊买卖合同纠纷案， 安徽省合肥市中级人民法院(2019)皖01民终10232号 [Jinan Kaige Internet Technology Co Ltd v Sun Chenghao Sales and Purchase Contract Dispute Case, the Intermediate People's Court of Hefei City, Anhui Province (2019) Wan 01 Min Zhong No. 10232].

This position was manifested in *Guan Biaofu v Shenzhen Biwang E-Commerce Ltd. Co*,[74] an appellate case heard by the Shenzhen Intermediate Court. Guan had entered into 'entrustment' contracts with the defendant, a Bitcoin mining firm. Under the contracts, Guan's investments in the defendant's mining projects entitled him to returns, including an entitlement to an agreed share of the new Bitcoins created from those projects. After the defendant ran into operational difficulties, the parties found themselves in dispute over how Guan's returns should be calculated. In the first-instance trial, the defendant relied upon, amongst other things, what was in essence an illegality defence. It was claimed that because Bitcoins did not warrant the protection of PRC law, the contracts entered into with Guan were null and void. The court of first instance rejected the claim, ruling that

> under the current [PRC] state policy on currencies, Bitcoin does not possess such attributes of a currency as fiat money and mandated acceptance. However, Bitcoin bears attributes of commercial property. Trades in Bitcoin do come with policy and business risks. However, contracts entered into by parties [to Bitcoin transactions] shall be effective provided that they are not violative of any mandatory provisions in national laws and administrative regulations.

The defendant was ordered to pay Guan the Bitcoin amount agreed in the contracts, and a subsequent appeal was dismissed.[75]

A similar view was taken in an appellate case heard in Anhui Province, *Feng Xuebao v Wang Lina*.[76] Feng and Wang had contracted for a joint investment in Bitcoins. Wang purchased Bitcoins and parked them with a cryptocurrency platform offering Bitcoin wallet services. Subsequently, the platform in question became dysfunctional, resulting in the total loss of the Bitcoins at issue. Feng brought an action against Wang seeking restitution of his principal on the basis of nullity of the co-investment agreement. At trial, Feng advanced a ground for nullity that was unconnected to the legality of Bitcoin but that the court of first instance rejected as lacking in factual support. On appeal, Feng based his illegality argument on the 2017 Circular banning all Bitcoin trading platforms, including the one involved in the present case. Feng further supported his case with reference to the fact that the crypto platform in question had been specifically named by the PRC authorities as having engaged in criminal activities, a fact that the appellate court confirmed. Nevertheless, the court rejected the legal relevance of that fact and refused to

74 关标福、深圳必旺电子商务有限公司委托合同纠纷案，广东省深圳市中级人民法院 (2019) 粤03民终10567号 [Guan Biaofu v Shenzhen Biwang E-Commerce Ltd. Co Entrustment Contract Dispute Case, the Intermediate People's Court of Shenzhen City, Guangdong Province (2019) Yue 03 Min Zhong No. 10567].

75 The defendant, i.e. the Bitcoin mining firm, did not appeal. Guan appealed on a ground that is irrelevant to the discussion in this chapter.

76 冯学宝、王丽娜确认合同效力纠纷案，安徽省六安市中级人民法院 (2019) 皖15民终2988号 [Feng Xuebao v Wang Lina Contract Validity Confirmation Dispute Case, the Intermediate People's Court of Liu'an City, Anhui Province (2019) Wan 15 Min Zhong No. 2988].

declare the contract in question null and void. Feng was held to be bound by his contract with Wang, and the restitution claim failed.

Principle of **pacta sunt servanda** *coming under siege?*

Illegality renders a contract null and void under PRC contract law, and therefore imposes substantive limitations upon the *pacta sunt servanda* principle, as demonstrated above. A contract will be void ab initio, and relief granted to the promisor, if declared by the PRC courts to be illegal or contrary to public policy. It is worth noting that the PRC courts in the two cases discussed below did not attempt to draw a conceptual distinction between illegality at formation and illegality in performance, a notable distinction under English contract law.[77] In any event, the crypto asset transactions in both cases had been entered into and implemented well after promulgation of the 2017 Circular. The real issue was therefore whether contravention of the Circular was illegal or contrary to public policy in light of the legal uncertainty flowing from it.

In *Wang Chenwei v Gu Panchen*,[78] Gu had entered into a contract with his co-worker Wang under which he 'entrusted' Wang with making investments in Bitcoins on his behalf. Wang agreed to deliver a 7.5% fixed monthly return on Gu's principal. Subsequently, the crypto platform on which Wang traded Bitcoins became obsolete, and the Bitcoins that had been purchased became inaccessible, resulting in the total loss of Gu's investments. Gu brought an action requesting the court to order the restitution of his principal, and he also sought an interest payment on the principal. The first instance court ordered the recovery of Gu's principal, but rejected his claim for an interest payment.

On appeal, Wang cited illegality as a defence, claiming that Gu's investments in Bitcoins did not warrant protection under PRC law and that Gu's claim for the return of his principal was ill-grounded. The gist of Wang's illegality defence was to call on the court to refuse to order the restitution of money transferred under the contract. The appellate court had no difficulty ruling the contract in question to be illegal. It ruled that the contractual relationship between Wang and Gu was void and 'did not deserve the protection of law', as it contravened the 2017 Circular. Nevertheless, the appellate court did not accept Wang's argument that restitution ought to be rejected. It noted that, as discussed above,[79] PRC law provides for the restitution of transferred property where the contract in question is found to be null and void. Hence, the first instance court's order for restitution was affirmed. The first instance court was also right to have rejected Gu's claim for an interest payment, the appellate court opined, as Gu himself was at fault for having

77 See e.g. Ewan McKendrick, *Contract Law* (13th ed, Macmillan Education UK 2019) 299–301.

78 王晨威与顾盼辰民间委托理财合同纠纷案，上海市第二中级人民法院 (2020) 沪02民终7306号 [Wang Chenwei v Gu Panchen Private Entrusted Wealth Management Contract Dispute Case, the Second Intermediate People's Court, Shanghai Municipality (2020) Hu 02 Min Zhong No. 7306].

79 See nn 59–60 and the accompanying text.

knowingly entered into an invalid contract with Wang, and was therefore liable for his own interest loss.

In *Chen Ji v Peng Hailin*,[80] Chen and Peng had entered into a contract whereby Chen 'entrusted' Peng with 100 Bitcoins to engage in crypto arbitrage trading[81] on Chen's behalf. In return, Peng agreed to pay Chen a fixed daily return on the Bitcoins at issue. When the arbitrage trading subsequently ran into difficulty, Chen sued Peng, seeking restitution of the 100 Bitcoins transferred under the contract in question. The court of first instance declared the contract to be null and void, as it violated the 2013 Notice and 2017 Circular. The court ruled that Peng's share of the fault was 70%, with Peng thus ordered to "return" 70 Bitcoins to Chen as a way of compensating Chen for his presupposed loss of the 100 Bitcoins in question.[82] On appeal, Peng cited, amongst other things, the illegality defence that Bitcoin investments were illegal and thus 'did not warrant any protection under the law'. Peng's claim was identical to that of Wang in *Wang Chenwei* in that it also called for the court to refuse to restore the parties to their pre-contractual positions. Although the appellate court affirmed that any violation of the 2017 Circular would render a contract void, it rejected Peng's appeal.

Concluding remarks

The principle of *pacta sunt servanda* is the cornerstone of modern contract law systems. Indeed, its significance goes beyond the legal discipline of contracts. It forms the foundation on which economic transactions are planned, executed and enforced. Foundational though it is, however, the *pacta sunt servanda* principle is subject to various 'vitiating' factors,[83] such as force majeure. The restrictive effect of these factors on *pacta sunt servanda* can loom large in times of crisis such as the COVID-19 pandemic.

Deviations from the *pacta sunt servanda* principle can also gain traction during other times of change, particularly at a time of rapidly evolving new technologies.

80 陈霁、彭海林合同纠纷案，江西省上饶市中级人民法院 (2020) 赣11民终902号 [Chen Ji v Peng Hailin Contract Dispute Case, the Intermediate People's Court of Shangrao City, Jiangxi Province (2020) Gan 11 Min Zhong No. 902].

81 Crypto arbitrage trading is the trading strategy of buying a digital asset on one exchange and selling it simultaneously on another on which the price is higher. See 'Crypto Arbitrage Trading: How to Make Low-Risk Gains' <www.coindesk.com/learn/crypto-arbitrage-trading-how-to-make-low-risk-gains/> accessed 31 March 2022.

82 Restitution of property is conceptually distinct from the liability to compensate the innocent party for his losses by the party at fault under PRC contract law, see nn 59–60 and the accompanying text. However, leading Chinese contract law treaties seem to suggest that where the original property transferred under a void contract is not returnable, the party at fault could be ordered to 'return' 'equivalent' property as a method of compensating the innocent party for his loss of the original property. See e.g. Liming Wang, 合同法研究 [*Research on Contract Law*] (3rd ed, China Renmin University Press, 2015) 729. The first instance court in the case seemed to have applied this jurisprudence.

83 Mindy Chen-Wishart, *Contract Law* (7th ed, Oxford University Press, 2022).

This chapter highlights one such change, that is, the dawn of the age of cryptocurrencies, and places it in the context of China's changing crypto regulatory landscape. The case study of China shows that when legal systems scramble to understand and respond to the advancement of new technologies, their efforts can create legal ambiguity that thrusts the *pacta sunt servanda* principle into a state of uncertainty. It remains to be seen how a new equilibrium can be attained to restore the principle to where it belongs, particularly in China, to offer the certainty and predictability that economic actors expect.

9 Post-employment non-compete agreements under the Taiwan Labour Standards Act and *pacta sunt servanda*

Yalun Yen

Introduction

Pacta sunt servanda *and its exceptions in Taiwan Civil and Labour Law*

In a civil law system, the maxim of *pacta sunt servanda* is traditionally regarded as self-evident. The basic notion is that promises are binding; commitments that have been made must be executed, and that agreements must be obeyed or respected when this maxim is applied to agreements.[1] *Pacta sunt servanda* originates from natural law and its precipitation in the rule of equity, serves public policy, and is the underlying doctrine supporting the modern concept of freedom of contract.[2]

The Taiwan Civil Code ('TCC') was strongly influenced by the German civil law system and, as the German Civil Code, does not explicitly stipulate *pacta sunt servanda*. However, the Taiwan Supreme Court has stated repeatedly that both of the parties to an agreement shall be bound after the agreement is legally concluded, and that neither party thereto is allowed to unilaterally rescind the agreement without consent of the other party or for other legitimate reasons.[3]

In accordance with TCC article 153, a contract or an agreement is entered into by parties whose expressions of intent concur. The parties to a contract shall be

1 Richard Hyland, 'Pacta Sunt Servanda: A Meditation' (1994) 34 Virginia Journal of International Law 405, 405–407. See also Stephen Hall, 'Pacta Sunt Servanda, the Common Law, and Hong Kong', ch 1 (in this volume).

2 Otto Kahn-Freund, 'Pacta Sunt Servanda – A Principle and its Limits: Some Thoughts Prompted by Comparative Labour Law' (1974) 48 Tulane Law Review 894, 894; KM Sharma, 'From "Sanctity" to "Fairness": An Uneasy Transition in the Law of Contracts?' (1999) 18 New York Law School Journal of International and Comparative Law 95, 95–98.

3 Taiwan Supreme Court, 18 Shang Zi No. 484 Civil Precedent, 18 Shang Zi No. 1495 Civil Precedent, 19 Shang Zi No. 985 Civil Precedent, 20 Shang Zi No. 632 Civil Precedent, 20 Shang Zi No. 1941 Civil Precedent, 30 Shang Zi No. 455 Civil Precedent, and 40 Shang Zi No. 1746 Civil Precedent (臺灣最高法院18年上字第484 號民事判例、18年上字第1495號民事判例、19年上字第985號民事判例、20年上字第632號民事判例、20年上字第1941民事判例、30年上字第455民事判例、40年上字第1946民事判例).

DOI: 10.4324/9781003358305-11

bound thereby based on freedom of contract. Freedom of contract is not unrestricted and may be constrained if justice requires. Legal control on standard form contracts in TCC article 247-1 and adjustments to contractual obligations due to change of circumstances under TCC article 227-2 are the two main paradigms of restrictions on freedom of contract in the TCC.[4]

The Taiwan Labour Standards Act ('TLSA') has been enacted to provide minimum standards for working conditions and to protect workers' rights and interests. Its article 1 provides that the terms and conditions of any employment agreement shall not be below the minimum standards provided in the TLSA. Therefore, the TLSA is a special statute for employment agreements provided in the TCC that will prevail over the provisions of the latter. In addition, in the event that any term or condition set forth in an employment agreement violates any mandatory or prohibitive provision of the TLSA, it shall be null and void.[5]

Pacta sunt servanda ***and non-compete agreements under Taiwan Labour Law***

However, prior to 2015, no provisions in the TLSA regulated non-disclosure and non-compete agreements entered into by and between employers and employees for the main propose of protecting employers' trade secrets. There have been many lawsuits related to misappropriation or protection of trade secrets in Taiwan based on alleged breaches of non-disclosure or non-competing agreements.[6] The courts in Taiwan have faced the challenge of determining the validity and scope of non-disclosure or non-compete agreements since the 1980s.

Almost all the scholars, practitioners and courts in Taiwan agree that under the doctrine of freedom of contract, an enterprise shall be free to enter into non-disclosure or confidentiality agreements with associated persons, i.e. its employees, managers, executives, or directors, to oblige them to keep the enterprise's technical information or trade secrets in confidence during or even after expiration

4 Tez-chien Wang, *The Principle of Obligations: Elementary Theory – Sources of Obligations, Contracts, and Management of Affairs without Mandate* (3rd ed, Sam Min Book, 2021) 91–92 (王澤鑑，債法原理：基本理論一債之發生、契約、無因管理 (3版，三民經銷 2021) 91–92); see also generally: Cheng-hsien Hsu, 'The Consequentialist Approach to the Regulation of Contracts: A Preliminary Study on Court Decisions' (2013) 135 Chengchi LR 87–173 (許政賢，契約結果導向的司法控制—初探民事裁判結果導向案例 (2013) 政大法學評論第135期87–173); Hung-hui Yang, 'On Construction of Obligation to Re-Negotiate when Circumstances Change' (2016) 97 Taipei ULR 1–78 (楊宏暉，論情事變更原則下重新協商義務之建構 (2016) 臺北大學法學論叢第 97 期 1–78).

5 Taiwan Supreme Court, 109 Tai Shang Zi No. 6 Civil Judgment (台灣高等法院109年台上字第6號民事判決).

6 Ya-Lun Yen, 'The Trend of Civil Lawsuits related to Trade Secrets Based on the Civil Judgments of Taiwan Supreme Court' (2016) 11 Taiwan Bar Journal 33, 45 (顏雅倫，從我國最高法院歷年民事判決看營業秘密民事案件實務趨勢 (2016) 全國律師第20卷第11期頁33，45).

of their employment or mandate agreements.[7] In fact, even without any explicit provisions or agreements, such persons shall bear non-disclosure or confidentiality obligations for their affiliated enterprises' trade secrets within the terms and after expiration of employment or mandate agreements, due to their concomitant obligations and post-contractual obligations based upon the good faith rule.[8]

Generally speaking, non-compete agreements refer to agreements entered into by enterprises and specific persons associated with such enterprises, i.e. employees, managers, executives or directors, and stipulate that such specific persons shall not operate, engage in, or be employed at businesses identical or similar to these enterprises within the terms of or after the expiration of employment (for employees) or mandate (for managers, executives, or directors) agreements, for the purpose of protecting trade secrets and business interests, or retaining the competitive advantages of such enterprises.[9]

Compared to non-disclosure agreements, non-compete agreements, especially those imposing post-employment obligations, are much more controversial. Since during the terms of employment or mandate agreements, employees, managers, executives or directors of enterprises owe loyalty or a fiduciary duty to their enterprises under the TCC and the Taiwan Company Act ('TCA'), so they do not

7 Chia-hui Wang, 'The Study of the New Labour Standards Act Article 9–1 for Non-Competition and Protection of Trade Secrets I' (2017) 1875 Judicial Weekly 2, 2 (王家惠，勞動基準法增訂條文第9條之1後對於競業禁止規定與營業秘密保護之探討（上） (2017) 司法周刊第1875期第2頁，2). In addition, according to TCC art 528, a contract of mandate is a contract whereby the parties agree that one of them, a principal, commissions the other party, a mandatory, to deal with his affairs, and the latter agrees to do so. In accordance with the Taiwan Company Act ('TCA') arts 29 and 192, the relations between the company and its managers, executives, and directors shall be governed by the provisions of the TCC pertaining to the mandate contracts. The TLSA does not apply to a mandate contract because the purpose of the TLSA is to protect workers from unfair working conditions, and so the TLSA only applies to employment agreements.

8 Geng-schenq Lin, *Contract Control – From John Rawls' Theory of Justice to Control on Non-Compete Provisions after Resignation* (1st ed, Han Lu Book and Publishing, 2009) 130 (林更盛，論契約控制：從Rawls的正義理論到離職後競業禁止約款的控制 (初版，翰蘆 2009) 130); Taiwan Supreme Court, 95 Tai Shang Zi No. 1076 Civil Judgment (台灣最高法院95台上字第1076號民事判決). Concomitant obligations in Taiwan contract law mean contractual obligations arising from good faith rule in the course of performance of contracts in order to protect creditors' contractual or other personal and property interests: see Taiwan Supreme Court, 100 Tai Shang Zi No. 2 Civil Judgment and 104Tai Shang Zi No. 799 Civil Judgment (台灣最高法院100台上字第2號民事判決與104台上字799號民事判決). Post-contractual obligations mean one party's independent obligations after the expiration of the contract for protecting the other party's personal and property interests, such as an employee's obligation not to disclose the employer's trade secrets even after expiration of the employment contract, see Taiwan Supreme Court, 95 Tai Shang Zi No. 1076 Civil Judgment (台灣最高法院95台上字第1076號民事判決). See also Juei-Lin Tsai, 'The Development of Independent Contract Theory I: Principle of Independence of Post-Employment Non-Compete Agreements' (2016) 297 Taiwan LJ 87, 88–91 (蔡瑞麟，獨立契約說之開展一離職後競業禁止契約獨立性之基本原理 (2016) 台灣法學雜誌第297期第87頁，88–91).

9 Labour of Ministry, Executive Yuan, Taiwan, *Reference Handbook for Concluding Non-Compete Agreements* (2nd ed, Labour of Ministry, Executive Yuan 2008) 1 (台灣行政院勞動部，簽訂競業禁止參考手冊 (2版，台灣行政院勞動部2008) 1); see also Taiwan Supreme Court 108 Tai Shang Zi. No. 2125 Civil Judgment (台灣最高法院108台上字第2125號民事判決).

operate or engage without consent to do so in businesses identical or similar to those of their associated enterprises due to self-interest or benefits for themselves or others.[10]

The validity of post-employment non-compete agreements has consistently sparked intense debates in Taiwan since the 1980s, which corresponded to rapid economic growth and development of the high-tech industry in Taiwan. To tackle the relevant issues, it is necessary to strike a balance among protection of employers' trade secrets and other legitimate business interests, freedom of employees to choose their jobs, contract enforceability, legal certainty, and the *pacta sunt servanda* rule. Invalidating a post-employment non-compete agreement under specific requirements or criteria is an exception to the *pacta sunt servanda* rule. In the following discussion, the term 'non-compete agreements' and the related issues will specifically refer to post-employment non-compete agreements unless otherwise noted.

This chapter first introduces the debates concerning non-compete agreements before 2015, including the criteria for determining their validity as developed by the courts in Taiwan, the subsequent divergence amongst courts with regard to the criteria used to review non-compete agreements, and the application of TCC article 247-1. Then, this chapter expounds on the enactment and impact of TLSA article 9-1, which stipulates the requirements of legally binding non-compete agreements. Next, this chapter further discusses three important issues concerning TLSA article 9-1, including the determination of legitimate business interests, the requirements for reasonable compensation for non-compete obligations, and whether the blue pencil rule is applicable to TLSA article 9-1(3). Finally, a suitable scheme for applying and amending TLSA article 9-1 based on the *pacta sunt servanda* rule, legal framework, and decisions regarding the validity and fairness of no-compete agreements is proposed.

The debates concerning the validity of non-compete agreements before 2015

The early development

Before 2015, in Taiwan, with the exception of the Taiwan Labour Contract Act articles 14 and 15, which has never been officially enforced, no other acts, provisions, or regulations have discussed or controlled non-compete provisions in labour contracts. The Taiwan Supreme Court 75 Tai Shang Zi No. 2446 Civil Judgment in 1986 was the Court's first decision on the validity of a non-compete agreement. In this

10 Labour of Ministry (n 9) 2–3. TCA art 23 (1) stipulates that the responsible person of a company shall have the loyalty and shall exercise the due care of a good administrator in conducting the business operation of the company; and if he or she has acted contrary to this provision, shall be liable for the damages to be sustained by the company there-from. The managers, executives, and directors of a company qualify for 'responsible persons' of a company described in the TCA art 8. In addition, the loyal duty of an employee is considered his or her concomitant obligation to his or her employer under the TCC.

case, the respondent (the employee) signed at the beginning of employment with the appellant (the employer), as required by the latter, a declaration that the respondent shall not operate, work for, or provide information to any business identical or similar to that of the appellant within two years after the expiration of employment; otherwise, the respondent would be liable for the damages arising from his breach. By resorting to the Taiwan Constitution article 15 for emphasising a person's right to work shall be protected and not be restricted by law except by such as may be necessary to prevent infringement upon the freedoms of other persons, to avert an imminent crisis, to maintain social order, or to advance public welfare, the Taiwan High Court supported the respondent's argument that this declaration was void in accordance with TCC article 72 because it was against public policy or morals.[11] However, the Taiwan Supreme Court opined that the right to work in the Taiwan Constitution article 15 is not a right that shall be protected absolutely. The Taiwan Supreme Court held that this non-compete agreement with limitations of occupational activities and two-year non-compete period was validly consented to by the respondent and then complied with the intent of the Taiwan Constitution article 15 with regard to protecting the right to work. Furthermore, the Taiwan Supreme Court stated that this non-compete agreement neither violated other mandatory or prohibitive laws, nor was it against public policy or morals, so this agreement was not declared null and void. The Taiwan Supreme Court in this case supported the validity of this non-compete agreement mainly based on the freedom of contract.[12]

After the Taiwan Supreme Court 75 Tai Shang Zi No. 2446 Civil Judgment, the Taiwan Supreme Court 83 Tai Shang Zi No. 1865 Civil Judgment affirmed the decision of the Taiwan High Court 81 Shang Geng Yi Zi No. 283 Civil Judgment and stated that a non-compete agreement shall be considered valid provided that its limitations on the geographical area and time period are reasonable. Even though the non-compete agreement of interest had no limitations on the non-compete area and period during which it was applicable, the Taiwan Supreme Court affirmed the Taiwan High Court's opinion that since in the complaints the employer only required the former employee not to compete for two years after the expiration of employment and this time period was reasonable, this non-compete agreement shall be valid within these two years. Nevertheless, except for reasonable non-compete areas and time periods, neither of these two decisions made by the Taiwan Supreme Court deliberated on any other substantial standard for reviewing the validity of non-compete agreements.

11 The Taiwan Constitution art 15 provides that the right of existence, the right to work, and the right of property shall be guaranteed to the people. The Taiwan Constitution art 23 states that all the freedoms and rights enumerated in the preceding articles shall not be restricted by law except by such as may be necessary to prevent infringement upon the freedoms of other persons, to avert an imminent crisis, to maintain social order or to advance public welfare. In addition, TCC article 72 stipulates that a juridical act which is against public policy or morals is void.

12 Yu-Fan Chiu and Che-Kun Liu, 'A Study on Non-Compete Clause: The Analysis on Elements and Legal Effects of the Labour Standards Act Article 9–1' (2020) 32 Soochow L R 1, 3 (邱羽凡、劉哲鯤，勞工離職後競業禁止條款之研究－勞動基準法第9條之一規範要件與法律效果之分析 (2020) 東吳法律學報第32卷第1 期第1頁，3).

Divergence of criteria for reviewing non-compete agreements

Accompanying Taiwan's rapid economic growth in 1980s and 1990s, the number of disputes concerning non-compete agreements increased dramatically. In 1997, the Taiwan Taipei District Court 85 Lao Su Zi No. 78 Civil Judgment[13] pointed out that non-compete agreements will be valid if their limitations on periods, areas, scope and methods are reasonable under general social notions and business practices and do not endanger the economic viability of obligors. The decision proposed five criteria for reviewing non-compete agreements. Then, this decision further expounded that the protection of the right to work set forth in the Taiwan Constitution article 15 required that the criteria for reviewing the reasonableness of a non-compete agreement included at least the following:

1. The enterprise or employer shall have interests, i.e. specialised knowledge or trade secrets, necessary to be protected by the non-compete agreement.
2. It is necessary to consider the former employee's position or status in the enterprise or firm. In the event that the former employee of interest has a low position, does not have special skills or techniques, and is not one of main business managers, the non-compete agreement shall be deemed null and void by reason of being against public policy or morals. Such former employee will not endanger his or her former employer's business even when he or she works for another enterprise or firm operating a business that is identical or similar to that of his or her former employer after his or her resignation.
3. The limitations on prospective employers, the period, area, and scope of occupations must be reasonable.
4. A non-compete agreement with compensation for the former employee's non-competition after employment is rarely deemed to be against policy and morals except under special circumstances.
5. When a former employee misuses his or her former employer's information or poaches its clients, engages in hostile or fraudulent competitive actions or competes with the former employer in violation of good faith, the former employee in breach of the non-compete agreement is not considered to be worthy of protection.[14]

13 This decision was later affirmed by Taiwan High Court 86 Lao Shang Zi No. 39 Civil Judgment (台灣高等法院86勞上易字第39號民事判決).

14 Some commentors thought that the judge of the Taiwan Taipei District Court 85 Lao Su Zi No. 78 Civil Judgment might have consulted the opinions of Japanese scholars and decisions and then introduced the aforesaid five criteria to Taiwan. It is clear that these five criteria for reviewing non-compete agreements are highly similar to the analytical framework used to review non-compete clauses of post-employment in Japan, see Zong-Lin He, 'A Comparative Study on Post-Employment Covenants Not to Compete between Taiwan and Japan' (Master Thesis, NTU College of Law 2011) 72–75 (何宗霖，我國與日本勞工離職後鏡業禁止約款效力之比較法研究 (國立台灣大學法律學院法律學系碩士論文 2011) 72–75).

TCC article 247-1 was enacted in 1999 to prohibit unfair standard form contracts in general. Since many employment agreements incorporating non-compete provisions are standard form contracts, the application of TCC article 247-1 will also influence the validity of non-compete agreements. TCC article 247-1 stipulates that if a contract has been constituted according to the provisions prepared by one of the parties in the form of contracts of the same kind, agreements that are obviously unfair in light of all the circumstances will be declared void if they include any of the following provisions: (1) a provision releasing or reducing the responsibility of the party who prepared the contract provisions, (2) a provision increasing the responsibility of the other party, (3) a provision making the other party waive his or her rights or restricting the party from exercising his or her rights, and (4) provisions that are gravely disadvantageous to the other party.

After the Taiwan Taipei District Court 85 Lao Su Zi No. 78 Civil Judgment and enactment of TCC article 247-1, the Taiwan Labour Commission of Executive Yuan, the Taiwan Ministry of Labour, issued an official letter in 2000 to explain the validity of non-compete agreements and published the *Reference Handbook for Concluding Non-Compete Agreements* in 2003. Both the letter and Reference Handbook adopted the five criteria set forth in the Taiwan Taipei District Court 85 Lao Su Zi No. 78 Civil Judgment. The Reference Handbook further emphasised and concluded that non-compete agreements shall be considered valid as long as they comply with freedom of contract, good faith, and the five criteria.[15]

However, there was still no consensus among the courts in Taiwan on the criteria for reviewing non-compete agreements. Even though the majority of the courts in Taiwan used the five criteria,[16] some courts ruled that a former employee's obviously unfair competitive actions or violation of good faith are not required for determining the validity of a non-competing agreement, but only one factor the courts could use to determine the amount of a penalty or damages.[17] Some courts in Taiwan only considered three criteria when reviewing the validity of non-competing agreements and further held that neither compensation for non-competition nor a former employee' competitive action violating good faith or breaching trust is a prerequisite of a valid non-compete agreement.[18] Some commentors even advocated that a non-compete agreement without compensation for the former employee's non-competition shall be declared null and void because

15 Joyce JM Chen, 'The Publication of Reference Handbook for Non-competition by Labour Commission of Executive Yuan' (2003) 5 Lee and Li LJ Bimonthly 1–3 (陳瑞敏，勞委會公布競業禁止參考手冊 (2003) 理律雜誌雙月刊2003年5月，1–3).

16 He (n 14) 65.

17 Wan-Ning Hsu, 'Determining the Validity of Post-Employment Covenants not to Compete before the Taiwan Labour Standards Act Article 9–1' (2021) 312 Taiwan LR 169, 172–173 (徐婉寧，勞動基準法第9條之1施行簽訂之離職後競業禁止條款效力之判斷 (2021) 月旦法學雜誌第312期第169頁，172–173).

18 Zong-Lin He, 'The Formation and Development of Reviewing Criteria for the Validity of Post-Employment Non-Compete Clauses in Judicial Practice of Taiwan' (2016) 6 Taiwan Bar Journal 83, 90–91 (何宗霖，我國實務上對勞工離職後競業禁止約款有效性審查標準之形成與演變 (2016) 全國律師第15卷第6期第83頁，90–91).

it is unfair to impose gratuitous non-compete obligations on a former employee. To avoid a huge imbalance between employers and employees,[19] the decisions adopting four or five criteria differed in terms of considering compensation for a former employee's non-competition either as a factor or as a condition of validity of a non-compete agreement. In addition, there were no coherent standards by which to determine if specific share issues, bonuses, severance pay, or any other benefits received by employees should be regarded as compensation for a former employee's non-competition.[20]

Then, in the Taiwan Supreme Court 99 Tai Shang Zi No. 599 Civil Judgment in 2010, the Taiwan Supreme Court stated that a non-compete agreement shall be lawful and effective in accordance with freedom of contract provided that the limitations set forth therein are reasonable, clear and necessary, and the employee's damage or harm arising from such limitations has been reasonably compensated for. In the subsequent Taiwan Supreme Court 103 Tai Shang Zi No. 793 Civil Judgment, the Taiwan Supreme Court further concluded that if employers are entitled to require employees to agree to non-compete agreements without any compensation during or after employment, employees' rights related to existence and work will not be sufficiently protected. Nevertheless, in the same decision, the Taiwan Supreme Court ruled that the employee in question voluntarily applied for retirement and received his pension of NTD 3,000,000, so it was ruled that he should be bound by the reasonable non-compete agreement even without other compensation. These two decisions of the Taiwan Supreme Court both emphasised the importance and necessity of reasonable compensation for non-compete obligations. However, the Taiwan Supreme Court did not expressly support the

19 Jiunn-Yann Chiou, 'Determining the Validity of Non-Compete Agreements/Taiwan Hsinchu District Court 98 Su Zi No. 438 Judgment' (2011) 189 Taiwan Law Journal 183, 184–185 (邱駿彥，競業禁止特約有效與否之認定/新竹地院98訴438 (2011) 台灣法學雜誌第189期第183頁，184–185); Wei-Lin Wang, 'Trade Secrets and Post-Employment Non-Compete Clauses－Comments on Taiwan Taipei District Court 97 Lao Su Zi No. 14 Civil Judgment' (2010) 186 Taiwan LR 193, 208 (王偉霖，營業秘密與離職後競業禁止約款－評台灣台北地方法院九十七年勞訴字第十四號判決 (2010) 月旦法學雜誌第186期第193頁，208); Geng-Schenq Lin, 'Control on Post-Employment Non-Compete Clauses－Giving Workers Appropriate Compensation or Not' (2009) 2 Taiwan Bar Journal 41, 44 (林更盛，離職後競業禁止約款的控制－是否給予勞方適當的補償 (2009) 全國律師第13卷第2期頁41，44); Tong-Shuan Yang, 'A Study on the Problem of Articles for Restraint on Competitive Practice Concerning Laborers' Inventions or Copyright's Works during the Working Time' (2005) 3 National Taiwan University Law Journal 333, 347 (楊通軒，勞工創刊物權益歸屬與競業禁止關係之研究 (2005) 國立臺灣大學法學論叢第 34 卷 第 3 期 第333頁， 347). However, Geng-Schenq Lin also emphasised that if the employee's professional competencies and economic sustainability are equivalent to those of an independent business entity, the non-compete agreements for such employee with reasonable restrictions could be considered lawful even without compensation to such an employee: ibid, 44, 52.

20 Hsu (n 17) 173–174. For example, in Taiwan Supreme Court 99 Tai Shang Zi No. 599 Civil Judgment, Taiwan Supreme Court disagreed with the opinion of the Taiwan High Court indicating that shares or options acquired or received by an employee during employment could be considered compensation for employees' non-compete obligations after expiration of employment.

other four criteria nor regarded compensation for non-competition to be one of essential elements of a valid and lawful non-compete agreement.

In conclusion, prior to 2015, the courts in Taiwan reached a consensus on three essential, critical requirements for a valid non-compete agreement. These included that the legitimate interests of employers must be protected; during employment, the employee's position or status should be sufficient for him or her to access or use the employer's trade secrets or specialised knowledge, which would in turn make it likely that the employee may endanger the employer's business through providing such information to a competitor after expiration of employment, and the reasonableness of limitations, in view of employers' legitimate interests, on prospective employers, the non-compete period, area, and scope of occupational activities set forth in the non-compete agreement.[21] In practice, the courts in Taiwan also used the criteria for non-compete agreements to review non-solicitation clauses that prohibit former employees from approaching their former employers' clients or making any deal with those clients.[22] According to one quantitative study of non-compete agreements in Taiwan, more than 80% of non-compete periods considered reasonable by the courts in Taiwan were less than 2 years.[23] In addition, when reviewing the validity of non-compete agreements, most courts in Taiwan also considered whether the non-compete agreements were obviously unfair under TCC article 247-1.[24] The aforesaid five criteria could be taken into consideration in interpretation and application of TCC article 247-1.[25]

TLSA article 9-1 and its critical issues

The impact of TLSA article 9-1

On 16 December 2015, TLSA article 9-1 was enacted. TLSA article 9-1(1) stipulates that an employer shall not enter into a post-employment non-compete agreement with an employee unless the following requirements have been met:

1 The employer has legitimate business interests that need to be protected (subparagraph 1);
2 the position or job of the employee entitles him or her to have access to or be able to use the employer's trade secrets (subparagraph 2);

21 ibid, 173; He (n 14) 78.

22 Chiu and Liu (n 12) 7–8.

23 Oliver Hung, Wei-Li Liu and Nicole Huang, 'Quantitative Analysis of the ROC Court Decisions on Trade Secret Infringements and Violation of Non-Compete Clauses' (2007) 2 Technology Law Review 1, 19 (洪榮宗、劉偉立、黃心苑，我國侵害營業秘密與競業禁止違約判決之量化研究 (2007) 科技法學評論第4卷第2期第1頁，19).

24 Yen (n 6) 46.

25 Geng-Schenq Lin, 'Reviewing Post-Employment Non-Compete Clauses in Standard Forms – Comments on Taiwan Supreme Court 94 Tai Shang Zi No. 1688 Judgment' (2006) 87 Taiwan LJ 249, 252 (林更盛，定型化離職後競業禁止約款的審查ー評最高法院九四年台上字第一六八八號判決 (2006) 台灣本土法學雜誌第 87 期第頁249，252).

3 the limitations on the period, area, scope of occupational activities, and prospective employers shall not exceed a reasonable range (subparagraph 3); and
4 the employer shall reasonably compensate the employee concerned who does not engage in competing activities for any losses incurred (subparagraph 4).

Moreover, TLSA article 9-1(2) stipulates that the reasonable compensation referred to in TLSA article 9-1(1) shall not include remuneration received by the employee during employment. Then, TLSA article 9-1(4) further requires the non-compete period not to exceed a maximum of two years. If the period is longer than two years, then it must be shortened to two years. Finally, in accordance with TLSA article 9-1(3), any agreement in violation of any of the provisions of TLSA article 9-1(1) will be null and void.

In addition, of the TLSA Enforcement Rules ('Enforcement Rules') articles 7-1, 7-2, and 7-3[26] impose more rigorous restrictions on non-compete agreements. The Enforcement Rules article 7-1 stipulates that a non-compete agreement be made in writing and sets forth the limitations described in TLSA article 9-1(1)(3) and (1)(4). Furthermore, the Enforcement Rules article 7-2 stipulates that 'a reasonable range' described in TLSA article 9-1(1)(3) shall be subject to the following requirements:

1 The limitation on the non-compete period shall not exceed the lifecycle of the trade secrets or technological information that the employer intends to protect, within a maximum of up to two years;
2 the limitation on the non-compete area shall be limited to the area in which the employer's actual business activities take place;
3 the limitation on the scope of non-competition shall be clearly specified and within a scope identical or similar to that of the employee's current occupational activities; and
4 the limitations on the employee's prospective employers within the non-compete period shall be clearly specified and limited to prospective employers whose business activities are identical or similar to and thus compete with those of the employer

The Enforcement Rules article 7-3(1) prescribes that the 'reasonable compensation' referred to in TLSA article 9-1(1)(4) is considered based upon the following concerns:

1 The amount of compensation per month shall be no less than 50% of one month's average wage of the employee at the time of resignation;
2 the amount of compensation shall be sufficient to support the resigned employee during the non-compete period;

26 The TLSA Enforcement Rules were ordained and promulgated by the Ministry of Labour in accordance with TLSA art 85.

3 the amount of compensation shall be equivalent to the loss incurred by the employee in compliance with the non-compete limitations on period, area, scope of occupational activities, and prospective employers; and
4 other matters relevant to the consideration of reasonable compensation criteria

The Enforcement Rules article 7-3(1) does not indicate how to solve the conflicts between these concerns. Nevertheless, since the first concern has a clear standard and has become the most dominant concern in the courts' decisions, an amount of compensation less than that described in the first concern will not be deemed reasonable. The Enforcement Rules article 7-3(2) requires that reasonable compensation shall be paid to the employee in a lump sum upon resignation or on a monthly basis after resignation.

TLSA article 9-1 adopts a four-criteria approach for the purpose of reviewing the validity of non-compete agreements and ensures that compensation for the non-compete obligations of a former employee shall be a prerequisite requirement of a valid and lawful non-compete agreement. Therefore, TLSA article 9-1 clarifies the criteria but has significantly reduced the discretion exercised by Taiwan's courts to determine the validity of non-compete agreements.[27] In 2020, the Taiwan Supreme Court 109 Tai Shang Zi No. 4 Civil Judgment even held that the requirements set forth in TLSA article 9-1 could be considered criteria for determining the fairness and validity of a non-compete agreement under TCC article 247-1, where the employee's resignation came into force before the enactment of TLSA article 9-1. A former employee's competing activities in violation of good faith are only relevant for determining whether a former employee will be held responsible for the damage suffered by the employer and the amount of damages resulting therefrom.[28]

However, although now it seems that TLSA article 9-1 has delineated a clear boundary of valid, effective non-compete agreements, debates about its application and interpretation remain. In the author's view, the three issues discussed in detail below and corresponding proposed revisions to the TSLA article 9-1 are still critical and urgent.

Employers' legitimate business interests

TLSA article 9-1(1)(1) stipulates that for a valid non-compete agreement, the employer must have legitimate business interests that require being protected, but TLSA article 9-1(1)(2) indicates the position or job of the employee is limited to one that entitles the employee to have access to or be able to use the employer's

27 Hsu (n 17) 175.

28 Some scholars argue that the courts in Taiwan should not trespass on legislative discretion and the determination that TLSA art 9-1 does not apply to non-compete agreements entered into before the enactment of TLSA art 9-1: ibid, 182–184.

'trade secrets', and not necessarily including all the employer's legitimate business interests. Such discrepancies between TLSA article 9-1(1)(1) and (1)(2) raise a serious question about whether an employer's legitimate business interests are limited to trade secrets.

Essentially, non-compete agreements consistently interweave with protection of trade secrets. However, the intent, requirements and applicability of TLSA article 9-1 and those of the Taiwan Trade Secret Act still differ. On the one hand, a lawful non-compete agreements with an employee shall not affect the employer's right to prevent misappropriation in accordance with the Taiwan Trade Secret Act. In the event that a trade secret is misappropriated or in danger of misappropriation, and reasonable constraints on a former employee's choice of occupations are necessary to prevent misappropriation, the owner of the trade secret is entitled to prohibit the former employee from working for or providing services to the owner's specific competitor under the Taiwan Trade Secret Act article 11[29] even after expiration of any non-competition period contained in a lawful and valid non-compete agreement.[30]

However, the function of a non-compete agreement may differ from that of the provisions of the Taiwan Trade Secret Act. As mentioned above, even without any explicit provisions or agreements about the confidentiality duty of employees, employees are obliged not to disclose or misappropriate their employers' trade secrets during the term of employment agreements and after expiration thereof, due to their concomitant obligations and post-contract obligations based upon the good faith rule. Even if a former employee engages in business activities identical or similar to that of his or her former employer, it doesn't mean this former employee will definitely disclose or misappropriate the former employer's trade secrets. Therefore, preventing employees from disclosing or misappropriating employers' trade secrets after the expiration of employment is not the only purpose and protection provided by a non-compete agreement.[30] Adoption of a non-compete agreement could reduce the risk of proving a former employee's actual misappropriation or disclosure of the employer's trade secrets, protect the employer's legitimate competitive advantages, and prevent unfair competition or poaching.

Prior to the enactment of TLSA article 9-1, most of the courts in Taiwan ruled that an employer's legitimate business interests may include special client relationships, prevention of malicious poaching, and some non-confidential information that leads to a competitive advantage, such as customer information, wholesale prices, prime cost, reservation price, manufacturing techniques,

29 The Taiwan Trade Secret Act art 11: 'If a trade secret is misappropriated, the injured party may request for the removal of such misappropriation. If there is a likelihood of misappropriation, a prevention may be requested. When requesting for a remedy available under the preceding paragraph, the injured party may request for the destruction or other necessary dispositions of products generated from the misappropriation or items used exclusively in the misappropriation'.

30 See Taiwan Supreme Court 104 Tai Shang Zi No. 1589 Civil Judgment (台灣最高法院104年度台上字第1589號民事判決).

training materials etc.[31] In 2014, the Taiwan Supreme Court 93 Tai Shang Zi No. 1633 Civil Judgment recognised that an employer's legitimate business interests entitled protection by a non-compete agreement are not limited to trade secrets, and the legitimacy of a non-compete agreement to prevent competitor poaching and the preservation of fair competition was acknowledged.[32]

In addition, since TLSA article 9-1 placed reasonable limits on non-compete agreements and required compensation for former employees' non-compete obligations, the employees' rights and interests have been reasonably protected. However, it is unnecessary to strictly exclude employers' legitimate business interests other than trade secrets from protection in non-compete agreements.[33] Therefore, TLSA article 9-1(1)(2) should be revised to include 'legitimate business interests' as the wording in TLSA article 9-1(1)(1), since this revision will eliminate any possible misinterpretations.

Certainly, whether specific techniques, information, knowledge, or client relationships are qualified to be identified as legitimate business interests as prescribed in TLSA article 9-1(1)(1) should be carefully reviewed and determined by the courts in Taiwan. In principle, general knowledge or skills that workers or employees can learn or acquire in the general course of work should not be considered an employer's legitimate business interests. Specialised knowledge or skills that workers or employees can learn or acquire only through employment by special employers constitute employers' legitimate business interests that should be protected by non-compete agreements.[34] Neither an employer's customer lists that can be acquired through the Internet or international trade exhibitions, nor quotations or sale and reservation prices that are not related to cost analyses, but rather only information easily obtained from markets when substitute products enter into markets that trigger price competition meet the minimum standard of trade secrets or legitimate business interests.[35] As for client relationships, when an employer, by investing time, money and resources, has established a long-term, stable relationship with a specific client, and this client relationship has obviously contributed to this employer's success or competitive advantage, it is legitimate to recognise the necessity of this employer's protecting this client relationship through the use of a non-compete agreement.[36] However, if an employer only intends to prevent

31 Wei-Lin Wang, 'Looking into the Practice Problems of Labour Standards Act Article 9–1 in View of Protecting Trade Secrets: Also Comments on Taiwan High Court 105 Zhong Lao Shang Zi No. 54 Civil Judgment and Lao Shang Zi. No. 38 Civil Judgment' (2018) 273 Taiwan LR 227, 235–236. (王偉霖，自營業秘密保護觀點觀察勞基法第九條之一實務問題－兼評臺灣高等法院一○五年度重勞上字第五四號民事判決、一○六年度勞上字第三八號民事判決 (2018) 月旦法學雜誌第 273 期第227頁，235–236).

32 Yen (n 6) 45.

33 Chiu and Liu (n 12) 15–16.

34 Wang (n 31) 202–204.

35 Taiwan Supreme Court 87 Tai Shang Zi. No. 2322 and 104 Tai Shang Zi No. 1654 Civil Judgment (台灣最高法院87年度台上字第2322號與104年台上字第1654號民事判決).

36 Che-Kun Liu and Yu-Fan Chiu, 'Discussion of The Criteria of Legitimate Operating Profit Under the Non-Compete Agreement of Post-Employment: Taking the Customer Relations as an Example' (2020) 297 Taiwan Law Review 70, 82–84 (劉哲鯤、邱羽凡，論勞工離職後競業禁止約定中正當營業利益之保護要件—以客戶關係為例 (2020) 月旦法學雜誌第297期第70頁，82–84); Yen (n 6) 45.

competition, forestall the former employee's approaching prospective clients, or impede the employee's resignation by enacting a non-compete agreement, these concerns could not be viewed as the employer's legitimate business interests.[37]

Reasonable compensation for post-employment non-compete obligations

Reasonable compensation for an employee's post-employment non-compete obligation is a requirement of a legal, effective non-compete agreement under TLSA article 9-1(1)(4). In addition, the Enforcement Rules article 7-3(1) prescribes that the amount of 'reasonable compensation' per month shall be no less than 50% of one month's average wage of the employee upon resignation. The Enforcement Rules article 7-3(2) requires that the reasonable compensation shall be paid to the employee in a lump sum upon resignation or on a monthly basis after resignation.

Even though it is widely acknowledged that reasonable compensation is a requisite for a lawful, valid non-compete agreement under TLSA article 9-1, requiring employers to pay reasonable compensation only after expiration of employment is still very controversial. Literally termed as 'remuneration' in the TSLA article 9-1(2), it may be paid in cash or in kind. Accordingly, TLSA article 9-1(2) and the Enforcement Rules article 7-3(2) have left virtually no wiggle room for an employer to pay reasonable compensation as remuneration for an employee's non-compete obligation during the term of the employment.[38] Therefore, some critics have asserted that an employer may be inclined to abandon the policy of giving an employee a generous remuneration, bonuses, options or shares within the term of employment in consideration of the cost arising from compensation for the employee's non-compete obligations.[39]

In addition, according to the Enforcement Rules article 7-3(1), the minimum reasonable compensation per month shall be no less than 50% of one month's average wage. The wages defined in TLSA article 2(1)(3) refer to remunerations that workers receive for services rendered, including wages, salaries and bonuses, allowances, and any other regular payments that may be computed on an hourly, daily, monthly, or piece-rate basis, as well as payable in cash or in kind. Hence, if a payment is made by an employer irregularly as this employer's unilateral effort to improve an employee's life or to encourage him or her, such payment shall be neither regarded as a consideration for the employee's service rendered, nor as a part of his or her wages.[40] Predictably, the meaning of a 'wage' has been the hotspot of many employment lawsuits since it is always a

37 Lin (n 8) 163.

38 Yen (n 6) 47.

39 Hsu (n 17) 175.

40 Taiwan Supreme Court 107 Tai Shang Zi No. 1709 Civil Judgment, 106 Tai Shang Zi No. 2679 Civil Judgment, 106 Tai Shang Zi No. 1215 Civil Judgment, and 104 Tai Shang Zi No. 728 Civil Judgment (台灣最高法院107年度台上字第1709號、106年台上字第2679號民事判決、106年台上字第1215號民事判決、104年台上字第728號民事判決).

contentious matter to distinguish between a regular payment and a favour in each individual case. The problem becomes more complicated in particular since a non-compete agreement without reasonable compensation is considered null and void under TLSA article 9-1(1)(4) and 9-1(3). Consequently, it would be wiser for the courts in Taiwan to acknowledge in principle the agreed calculation of one month's average wage of the employee upon resignation in the non-compete agreement and simultaneously consider whether the agreed amount of compensation is sufficient to support the employee during the non-compete period and equivalent to the loss incurred by the employee in accordance with the Enforcement Rules article 7-3(1)(2) and 7-3(1)(3).

The blue pencil rule and TLSA article 9-1(3)

Prior to the enactment of TLSA article 9 - 1 in 2015, a few courts in Taiwan ruled that, under the exception set forth in TCC article 111,[41] if any part of a non-compete agreement is considered unreasonable, the other part thereof could be still valid and enforceable, except for the unreasonable part thereof. For example, the Taiwan Supreme Court 103 Tai Shang Zi No. 2215 Civil Judgment supported the premise that the non-compete agreement in that case was read down to exclude the limitations therein that were not reasonable. Some scholars strongly criticised both the courts' application of TCC article 111 and the adoption of the blue pencil rule. They argued that a non-compete agreement with unreasonable limitations should be considered null and void as a whole. The adoption of the blue pencil rule may tempt employers, who would have stronger bargaining power, to seek to expand the limitations on periods, areas, scopes of occupational activities, or prospective employers in their drafts of non-compete agreements because the courts in Taiwan would be responsible for delineating the reasonable boundaries of non-compete agreements.[42]

In accordance with TLSA article 9-1(3), any non-compete agreement that does not meet one of the four requirements set forth in TLSA article 9-1(1) is deemed null and void. Hence, some pundits have proposed that the whole of a non-compete agreement shall be null and void when any limitation on the period, area, scope of occupational activities, or prospective employers in a non-compete agreement exceeds a reasonable range. Some observers have further pointed out that TLSA article 9-1(3) may induce the courts in Taiwan to interpret and apply TLSA article 9-1 strictly, which would in turn increase the likelihood that the courts nullify non-compete agreements.[43] For example, the Taiwan High Court 106 Lao Shang Zi. No. 38 Civil Judgment held that the limitation on prospective employers in the

41 TCC art 111 states: 'If a part of a juridical act is void, the whole juridical act is void; however, if the juridical act could exclude the void part, the other part could remain valid'.

42 Geng-Schenq Lin, 'On the Excessive Limitation of the Non-Compete Clause' (2009) 5 Chung-Hsing ULR 77–112 (林更盛，限制過當的離職後競業禁止約款的效力 (2009) 興大法學第5期 77–112).

43 Wang (n 31) 243–244.

non-compete agreement corresponded to and intertwined with the compensation, penalty, and the former employee's non-compete obligation therein. Therefore, to preserve part of a non-compete agreement would violate the purpose of this agreement, the exception TCC article 111 should not apply in this case.

Nevertheless, the resolution of the 107 Legal Conference of Taiwan High Court and Its Branches, Civil Proposals No. 7 ('The Resolution of 107 Legal Conference') stated that if the limitations on the period, area, scope, and competing methods set forth in a non-compete agreement are beyond a reasonable range under social norms and business practices, only the unreasonable part violates TLSA article 9-1(1)(3) and shall then be null and void. However, the reasonable part thereof shall be valid since this part will not endanger workers' right to work and could secure the employer's business interests in terms of promotion of economic development.

TLSA article 9-1 is an exception to the *pacta sunt servanda* rule. The Resolution of 107 Legal Conference, with the existence of reasonable compensation as a precondition, took the stance that all interests involved could be balanced and the *pacta sunt servanda* rule simultaneously respected without unduly jeopardising workers' right to work. According to TLSA article 9-1(1)(4), reasonable compensation is a prerequisite for a valid non-compete compensation, and the Enforcement Rules article 7-3 has set minimum standards for reasonable compensation. Therefore, the requirements related to reasonable compensation contain effective and relatively clear standards by which to determine the validity of non-compete agreements and protect employers' interests and rights. Nevertheless, the reasonableness of the limitations on the period, area, scope of occupational activities and prospective employers in a non-compete agreement may vary during a long term of employment due to the likelihood of an unexpected change in the employer's line of business or the employee's status or position. In the event that the red pencil rule is adopted to interpret the TSLA article 9-1(1)(3), i.e. any unreasonable part of limitations in a non-compete agreement leads to the invalidity of the entire non-compete agreement, this approach will overly weaken the *pacta sunt servanda* rule and increase the likelihood that a non-compete agreement is unnecessarily declared null and void under TLSA article 9-1(3).

Hence, if an employer has the legitimate business interests that require protection, the employee has access to or uses trade secrets due to his or her position or job tasks, and the employer has promised to or has reasonably compensated the employee according to the non-compete agreement, then only any unreasonable parts of the limitations on the period, areas, scopes, and ways in which the non-compete agreement is implemented will be invalidated by reference to TCC article 111 and TLSA article 9-1(1)(3) combined with TLSA article 9-1(3). This approach of reading down excessive agreements will allow courts in Taiwan to properly balance both employer and employee interests based on all the circumstances during and after the period of employment ends. The adoption of the blue pencil rule also helps to avoid thorny problems that could arise from nullifying the entire non-compete agreement, such as whether the employee is entitled to receive compensation for his or her non-compete obligations under the non-compete agreement until the court decides on the validity of the non-compete agreement, or if the employee must return the received compensation in accordance with TCC article 113[44] or 179[45] if the entire non-compete agreement is declared null and void.

Notwithstanding the foregoing, it would be welcome if TLSA article 9-1(1)(3) was amended to make clearer that the blue pencil rule applies. This could occur by adding an exception or a proviso to the provision that if any part of the limitations described in TLSA article 9-1(1)(3) is found to be unreasonable in any respect, a court may limit the agreement to render it reasonable in light of the circumstances.[46]

Conclusions

The courts in Taiwan have been facing the challenges of non-compete agreements since 1980s. Initially, the Taiwan Supreme Court showed particular respect to freedom of contract and the *pacta sunt servanda* rule when reviewing non-compete agreements. Then, the Taiwan Supreme Court required a valid non-compete agreement to be reasonable. The criteria for reviewing agreements developed by lower courts and the application of TCC article 247-1 helped the Taiwan Supreme Court elaborate on the reasoning related to determining the validity of non-compete agreements. The enactment of TLSA article 9-1 in 2015 clarified these criteria but reduced the discretion of Taiwan's courts significantly. However, an overly stringent construction and application of TLSA article 9-1 may unnecessarily weaken the *pacta sunt servanda* rule and disregard the legitimate function of non-compete agreements. For the purpose of better balancing the interests of both employers and employees, it would also be helpful to amend TLSA article 9-1, including the explicit adoption of the blue pencil rule.

44 TCC art 113 states: 'When a party who made a void juridical act knew or might have known that it was void, he shall be liable to bring the status of matters to their original condition or to compensate for any injury arising therefrom'.

45 TCC art 179 states: 'A person who acquires interests without any legal grounds and prejudice toward the other party shall be bound to return it. The same rule shall be applied if a legal ground existed originally but subsequently disappeared'.

46 The similar suggestion about adding an exception in TLSA art 9-1(1)(3), see Wang (n 31) 244.

10 *Pacta sunt servanda* and the consumer's right of withdrawal

*Geraint Howells**

Rise of the right of withdrawal in Europe

Pacta sunt servanda is a cornerstone of contract law. Parties should be bound to the deal struck otherwise the value of the agreement is undermined. It sounds like it should be (and is) a logical foundation of the private law of contracts. Therefore, it is quite remarkable how easily, in the context of consumer contracts, EU law has weakened such a foundational principle.[1] Numerous EU directives have given the consumer the right to withdraw from the contract within a set period without having to give a reason and even if the goods or services fully conform with the contract. The terms 'right of withdrawal' and 'right of cancellation' tend in this context to be used interchangeably. UK law, which knew of such rights even before joining the EU, prefers to call it a right to cancel, whereas EU law prefers to describe it as a right of withdrawal.[2] They amount in essence to the same thing, but different terminology has been useful to allow both to be distinguished when the UK and EU rights existed in parallel but were not identical.[3]

The contract only becomes fully irrevocable via the right of withdrawal once the withdrawal period has passed. The consumer remains able to accept goods within the withdrawal period without that affecting their right to withdraw. Contracts can have legal effects during that period; for example, exceptions to the right to withdrawal apply where goods and services are supplied in an emergency situation or the seal is broken on audio-visual materials.[4] Therefore it seems like the contract must have been formed before the withdrawal period commenced.

* The author would like to thank Jonathon Watson for his help in preparing this chapter.

1 See also Horst Eidenmüller, 'Why Withdrawal Rights?' (2011) 1 ERCL 1, 2.

2 See in this respect the differing terminology in the UK Consumer Contracts (Information, Cancellation and Additional Charges) Regulations 2013 SI 2013/3134 and in the EU Directive 2011/83/EU of the European Parliament and of the Council of 25 October 2011 on consumer rights [2011] OJ L304/64 ('Consumer Rights Directive'). For a broader comparison, see Christian Twigg-Flesner, Reiner Schulze and Jonathon Watson, 'Protecting rational choice: information and the right of withdrawal' in Geraint Howells, Iain Ramsay and Thomas Wilhelmsson (eds), *Handbook of Research on International Consumer Law* (2nd ed, Edward Elgar, 2018) 111, 127–128.

3 See the Consumer Credit Act 1974, ss 66 et seq.

4 Consumer Rights Directive (n 2) art 16.

DOI: 10.4324/9781003358305-12

The right of withdrawal imposes conditions for the unravelling of the concluded contract. It is a clear breach of the *pacta sunt servanda* principle.

The first EU right of withdrawal for consumers was granted in the Doorstep Selling Directive in 1985.[5] At the other extreme of selling methods, the EU granted a right of withdrawal for distance selling for consumer goods and services in general in 1997[6] and for financial services in 2002.[7] The general rights of withdrawal based on selling methods were rationalised in the Consumer Rights Directive in 2011.[8] Other examples of such rights are found in the Life Assurance Directive 1990[9], due to the complexity and importance of the transaction, and for timeshares, where they can be seen as part of a project to clean up the image of the sector.[10]

The Consumer Rights Directive sought to bring some order to the right of withdrawal in EU law as the rules had been developed in a haphazard patchwork manner.[11] It created a common framework for distance and off-premises contracts, the latter including doorstep selling. It introduced a 14-day cooling-off period that is becoming the norm across other areas of the consumer *acquis*.[12] The 14-day period runs from the signing of the contract in the case of services or from delivery where the contract is for goods.[13] Withdrawal can be effected by making a clear statement to that effect or by using the form that must be provided.[14] It is effective when sent

5 Council Directive 85/577/EEC of 20 December 1985 to protect the consumer in respect of contracts negotiated away from business premises [1985] OJ L372/31.

6 Directive 97/7/EC of the European Parliament and of the Council of 20 May 1997 on the protection of consumers in respect of distance contracts [1997] OJ L144/19. As an aside it is interesting to remember that this Directive was introduced before advent of internet selling.

7 Directive 2002/65/EC of the European Parliament and of the Council of 23 September 2002 concerning the distance marketing of consumer financial services [2002] OJ L271/16 ('Distance Marketing of Financial Services Directive').

8 See n 2.

9 Council Directive 90/619/EEC of 8 November 1990 on the coordination of laws, regulations and administrative provisions relating to direct life assurance [1990] OJ L330/50.

10 Directive 94/47/EC of the European Parliament and the Council of 26 October 1994 on the protection of purchasers in respect of certain aspects of contracts relating to the purchase of the right to use immovable properties on a timeshare basis [1994] OJ L280/83 ('Timeshare Directive'); repealed by Directive 2008/122/EC of the European Parliament and of the Council of 14 January 2009 on the protection of consumers in respect of certain aspects of timeshare, long-term holiday product, resale and exchange contracts [2009] OJ L33/10.

11 For detail see Elizabeth Hall, Geraint Howells and Jonathon Watson, 'The Consumer Rights Directive – An Assessment of its Contribution to the Development of European Consumer Contract Law' (2012) 8 ERCL 139.

12 Consumer Rights Directive (n 2) art 9(2); Distance Marketing of Financial Services Directive (n 7) art 6(1); Timeshare Directive (n 10) art 6(1); Directive 2008/48/EC of the European Parliament and of the Council of 23 April 2008 on credit agreements for consumers [2008] OJ L133/66 ('Consumer Credit Directive') art 14(1).

13 Consumer Rights Directive (n 2) art 9(2); Distance Marketing of Financial Services Directive (n 7) art 6(1); Timeshare Directive (n 10) art 6(2); Consumer Credit Directive (ibid) art 14(1).

14 Consumer Rights Directive (n 2) art 11; art 6(1); Timeshare Directive (n 10) art 7.

even if only received after the 14-day period has expired.[15] The consumer should be reimbursed the price paid under the contract, including delivery costs (except any premium delivery service).[16] A consumer who returns goods after withdrawing normally bears the costs of return, unless the trader agrees to collect them, or the goods were given immediately in an off-premises contract and cannot be returned by post or the trader failed to provide information concerning the costs of returning goods.[17]

The trader can claim compensation for the diminution in value resulting from the consumer handling of the goods beyond what is necessary to establish the nature, characteristics and functioning of the goods.[18] This is said to mean the consumer should only use the goods as they would be allowed to in a shop.[19] This makes sense for some products such as the example in the recital of garments where the consumer should only be able to try them on and not wear them. However, for other products the consumer may naturally test their functioning to an extent beyond allowed in the shop.[20] For example, they might use an appliance. If it proves unsuitable then it would seem unfair to impose a reduction in the sum reimbursed. In many cases, it will be hard in any event to prove the extent to which the consumer has used the products.

One of the thorny issues under the old *acquis* was the extent to which the withdrawal period was extended for failure to properly inform the consumer. The case law held that until the information rules were fulfilled the right of withdrawal under the Doorstep Selling Directive continued to exist.[21] This was potentially an indefinite extension. The Consumer Rights Directive tried to scale this back by imposing a maximum 12-month extension. However, it might have been too restrictive to allow this extension only where there had been a failure to inform of the right of withdrawal. Failure to disclose other material facts may cause the consumer not to withdraw within the 14-day period where they would have done so had all required information been given. The new solution can be seen as a practical compromise, but there is potential for abuse if the consumer is not directed to onerous terms until the withdrawal period has expired. Rules on incorporation of terms will have to be invoked to achieve fair outcomes.

The right of withdrawal is a very powerful weapon in the hands of the consumer. It can be exercised without the need to give reasons. Indeed, you can

15 Consumer Rights Directive (n 2) art 11(2); Consumer Credit Directive (n 12) art 14(3). See also Reiner Schulze and Fryderyk Zoll, *European Contract Law* (3rd ed, Nomos 2021) 166.
16 Consumer Rights Directive (n 2) art 14(1); Distance Marketing of Financial Services Directive (n 7) art 7(4).
17 Consumer Rights Directive (n 2) art 14(1).
18 Consumer Rights Directive (n 2) art 14(2).
19 ibid, Recital 47.
20 ibid.
21 Case C-481/99 *Heininger v Bayerische Hypo- und Vereinsbank AG* ECLI:EU:C:2001:684; Case C-350/03 *Schulte v Deutsche Bausparkasse Badenia* AG ECLI:EU:C:2005:637; Case C-350/03 *Crailsheimer Volksbank eG v Conrads* ECLI:EU:C:2005:640; cf Case C-412/06 *Hamilton v Volksbank Filder eG* ECLI:EU:C:2008:215.

even use the right if you view goods in the showroom, but then return home and order the same goods online. A German consumer who subsequently found the goods cheaper even used the threat of exercising the right of withdrawal to renegotiate the price.[22] The right has also been used to circumvent a trader's resistance to repairing defective goods.[23] Therefore, the granting of such strong rights has been balanced with the interest of traders by providing exclusions for situations where it would be unfair to traders to grant such a right: where a consumer gives express prior consent to the supply of services or digital services and acknowledges that the right of withdrawal will be lost upon supply; financial services and alcohol where prices fluctuate; personalised goods; perishable goods; emergency services; papers, magazines etc.; auctions; travel, accommodation and leisure services for specific dates; sealed goods when unsealed (that are not suitable for return due to health protection or hygiene reasons or in the case of audio or video recordings and software) and goods that have become inseparably mixed.[24] These exemptions have generated some jurisprudence from the Court of Justice of the European Union ('CJEU'). In *easyCar*,[25] contrary to the Opinion of Advocate General Stix-Hackl,[26] a car hire contract was held to be excluded from requiring the right as it was considered a transport service under the Distance Selling Directive.[27] In *Möbel Kraft*,[28] a kitchen ordered to specification was exempt even though production of it had not yet started. By contrast in *Slewo*[29] a mattress was not exempt when the protective packaging had been removed as it was not held to be a product that had been sealed for personal hygiene reasons.

Rights of withdrawal in Asia

As a European consumer lawyer, I had become so accustomed to the widespread availability of the right of withdrawal that it came as a shock to discover on moving to Asia in 2014 that such rights were much less common in Asia. However, Asia is not unique in that respect, for such rights are also less well developed in other areas of the world, even in regions such as North America and Australasia, that have a long history of adopting consumer laws.[30] It is, in fact, Europe with its extensive patchwork of rights of withdrawal that is the outlier. Where rights

22 BGH NJW 2016, 1951. The German BGH has also highlighted that in some cases the exercise of a right of withdrawal may be contrary to good faith, BGH NJW 2019, 66.

23 See Case C-489/07 *Pia Messner v Firma Stefan Krüger* ECLI:EU:C:2009:502.

24 Consumer Rights Directive (n 2) art 16. For detail on the exceptions see Jonathon Watson, 'Withdrawal Rights' in Christian Twigg-Flesner (ed), *Research Handbook on EU Consumer and Contract Law* (Edward Elgar, 2016) 241, 253–258.

25 Case C-366/03 *easyCar (UK) Ltd v Office of Fair Trading* ECLI:EU:C:2005:150.

26 ECLI:EU:C:2004:716.

27 Car rental services are now expressly mentioned in Consumer Rights Directive (n 2) art 16.

28 Case C-529/19 *Möbel Kraft GmbH & Co. KG v ML* ECLI:EU:C:2020:846.

29 Case C-681/17 *slewo – schlafen leben wohnen GmbH v Sascha Ledowski* ECLI:EU:C:2019:255.

30 See the comparative comments in Twigg-Flesner, Schulze and Watson (n 2).

of withdrawal exist in Asia they tend to be in the context of doorstep and other forms of direct selling with only isolated instances of the right applying to distance selling.[31] China, South Korea, Taiwan and Thailand have adopted a right of withdrawal which applies to internet sales, and such rights are being proposed in Macau.[32] Japan seeks to develop a nuanced approach by allowing the trader not to offer a right of withdrawal in internet sales, but only if this is made clear to the consumer.[33]

Hong Kong

Hong Kong will be focused upon. This is not only because this project originates in Hong Kong, but also because there have been some interesting debates about introducing the right in that jurisdiction. Currently there are no statutory rights of withdrawal for consumers in Hong Kong. However, there are some voluntary schemes (for instance in relation to insurance, telecommunications, some financial products and where there is direct selling) and some traders (online and offline) have developed their own 'goodwill' returns policies offering exchange, replacement, credit notes or refund.

Discussion of introducing a right of withdrawal originally arose out of the 2010–11 government consultation on the reform of the unfair trading practices law.[34] A proposal was made to introduce cooling-off periods for goods and services contracts of more than six months duration and for contracts concluded during unsolicited visits to the consumer's home.[35] This was not introduced due to opposition from the business community. More recently, the Consumer Council issued 'A Report to Advocate Mandatory Cooling-Off Period in Hong Kong'.[36] It recommended a seven-day cooling off period for off-premises contracts,[37] distance contracts (other than online contracts) and for fitness centres, beauty treatments, and timeshares. The exclusion of online transactions under the latest proposal is surprising given that is one of the most important everyday uses of the EU right. It is all the more curious because in the past the Consumer Council had supported such a right for online trade in order to enhance consumer confidence.[38] This change of heart is explained as being based on consumer

31 See Meika Atkins and Eileen Webb, 'Information Duties and the Right to Withdrawal' in Geraint Howells and others (eds), *Consumer Protection in Asia* (Hart, 2022).

32 See the national reports in Howells and others, ibid.

33 Hisakazu Hirose, Karl-Friedrich Lenz and Shiraishi Tadashi, 'Japan' in Howells and others (n 31).

34 Commerce and Economic Development Bureau (Hong Kong), Commerce, Industry and Tourism Branch, 'Public Consultation Paper on Legislation to Enhance Protection for Consumers Against Unfair Trade Practices' (15 July 2010).

35 Consumer Council (Hong Kong), 'Report on Public Consultation Paper on Legislation to Enhance Protection for Consumers Against Unfair Trade Practice' (2011).

36 Consumer Council (Hong Kong), 'A Report to Advocate Mandatory Cooling-off Period in Hong Kong' (April 2018).

37 This is another term for a cancellation or withdrawal period.

38 Consumer Council (2011) (n 35) viii.

satisfaction with online shopping, the competitive market and small margins that may be threatened by the granting a cooling-off period as well as problems of defining online shopping and legal difficulties arising from cross-border transactions. These reasons do not seem very compelling as European online businesses cope perfectly well with these rules. In any event, such contractual rights are commonly found in voluntary codes or provided due to company policy. The lack of knowledge about the quality of online goods would seem to be a reason why consumers should be granted protection. If there is a view that consumers should bear the risk in low value transactions, this could be addressed by a tailored exemption. However, general consumer law would continue to apply even to low value goods. The Hong Kong government has recently signalled plans to introduce the right of withdrawal for fitness and beauty services where pre-paid plans are entered into for more than HKD 3,000 (around GBP300). This is in response to some very high-profile cases involving poor commercial practices in the Hong Kong fitness and beauty industry.[39] The discussion below about the value of the right and also criticisms about it should be very relevant for Hong Kong and other Asian countries. It is also important for the EU to reflect on whether its law in this area strikes the right balance.

Rationales for providing a right of withdrawal

The classic rationale for providing a right of withdrawal is to counter aggressive selling practices. The image of the pushy doorstep seller taking advantage of the surprised consumer's natural desire to be polite to visitors in their own home lay behind the first European right of withdrawal adopted in the context of doorstep selling.[40] This element of surprise is also relevant to some forms of distance selling, such as telephone marketing that can catch the unwary consumer and involve skilled sellers aggressively marketing goods. The granting of a right of withdrawal for timeshares was also a response to high-pressure selling techniques. It is also an example of how the introduction of a consumer protection measure can assist an industry's efforts to improve its image. Another rationale for providing the right of withdrawal addresses a different set of concerns and relates to redressing the asymmetry of information between seller and consumer. This is particularly acute when buying goods at a distance without the ability to inspect them. It is hard to tell the quality of materials or their build at a distance, and even colours can appear very different in reality rather than when pixelated. In this sense the right of withdrawal can be viewed as a corollary of the EU's policy of providing

39 Chris Lau, 'Hong Kong Chief Executive Eooks to Improve Consumer Protection In Wake of California Fitness Collapse' (*SCMP*, 14 July 2016) <www.scmp.com/news/hong-kong/law-crime/article/1989868/hong-kong-chief-executive-looks-improve-consumer-protection> accessed 27 April 2022; 'Too much chaos in the beauty industry' (*orientaldaily.on.cc*, in Chinese); see Mateja Durovic, Geraint Howells and André Janssen, 'Hong Kong' in Howells and others (n 31).

40 European Commission, 'Proposal for a Council Directive to protect the consumer in respect of contracts which have been negotiated away from business premises' COM(76) 544. See Doorstep Selling Directive (n 5) art 5.

consumers with more information to make better informed choices.[41] This problem can be exacerbated when the consumer is caught by surprise by a trader making an offer in situations where situational monopolies are created so the consumer is forced to make a decision with limited information about any alternatives.

There are in truth several motivations for providing rights of withdrawal in the various settings. The utility of the right also varies depending on the nature of the goods and services. At times the complexity of a product and its importance to the consumer seems to be the justification for the right, as in the case of life assurance. However, it is with respect to these types of credence goods and services that the right of withdrawal does not work well for it is unlikely the consumer can make any better-informed decision within the withdrawal period than at the time of contracting. What is probably needed in such circumstances are means for the consumer to exit the contract post-contractually where the contract is long term. The right of withdrawal works well for search goods where the consumer needs to find out if the goods meet his or her needs. For some search elements the right of withdrawal may seem superfluous as the consumer could identify them immediately from the information provided even without being physically present, others may only be discoverable when the consumer has the goods in his or her possession. The right is perhaps best suited to allow the consumer to assess experience goods, but the limitation on the testing of goods, before compensation is payable, to the extent they could be tested in a shop[42] means that goods can only be experienced to a certain degree. You would not, for instance, try out a vacuum cleaner in a shop, but if you used it at home and decided it was not appropriate within the first 14 days compensation due for the use might be payable. This rule may inhibit some consumers from exercising the right of withdrawal, but equally may be of little use to businesses for they will find it hard to establish evidence of the extent of use.[43]

Critique of the right of withdrawal

The right of withdrawal is welcomed by many consumer activists as a tool to allow the consumer to take action where they regret a purchase. It can be used to redress aggressive practices by traders and also helps ensure contracts meet consumers' needs. It can be seen as particularly valuable as it is a self-help remedy. The consumer can simply invoke the right without the need to go to court, though that may be necessary if the trader refuses to refund money, but depending on the payment system used, chargeback systems may assist the consumer in seeking reimbursement where a trader is uncooperative.

41 See Schulze and Zoll (n 15) 159–160; Twigg-Flesner, Schulze and Watson (n 2) 124–126; Watson (n 24) 242–245.

42 Consumer Rights Directive (n 2) Recital 47. See in this respect *Messner* (n 23) [29].

43 See the comments by Advocate General Trstenjak in Case C-489/07 *Pia Messner v Firma Stefan Krüger* ECLI:EU:U:2009:98, [36], [107]–[108].

However, the value of the right of withdrawal has also been questioned. Take up of the right has at times been relatively limited and probably consumers make use of the right more often when it is granted under a commercial policy. There are various factors for this. Consumers may be unwilling to challenge traders. This is most likely to be the case at both ends of the selling tactics continuum: both where traders have been aggressive so consumers may not feel confident dealing with them and where companies have used sales staff who become 'fictive friends' whom the consumers do not want to let down by withdrawing their custom. Psychologically, consumers may even find it hard to admit they made a mistake. Most people like to believe their purchasing choices were good. Moreover, despite the information requirements, consumers may not be aware of the right. Equally, they may be uncertain of how to assert the right, even if this is assisted by providing a withdrawal form, as required.[44] The complexity of the law may put people off. It has spawned a surprising number of cases before the CJEU.[45] Recent reforms at the EU level are helping to make the law simpler, such as more standardisation of the withdrawal period, but uncertainty about practicalities such as whether there will be any deduction for use of the goods is another factor that might make consumers hesitate before invoking the right.[46] For many consumer goods of low value, even the limited effort needed to exercise the right of withdrawal may simply deter them from exercising their rights, particularly where there are costs associated with returning the goods. These criticisms question the effectiveness of the right of withdrawal. Another set of criticisms challenge the appropriateness of the right of withdrawal, at least its current form.

In Europe, one does not commonly hear direct criticism that the right of withdrawal breaches the principle of *pacta sunt servanda*.[47] Doubtless some free-market scholars and lawyers do think that and would prefer a more liberal market-based approach. Most though probably accept consumer protection justifies some limited inroads into the principle. The argument that the right of withdrawal makes it difficult for businesses to plan as contracts can be unravelled is sometimes raised, but is not very strong given the limited time the right is available for (if information duties are complied with) and evidence of at best moderate take-up on the right. The image of consumers abusing their right to withdraw is often raised,[48] but there seems to be no strong empirical evidence to demonstrate that abuse is widespread. It has been questioned whether the rationales justifying the right apply in all cases where the right is granted.[49] For instance, some search goods purchased over the internet may not need such a right as the consumer knew exactly what

44 Consumer Rights Directive (n 2) Annex I B; Timeshare Directive (n 10) Annex V.

45 On case law, see Watson (n 24) 249–250.

46 *Messner* (n 23).

47 See Twigg-Flesner, Schulze and Watson (n 2) 124 with further references, explaining that the right of withdrawal restricts the principle of *pacta sunt servanda* but also protects freedom of contract.

48 *Messner* (n 23). See also Watson (n 24) 247 referring to the practice of blocking the accounts of consumers who exercise the right of withdrawal too frequently when contracting with the trader.

49 Eidenmüller (n 1) 7 et seq.

they were getting and was under no pressure. However, a counterargument is that consumer law needs to be kept simple and introducing exceptions will make the law unduly complex. For these types of goods purchased in such circumstances it is in fact less likely the consumer will exercise their right of withdrawal as their expectations will be met. Any suggestion that the right will be exercised so often that it might affect trade, especially in low value goods, as noted by the Hong Kong Consumer Council in the context of e-commerce,[50] could be met by excluding items below a certain price.

In recent times the right of withdrawal has faced two novel and engaging critiques. One derives from law and economics and the ability of data science to produce more efficient legal solutions. The right of withdrawal is in effect an insurance. The costs associated with granting it (compliance costs) and resulting from its use by consumers have to be factored into the price of goods and services.[51] It is argued that not all consumers want to have to pay for this protection and that developments in data science mean it is not necessary for them to have more protection than they want to pay for forced upon them. Personalised law, it is argued, unlocks the potential for the law to be aligned with the preferences of consumers. Another challenge comes from the environmental lobby that claims the right of withdrawal can lead to waste and excessive transportation of goods. It is these two modern challenges that will be focused on in the remainder of the essay.

Personalising the right of withdrawal

The right of withdrawal is therefore under challenge from two of the most significant research areas of our time: data and environmental sustainability. The possible implications of big data and machine learning on the structure of any right of withdrawal will be discussed first.

Each consumer will have their own appetite for risk when purchasing goods and services. Equally, we all have a sense of the extent of our own ability to protect ourselves from risk by making informed decisions in the marketplace. The right of withdrawal mitigates the risk of making a bad decision, but at a price. Consider, for instance, an area where there is a marketplace for the right of withdrawal, such as hotel bookings. Typically, consumers can choose to book a non-refundable room or have the right to cancel for which there is often, but not always, a charge. Consumers have to assess how much the right is worth to them. That may be difficult to assess. It may be that this right is more valuable to some consumers than others. Those whose plans are subject to change will find the right to cancel most valuable and would therefore be more likely to opt to pay for such a right. That exposes the adverse selection problem inherent in an optional right of withdrawal: it is more valuable and hence more likely to be purchased

50 *Consumer Council (Hong Kong)* (n 36) 59.

51 Georg Borges and Bernd Irlenbusch, 'Fairness Crowded Out by Law: An Experimental Study on Withdrawal Rights' (2007) 163 Journal of Institutional and Theoretical Economics 84, 100.

by those who are most likely to use it. This in turn forces up the price at which the right can be offered. The statutory rights of withdrawal are mandatory. It is a cost imposed on all businesses, which is therefore spread across all consumers. Of course, in some way the cost of the right will need to be factored into the price paid by consumers. However, as it applies to every unit the price impact is likely to be limited.

Nevertheless, it could be argued that not all consumers will want the right or, at least, not all would want it with the same characteristics as required by law.[52] For instance, some may prefer a shorter withdrawal period if the price was reduced. One could imagine a range of possible choices offering different levels of protection. In this age of mass data and machine learning we arguably have enough information about individuals to apply a withdrawal right (with associated costs) correlated to each person's needs.[53] Indeed the appetite for a right of withdrawal might vary depending on context. People may take different views on the need when purchasing over the internet, on the doorstep or when buying a timeshare. Artificial intelligence (AI) machine learning technology might even be able to discover our true preferences for such rights better than we can articulate them ourselves.

However, there are barriers and concerns about the personalisation of the right of withdrawal in this manner. It assumes consumers are able properly to calculate the value of the right of withdrawal, but consumers may not know how to value their consumer rights. It is highly likely that when faced with a higher price they will not see the full value in the right as they will be overly optimistic about the chance that they personally will not need to avail themselves of the right. This is one reason why consumer laws need to be mandatory. Their value is simply not sufficiently appreciated as it is a future benefit that is discounted in comparison to an immediate saving.[54] The argument that this weakness can be remedied by using AI to reveal consumers' true preferences in a manner that is better than consumers know them themselves is fragile. AI has to rely on imperfect, irrational past conduct and decisions of consumers. In any event the adverse selection risk remains as those who are more likely to use the right will select it and this will push up cost. There is therefore only limited risk spreading. In any event the result might be very messy. Consumers might have different preferences for different rights of withdrawal – doorstep, internet, timeshare. Seeking to accommodate all the preferences will create a risk of confusion. Effective enforcement of consumer rules relies upon consumer education, which in turn benefits from there being clear simple rules. Enforcement of the right of withdrawal is likely to become even more problematic if there are no clear rules, but rather variable rules depending on each individual and the different circumstances.

52 Eidenmüller (n 1) 24.

53 Omri Ben-Shahar and Ariel Porat, 'Personalizing Mandatory Rules in Contract Law' (2019) 86 University of Chicago Law Review 255.

54 Kris Kirby and R J Herrnstein, 'Preference Reversals Due to Myopic Discounting of Delayed Reward' (1995) 6 Psychological Science 83.

The same logic of personalisation could be applied to every consumer right – not just the right of withdrawal. This personalisation philosophy would undermine mandatory consumer law and hasten the return to *laissez-faire* market regulation. Some argue the answer is that there should be an optional mandatory consumer law, to protect against consumer law being not too easily wiped out by market forces.[55] But mandatory consumer law reflects a consensus on what the best rules are for society in general. Introducing optionality exposes consumers to the risk that they make the wrong choice about what level of legal protection is desirable. Optionality would increase the cost as the risk is not spread across all consumers. It would reduce the effectiveness of enforcement by introducing complexity. Personalisation of law is an intriguing topic and there may be uses for it particularly in the drafting of commercial contracts. However, even if it could be applied to the right of withdrawal it should not be (assuming, of course, the right of withdrawal is in principle supported). To be accessible and effective, consumer law needs clear, easily understood rules. Personalising the law would make it very complicated for consumers to understand their individual rights and risks them being over optimistic about their (lack of) need for protection.

The environmental challenge

If the data-driven challenge to the right of withdrawal is relatively easy to counter, the environmental concerns perhaps need closer attention. There is certainly something counter-intuitive about promoting a green agenda and at the same time promoting e-commerce where goods are transported great distances and can be returned at the whim of the consumer. Terryn and Van Gool have done a good job of focusing attention on the environmental impact of the right of withdrawal for distance sales.[56] However, it is noteworthy that commercial pressures often drive traders to grant such rights voluntarily. These voluntary rights of withdrawal can offer even more extended rights than the legal requirements. For instance, some of the most egregious examples of consumers ordering multiple items to test at home and then returning the unwanted items are facilitated due to company free returns policies. This goes beyond the rights afforded by law. Even the EU Consumer Rights Directive places the cost of returning the goods normally on the consumer.[57]

However, if you believe in the right of withdrawal, it is hard to find a solution that would reduce waste and yet retain the essence of the right. Reducing the 14-day withdrawal period will probably not greatly affect the use of the right; for, as Terryn and Van Gool note, most rights of withdrawal are exercised quickly.

55 Eidenmüller (n 1) 13; see also Gerhard Wagner, 'Mandatory Contract Law: Functions and Principles in Light of the Proposal for a Directive on Consumer Rights' (2010) 3 Erasmus Law Review 47, 68.

56 Evelyne Terryn and Elias Van Gool, 'The role of European consumer regulation in shaping the environmental impact of e-commerce' (2021) 10 EuCML 89.

57 Consumer Rights Directive (n 2) art 14(1). Note, however, that under Consumer Rights Directive art 13 the trader is to reimburse the costs of delivery.

One might, moreover, conjecture that the longer periods to exercise the right tend to assist some vulnerable consumers whose entry into unwanted contracts may take some time to come to the attention of their family and carers. The move towards an increasingly standardised 14-day period has the positive impact of helping to promote clarity about consumer rights.

Terryn and Van Gool also argue that allowing testing of the functioning of goods allows the goods to be used beyond the degree available in bricks and mortar transactions. But the Recital 47 to the Consumer Rights Directive in fact states that should not be allowed without the consumer being liable for any diminution in value. Probably, in reality the position is that you might be able to test the functioning of some goods in shops, but you are just less likely to do so. If you can test goods out more easily at home why should you not be allowed to check how they work and withdraw from the contract if you are unhappy? In any event imposing legal limits may not be very helpful as the authors themselves concede proving the extent of use will be hard for traders to establish. Barring obvious examples of misuse, such as drinks spilled on clothing, this is a very difficult limitation in practice.

It is possible to restrict the scope of the right. Terryn and Van Gool take aim at the *Slewo* decision and argue that it may have had a different outcome had the environmental impact been taken into account.[58] But that does not seem fair as the exception concerned whether the removal of the cover from the mattress had any impact on personal hygiene such that the goods should not be allowed to be returned. That is an essentially factual decision. If it does not affect personal hygiene there seems no more justification for excluding mattresses than any other product. Should the environmental impact therefore be taken on board in all cases? If so, what weight should be allocated to it versus the value of promoting more informed consumers and allowing them to seek relief from decisions made under pressure?

Broader arguments have also been put forward about amending the right of withdrawal to reduce its negative environmental impact, but many of these would take the heart out of the right.[59] Requiring there to be justification for invoking the right, such as a lack of conformity, would radically change the utility of the right. In many countries there is already the right to reject the goods and terminate the contract where they are non-conforming.[60] The additional right of withdrawal might provide some extra protection in countries where the right to cure exists prior to the consumer being able to terminate.[61] However, the rationales for a right of withdrawal are different from the remedies available for non-conformity and it would be unfortunate if the right to withdrawal should be dependent upon there

58 Terryn and Van Gool (n 56) 98.

59 ibid, 97 et seq.

60 Such as in the UK, Consumer Rights Act 2015, ss 20 et seq. (for consumer contracts).

61 As the general approach favoured under EU consumer sales law, see Directive (EU) 2019/771 of the European Parliament and of the Council of 20 May 2019 on certain aspects concerning contracts for the sale of goods [2019] OJ L136/28.

being non-conformity. Making the right of withdrawal optional has already been shown to be problematic as consumers may not properly appreciate the value of the right.[62] Making it a requirement that firms offer such a right but allowing consumers to opt out merely mitigates, but does not remove, the risk that consumers will too easily sign away their rights. Such a voluntary approach could be applied to any consumer right and it might represent a slippery slope back into a *laissez-faire* consumer contract law. Terryn and Van Gool also consider whether the exercise of the right should be made subject to a good faith condition.[63] It is easy to be frustrated with consumers who purchase numerous products merely to have the advantage of selecting at home and disregard the environmental costs of transporting the goods and returning them.[64] However, the boundaries of good faith may be hard to police. In some instances, such as where people have difficulty accessing shops, extensive exercise of withdrawal rights may not be in bad faith. It also seems potentially unfair to invoke a technical legal rule against consumers who may at best know they have the right of withdrawal, but not be aware of caveats concerning having to exercise the right in good faith, or fully comprehend what a good faith requirement would demand. This also seems overly elaborate as, Terryn and Van Gool concede, commercial returns policies are often in any event more generous than the statutory rules.[65] Educating consumers to consider the environmental impact of e-commerce seems a realistic way forward so that they might, for instance, only order goods they are seriously considering purchasing and use green delivery options such as bunching deliveries to avoid unnecessary journeys. Obligations might also be placed on traders to ensure the returned goods are handled in an environmentally sustainable way as there are reports that many returned goods are simply binned.[66]

The future of the right of withdrawal (in Asia, especially Hong Kong)

The contrast is stark between the central role the right of withdrawal has played in the development of the consumer *acquis* and the limited enthusiasm for it outside Europe, including in Asia. Doubtless the inroad into the principle of *pacta sunt servanda* may explain the reluctance of some legal systems to embrace this pro-consumer attribute of contract law. However, Europe has shown clear (if varied) rationales for retaining the right. It now plays an important role in providing confidence to European e-consumers. It is this role in promoting e-commerce that one might expect to be a driver for the right of withdrawal to become more

62 Eidenmüller (n 1); Terryn and Van Gool (n 56) 98.

63 Terryn and Van Gool (n 56) 98.

64 If firms wanted to, they might blacklist customers who abuse these right and there seems to be some evidence that this is happening: see Watson (n 24) 247.

65 Terryn and Van Gool (n 56) 95.

66 See Ajit Niranjan, 'Online retailers are destroying goods but won't say how much ends up as trash' (*Deutsche Welle*, 7 February 2020) <https://p.dw.com/p/3XMp5> accessed 21 February 2022.

widely available in Asia. E-commerce was once viewed as a medium for small businesses to reach mass markets. The reality is often that consumers seek out the security of transacting through familiar names. Using platforms is often the only way small traders can access the market effectively. However, the right of withdrawal does give consumers some security when contracting with unknown traders, especially if using a card that offers a chargeback facility for breach of contract. The right of withdrawal retains value as part of the arsenal of instruments available to consumers.

It is surprising that the right of withdrawal is not more widely seen as part of the regulatory environment in Asia, particularly in relation to promoting internet sales. Hong Kong has challenged the desirability of applying the right to e-commerce. The most legitimate concern – that the right is disproportionate for low value products – could be addressed by applying a threshold test before the right is made available.

Hong Kong seems on the verge of adopting rights of withdrawal for fitness centre and beauty clinic contracts. These do not give rise to environmental concerns as these contracts are for services rather than goods that therefore do not involve transportation. However, they do highlight why the right should be mandatory and not left to individual choice. One can imagine some consumers of these services being overly optimistic about their likelihood of using pre-paid packages to the planned extent.[67] If these rights of withdrawal are introduced as a first tentative step, more such rights may follow.

Conclusion

The right of withdrawal is certainly a complex legal tool. It is interesting that the tenor of the European debate ebbs and flows between fears consumers will not make use of it and concerns that it will be overused. There is a need for a review of its effectiveness and such an analysis based on European experience might be useful for discussions about the right globally. The market has embraced the right and it is suggested that statutory rights have a role to play in protecting the vulnerable and promoting confidence in the market, especially with regard to e-commerce and sectors that have at times had a bad reputation such as timeshare and consumer credit. Pressures to adapt it fundamentally due to movement towards personalisation of the law or to respond to green concerns have been shown to be problematic as they would undermine the right. Rights of withdrawal are not, however, a panacea for all consumer problems and need to form part of a holistic consumer protection policy. In this important area of market law, consumer protection has to-date prevailed over the doctrine of *pacta sunt servanda*.

67 Cf *OFT v Ashbourne Management Services Ltd* [2011] EWHC 1237 (Ch).

11 Contract enforcement during the Global Financial Crisis

Lessons for the coming tsunami

Kingsley Ong

'That which has been *is* what will be,
That which is done *is* what will be done,
And there is nothing new under the sun.'
— Ecclesiastes 1:9

A Introduction[1]

In any financial crisis, there will always be two competing groups of concerned parties. The first group will be worried and want to be reassured that their contracts are enforceable so that they can recover their money or assets. The second group will be desperate to exit their contractual obligations because they have difficulties to perform.

In the 2008 global financial crisis, I was counsel to and represented, among others, the Hong Kong liquidators of Lehman Brothers and MF Global. In this paper, I share seven lessons from my experience in dealing with contract enforcement during the global financial crisis.

1 The law is stated as at 17 September 2022. All websites were last accessed on this date.

DOI: 10.4324/9781003358305-13

B Seven lessons

I Lesson 1: Financial contracts are complicated, mistakes can be very costly

In 2002, the legendary investor Warren Buffet warned that derivatives (a type of complex financial contracts)[2] were 'financial weapons of mass destruction'.[3] Warren Buffet cited their volatility, leverage, opaqueness, potential to 'exacerbate trouble' due to 'pile-on effect'[4] from margin call provisions, potential to cause a 'daisy-chain risk'.[5] Financial contracts can indeed be complicated, and mistakes can be very costly as the following two examples show.

First, complex financial contracts, namely derivatives and securitisations, were blamed to have caused the 2008 global financial crisis.[6] During that time, the amount of outstanding over-the-counter (OTC) derivative trades in the market had become so huge that a crisis in the derivatives markets could easily cause a crash and result in a run among investors in the primary markets.[7]

Second, the Ohio case of *AEP Energy Services, Inc. v Bank of Montreal* (S.D. OH) provides another example of the volatility of derivative contracts. In that

2 Derivatives are financial contracts whose value is derived from the underlying or 'notional value' of the referenced asset (e.g. currencies, shares, commodities, etc). These financial instruments are usually highly leveraged and volatile, subject to huge profits (or losses) in the blink of an eye. Prior to the 2008 global financial crisis, derivatives were relatively unregulated. While derivatives exhibit certain characteristics that are similar to heavily regulated industries like insurance or gambling, there were differences. For example, in 1997, the International Swaps and Derivatives Association (ISDA) obtained a legal opinion from Robin Potts QC distinguishing credit derivatives from insurance (and therefore argued that derivatives were not subject to insurance regulations): see <www.isda.org/a/BNEDE/edcreditderivatives.pdf>. In Hong Kong, section 29 of the Gambling Ordinance (Cap. 148) excludes derivatives contracts. Section 404 of the Securities and Futures Ordinance (Cap. 571) also provides that the Gambling Ordinance does not apply to any transaction or activity regulated by the Securities and Futures Ordinance. For a further background on derivatives, see Kingsley Ong, 'The ISDA Master Agreement: Insolvency Stalemate and End-game Solutions for Hong Kong Liquidators' (2010) 40 Hong Kong Law Journal 337.

3 Berkshire Hathaway Inc, *Annual Report 2002*, p 15. See <www.berkshirehathaway.com/2002ar/2002ar.pdf>.

4 ibid, 14.

5 ibid, 14.

6 Although unsound lending practices are generally considered the primary cause of the global financial crisis, securitisation, collateralised debt obligations (CDOs) and derivatives (e.g. credit default swaps) have been blamed for spreading the losses much further. In 2009, the G20 countries agreed to reforms in the over-the-counter (OTC) derivatives market, including central clearing, reporting of all transactions to trade repositories, higher capital and margin requirements for non-centrally cleared transactions. These reforms were implemented globally through legislative and regulatory measures, such as the Dodd-Frank Wall Street Reform and Consumer Protection Act (Dodd-Frank Act) in USA, and the European Market Infrastructure Regulation (EMIR) in the EU.

7 In June 2008, OTC derivative notional value was estimated to be about US$683 trillion: Stephen Figlewski, Roy C Smith and Ingo Walter, 'Geithner's Plan For Derivatives' *Forbes* (18 May 2009) <www.forbes.com/2009/05/18/geithner-derivatives-plan-opinions-contributors-figlewski.html?sh=fc2e5ab5d316>.

case, the parties entered into a 1992 ISDA Master Agreement[8] to document natural gas commodity derivatives. On 10 February 2003, an 'additional termination event' occurred under the contract due to AEP's credit rating downgrade. On 13 March 2003, based on the mark-to-market value of the contract, AEP was US$49 million in-the-money (meaning AEP was entitled to receive a US$49 million payout from Bank of Montreal (BMO) if the contract were terminated). BMO terminated the contract on 14 March 2003. On 24 March 2003, BMO sought payment of US$34 million from AEP. In other words, there was a swing of US$83 million in the mark-to-market value (from minus US$49 million to plus US$34 million for BMO) in a very short time.

II Lesson 2: Be prepared for radical changes that impact contract enforcement during a financial crisis

1 General

In a time of great systemic financial distress, be prepared for radical changes which can affect contract enforcement. In a financial crisis, politicians will focus on financial stability – the rule of law and certainty of contracts will be of lesser priority. Below are some examples of such 'Black Swan' events, where the 'unthinkable' became reality during a major financial crisis.

2 Restrictions on private ownership of gold

(A) USA

The stock market crash of 28 October 1929 resulted in multiple bank failures and led to the Great Depression – the 'longest, deepest, and most widespread depression of the 20th century'.[9]

Many people started holding physical gold as protection against inflation and deflation. This made it difficult for the US Federal Reserve to maintain the gold standard and stabilise the economy. The Fed was constrained from increasing money supply as a result of gold 'hoarding' by the public, and this was viewed as a threat to the stability of the US financial system.[10]

In 1933, the US Government suddenly decided to nationalise gold. On 5 April 1933, US President Franklin D. Roosevelt signed the US Presidential Executive Order 6102 to 'prohibit the hoarding of gold coin, gold bullion, and gold

8 The ISDA Master Agreements are pre-printed forms and are not amended themselves (save for writing in the names of the parties on the front and signature pages). The counterparties would select certain options and (if desired) modify sections of the relevant Master Agreement in a manually produced Schedule. See Ong (n 2) 338.

9 Charles Duhigg, 'Depression, You Say? Check Those Safety Nets' *The New York Times* (23 March 2008) <www.nytimes.com/2008/03/23/weekinreview/23duhigg.html>.

10 Andrew Hecht, 'The Relationship between Gold and the US Dollar' *The Balance* (18 June 2021), <www.thebalance.com/gold-prices-and-the-u-s-economy-3305656>.

certificates within the continental United States'. The Executive Order further provides that:

> Section 2. All persons are hereby required to deliver on or before May 1, 1933, to a Federal Reserve Bank . . . all gold coin, gold bullion and gold certificates now owned by them or coming into their ownership on or before April 28, 1933.
> Section 3. Until otherwise ordered, any person becoming the owner of any gold coin, gold bullion, or gold certificates after April 28, 1933, shall, within three days after receipt thereof, deliver the same in the manner prescribed in Section 2.[11]

Under the *US Trading with the Enemy Act 1917* (and later amended by the *Emergency Banking Relief Act* of March 9, 1933[12]), violation of the order was punishable by fine up to US$10,000, up to 10 years in prison, or both.

To protect against inflation, during the Great Depression, many business contracts contained 'gold clauses'. Such clauses allowed creditors to have the option to receive payment in gold or gold equivalent. Gold clauses were made unenforceable by the *US Gold Reserve Act* of 1934.

It was only on 31 December 1974 that private ownership of physical gold coins and bars was legalised again in the USA.

(B) AUSTRALIA

The nationalisation of physical gold during the Great Depression is not unique. The Australian *Banking Act 1959*[13] creates a similar regime in Australia. Section 40(2) of the Australian *Banking Act 1959* provides:

> Where the Governor-General is satisfied that *it is expedient so to do, for the protection of the currency or of the public credit of the Commonwealth* the Governor-General may, by Proclamation, declare that this Part, or such of the provisions of this Part as are specified in the Proclamation, shall come into operation, and this Part, or the provisions so specified, shall thereupon come into operation.[14]

Section 42 of the Australian *Banking Act 1959* adds:

> Subject to this Part, a person who has any gold in the person's possession or under the person's control, not being:
>
> (a) gold coins the total value of the gold content of which does not exceed the prescribed amount; or

11 US Executive Order 6102, ss 2 and 3.
12 Text at <https://catalog.archives.gov/id/299829>.
13 Text at <www.legislation.gov.au/Details/C2021C00574>.
14 Emphasis added.

> (b) gold lawfully in the possession of that person for the purpose of being worked or used by that person in connexion with the person's profession or trade;
>
> shall deliver the gold to the Reserve Bank, or as prescribed, within one month after the gold comes into the person's possession or under the person's control or, if the gold is in the person's possession or under the person's control on any date on which this Part comes into operation, within one month after that date.

These provisions allow the Australian Government in time of crisis to seize physical gold from private citizens and to pay compensation in paper currency.[15]

(C) UK

State restrictions on physical gold ownership also occurred in the UK. Under the UK's *Exchange Control (Gold Coins Exemption) Order 1966*,[16] all UK residents were limited to four gold coins minted after 1837. Anything in excess of that had to be surrendered for sale to an authorised dealer at a price authorised by the Bank of England. This regulation was put forward at a time of economic crisis and soaring inflation.[17] The restriction on gold ownership was removed in April 1971, and the Exchange Control Act was repealed completely by Margaret Thatcher's government in 1979, allowing British citizens to freely trade and possess gold bullion again.[18]

3 Currency controls – the 1997 Asian Financial Crisis

In 1995, the daily volume of derivatives-based foreign currency transactions reached US$1.3 trillion.[19] Leveraged currency trading[20] was particularly prevalent in Southeast Asia. On 2 July 1997, institutional derivatives players, notably George Soros, sold off their leveraged holdings of the Thailand currency, resulting in a 38% collapse of the Thai baht and an inflation rate of 65%. This started a run on Asia's financial institutions, leading to the collapse of over 150 Asian banks, securities firms and insurance companies.

15 *Banking Act 1959* (Cth) ss 43–44.

16 S.I., 1966, No. 438; text at <www.legislation.gov.uk/uksi/1975/609/contents/made>.

17 See UK Parliament, House of Commons, Debate 13 June 1966, Hansard vol 729 col. 1173–95 <https://api.parliament.uk/historic-hansard/commons/1966/jun/13/exchange-control-gold-coins>.

18 Joseph P Collins, 'British Abolish Controls On Foreign Currency' *The New York Times* (24 Oct 1979) <www.nytimes.com/1979/10/24/archives/british-abolish-controls-on-foreign-currency-some-outflows-are.html>.

19 Norm Franz, *Money and Wealth in the New Millennium: A Prophetic Guide to the New Word Economic Order* (Ascension Publishing, 2001) 99.

20 This involves the use of borrowed money to invest in forex trading.

In response to the 1997 Asian Financial Crisis, on 1 September 1997, Malaysia suddenly imposed currency controls.[21] Malaysia's unexpected currency controls triggered frustration and force majeure, and caused the termination of many foreign currency contracts linked to the Malaysian ringgit.

4 2008 Global Financial Crisis

The 2008 Global Financial Crisis led to the near-collapse and government rescues of powerful and highly regarded financial institutions like Bear Stearns, Bradford & Bingley, Citigroup, Fannie Mae, Freddie Mac, HBOS/Lloyds Banking Group, IndyMac, Merrill Lynch/Bank of America, Northern Rock, The Royal Bank of Scotland, Wachovia and Washington Mutual. It culminated in the unprecedented collapse of the Lehman Brothers empire and the Icelandic banks (Kaupthing, Glitinir and Landsbanki). The 2008 Global Financial Crisis is probably the worst financial crisis since the 1929 Great Depression.[22]

As a result of the 2008 Global Financial Crisis, governments around the world sought to mitigate any future systemic risks to the global financial markets caused by OTC derivatives. They started to regulate OTC derivatives, forcing such contracts to be centrally cleared and reported to regulators, and forcing non-centrally cleared OTC derivatives to be subject to additional margin requirements.[23] The EU adopted the *European Market Infrastructure Regulation 648/2012*[24] and the US introduced *Dodd-Frank Wall Street Reform and Consumer Protection Act* of 2010[25] respectively. Other jurisdictions implemented the IOSCO recommendations through their own local laws and regulations.[26]

5 COVID-19 crisis – mandatory forbearance and standstill legislation

As a result of the COVID-19 pandemic, various governments and regulators have encouraged creditors to give forbearance to debtors. For example, in China, the China Banking and Insurance Regulatory Commission has asked lenders to allow

21 Bloomberg News, 'International Business; Malaysia Imposes Controls On Trading in Its Currency' *The New York Times* (2 September 1998) <www.nytimes.com/1998/09/02/business/international-business-malaysia-imposes-controls-on-trading-in-its-currency.html>.

22 For more background information, Alastair Hudson, *The Law of Finance* (2nd ed, Sweet & Maxwell, 2013), 1311–1350.

23 Basel Committee on Banking Supervision, Board of the International Organization of Securities Commissions, 'Margin requirements for non-centrally cleared derivatives', March 2015 <www.iosco.org/library/pubdocs/pdf/IOSCOPD480.pdf>.

24 [2012] EU OJ L201/1 <https://eur-lex.europa.eu/legal-content/EN/TXT/?uri=CELEX%3A32012R0648>.

25 124 Stat. 1376 <www.govinfo.gov/app/details/STATUTE-124/STATUTE-124-Pg1376>.

26 See n 2 above. See also: Hong Kong Monetary Authority, *Non-centrally Cleared OTC Derivatives Transactions – Margin and Other Risk Mitigation Standards*, CR-G-14, September 2020 <www.hkma.gov.hk/media/eng/doc/key-functions/banking-stability/supervisory-policy-manual/CR-G-14.pdf>.

payment extensions to borrowers.[27] In February 2020, it was reported that China issued a 'record number of force majeure certificates' to exempt local exporters from fulfilling contracts with overseas buyers.[28] As at 3 March 2020, it was reported that China had issued 4,811 force majeure certificates covering contracts worth CNY373.7 billion due to the pandemic.[29]

On 16 April 2020, the PRC Supreme People's Court (SPC) issued the *Guiding Opinions of the Supreme People's Court on Several Issues Concerning Properly Handling Civil Cases Related to COVID-19 Epidemic in Accordance with the Law (I)*.[30] On 13 May 2020 the SPC issued the *Guiding Opinions of the Supreme People's Court on Several Issues Concerning Properly Handling Civil Cases Related to COVID-19 Epidemic in Accordance with the Law (II)*.[31] These SPC guiding opinions provided guidance to the People's Courts on handling COVID-19 related cases, including suspension of the enforcement application period.[32]

On 1 January 2021, the PRC Civil Code came into force. The PRC Civil Code provides that there shall be no civil liability in respect of civil obligations that fail to be performed due to force majeure.[33] Contract parties may terminate the contract if the purpose of the contract is rendered impossible to achieve due to force majeure.[34] If a contract cannot be performed due to force majeure, the liabilities shall be exempted.[35]

Other jurisdictions have taken more drastic measures, and passed legislation to impose mandatory forbearance ('standstill legislation').[36] For example, the UK

27 On 26 January 2020, see Fitch Ratings, 'What Investors Want to Know: Coronavirus Impact on Structured Finance in Asia-Pacific' (13 March 2020) 2 <www.fitchratings.com/research/structured-finance/what-investors-want-to-know-coronavirus-impact-on-structured-finance-in-asia-pacific-12-03-2020>.

28 Sun Yu and Xinning Liu, 'China issues record number of force majeure certificates' *Financial Times* (28 February 2020) <www.ft.com/content/bca84ad8-5860-11ea-a528-dd0f971febbc>.

29 Huileng Tan, 'China invokes 'force majeure' to protect businesses – but the companies may be in for a "rude awakening"' *CNBC* (6 March 2020) <www.cnbc.com/2020/03/06/coronavirus-impact-china-invokes-force-majeure-to-protect-businesses.html>.

30 Supreme People's Court, *Guiding Opinions of the Supreme People's Court on Several Issues Concerning Properly Handling Civil Cases Related to COVID-19 Epidemic in Accordance with the Law (I)* 最高人民法院关于依法妥善审理涉新冠肺炎疫情民事案件若干问题的指导意见（一）. For further discussion, see Siyi Lin, 'Exceptions to *pacta sunt servanda* in the Chinese Civil Code', ch 2 (in this volume).

31 Supreme People's Court, *Guiding Opinions of the Supreme People's Court on Several Issues Concerning Properly Handling Civil Cases Related to COVID-19 Epidemic in Accordance with the Law (II)* 最高人民法院关于依法妥善审理涉新冠肺炎疫情民事案件若干问题的指导意见（二）.

32 Keith Brandt and Raymond Zhu, 'Implementation Of The Interim Measures Arrangement Between Hong Kong SAR And Mainland China' *Hong Kong Lawyer* (November 2020) <www.hk-lawyer.org/content/implementation-interim-measures-arrangement-between-hong-kong-sarand-mainland-china>.

33 Article 180, PRC Civil Code.

34 Article 563, PRC Civil Code.

35 Article 590, PRC Civil Code.

36 Kingsley Ong and Stan Ho, 'The Impact of COVID-19 on Asset-Backed Securitisations in Asia' in *The Securitisation & Structured Finance Handbook 2021* (11th ed, Capital Markets Intelligence, 2020), ch 7.

Coronavirus Act 2020[37] introduced various new laws, including forcing landlords to wait at least three months before initiating eviction proceedings for non-payment of rent for private and social accommodation.[38]

Singapore introduced the *COVID-19 Measures (Temporary Measures) Act 2020*[39] ('Singapore COVID-19 Act') on 7 April 2020. The Singapore COVID-19 Act allowed for a temporary suspension of obligations to perform 'scheduled contracts'[40] that were 'materially affected by COVID-19'.[41] The following were prohibited during the prescribed period:

- Enforcement of security over movable and immovable property related to business[42]
- Termination of a scheduled contract where the party is unable to pay rent or other moneys[43]
- Call on performance bonds in construction related contracts[44]
- Payment of liquidated damages in the event of delay or failure in performance of supply contracts[45]

Certain mandatory forbearance requirements under the Singapore COVID-19 Act were extended to 30 September 2021,[46] and then further extended to 31 March 2022.[47]

In Hong Kong, the Hong Kong Monetary Authority encouraged Hong Kong banks to take a 'sympathetic stance' when dealing with customers facing financial difficulty.[48] On 23 February 2022, to help businesses survive the fifth wave

37 Text at <www.legislation.gov.uk/ukpga/2020/7/contents/enacted>.

38 This became effective on 26 March 2020. The latest UK Coronavirus Act March 2022 report is available here: <www.gov.uk/government/publications/coronavirus-act-report-march-2022>.

39 Text at <https://sso.agc.gov.sg/Act/COVID19TMA2020>.

40 This term is defined in the Singapore COVID-19 Act, Schedule 1.

41 ibid, s 9(1). See further Wayne Courtney, 'Contracts in the time of COVID-19: common law and statutory solutions in Singapore', ch 6 (in this volume).

42 ibid, s 5(3).

43 ibid, s 5(3).

44 ibid, s 6(2) and (4).

45 ibid, s 6(5).

46 COVID-19 (Temporary Measures) (Amendment No. 2) Act 2021 <https://sso.agc.gov.sg/Acts-Supp/9-2021/Published/20210419?DocDate=20210419>.

47 The relief currently applies to construction contracts and supply contracts and the prescribed period is extended to 28 February 2022 (Additional relief for inability to perform construction contract or supply contract and Temporary Measures for cost-sharing in construction contracts) and 31 March 2022 (Reliefs for construction contracts affected by increase in foreign manpower salary costs).

48 Chad Bray and Enoch Yiu, 'Hong Kong banks to offer relief on mortgages, credit cards, corporate loans as coronavirus outbreak weighs on economy' *South China Morning Post* (6 February 2020) <www.scmp.com/business/banking-finance/article/3049396/hong-kong-banks-offer-relief-mortgages-credit-cards/>.

of COVID-19, the Hong Kong government originally announced that SMEs[49] in certain sectors will be allowed to defer their retail and office rental payments by up to six months.[50] It was also reported that the Hong Kong Monetary Authority (HKMA) may direct banks to give some flexibility to owners of premises facing mortgage repayment difficulties. The original plan was to grant mandatory relief measures for an initial three months, which may be extended by a further three months, giving a total of six months relief. This is not without controversy,[51] and eventually the Hong Kong government only approved rent deferral for three months with no extension option.[52]

6 2022 Russia-Ukraine conflict

At the time of writing, the economic fallout from the Russia-Ukraine military conflict (which started on 24 February 2022)[53] is still playing out.[54] However, there are already several reported black swan events that have created uncertainty for contract enforcement.

It was reported that in 2021, Russia accounted for 9.2% of the world's total nickel mining production, and holds 7.5 million tonnes of nickel in reserves. Before the military conflict, in early January 2022, nickel prices were trading at US$20,700 per tonne. On 24 February 2022, in response to the Russian offensive, the nickel price rose to above US$26,000 per tonne. On 8 March 2022, the nickel

49 Small and medium-sized enterprises.

50 Lam Ka-sing and Sandy Li, 'Budget 2022–2023: Hong Kong's rents deferment plan for certain SMEs only a short-term solution, industry observers say' *South China Morning Post* (23 February 2022) <www.scmp.com/business/article/3168051/budget-2022-23-hong-kong-offers-office-and-retail-rental-relief-citys>.

51 Cannix Yau and Natalie Wong, 'Finance chief's rental deferral plan for small Hong Kong firms in trouble as Carrie Lam wants cabinet to decide whether to support bill' *South China Morning Post* (9 March 2022) <www.scmp.com/news/hong-kong/hong-kong-economy/article/3169872/finance-chiefs-rental-deferral-plan-small-hong>.

52 Natalie Wong and Lilian Cheng, 'Carrie Lam gives green light to Hong Kong's controversial rent deferral plan despite lobbying by developers and landlords' *South China Morning Post* (15 March 2022) <www.scmp.com/news/hong-kong/hong-kong-economy/article/3170536/carrielam-gives-green-light-hong-kongs>. The Temporary Protection Measures for Business Tenants (COVID-19 Pandemic) Ordinance came into force on 1 May 2022, and implemented mandatory forbearance for business tenants from 1 May 2022 to 31 July 2022.

53 Russia commenced military action in Ukraine on 24 February 2022, shaking financial markets and raising concerns about the global economy: Chris Giles, Jonathan Wheatley and Valentina Romei, 'How will Russia's invasion of Ukraine hit the global economy?' *The Financial Times* (25 February 2022), <www.ft.com/content/a6227910-751b-443c-883f-2ed41a828426>. On the Ukraine conflict, see Council on Foreign Relations, Global Conflict Tracker, Conflict in Ukraine: see <www.cfr.org/global-conflict-tracker/conflict/conflict-ukraine>.

54 Julian Borger, 'Ukraine crisis: miscalculation could trigger unintended wider conflict' *The Guardian* (13 February 2022) <www.theguardian.com/world/2022/feb/13/ukraine-crisis-miscalculation-could-trigger-unintended-wider-conflict>. See also Aila Slisco, 'Donald Trump Predicts "China's Going to Be Next", Will Invade Taiwan' *Newsweek* (22 February 2022) <www.newsweek.com/donald-trump-predicts-chinas-going-next-will-invade-taiwan-1681616>.

market price spiked to over US$100,000 per tonne before the London Metal Exchange (LME) was forced to step in and halt trading to avoid a systemic meltdown. This price spike was accelerated by market participants rushing to unwind their hedges to cut their losses. Commentators described the events as 'unprecedented', 'never happened before in the history of the nickel market', 'the mother of all short squeezes'.[55] Noting the cancellation of nickel trading contracts, Mark Thompson, executive vice chairman of the trading firm Tungsten West, tweeted that '*to cancel Nickel trades between willing buyers and sellers is unforgivable. UNFORGIVABLE.*'.[56]

Separately, it was widely reported that the assets of Russian oligarchs (who are private citizens) were suddenly seized and converted[57] due to their perceived association with Russian President Vladimir Putin.[58] This controversial action could arguably be a breach of fundamental social contract theory,[59] *pacta sunt servanda* and rule of law principles. Unsurprisingly, China was reported to be making contingency plans to 'protect the country's overseas assets from US-led sanctions similar to those imposed on Russia for its invasion of Ukraine'.[60]

In another development that sent shockwaves for *pacta sunt servanda* principles, on 16 September 2022, the German government suddenly seized control of three refineries owned by the Russian oil company Rosneft, and declared the move as 'unavoidable' and 'to safeguard Germany's energy supply'.[61]

55 Will Daniel, 'This has never happened before in the history of the nickel market': 145-year-old exchange halts trading as price more than doubles', *Fortune* (10 March 2022) <https://fortune.com/2022/03/09/nickel-trading-halted-price-doubles-russia-ukraine-invasion-short-squeeze/>.

56 Reported in: Will Daniel, 'Nickel trading on the London Metal Exchange just melted down for a third time: "Credibility is very quickly slipping through their fingers"' *Fortune* (18 March 2022) <https://fortune.com/2022/03/17/nickel-trading-shut-down-london-metal-exchange-credibility-slipping/>. On 6 June 2022, it was reported that the London Metal Exchange was facing a wave of law suits for its decision to cancel nickel trades: see 'London Metal Exchange Sued for $456m Over Cancelled Trades' *The Guardian* (6 June 2022) <https://www.theguardian.com/business/2022/jun/06/london-metal-exchange-sued-cancelled-trades-elliott-management>.

57 Conversion is a tort which occurs when one person interferes with the personal property of another, for example by taking it or withholding it without lawful justification.

58 Catie Edmondson, 'House Passes Bill Urging Biden to Sell Seized Russian Yachts to Aid Ukraine' *New York Times* (27 April 2022) <www.nytimes.com/2022/04/27/us/politics/biden-russia-sanctions.html>.

59 For a discussion on social contract theory, see: Fred D'Agostino, Gerald Gaus and John Thrasher, 'Contemporary Approaches to the Social Contract' in Edward N Zalta (ed), *The Stanford Encyclopedia of Philosophy* (Winter 2021 Edition) <https://plato.stanford.edu/archives/win2021/entries/contractarianism-contemporary/>.

60 Sun Yu, 'China meets banks to discuss protecting assets from US sanctions' *Financial Times* (1 May 2022) <www.ft.com/content/45d5fcac-3e6d-420a-ac78-4b439e24b5de>.

61 'Germany seizes control of Rosneft oil refineries' *Financial Times* (16 September 2022) <https://www.ft.com/content/c1c66e25-ba3c-464e-bca8-b3fa70ebb747>

III Lesson 3: Get the basics right

Legal requirements to create enforceable contracts (e.g. offer, acceptance, consideration, intention to create legal obligations, etc.) apply to all agreements, whether simple or complex. Before even considering whether a contract has all the necessary elements to be enforceable, the contracting parties should also consider the following checklist:

- Does your counterparty have capacity to enter into the contract? For example, a contracting party that is subject to a winding up petition may not have capacity to enter into a new contract even if no winding up court order has been made yet.[62]
- Did your counterparty properly authorise/approve the contract?
- Was the contract duly executed?

In *Au Wai Ming v Kam Tze Ming Alfred*,[63] a Hong Kong Court of Appeal case, a deed of release was executed by a first mortgagee company in two capacities. First in its own right, second as attorney for the first mortgagee. Although the document bore two signatures of the company, there was only one common seal affixed (instead of two). The Hong Kong Court of Appeal held (by majority) that the execution was defective. Under s 127(4) of the *Companies Ordinance* (Cap. 622),[64] if a person is to sign a document on behalf of two or more companies, the person must sign the document separately in each capacity.

In *R (on the application of Mercury Tax Group) v HMRC*,[65] an English judge took the view that s 1(3) of the *Law of Property (Miscellaneous Provisions) Act 1989* (UK)[66] requires a deed to be executed by an individual in its final version. Therefore, the practice of having pre-signed signature pages to be inserted into a contract later may result in the contract not being properly executed and therefore becoming void. Following this case, the Law Society Company Law Committee and The City of London Law Society Company Law and Financial Law Committees prepared guidance on execution by virtual signings that are governed by English law.[67]

During the COVID-19 pandemic, electronic signings (where parties enter into contracts electronically rather than using wet-ink signatures) are becoming more popular.[68] In Hong Kong, electronic contracts are regulated by the *Electronic*

62 E.g. under Hong Kong Companies (Winding Up and Miscellaneous Provisions) Ordinance (Cap. 32) s 182.

63 [2009] 4 HKC 469.

64 Text at <www.elegislation.gov.hk/hk/cap622>.

65 [2008] EWHC 2721 (Admin).

66 Text at <www.legislation.gov.uk/ukpga/1989/34/contents>.

67 The Law Society, *Practice note: Execution of documents by virtual means* (May 2020) <www.lawsociety.org.uk/topics/business-management/execution-of-documents-by-virtual-means>.

68 Docusign, 'The Current State of Electronic Signature Technology', 5 March 2021 <www.docusign.com/blog/the-current-state-electronic-signature-technology>.

Transactions Ordinance (Cap. 553). It is worth noting that certain types of contracts cannot be concluded electronically (and still require wet-ink signatures), such as the creation of powers of attorney, wills and trusts.[69]

The above examples demonstrate that overlooking basic contract law issues can be costly. The only difference between a simple contract and a high-value complex financial contract is that the mistake will cost even more dearly in the latter scenario.

IV Lesson 4: Attention to detail is critical

An example of this lesson can be found in the case of *High Risk Opp. HUB Fund Ltd. v Credit Lyonnais*.[70] In this US case, the issue in dispute was whether Credit Lyonnais properly valued contracts through the 'market quotation' procedure under the 1992 ISDA Master Agreement.

Under the 1992 ISDA Master Agreement, section 14 (*Definitions*) provides:

> '**Market Quotation**' means . . . an amount determined on the basis of **quotations from Reference Market-makers**. Each quotation will be for an amount, if any, that would be paid to such party (expressed as a negative number) or by such party (expressed as a positive number) in consideration of an agreement between such party (taking into account any existing Credit Support Document with respect to the obligations of such party) and the quoting Reference Market-maker to enter into a transaction (the 'Replacement Transaction') that would have the effect of preserving for such party the economic equivalent of any payment or delivery (whether the underlying obligation was absolute or contingent and assuming the satisfaction of each applicable condition precedent) by the parties under Section 2(a)(i) in respect of such Terminated Transaction or group of Terminated Transactions that would, but for the occurrence of the relevant Early Termination Date, have been required after that date. . . . The party making the determination (or its agent) will request each Reference Market-maker to provide its quotation to the extent reasonably practicable as of the **same day and time** (without regard to different time zones) on or as soon as reasonably practicable after the relevant Early Termination Date. The day and time as of which those quotations are to be obtained will be selected in **good faith** by the party obliged to make a determination under Section 6(e), and, if each party is so obliged, after consultation with the other. **If more than three quotations are provided**, the Market Quotation will be the arithmetic mean of the quotations, **without regard to the quotations having the highest and lowest values**. If **exactly three such quotations** are provided, the Market Quotation will be the **quotation remaining after disregarding the highest and lowest quotations**. For this purpose, if more than one quotation has the

69 Electronic Transactions Ordinance (Cap. 553), Schedule 1.
70 Index No. 600229/00, N.Y. Sup. Ct. July 07, 2005.

> same highest value or lowest value, then one of such quotations shall be disregarded. If **fewer than three quotations** are provided, it will be deemed that the Market Quotation in respect of such Terminated Transaction or group of Terminated Transactions **cannot be determined.**'
>
> '**Reference Market-makers**' means **four** leading dealers in the relevant market selected by the party determining a Market Quotation in good faith (a) from among dealers of the highest credit standing which satisfy all the criteria that such party applies generally at the time in deciding whether to offer or to make an extension of credit and (b) to the extent practicable, from among such dealers having an office in the same city.

This dispute involved a non-deliverable forward currency contract,[71] based on the exchange rate between the US dollar and the Russian ruble. The contract was documented using the 1992 ISDA Master Agreement. Credit Lyonnais declared early termination following High Risk's insolvency. Credit Lyonnais then contacted 13 market-makers to obtain valuations. This is despite the 1992 ISDA Master Agreement providing that quotations should be obtained from only 4 market-makers. Credit Lyonnais also instructed the market-makers to consider the existence of exchange risk as a factor in valuing the contracts, and followed up with phone calls to several of the market makers. This is despite there being no mention of exchange risk in the 'market quotation' procedure under the 1992 ISDA Master Agreement.

High Risk sued Credit Lyonnais and claimed that the market quotations were not obtained in good faith. The Court held that Credit Lyonnais failed to act in good faith because it interfered with the market-makers' independence in valuing the contracts (inconsistent with the provisions of the 1992 ISDA Master Agreement), and the market quotations were therefore invalid.[72]

When considering the enforceability of contracts, attention to detail is critical especially in the case of high value financial contracts, where a seemingly small mistake can become very costly.

V Lesson 5: 'Market practice' or 'market standard' does not necessarily reflect the law

1 General

There is a timeless idiom about 'strength in numbers'. The comfort that comes from following the crowd has resulted in many market participants always seeking to follow 'market standard' or 'market practice', and the assumption that

71 A non-deliverable forward currency contract is a cash-settled forward contract where the notional amount is never exchanged.

72 The practical consequence of this is that the fallback 'Loss' method was used for calculating settlement amounts, in accordance with the 1992 ISDA Master Agreement.

following 'market practice' will always be safe. While this may be the case most of the time, for some of the time it can prove costly. In particular, 'market practice' or 'market standard' will always get tested during a severe financial crisis as the following examples demonstrate.

2 *Waterfall flip clauses*

The US case of *Lehman Brothers Special Financing Inc v BNY Corporate Trustee Services Ltd*[73] provides an example of so-called 'waterfall flip clauses'. The case relates to a credit-linked synthetic securitisation programme,[74] where Lehman Brothers Special Financing Inc. (LBSF) was the swap counterparty. Under the contractual terms of the transaction documents, the priority of payments (the 'waterfall') provides that LBSF's interests (as swap counterparty) ordinarily rank ahead of noteholders' interests. However, the transaction documents provided that, upon the occurrence of an event of default on the part of LBSF under the swap documents, the waterfall positions were to be reversed such that LBSF's interest would rank subordinate to the noteholders' interest (i.e. the waterfall priority positions are 'flipped' under such circumstances).

Such a waterfall 'flip clause' is market-standard in the securitisation industry. The primary objective of this clause is to disincentivise default by a swap counterparty and ensure that the defaulting swap counterparty does not benefit from its own default by continuing to be paid at a senior position in the waterfall. There have been positive legal opinions issued by leading law firms and plenty of market confidence in the enforceability of flip clauses. The enforceability of flip clauses formed an important basis for the credit ratings of securitisation bonds.[75]

LBSF was a US entity that went into bankruptcy in US, whereas the contracts related to the securitisation in question were governed by English law. Proceedings were brought in the US and in England by LBSF to challenge the validity of the flip clause. LBSF sought to argue that the flip clause breached anti-deprivation laws and was against public policy by unfairly depriving creditors of LBSF in LBSF's insolvency.[76]

The UK Supreme Court upheld the judgments of the Court of Appeal and High Court, and decided that the 'flip clause' was effective and enforceable, and not contrary to public policy.[77]

73 US Bankruptcy Court, Southern District of New York, Adversary Proceeding No 09–01242 (JMP). US Bankruptcy Court judgment handed down on 25 January 2010.

74 Credit-linked synthetic securitisation programmes issue credit-linked notes with an embedded credit default swap that allows the issuer to transfer specific credit risks to credit investors.

75 For further discussions, see Ong (n 2).

76 The modern rationale for the anti-deprivation principle is that a removal of assets from the insolvent estate infringes insolvency laws that provide for distributions in an insolvency to be made to unsecured creditors on a *pari passu* basis.

77 *Belmont Park Investments PTY Ltd v BNY Corporate Trustee Services Ltd* [2011] UKSC 38, [2012] 1 AC 383.

However, in an opposing decision, the US Bankruptcy Court held that the flip clause was 'unenforceable and violates the ipso facto provisions of the [US] *Bankruptcy Code*'.[78] This shocked the industry, which had relied on 'market practice' and 'market standard', and assumed the integrity and enforceability of such 'flip clauses' at that time.[79]

It is interesting to note that a few years later before the same US Court in the case of *Lehman Brothers Special Financing Inc. v. Bank of America N.A.*, the earlier ruling in *In Re: 09-01242-jmp Lehman Brothers Special Financing Inc. v BNY Corporate Trustee Serviced Limited* was not followed.[80] On appeal by LBSF to the Second Circuit District Court,[81] the Second Circuit upheld the lower court decision to enforce the flip clause and declared that the flip clause is protected under section 560 of the US *Bankruptcy Code* and therefore enforceable even in bankruptcy. The US Court eventually recognised the market practice and purpose of the flip clause – but the opportunity to reconsider the case only came eight years after its 2010 decision and would provide little comfort to the aggrieved parties of the original litigation.

3 ISDA insolvency stalemate

The US *Metavante* case provides another example of a challenge to the 'market standard'. The US Bankruptcy Court handed down its judgment in this case on 17 September 2009 based on the following facts: Lehman Brothers Holding Inc. (LBHI) sought to compel Metavante Corporation to perform its obligations under a swap contract[82] (documented using an ISDA Master Agreement[83]) between Metavante and LBSF guaranteed by LBHI. At that time, Metavante would be substantially out of the money (i.e. Metavante would be required to pay LBHI under the derivative contract) if the swap transactions under its swap agreement with LBSF were terminated. However, relying on certain provisions (as explained below) in the ISDA Master Agreement, Metavante refused to terminate the ISDA contract.

78 *In Re: 09–01242-jmp Lehman Brothers Special Financing Inc. v BNY Corporate Trustee Services Limited*, US Bankruptcy Court, Southern District of New York, Adversary Proceeding No 09–01242 (JMP), Judgment dated 25 January 2010, p 7.

79 Moody's and Fitch warned (on 28 and 29 January 2010, respectively) that Judge Peck's ruling may adversely impact the ratings of transactions with US domiciled counterparties.

80 *Lehman Brothers Special Financing Inc. v. Bank of America National Association*, No. 17-cv-01224, 2018 WL 1322225 (S.D.N.Y. March 14, 2018).

81 *Lehman Brothers Special Financing Inc. v Bank of America National Association*, No. 18–1079, 2020 WL 4590247 (2d Cir. Aug. 11, 2020).

82 A swap is an agreement between two parties to exchange sequences of cash flows for a set period of time.

83 cf. n 8 above.

Metavante relied on section 2(a)(iii) of the 1992 ISDA Master Agreement to suspend its payment obligations to LBSF. This section provides as follows:

> 2(a)(iii). Each obligation of each party under Section 2(a)(i) is subject to (1) the condition precedent that no Event of Default or Potential Event of Default with respect to the other party has occurred and is continuing, (2) the condition precedent that no Early Termination Date in respect of the relevant Transaction has occurred or been effectively designated and (3) each other condition specified in this Agreement to be a condition precedent for the purpose of this Section 2(a)(iii).

Section 2(a)(iii) permits a party to suspend the performance of its payment and delivery obligations under the ISDA contract if an Event of Default or Potential Event of Default has occurred and is continuing in respect of its counterparty. LBSF was in US bankruptcy proceedings and therefore subject to an Event of Default.[84] Under section 6 of the ISDA Master Agreement, only the non-defaulting party can terminate the ISDA contract following an Event of Default. Metavante refused to terminate while it waited for the market value of the swap transactions to move in its favour, and relied on section 2(a)(iii) to suspend its payment obligations in the interim.

The purpose of section 2(a)(iii) is to protect the close-out netting rights of the non-defaulting party.[85] According to ISDA, close-out netting promotes financial system stability and has reduced over-the-counter derivatives credit exposure by over 85%. Without the benefits of netting, banks worldwide might face a capital shortfall of over US$500 billion.[86] Given the importance of close-out netting, and the ISDA Master Agreement being one of the world's most recognised 'market standard' financial contracts in the world, nobody previously doubted the enforceability of section 2(a)(iii). The enforceability of section 2(a)(iii) was confirmed by the Australian New South Wales Court of Appeal in *Sims and Singleton as Liquidators of Enron Australia Pty Ltd v TXU Electricity Ltd*.[87] It was also upheld by the English Court of Appeal in *Lomas v JFB Firth Rixson Inc*.[88]

However, in the *Metavante* decision, the US Bankruptcy Court handed down a judgment in favour of LBSF. The US Bankruptcy Court decided that section 2(a)(iii) of the ISDA Master Agreement was unenforceable, and ordered Metavante to perform its obligations under the ISDA contract without regard to any defaults by LBSF. Metavante was also ordered to pay default interest on such payment

84 Under ISDA Master Agreement s 5(a)(vii).

85 For further discussion on close-out netting, see Ong (n 2) 341.

86 ISDA, The Importance of Close-out Netting (1 February 2010) <www.isda.org/2010/02/01/the-importance-of-close-out-netting/>.

87 [2005] NSWCA 12.

88 [2012] EWCA Civ 419.

obligations and make all other payments under the ISDA contract.[89] The decision was reasoned on the basis that Metavante's unilateral cessation of its payment obligations following LBSF's bankruptcy filing violated US bankruptcy law. The US *Bankruptcy Code* section 365(e)(1) provides that parties are prohibited from suspending their performance obligations solely on account of the bankruptcy filings of its counterparties.[90]

The *Metavante* ruling had extensive implications in US insolvency proceedings involving derivative transactions.[91] On 19 June 2014, ISDA[92] published an amendment to section 2(a)(iii) of the ISDA Master Agreement,[93] in order to address the *Metavante* ruling.[94] What used to be regarded as 'market standard' thereby became amended.

VI Lesson 6: Don't assume 'similar' contracts will achieve identical end results

It is not always safe to assume that a previous legal precedent set under a 'similar' financial contract will yield the same end result. In fact, relying on such an assumption is rather dangerous.

One of the reasons for the popularity of the ISDA Master Agreement[95] has been attributed to reducing the 'basis-risk', because secondary trades also use the same documents.[96] Derivatives market players usually enter into secondary or back trades to hedge their positions in their primary or front trades. If the primary and secondary trade contracts are different, there will be a 'basis risk' and this may not be a perfect hedge. The purpose of having back-to-back contracts is to hedge against losses, i.e. losses under the front contract are hedged against profits from the back contract. However, if the front and back contracts are not a perfect hedge, the contracting party relying on the back contract as a hedge may not be properly protected. Such arbitrage leakage becomes particularly profound and exacerbated in a severe financial crisis when markets are extremely volatile.

When ISDA introduced a new version of its Master Agreement in 2002, it was intended to improve on the original 1992 version. There was no intention to create

89 It is estimated that this amounted to US$6.6 million plus an unspecified amount of default interest.

90 The text of US *Bankruptcy Code* s 365(e)(1) can be found at <https://codes.findlaw.com/us/title-11-bankruptcy/11-usc-sect-365.html>.

91 LBHI has indicated that it has about US$24 billion of unpaid receivables under derivative contracts with approximately 4,000 counterparties. For further discussion on the impact, see Ong (n 2) 347.

92 cf. n 8.

93 ibid.

94 ISDA, Amendment to the ISDA Master Agreement for use in relation to Section 2(a)(iii) and explanatory memorandum (19 June 2014) <www.isda.org/2014/06/19/amendment-to-the-isda-master-agreement-for-use-in-relation-to-section-2aiii-and-explanatory-memorandum/>.

95 See n 8.

96 See Ong (n 2) 338.

any 'basis risk' for those using different versions of the ISDA Master Agreement in their primary and secondary trades.

One key difference between the 1992 and 2002 ISDA Master Agreement is the close-out calculations upon an early termination of the contract. Under the 1992 ISDA Master Agreement, there are two calculation methods on early termination, namely 'Loss' and 'Market Quotation'.[97] 'Loss' is the fallback if 'Market Quotation' calculation method fails.[98] Under the 2002 ISDA Master Agreement, 'Loss' and 'Market Quotation' methods have been replaced by 'Close-out Amount'.

The definition of 'Close-out Amount' in the 2002 ISDA Master Agreement takes into account certain factors, such as the 'then prevailing circumstances', 'economic equivalence', using 'commercially reasonable procedures' to obtain a 'commercially reasonable result', the 'creditworthiness of the Determining Party', etc. These factors were absent in the 1992 ISDA Master Agreement calculation methods.

In *Australia and New Zealand Banking Group Ltd v Société Générale*,[99] the UK Court of Appeal considered a valuation dispute using the Loss method under the 1992 ISDA Master Agreement. In that case, *Société Générale* had back-to-back hedges, which suffered big losses due to the 1998 Russian banking moratorium. It was held that such losses on hedge trades should be excluded from the Loss calculation because such losses were caused by the Russian banking moratorium, not by the termination of ANZ-*Société Générale* trades.

In *Lehman Brothers International (Europe) (In Administration) v Lehman Brothers Finance S.A.*,[100] there was a close-out valuation dispute[101] between Lehman Brothers entities arising under the 2002 ISDA Master Agreement. In that case, there was an intercompany side letter between the insolvent Lehman entities which provided that intercompany transactions terminated automatically at the same time as corresponding Lehman Brothers International (Europe) (LBIE) client trades,[102] and that termination payments due from LBIE to LBF were only payable if the client paid LBIE for the client trades. The issue to be determined was whether this intercompany side letter should be applied for purposes of calculating the close-out amount under the 2002 ISDA Master Agreement. The High Court initially followed *ANZ v Société Générale* and held that this intercompany side letter should be excluded from the calculation of close-out amount. On appeal, the English Court of Appeal overruled the High Court decision and held

97 See discussion of 'Market Quotation' in Section 2.4 of this Chapter.

98 Section 6(e) of the 1992 ISDA Master Agreement.

99 [2000] EWCA Civ 44, [2000] 1 All ER (Comm) 682.

100 [2013] EWCA Civ 188.

101 This refers to a dispute in the close-out valuation amounts.

102 'Client trades' refer to trades between Lehman affiliates and external street counterparties (which are unaffiliated to Lehman).

that the 2002 ISDA Master Agreement was different from the 1992 ISDA Master Agreement and requires a 'commercially reasonable result':

> the first standardised terms of business for use with all types of derivative transactions produced by ISDA were issued in 1992. The terms as to the consequences of early termination were revised in 2002. The reason for this appears to have been that the provisions of the 1992 Master Agreement did not produce a closing out which met regulators' requirements with regard to the capital base of the market participants. . . . For the first time, the calculation of the liabilities due on closing out had to be carried out "in order to produce a commercially reasonable result". The fact that it had to be expressly stated suggests that the drafting had not always met commercial expectations in the past, and that ISDA wanted a new approach to be adopted.[103]

The 2002 ISDA Master Agreement also allows quotations to 'take into account creditworthiness of the Determining Party'. Therefore, the intercompany side letter was a material term and must be taken into account in the calculation valuation. Lady Justice Arden in the Court of Appeal concluded as follows:

> For the detailed reasons given below, I would hold that this appeal succeeds and that the Side Letter should be taken into account for the purposes of determining the value of replacement transactions under the 2002 Master Agreement closing out provisions. I reach this conclusion by the following steps:
>
> (1) The 2002 Master Agreement should be interpreted (a) according to its own terms and (b) taking into account all the relevant background.
> (2) The reasons for the changes shown in the 2002 Master Agreement given in the User's Guide to the ISDA 2002 Master Agreement published by ISDA in 2003 . . . suggest that those changes were regarded as more important than the preservation of the 'value clean' principle in the form in which it existed in the 1992 Master Agreement.
> (3) The 'value clean' principle appears in the 2002 Master Agreement in a different context from that in which it appeared in the 1992 Master Agreement.
> (4) Where more than one meaning is possible the court should prefer that which is more consistent with business common sense and

103 *Lehman Brothers International (Europe) (In Administration) v Lehman Brothers Finance S.A.* [2013] EWCA Civ 188 [10] (Arden LJ).

the judge's application of the 'value clean' principle conflicts with business common sense.

(5) Words should generally be given their natural meaning.
(6) 'Material terms' are those that impact on pricing and (but for the judge's ruling on the 'value clean' principle) they would in the present case include the terms of the Side Letter.
(7) The judge's restriction on the meaning of 'option rights' is not justified by the words used to describe option rights in the definition of Close-out Amount or by the User's Guide.
(8) The inclusion in the Close-out Amount of permission to the Determining Party to take account of its own creditworthiness involves a clear departure from the 'value clean' principle.
(9) The words 'assuming satisfaction of the conditions precedent in clause 2(a)(iii)' cannot be taken to deprive the references to 'material terms' and 'option rights' of the weight that they would otherwise have.[104]

These examples show that contracting parties of derivatives contracts must carefully consider that there may not be a perfect legal hedge in their primary and secondary trades if they use different versions of the ISDA Master Agreement.

VII Lesson 7: Practical considerations

While every financial crisis presents unique new issues, from a contract enforcement perspective, there are three things that can be done to be better prepared.

First, in a financial crisis, markets become very volatile. Time is of the essence, and decisions must be made quickly. Delays or mistakes can be very costly. First and foremost, it is important to have a complete and up-to-date set of all the relevant legal contracts available. This would include all amendments, supplements or restatements to the main contracts and security documents. A complete set of documents is necessary to make informed decisions quickly or to take advice promptly. Avoid scrambling to find documents when the markets start collapsing.

Second, establish good relationships with experienced and trusted lawyers so that legal support can be obtained quickly. Whether seeking to enforce contracts, or to avoid contracts, it is very likely that legal advice will be needed. The best lawyers may be conflicted and could end up acting against you if you approach them too late.

Third, reduce debt and leverage. Having fewer creditors trying to enforce contracts against you in a time of financial turmoil, when liquidity and funding are very tight, is always a good thing.

104 ibid, 7 (Aikens LJ agreeing in a separate judgment; Munby PFD agreeing with both).

C Conclusion

At the time of writing this chapter, we are on the cusp of a new global financial crisis arising from a convergence of the COVID-19 global pandemic, the Russia-Ukraine war, the pressure of rising interest rates,[105] hyper-inflation,[106] a global energy and commodity crisis,[107] and a looming global food shortage crisis.[108] The combination of all these crises has the potential to create a perfect storm, which could dwarf the 2008 GFC or even the 1929 Great Depression.[109]

There is still plenty of forbearance (voluntary and mandatory), and we could be only in the early stages of a full blown global financial crisis. Forbearance may delay a financial crisis temporarily. However, forbearance, whether mandatory or voluntary, cannot last indefinitely. I have previously argued that any unreasonable extended forbearance may have wider repercussions for the bond and hedging markets, and create broader systemic risks to the global financial markets.[110]

Will the lessons from earlier financial crises make the markets better prepared for the next one? I believe Ecclesiastes 1:9 holds the answer.

105 Brian O'Connell and Benjamin Curry, 'What Happens When The Fed Raises Interest Rates?' *Forbes* (5 April 2022) <www.forbes.com/advisor/investing/fed-raises-interest-rates/>.

106 Jameson Lopp, 'How To Prepare For Hyperinflation' *Forbes* (6 March 2022) <www.forbes.com/sites/jamesonlopp/2022/03/06/how-to-prepare-for-hyperinflation/?sh=131f6f6b42d3>.

107 Luís Pinheiro de Matos, Ricard Murillo Gili, 'The energy crisis in Europe' *CaixaBank Research* (13 January 2022) <www.caixabankresearch.com/en/economics-markets/commodities/energy-crisis-europe>.

108 ET Spotlight Special, 'Ukraine invasion: Biden warns of significant food shortage risk following sanctions on Russia' *The Economic Times* (25 March 2022) <https://economictimes.indiatimes.com/news/international/us/ukraine-invasion-biden-warns-of-significant-food-shortage-risk-following-sanctions-on-russia/articleshow/90447961.cms?from=mdr>.

109 Marco Quiroz-Gutierrez, 'Deutsche Bank just predicted "a major recession" weeks after forecasting a "mild" one' *Fortune* (27 April 2022) <https://fortune-com.cdn.ampproject.org/c/s/fortune.com/2022/04/27/deutsche-bank-major-recession-2023-inflation-federal-reserve/amp/>.

110 Ong and Ho (n 36) 42.

Part C

Pacta sunt servanda in international law

12 Invoking COVID-19 to suspend or terminate the operation of a treaty

Hanh Hong Pham and Huong Thi Thu Phung

Introduction

In March 2020, the World Health Organization (WHO) recognised COVID-19 as a global pandemic. Obviously, COVID-19 has created a global crisis in many aspects, from economic, medical to social. Until now, most countries and territories around the world have had many cases of infection and death from COVID-19. Accordingly, state parties implement many different measures to prevent and limit the spread of COVID-19 and protect the safety of the community. In some cases, the emergence of COVID-19 or public health responses also affected the ability of a State party to fulfil their international legal obligations.

According to the principle of *pacta sunt servanda*, all international treaties that come into force are legally binding on the state and the state must implement them in good faith: Article 26 of the 1969 Vienna Convention on the Law of Treaties (VCLT).[1] However, a party may invoke objective or subjective factors that affect the validity of a treaty without being seen as violating this principle. This can be considered an exception to the principle of *pacta sunt servanda*. One of those exceptions is the case of 'a fundamental change of circumstances'. Under the provisions of the VCLT, a party may invoke a fundamental change of circumstances (article 62) to temporarily suspend or terminate a treaty if the following conditions are satisfied: (1) the change must be of a circumstance that existed at the time of the conclusion of the treaty; (2) that change must be a fundamental one; (3) it must also be one not foreseen by the parties; (4) the existence of those circumstances must have constituted an essential basis of the consent of the parties to be bound by the treaty; and (5) the effect of the change must be radically to transform the scope of obligations still to be performed under the treaty.

This chapter pursues the following objectives:

- To examine the conditions of the "fundamental change of circumstances" under the 1969 Vienna Convention on the Law of Treaties

1 Convention on the Law of Treaties (Vienna, 23 May 1969) 1155 UNTS 331, entered into force 27 January 1980 (VCLT).

DOI: 10.4324/9781003358305-15

- To assess the ability to invoke COVID1 - 19 as the "fundamental change of circumstances"
- To suggest suspending the operation of some treaties to which Vietnam is a member on the basic of invoking COVID-19 as a "fundamental change of circumstances".

To resolve these objectives, the chapter firstly analyses four conditions of the 'fundamental change of circumstances' stipulated in the VCLT by examining the relevant judgments of international courts. Furthermore, the chapter evaluates in what circumstances the COVID-19 can amount to a fundamental change of circumstances by comparing the conditions of the 'fundamental change of circumstances' with the COVID-19 and its effect of this pandemic to the world. Lastly, it recommends Vietnam to temporarily suspend certain treaties due to a 'fundamental change of circumstances' relating to COVID-19.

The 'fundamental change of circumstances' under the 1969 Vienna Convention on the Law of Treaties

Article 26 of the VCLT codified one of the fundamental principles of international law, the principle of *pacta sunt servanda*, when it stated: 'Every treaty in force is binding upon the parties to it and must be performed by them in good faith'. However, the VCLT also recognises a number of exceptions that the parties can invoke to suspend or terminate the implementation of the treaty without this being considered a violation of this principle, and one of them is the case of a 'fundamental change of circumstances'.

Article 62(1) of the VCLT provides:

> A fundamental change of circumstances which has occurred with regard to those existing at the time of the conclusion of a treaty, and which was not foreseen by the parties, may not be invoked as a ground for terminating or withdrawing from the treaty unless:
>
> (a) the existence of those circumstances constituted an essential basis of the consent of the parties to be bound by the treaty; and
>
> (b) the effect of the change is radically to transform the extent of obligations still to be performed under the treaty.

In other words, in order to have grounds for the suspension or termination of the implementation of the treaty, a party may invoke a fundamental change of circumstances when the following conditions are met:

Firstly, the circumstances must change after the treaty's signing and the parties did not anticipate this change in advance. In other words, the parties did not anticipate that change in circumstances at the time of the conclusion of the treaty.

In the case concerning the *Gabčíkovo-Nagymaros Project* between Hungary and Slovakia, Hungary cited a change in environmental awareness and the development of standards and regulations in international environmental law as such a fundamental change of circumstances and argued on that basis for a temporary suspension of construction activities in Nagymaros and Gabčíkovo as agreed in the Treaty of Budapest on 16 October 1977 on the construction and operation of the Gabčíkovo-Nagymaros Dam System ('the 1977 Treaty'). Specifically, Hungary alleged, in relation to the operations in Nagymaros that the country did not have adequate knowledge of the consequences from environmental risks (para 35), in relation to the activities at Gabčíkovo that the environmental, ecological and water quality impacts were not properly taken into account during the design and construction period, and at the same time that, due to the complexity of ecological processes and the lack of measurement data as well as related calculations, the impacts on the environment had not been assessed (para 56).

However, in its ruling, the United Nations International Court of Justice (ICJ) held:

> The Court does not consider that new developments in the state of environmental knowledge and of environmental law have been completely unforeseen. What is more, the formulation of articles 15, 19 and 20 [of the 1977 Treaty] was designed to accommodate change, made it possible for the parties to take account of such developments and to apply them when implementing those treaty provisions.[2]

Secondly, the change of circumstances must be fundamental.

This condition was explained by the ICJ in the *Fisheries Jurisdiction Case.*[3] In 1961, the Government of Iceland and the Government of the United Kingdom of Great Britain and Northern Ireland (Exchange of Notes) exchanged notes on fishery limits. This exchange of notes contained a compromissory clause, which gave a right to refer disputes to the ICJ.[4] In 1971, Iceland notified the United Kingdom that it intended to extend its fisheries jurisdiction to 50 nautical miles, contrary to the 12 nautical miles agreed in the Exchange of Notes 1961. Therefore, the United Kingdom initiated proceedings against Iceland before the ICJ on 14 April 1972. Iceland denied that the Court had jurisdiction and substantiated its claim by relying on a unilateral termination of the compromissory clause.

In the letter of 29 May 1972 to the Registrar, the Minister for Foreign Affairs of Iceland referred to 'the changed circumstances resulting from the ever-increasing exploitation of the fishery resources in the seas surrounding Iceland'[5]. According to

2 *Gabčikovo-Nagymaros Project* (*Hungary v Slovakia*), Judgment, Merits [1997] ICJ Rep 7, [104].

3 *Fisheries Jurisdiction (United Kingdom v Iceland)*, Jurisdiction of the Court, Judgment [1973] ICJ Rep 3.

4 Exchange of Notes constituting an agreement settling the fisheries dispute between the Government of Iceland and the Government of the United Kingdom of Great Britain and Northern Ireland, 397 UNTS 276 <https://treaties.un.org/doc/Publication/UNTS/Volume%20397/volume-397-I-5710-English.pdf>.

5 *Fisheries Jurisdiction (United Kingdom v Iceland),* Jurisdiction of the Court, Judgment [1973] ICJ Rep 3.

Iceland's argument, the increased exploitation of fisheries and the danger of further exploitation as a consequence of technical development resulting in increased fishing capacity endangered the vital interests of the people of Iceland.[6] Therefore, Iceland claimed that, 'because of the vital interests of the nation and owing to changed circumstances, the Notes concerning fishery limits exchanged in 1961 are no longer applicable and that their provisions do not constitute an obligation for Iceland'.[7]

Iceland cited 'vital interests' as a fundamental change to the termination of the ICJ dispute settlement clause in the Exchange of Notes 1961. The ICJ adopted an interpretation that corresponded to the traditional view that 'the changes of circumstances which must be regarded as fundamental or vital are those which imperil the existence or vital development of one of the parties'.[8] Applying this test, the ICJ held that

> the alleged changes could not affect in the least the obligation to submit to the Court's jurisdiction, which is the only issue at the present stage of the proceedings. It follows that the apprehended dangers for the vital interests of Iceland, resulting from changes in fishing techniques, cannot constitute a fundamental change with respect to the lapse or subsistence of the compromissory clause establishing the Court's jurisdiction.[9]

As explained by the ICJ, a change is considered fundamental if it is related to the dispute and if *it completely affects the obligations to be fulfilled by the treaty*.

Thirdly, the existence of the circumstances must be the essential basis for the parties to agree to the treaty.

In order to determine this condition, international courts often consider the connection between the circumstances that existed at the time of conclusion of the treaty and the object and the purpose of the treaty; thereby, assessing whether such circumstances form an essential basis for the consent of the parties.

In the *Gabčíkovo-Nagymaros Project* case between Hungary and Slovakia, the ICJ suggested that the political situation was undoubtedly relevant to the signing of the 1977 Treaty. However, the ICJ went on to 'recall that the Treaty provided for a joint investment program for the production of energy, the control of floods and the improvement of navigation on the Danube. In the Court's view, the prevalent political conditions were thus not so closely linked to the object and purpose of the Treaty that they constituted an essential basis of the consent of the parties.'[10]

The *Case C-162/96*[11] before the Court of Justice of the European Communities is another illustration of this condition. In April 1980, the European Economic

6 ibid, 37.
7 ibid.
8 ibid, 38.
9 ibid, 40.
10 *Gabčíkovo-Nagymaros Project* (Hungary v Slovakia), Judgment, Merits [1997] ICJ Rep 7, [104].
11 *A. Racke GmbH & Co. v Hauptzollamt Mainz*, Case C-162/96, Judgment, 16 June 1998, ECR 1998 I-03655, ECLI:EU:C:1998:293, [23].

Community concluded a Cooperation Agreement with the Socialist Federal Republic of Yugoslavia ('SFRY'). Article 1 of the Cooperation Agreement stated that the objective of the Agreement was to promote overall cooperation between the parties with a view to contributing to the economic and social development of the SFRY. Article 22 provided for preferential tariff treatment of imports of wine from the SFRY into the Community.[12]

In 1991 an armed conflict broke out in Yugoslavia which, over time, led to the dissolution of the SFRY and declarations of independence by four of its six republics.[13] On 11 November 1991, the European Council passed Regulation No. 3300/91 suspending the Cooperation Agreement between the Community and SFRY (Suspension Regulation), including the trade concessions granted by, or pursuant to, the Cooperation Agreement.[14]

Racke GmbH & Co. ('Racke') was a wine importer which imported wine from Serbia and hence benefited from tariff preferences on imports of wine from Yugoslavia until the Council adopted the Suspension Regulation. In proceedings in the German courts, Racke claimed that the Cooperation Agreement with Yugoslavia did not permit the Council to suspend its operation, and that the decision to do so was not in conformity with certain rules of general international law. The argument focused in particular on rules of customary international law which are also contained in the VCLT, including the principle of *pacta sunt servanda* and the rule that a treaty may under certain conditions be terminated by reason of a fundamental change of circumstances.[15] In the light of those considerations, the German Federal Finance Court (*Bundesfinanzhof*) decided to stay the proceedings and referred to the Court of Justice for a preliminary ruling two questions concerning the validity of the Suspension Regulation.[16]

Applying article 26 of the VCLT as customary law,[17] the Court answered the question about the validity of Suspension Regulation by determining whether a fundamental change of circumstances existed. In identifying the circumstances that constituted the essential basis of the parties' consent to the treaty, the ECJ examined specifically the stated purpose of the Agreement. The Court quoted from the Preamble of the Cooperation Agreement, which stated that the object

12 Cooperation Agreement Between The European Economic Community And The Socialist Federal Republic Of Yugoslavia: Final Act (1980) <https://op.europa.eu/en/publication-detail/-/publication/1b7c7231-a198-468d-873b-4a46d5479e62/language-en> accessed 30 March 2022.

13 United Nations, International Criminal Tribunal For The Former Yugoslavia, 'What Is The Former Yugoslavia?' (Webpage) <www.icty.org/en/about/what-former-yugoslavia> accessed 29 March 2022.

14 Council Regulation (EEC) No 3300/91 of 11 November 1991 suspending the trade concessions provided for by the Cooperation Agreement between the European Economic Community and the Socialist Federal Republic of Yugoslavia [1991] EU OJ L 315/1.

15 *A. Racke GmbH & Co. v Hauptzollamt Mainz*, Case C-162/96, Opinion of Mr Advocate General Jacobs, 4 December 1997, ECR 1998 I-03655, ECLI:EU:C:1997:582.

16 *A. Racke GmbH & Co. v Hauptzollamt Mainz*, Case C-162/96, Judgment, 16 June 1998, ECR 1998 I-03655, ECLI:EU:C:1998:293, [23].

17 ibid, 24.

of the Agreement was to 'promote the development and diversification of economic, financial and trade cooperation in order to foster a better balance and an improvement in the structure of their trade and expand its volume and to improve the welfare of their populations'.[18] Article 1 of the Agreement stipulated that the object of the Agreement is to 'promote overall cooperation between the contracting parties with a view to contributing to the economic and social development of the Socialist Federal Republic of Yugoslavia and helping to strengthen relations between the parties'.[19] On the basis of the broad goals in the Preamble and article 1 of the Agreement, the ECJ affirmed that 'the maintenance of a situation of peace in Yugoslavia, indispensable for neighbourly relations, and the existence of institutions capable of ensuring implementation of the cooperation envisaged by the Agreement throughout the territory of Yugoslavia constituted an essential condition for initiating and pursuing that cooperation'.[20] The Court furthermore considered that the Community did not make a manifest error of judgment when it concluded that the hostilities in Yugoslavia and their effect on the relationship with the Community radically transformed the effect of the parties' obligations under Agreement. Therefore, the ECJ concluded that the Suspension Regulation could be based on fundamentally changed circumstances, as defined under by VCLT, and was therefore not invalid.

Fourthly, the impact of that change of circumstances must have had the effect of fundamentally affecting the extent of obligations still to be performed under the treaty.

In the *Fisheries Jurisdiction Case*, the ICJ explained this condition as follows:

> In order that a change of circumstances may give rise to a ground for invoking the termination of a treaty it is also necessary that it should have resulted in a radical transformation of the extent of the obligations still to be performed. The change must have increased the burden of the obligations to be executed to the extent of rendering the performance something essentially different from that originally undertaken.[21]

In the Gabčíkovo-Nagymaros Project case, the ICJ used this standard to examine whether the changes in political, economic and environmental circumstances relied upon by Hungary were sufficient, either individually or collectively, in fundamentally altering the extent of Hungary's obligations under the treaty.[22] The Court held that, although the estimated benefits from the project in 1992 have decreased compared to the time of the treaty's signing in 1977, this did not result in a complete change of the burden of the obligations of the parties under the

18 Cooperation Agreement (n 12).

19 ibid.

20 ibid.

21 *Fisheries Jurisdiction (United Kingdom v Iceland)*, Jurisdiction of the Court, Judgment [1973] ICJ Rep 3, [43].

22 *Gabčíkovo-Nagymaros Project (Hungary v Slovakia),* Judgment, Merits [1997] ICJ Rep 7, [104].

treaty. It also held that the changes to the political situation were not so closely linked to the object of the treaty that they formed an essential basis of the parties' consent and that the environmental developments were not unforeseen by parties and could be accommodated when implementing the treaty.[23] Importantly, the Court pointed out that 'the stability of treaty relations requires that the plea of fundamental change of circumstances be applied only in exceptional cases'.[24]

This aspect of the ICJ's decision was referred to in *Case C-162/96*, when the ECJ considered whether there had been a fundamental change in circumstances. The ECJ held that, although it was true that 'there was a certain volume of trade that had to continue with Yugoslavia and that the Community could have continued to award tariff concessions', there was 'no point in continuing to grant preferences, with a view to stimulating trade, in circumstances where Yugoslavia was breaking up'.[25]

The ability to invoke COVID-19 as a 'fundamental change of circumstances' in accordance with the VCLT

The SARS-CoV-2 virus that causes COVID-19 in humans is a coronavirus that is suspected to have originated from the modified wildlife coronavirus.

Applying article 62(1) of the VCLT, the COVID-19 pandemic may be invoked as a fundamental change of circumstances provided the criteria examined above are established:

Firstly, the appearance of COVID-19 is completely unpredictable.

Secondly, COVID-19 is a fundamental change. COVID-19 may affect the implementation of a country's international commitments in a number of ways:

In order to control the spread of COVID-19 in the community, many countries have adopted, or did adopt, strict measures to prevent the influx of the disease and limit the spread of COVID-19 between countries or regions. These measures had in common that they affected domestic as well as international mobility between countries, such as border closures, stopping entry activities for foreigners, mandatory quarantine requirements for people entering a national territory. Border closures effectively suspend the entry of foreigners except for some special cases such as holders of diplomatic passports or official passports. The application of these measures may have affected the performance of national obligations with respect to the entry and/or cross-border movement of foreigners.

International treaties relating to entry and/or cross-border movement of foreigners mainly consist of three groups: treaties can provide for visa exemption for

23 ibid.

24 ibid.

25 *A. Racke GmbH & Co. v Hauptzollamt Mainz*, Case C-162/96, Judgment, 16 June 1998, ECR 1998 I-03655, ECLI identifier: ECLI:EU:C:1998:293, [57].

individual foreigners when entering the national territory for a certain period of time (also popularly known as agreements on visa-free entry); treaties can allow foreigners to freely travel and reside between the countries that are party to that treaty (typically in the case of the countries of the Schengen area in Europe) and, thirdly, treaties on cooperation in the fields of labour, culture, education, etc. can include provisions on receiving foreign experts directly to work in the country. To implement these treaties, it is required that the country opens its borders, allows foreigners covered by the treaty to enter, reside for a certain period of time, and enable export activities of goods, nationals' citizens and citizens of the contracting parties to the treaty.

Border control or closure measures have been enacted to ensure the safety of the community in the context of the ongoing COVID-19 pandemic. In this case, *COVID-19 can be considered as a fundamental change of circumstances that affects the implementation of international commitments of the country related to the entry and residence of foreigners*.

Furthermore, in response to the impact of COVID-19 on the national economy and society and to protect national security and other public interests, a country can issue regulations affecting international commitments of the country in the field of trade liberalisation, including investment, services or goods.

In accordance with investment commitments in free trade agreements or investment agreements, a Contracting Party may be under an obligation to open and liberalise investment to foreign investors in the fields covered by the agreements. Such agreements are based on the elimination of discriminatory measures and investment-restrictive measures. For example, the ASEAN Comprehensive Investment Agreement (ACIA) stipulates that member states will open and liberalise investment in areas including industrial production, agriculture, fisheries, forestry, mining and quarrying, associated services of the foregoing and any other areas agreed upon by all Member States.[26] In addition to the specific fields listed above, ASEAN countries can also liberalise investment in other areas that are agreed with other members. Under normal socio-economic conditions, investment liberalisation brings many benefits to the country. However, following the impact of COVID-19 on all socio-economic aspects, the liberalisation of investment in some fields may affect the public order and interests of the country. For example, transportation is one of the economic sectors strongly affected by the pandemic because of the restrictions on domestic and foreign movement enacted by the country to prevent the spread of the disease. The disruption of transport activities due to the implementation of national lockdown measures had knock-on effects for related economic sectors, including the energy industry. Specifically, the decrease in transportation and circulation demand reduced oil demand, which led to lower oil prices. Gasoline and oil inventories of refineries increased rapidly because customers delay receiving goods because of the difficult consumption

26 ASEAN Comprehensive Investment Agreement, art 3 <http://investasean.asean.org/files/upload/Doc%2005%20-%20ACIA.pdf> accessed 24 April 2022.

patterns. For example, in Vietnam, in the first three months of 2020, the revenue of the Vietnam National Oil and Gas Group (PVN) decreased by 13,194 billion VND (equivalent to 13%) compared to the same period in 2019; total profit after tax decreased by VND 4,580 billion (equivalent to 51%) compared to the same period in 2019.[27]

If investment in transportation and energy industries were continued to liberalise as committed to earlier in the trade agreements, foreign enterprises with many advantages in capital compared to domestic enterprises may gain control over sectors that are considered as essential infrastructure of the economy. This could seriously affect national security and other vital national interests.

An example that demonstrates changes to a country's law on investment liberalisation regime is the issuance of three Royal Decree-Laws by Spain to amend the current regulations on foreign investment in response to the COVID-19 pandemic and in order to prevent opportunistic foreign investments in critical sectors, such as national security and public health. This followed a recommendation of the European Commission that Member States advance the application of Foreign Direct Investment (FDI) Screening Regulation (EU) 2019/452,[28] which aimed at controlling FDI in the Union likely to affect security or public order.[29]

Decree-Royal Law 8/2020 on 17 March 2020 on urgent and extraordinary measures to confront the economic and social impact of COVID-19 introduces a new article 7bis into Law 19/2003, suspending the liberal FDI regime in Spain, especially related to some important industries. Accordingly, FDI will have to be pre-approved by the Spanish Council of Ministers if it falls under any of the following circumstances:

- The foreign direct investment concerns a company that operates in one of the strategic sectors set by Law 19/2003 (critical infrastructures, critical technologies and dual-use technologies, key inputs supply, industries with access to sensitive information, media, defence, food security, health care, electricity production and supply of hydrocarbons among others); or
- The foreign direct investment is carried out by a foreign State-controlled investor or by an investor who has already carried out an investment affecting public order or health in another Member State; or
- The foreign direct investment is carried out by an investor that poses a high risk of conducting illegal activities affecting public health or public order.

27 Vietnamese Government, Committee for Management of State Capital at Enterprises, 'The impact of the COVID-19 epidemic on the production and business activities of 19 corporations and corporations under the management of the Commission' [2020] Document No. 561/UBQLV-TH.

28 Regulation (EU) 2019/452 of the European Parliament and of the Council of 19 March 2019 establishing a framework for the screening of foreign direct investments into the Union [2019] EU OJ L 79I/1.

29 Ashurst Spain, 'Restrictions on Foreign Direct Investments in Spain' (*Ashurst*, website, 26 November 2020) <www.ashurst.com/en/news-and-insights/legal-updates/rdl-8-2020---suspension-of-direct-foreign-investment/> accessed 26 April 2022.

Under new article 7bis of the Royal Decree-Law 8/2020, authorisation in the above circumstances is required if all the FDI results in the investor acquiring a shareholding equal to or greater than 10% of a Spanish company (listed or unlisted), or where it acquires effective control over the company, provided that one of the following circumstances occurs: The investment is carried out by residents of countries outside the EU and EFTA or the investment is carried out by a EU or EFTA resident whose beneficial owner is a non-EU or EFTA resident.

Royal Decree-Law 11/2020 on 31 March 2010 introduced two non-fixed-term temporary measures:

- It introduced a EUR 1,000,000 threshold below which FDI is not subject to scrutiny, irrespective of the investor and sector of activity
- It introduced a fast-track scrutiny mechanism for FDI between EUR 1,000,000 and EUR 5,000,000. According to this law, clearance for those investments must be granted or denied within 30 days following the request for approval

According to Royal Decree-Law 34/2020 on 17 November 2020, during the period between 19 November 2020 and 30 June 2021, investments made by residents of countries in the European Union (EU) and the European Free Trade Association (EFTA) and investments made by Spanish residents whose beneficial ownership belonged to non-EU or non-EFTA residents, are considered to be FDI (provided they meet the conditions set by Royal Decree 8/2020).

Changes in the regulation of Spanish legislation on FDI control in some sectors may allow the country to temporarily disregard its commitments on investment liberalisation in these areas between Spain and non-EU and non-EFTA countries.

In the field of trade in services, commitments to regulate the temporary presence of natural persons who are nationals of the contracting parties such as business visitors, intra-enterprise movers, service providers are part of commitments on trade liberalisation in services. However, the implementation of these commitments is also likely to be impossible in the context of COVID-19 while countries apply measures to limit movement both within and between countries to control diseases.

In the field of trade in goods, many countries have issued regulations prohibiting or restricting the export of a number of goods due to COVID-19, such as medical equipment, personal protective equipment to ensure sufficient supply for domestic needs during the pandemic. For example, on 14 March 2020, the European Union issued Regulation 2020/403, which prohibited the export of personal protective equipment including face shields, protective spectacles and visors, mouth-nose-protection equipment and protective garments without an export license by the competent authority.[30] On 10 April 2020, the US Federal Emergency Management

30 Commission Implementing Regulation (EU) 2020/402 of 14 March 2020 making the exportation of certain products subject to the production of an export authorisation [2020] EU OJ L 77I/1. This regulation is no longer in force.

Agency (FEMA), on the instruction of the White House, published a temporary final rule on imposing export restrictions on respiratory filters, face masks, protective gloves and respirators without a FEMA-permit.[31] In essence, when export restrictions or bans in the above cases are applied, they may affect commitments on the liberalisation of trade in goods in trade agreements with which the parties are members.

Thirdly, COVID-19 and consequences arising from COVID-19 fundamentally change the scope of obligations that must still be fulfilled under the treaty.

The effects of COVID-19 can create a massive 'burden' for countries that seek to solve domestic problems as well as fulfil certain international commitments in the current context. At the time of signing, the provisions of the treaty create a legal basis for cooperation activities between countries, thereby creating conditions to promote the economic and social development of the parties. However, due to COVID-19, the implementation of some international commitments will not achieve the purpose intended at the time of signing. On the contrary, it may cause difficulties for the country in particular with respect to international commitments relating to the freedom of movement or facilitation of the free movement of natural persons between countries, including natural persons subject to commitments in the field of commercial services. If the commitment is fulfilled, the country must allow foreigners of other committed parties to enter and temporarily reside in the national territory or move through land border gates open for commerce. This can expose the country to the risk of not being able to control the spread of the disease. More dangerously, if foreigners are allowed to enter or move across national borders from places identified as serious epidemic areas, they may introduce new virus variants, putting further strain on the public health systems. Therefore, to ensure safety, the country may be temporarily unable to fulfil its international commitments on allowing foreigners to enter, reside in the national territory or move through border gates that opened to commerce between two countries that share a common border. Similarly, ongoing commitments on investment liberalisation in some fields may affect a country's security and national interests such as where investment concerns essential infrastructure, energy, technology, etc and investment may lead to the predominance of foreign investors over domestic investors in these fields. This can create negative dynamics for the country. In the area of trading goods, an unrestricted or limited export of medical products may result in inability to meet domestic demand as COVID-19 spreads. This will seriously affect the country's disease prevention, control and treatment activities. In these cases, *COVID-19 has the potential to fundamentally alter certain national obligations whose performance has become impossible due to the emergence of this pandemic.*

31 US Federal Register, *FEMA Prioritization and Allocation of Certain Scarce or Threatened Health and Medical Resources for Domestic Use*, 10 April 2020 <www.govinfo.gov/content/pkg/FR-2020-04-10/pdf/2020-07659.pdf>. This rule is no longer effective.

Temporarily suspending or terminating the implementation of a treaty on the basis of a 'fundamental change of circumstances'

Under the provisions of article 62 of the VCLT, a party may invoke a 'fundamental change of circumstances' to terminate or temporarily suspend the implementation of the treaty.

Termination or suspension of a treaty may extend to the entire treaty or be limited to certain clauses of the treaty. However, under article 44 VCLT, the termination or suspension of certain provisions of the treaty is available only if this clause can be separated from the rest of the treaty; the acceptance of such clause is not the primary basis of the consent of one or the other parties to be bound by the treaty as a whole, and the continuation of the implementation of the remainder of the treaty would not be unjust.

If the treaty specifically provides for the consequences of termination, the consequences for the parties of the termination of the treaty shall be resolved in accordance with the provisions of that treaty.[32] If the treaty does not deal with the consequences of terminating the treaty or the parties do not agree on different consequences of terminating the treaty, termination of the treaty will release the parties from any obligation to implement the treaty. In other words, after termination of the treaty, the parties will no longer need to perform their treaty obligations. However, under article 70(1) of the VCLT, the termination of the treaty does not affect any rights, obligations or legal situation of the parties created through the execution of the treaty before the treaty was terminated. In accordance with article 70(2), these legal consequences apply, where a State withdraws from or denounces a multilateral treaty, in the relationship between that State and each Contracting Party from the date at which the withdrawal or denunciation take effect.

Unless the suspension of the operation of a treaty was provided for by the treaty or is otherwise agreed to by the parties, article 72(1)(a) of the VCLT the suspension relieves the parties of their obligations during the period of suspension. In case of suspension of the entire treaty, the parties need not implement any the provisions of the treaty during the suspension period. However, if only one or several provisions of the treaty are suspended, the exemption from performance of the obligations in the treaty shall only apply to this provision, or these provisions, whereas the other provisions must still be fulfilled normally. In the event that the operation of a treaty is suspended only between some of the parties, the consequences of the suspension shall apply only between the parties concerned. The suspension of operation of the treaty does not affect the legal relations between the parties established by the treaty, as stated in article 72(1)(b) of the VCLT. In the

32 See, for example, Council of Europe, European Convention for the Protection of Human Rights and Fundamental Freedoms, as amended by Protocols Nos. 11 and 14, entry into force 4 November 1950, ETS 5, art 58 <www.echr.coe.int/documents/convention_eng.pdf> accessed 27 March 2022.

Draft Articles on the Law of Treaties with commentaries, the International Law Commission emphasised that: 'This provision is intended to make it clear that the legal nexus between the parties established by the treaty remains intact and that it is only the operation of its provisions which is suspended'.[33]

Invoking COVID-19 to suspend the implementation of a number of treaties for Vietnam

In Vietnam, the COVID-19 pandemic has had a serious socio-economic impact on Vietnam. While the Gross Domestic Product grew in 2019 at a rate of 7.02%, GDP in 2020 only increased by 2.91%,[34] GDP in 2021 only increased by 2.58%.[35] This was the lowest level of the years in the period 2011–2021. Its impact has been multi-dimensional on all areas of the socio-economy. Long-term social distancing solutions disrupted supply chains, leading to a sharp decline in both the demand and supply sides, across the industrial, agricultural and service sectors, causing a recession in investment and trade as well as in consumption, which also had a great impact on tourism and services.

As said above, COVID-19 affected the ability of Vietnam as well as many other countries to fulfil its international commitments related to the movement and entry of foreigners into the country's territory because of the risk it posed to the country's disease control.

Vietnam is a party to a number of treaties that directly regulate the movement of foreigners to Vietnamese territory, namely those related to the entry and temporary residence of foreigners, cross-border movement and transit, which includes trade agreements with provisions governing the movement of nationals of one Contracting Party to the territory of the other Contracting Party. The most prominent of these treaties include the following:

i) Border trade agreements between Vietnam and neighbouring countries. For example, the Border Trade Agreement between the Government of Vietnam and the Government of Laos contains regulations on opening various types of border gates between two countries, including international border gates, national border gates, local border gate and secondary border gate.[36]
ii) Trade agreements, which also regulate the temporary presence of natural persons for business purposes in trade in services, such as the Comprehensive

33 United Nations, Draft Articles On The Law Of Treaties With Commentaries (1966) art 68 <https://legal.un.org/ilc/texts/instruments/english/commentaries/1_1_1966.pdf> accessed 24 April 2022.

34 Vietnam, General Statistics Office (2021), Report on socio-economic situation in the fourth quarter and 2020.

35 Vietnam, General Statistics Office (2022), Report on socio-economic situation in the fourth quarter and 2021.

36 Border Trade Agreement between Laos and Vietnam (2015), art 3 <https://wtocenter.vn/chuyen-de/13042-border-trade-agreement-between-laos-and-vietnam> accessed 27 March 2022.

and Progressive Agreement for Trans-Pacific Partnership (CPTPP),[37] EU-Vietnam Free Trade Agreement (EVFTA)[38] and the ASEAN Agreement on Movement of Natural Persons (MNP).[39] According to these agreements, each member State, on the basis of its schedule of commitments, shall permit natural persons belonging to the group for the purpose of doing business in the trade in services. As such, service providers, business customers for the purpose of establishment, contract service providers, independent experts, intra-enterprise movers, etc. may enter and reside temporarily in the territory of the member country for a certain period of time. Specifically, according to article 4 of the MNP, each member state, in accordance with its schedule of commitments, will allow natural persons of other States, including business visitors, services under a contract, intra-corporate transferees to enter and reside temporarily in his or her territory when they complete the application procedures for an immigration applicant and meet all the requirements conditions for entry or temporary residence of the country. Similarly, according to the provisions of Chapter 12 of the CPTPP Agreement on temporary entry for business visitors, each signatory will make its specific commitment on the temporary entry of business visitors, including by stating conditions and restrictions on entry and temporary entry and the length of stay for each group. Furthermore, each Contracting Party shall grant temporary entry permits or temporary extension of entry to business visitors of the other Contracting Party in accordance with the commitments it has made: Article 12.4. To implement the above Agreements, Vietnam has issued specific commitments on temporary entry for business visitors of the signatories under the CPTPP Agreement,[40] the EVFTA[41] or the MNP.[42] For example, according to Vietnam's commitment to temporary entry for business guests, service offerors of a CPTPP signatory may enter and be granted residence permits in Vietnam for no more than six months provided that such services are not directly sold to the public and the offerees are not directly involved in providing services.

37 Comprehensive and Progressive Agreement for Trans-Pacific Partnership <www.sice.oas.org/tpd/tpp/tpp_e.asp#Text> accessed 24 April 2022.

38 Free Trade Agreement between the European Union and the Socialist Republic of Viet Nam [2020] EU OJ L186/3.

39 ASEAN Agreement on the Movement of Natural Persons <https://asean.org/wp-content/uploads/images/2013/economic/ASEAN%20MNP%20Agreement.pdf> accessed 24 April 2022.

40 Comprehensive and Progressive Agreement for Trans-Pacific Partnership, Annex 12-A 'Viet Nam's schedule of commitments for temporary entry for business persons' <http://cptpp.moit.gov.vn/data/e0593b3b-82bf-4956-9721-88e51bd099e6/userfiles/files/12-A_%20Viet%20Nam%20Temporary%20Entry%20for%20Business%20Persons.pdf> accessed 17 March 2022.

41 Free Trade Agreement between the European Union and the Socialist Republic of Viet Nam, Annex 8-B 'Vietnam's specific commitment schedule', [2020] EU OJ L186/1111.

42 ASEAN Agreement on the Movement of Natural Persons, Annex 1 – Viet Nam 'Viet Nam's schedule of movement of natural persons commitments' <https://asean.org/wp-content/uploads/images/2013/economic/asean_mnp_agreement/ASEAN%20MNP%20Schedule%20-%20Vietnam.pdf> accessed 25 March 2022.

In order to ensure the safety during the pandemic and not to be considered a violation of the treaty and to ensure safety for country, Vietnam can invoke COVID-19 as a fundamental change of circumstances to *temporarily suspend* the implementation of some international commitments relating to the movement of foreign people. In particular:

Firstly, temporarily suspending the terms of admission of experts, researchers, lecturers, artists, etc. in cultural-educational cooperation agreements between Vietnam and other countries during the complicated situation, except for experts in the medical field to participate in the treatment and response to COVID-19 in Vietnam.

Secondly, temporarily suspending the implementation of provisions in border trade agreements between Vietnam and other countries sharing a land border on opening main and auxiliary border gates for personal entry and exit activities, transportation products, except for certain cases. Therefore, temporarily closing main border gates and auxiliary border gates for individuals' entry and exit activities and goods transportation; stop entry and exit for individuals at international border gates, unless permitted by competent authorities.

Thirdly, temporarily suspending the implementation of regulations on temporary entry for business visitors in the field of trade in services in trade agreements. Accordingly, temporarily suspending entry permits for business visitors of the contracting parties for a certain period of time until the complicated situation of the epidemic is improved.

The grounds for this invoking are:

Firstly, there have been more than 200 countries and territories where COVID-19 cases have appeared, including all members of CPTPP as well as MNP.

Secondly, Vietnam has been through four waves of COVID-19, with all provinces and cities of Vietnam recording many cases of COVID-19. In particular, the number of infections in Vietnam increased continuously in the period from April 2021 to the end of 2021, and the period from February 2022 to the end of March 2022.[43] The Vietnamese health system coped well in the first three waves, as the number of cases were small and the Government responded well to the epidemic. When the Delta and the Omicron strain spread to Vietnam, the number of patients spiked, the health system faced many difficulties in disease control, medical examination and treatment for the people. In this situation, the prevention and control of the spread of the disease has become an increasingly urgent requirement of Vietnam.

43 Vietnamese Ministry of Health, Anti-epidemic bulletin of COVID-19' (*Covid19.gov.vn*, 2022) <https://covid19.gov.vn/?gidzl=JCK4EMNaV3rFqWqvOV9qEaZQ0JvyzIKv0jvTQdpp93q5tmSxVlyZEW7G06uigda_0u9TFMOQ640oP-LtFW> accessed 30 March 2022.

Thirdly, the spread and danger of COVID-19 along with Vietnam's conditions in response and control pandemic have caused the continuation of these international commitments to be fundamentally changed from the time of signing. That is, while removing barriers had the purpose of promoting the liberalisation of service trade among members or increasing corporation among states, the implementation of these measures during the pandemic could cause the epidemic to spread and diminish the country's ability effectively to respond to the epidemic.

Due to the above reasons, Vietnam can temporarily suspend the implementation of its commitments to suspend entry for citizens of member States subjects to these treaties in order to ensure the safety of Vietnam. The duration of the temporary suspension will depend on the evolution of COVID-19, the development of the global health system in response to the pandemic, and the ability to control and treat epidemics at member states.

In fact, during the complicated development of COVID, Vietnam has temporarily stopped entry activities for foreigners for a certain period of time which includes stopping the entry and exit of foreigners who are nationals of the Contracting Parties. For example, Directive No. 16/CT-TTg implemented urgent measures to prevent and control the COVID-19 epidemic on 31 March 2020 to 'temporarily close main border gates, auxiliary border gate for people crossing from 00:00 on April 1st, 2020 on the border with Laos and Cambodia' (para 7). Likewise, the Lao Government announced the closure of all main border gates and auxiliary border gates on the entire Vietnam-Laos border route from 19 March to 20 April 2020; completely closed all international border gates in operation from 3 April to 19 April 2020 and did not allow any individual to enter or exit through these border gates, except for product transportation or export-import in case of emergency.[44] The measures taken by Laos and Vietnam were in fact temporarily suspending the implementation of article 3 of the Border Trade Agreement between the Government of Vietnam and the Government of Laos.[45]

In this case, there was no statement citing COVID-19 as a fundamental change of circumstances, when imposing measures to limit or suspend cross-border movement, or suspend the entry of foreigners, except in special cases, who have temporarily suspended the implementation of the provisions on the movement of nationals of the contracting parties related to international treaties. When Vietnam applied the above measures to suspend the treaty, there was no objection from other countries. Because, in the period of 2020 and 2021, when the vaccine coverage rate was still low, border closure was a common measure considered by many countries to control the spread of the pandemic. However, if a dispute

44 'Laos Closes All Border Gates of Laos – Vietnam' *Dang Cong San*, 5 April 2020 (https://dangcongsan.vn, 2020) <https://dangcongsan.vn/thoi-su/lao-dong-tat-ca-cac-cua-khau-tuyen-bien-gioi-lao-viet-nam-552088.html> accessed 18 March 2022.

45 Border Trade Agreement between Laos and Vietnam (n 40), art 3.

had arisen, Vietnam could have invoked COVID-19 as a fundamental change of circumstances so as to prove that it has not violated international commitments related to import and export or move to the cross-border of foreigners.

Conclusion

Since the COVID-19 pandemic broke out in Wuhan (China) at the end of November 2019, COVID-19 has directly created a global health crisis, and at the same time caused serious impact to the economy and society of each country. Due to its severity, the COVID-19 pandemic has also had the potential to fundamentally affect the implementation of international treaties. The emergence of COVID-19 was not foreseen by any country. Yet, it is only possible to invoke COVID-19 as a fundamental change of circumstances if COVID-19 has the effect of radically transforming the extent of obligations to be performed under a treaty when compared to the implementation as initially envisaged.

Most countries in the world have responded to COVID-19 by adopting measures that directly affected the movement among regions or countries, and sometimes even within a country, to prevent the spread of the epidemic. In the event that a country has international commitments regarding the movement of individuals among countries, the implementation of these commitments in the context of COVID-19 can have serious consequences for the safety and security of the country. The original goal of promoting the liberalisation of service trade among countries, and increase their wealth, could not be achieved during this time, because free movement in times of a pandemic would cause the virus to spread, affect public health and diminish its economic well-being. In other words, COVID-19 has caused the continued implementation of these international commitments to be fundamentally changed from the time the treaty was signed. For the above reasons, COVID-19 can be invoked as a fundamental change of circumstances for the country to close its borders, temporarily suspend the implementation of international commitments related to freedom of movement – a measure that countries have universally implemented during 2020 and 2021.

From the beginning of 2022, many countries have announced plans to reopen their borders. However, in the future, there may be pandemics whose severity could be similar to or even worse than COVID-19. In this case, citing COVID-19 as an alternative fundamental change of circumstances would be seen as a useful precedent for states when dealing with similar issues related to the implementation of international commitments.

13 Treaties and *pacta sunt servanda*

A shared concept for the PRC?

Noble Po-kan Lo

Introduction

This chapter examines the understanding of the People's Republic of China (PRC) of adherence to treaties in the light of the importance of the doctrine of *pacta sunt servanda*, which requires that treaty obligations into which states have entered are to be carried out in good faith.

The PRC generally acknowledges the doctrine of *pacta sunt servanda* and honours its treaty commitments with neighbours and partners around the world. However, Chinese approaches to the notion of *pacta sunt servanda* also incorporate a belief that some historical treaties from colonial times, the 19th century in particular, were the result of coercion, imposed upon the threat of force, or not reciprocal in nature.[1] Some scholars suggest that these treaties, which the PRC ascribes to a class of what is sometimes called 'unequal'[2] treaties, can be justifiably abrogated, as an exception to the general rule of *pacta sunt servanda*.[3] Rather unsurprisingly, this causes tension between China and other states which take a different view of this principle, particularly those with which China historically entered into such unequal treaties. The respective countries' interpretation even of modern agreements such as the Sino-British Joint Declaration on Hong Kong of 1984 is case in point. China considers the Treaty of Nanking of 1898, in which Hong Kong was ceded to Britain, an 'unequal treaty' and considers that the Sino-British treaty of 1984 in respect of what is now the Hong Kong Special Administrative Region (or HKSAR) necessarily reflects this.[4] For the United Kingdom, the failure of China

1 Katherine A Greenberg, 'Hong Kong's Future: Can the People's Republic of China Invalidate the Treaty of Nanking as an Unequal Treaty?' (1983) 7 FILJ 534.

2 Matthew Craven, 'What Happened to Unequal Treaties? The Continuities of Informal Empire' (2005) 74 NJIL 355, 337.

3 Jianfeng Li, 'Equal or Unequal: Seeking a New Paradigm for the Misused Theory of "Unequal Treaties" in Contemporary International Law' (2016) 38 HJIL 465, 469.

4 Huo Zhengxin, 'UK Cannot Question HK Security Law' (*Embassy of the People's Republic of China in Poland*, 2020) <www.mfa.gov.cn/ce/cepl//pol/zbwx/t1797292.htm> accessed 23 November 2021.

DOI: 10.4324/9781003358305-16

to adhere to the Sino-British Joint Declaration meanwhile represents a breach of their treaty obligations, contrary to the doctrine of *pacta sunt servanda*.[5]

From this, it is clear that though *pacta sunt servanda* may remain the foundation stone of international law in China as it is in the rest of the world. However, in some situations China's historical relationship with the rest of the world affects the way in which *pacta sunt servanda* is perceived in China. This chapter will explain the nature of *pacta sunt servanda* as a rule of international law and then consider China's approach to the rule, in particular in relation to historical treaties that it regards as 'unequal'.

Pact sunt servanda in public international law

The rule of *pacta sunt servanda* stands at the very heart of public international law.[6] The principle has long been accepted as part of customary international law and constitutes *jus cogens* (a peremptory norm) so that it is accepted by civilised nations. Such norms create obligations *inter erga omnes* – regardless of whether or not any given state has accepted the doctrine.[7] As Janis suggests, 'probably no rule better fits the definition of the norm of *jus cogens* than *pacta sunt servanda*'.[8] A similar consequence arises from the almost universal application of the Vienna Convention on the Law of Treaties 1969 (VCLT), which adopts *pacta sunt servanda* as expressed in its article 26:

> Every treaty in force is binding upon the parties to it and must be performed by them in good faith.[9]

The principle of *pacta sunt servanda* was argued as far back as 1945 by Kunz to be a peremptory norm of international law.[10] This was recognised by its inclusion in the VCLT. However, as a *jus cogens* norm, it overrides other forms of international law, as a form of *lex superior*.[11] Thus, *pacta sunt servanda* is applied regardless of other obligations suggested by parties to be in existence, such as in treaties. This is again accepted by the VCLT, which in article 53 states that where a treaty conflicts with a peremptory norm of international law, the treaty will be void.

5 Gregory S Gordon, 'When "One Country, Two Systems" Meets "One Person, One Vote": The Law of Treaties and the Handover Narrative through the Crucible of Hong Kong's Election Crisis' (2015) 16 MJIL 344.
6 Hugh Thirlway, *Sources of International Law* (OUP 2014) 32.
7 Ulf Linderfalk, 'The Legal Consequences of *Jus Cogens* and the Individualisation of Norms' (2020) 33 LJIL 893, 894.
8 Mark W Janis, 'The Nature of Jus Cogens' in Larry May and Jeff Brown (eds), *Philosophy of Law: Classic and Contemporary Readings* (Blackwell, 2010) 185.
9 Convention on the Law of Treaties (Vienna, 23 May 1969) 1155 UNTS 331, entered into force 27 January 1980 (VCLT), art 26.
10 Josef L Kunz, 'The Meaning and the Range of the Norm *Pacta Sunt Servanda'* (1945) 39 AJIL, 180.
11 Jean d'Aspremont, '*Jus Cogens* as a Social Construct without Pedigree' (2015) 46 NYIL 85, 114.

China is a member of the United Nations and has both signed and ratified the VCLT. As a result, China is bound by the VCLT, including the application of *pacta sunt servanda*. Also, China, as a state with an international legal personality, will be bound by the doctrine as a result of its application of *erga omnes* and considering the status of *pacta sunt servanda* as a peremptory norm of public international law.[12]

However, *pacta sunt servanda* has never been universally accepted as being without exceptions, or absolute in nature. The doctrine of *rebus sic stantibus* allows parties to withdraw from a treaty or terminate a treaty obligation in the event of some fundamental changes in circumstances which render the treaty obligation obsolete.[13] This too has been translated into the VCLT: article 62(1) gives states a right to terminate or withdraw from a treaty if such a fundamental and unforeseeable change in circumstances not anticipated by the parties radically transforms the nature of their obligations.[14]

One of the early fathers of 20th-century public international legal thought, Hersch Lauterpacht, noted as early as 1933, that though –

> the rule that compacts must be kept is certainly one of the bases of the legal relations between the members of the community . . . the notion that in certain cases the law will refuse to continue to give effect to originally valid contracts is common to all systems of jurisprudence.[15]

This observation is vital to the general acceptance by states of international law. It is true that *pacta sunt servanda* is necessary to ensure that states enter into treaties in the first place. However, the lack of flexibility, or the lack of acknowledging political realities, in which states and their relative power and position *vis-à-vis* one another evolve over time mean that treaties would be likely to be regarded as being unhelpful, resulting in greater uncertainty, and a breakdown in the international order itself.[16]

Thus, it is fair to suggest that *pacta sunt servanda* is not 'impregnable' even when a treaty is carefully drafted by the parties.[17] After all, the VCLT makes provisions for the denunciation or withdrawal from a treaty if that treaty itself does not provide any such outlet for denunciation or withdrawal; if the parties intend to 'admit the possibility' of denunciation or withdrawal; if such a right of denunciation might be inferred as a result of the nature of the treaty.[18] Though such

12 Li Hapoei, 'Jus Cogens and International Law' in Sienho Yee and Wang Tieya (eds), *International Law and the Post-Cold War World: Essays in Memory of Li Hapoei* (Routledge, 2001) 499–522.

13 Hersch Lauterpacht, *The Function of Law in the International Community* (Clarendon, 1933) 213.

14 VCLT (n 9) art 62(1).

15 Lauterpacht (n 13) 273.

16 Bhek Pati Sinha, *Unilateral Denunciation of Treaty Because of Other Violations of Obligations by Other Party* (Martinus Nijhoff, 1966) 88.

17 ibid.

18 VCLT (n 9) art 56(1)(a)(b).

a denunciation is an accepted mechanism in the VCLT, it should be noted that, in general terms, where the treaty is signed by the parties, the opportunity for such a renunciation, or unilateral withdrawal from the treaty, is made significantly more difficult by the peremptory norm of *pacta sunt servanda*. This difficulty is compounded by the fact that the conditions under which such a withdrawal is permitted in the VCLT are restricted by what is intended at least, to be the VCLT's exhaustive provisions for the withdrawal or renunciation from the treaty.[19]

China's approach to *pacta sunt servanda*

The PRC's approach to treaties, and to the recognition of *pacta sunt servanda*, is broadly consistent with obligations being fulfilled in good faith and being treated as binding.[20] Issues have, nevertheless, arisen most commonly in the sphere of border disputes between the state and its neighbours. These have in fact been rather numerous over the years, owing to geographic and historical challenges faced by China in the region and to the country's vast size. As Pan notes, the failure of the PRC to have settled all of these disputes in the past 50 years or so has been considered a 'prominent disappointing feature' in the state's history.[21] According to Pan, part of this failure stems from the PRC's approach to international law itself.[22] This can be seen as early as the 1960s when the PRC engaged in a number of border disputes with the neighbouring Soviet Union, which then flared up in 1969 into a live exchange of fire between troops from both sides. While the Soviet Union sought to rely on *pacta sunt servanda*, the PRC demanded that it 'recognise the unequal nature of the existing treaties' as a precondition for beginning negotiations over the border delimitation and boundary issues.[23] This is a precursor to one of the key Chinese exceptions to *pacta sunt servanda* in the form of 'unequal treaties', which will form the focus of this chapter.

The issue of 'unequal treaties' can arise when a foreign state seeks to hold China to a treaty obligation agreed to by a predecessor state to the PRC itself. This situation can be distinguished from the approach taken by the PRC to treaty obligations into which it has itself entered. This was acknowledged as early as 1967 by Lee, who noted that treaties form the basis of Chinese adherence to international law in which there is largely a 'Western' focus. According to Lee, it was

19 Laurence R Helfer, 'Terminating Treaties' in Duncan Hollis (ed), *The Oxford Guide to Treaties* (OUP, 2012) 634.

20 Junwu Pan, *Toward a New Framework for Peaceful Settlement of China's Territorial and Boundary Disputes* (Martinus Nijhoff, 2009) 71.

21 ibid.

22 ibid.

23 Thomas Robinson, 'China Confronts the Soviet Union: Warfare and Diplomacy on China's Inner Asian Frontiers' in Roderick MacFarquhar and John K Fairbank (eds), *The Cambridge History of China, Vol 15: The People's Republic Part 2: Revolutions within the Chinese Revolution, 1966–1982* (CUP, 1991) 271.

> understandable that China might feel reluctant to be bound by Western customary law, in the making of which it did not participate. Treaties, on the other hand, as expressions of consent, remain the logical source of international law for China.[24]

For this reason, with the exception of unequal treaties, the state has been a proponent of *pacta sunt servanda* in respect of treaties into which it has entered.[25] It might be said that China's relations with its neighbours as well as its honouring of boundaries have been relatively stable in most cases in which the PRC itself has entered into an agreement. The Chinese Foreign Ministry has reaffirmed its commitment to the doctrine in recent years, stating in a press release that China is 'observing international law in the truest sense'; it is upholding the 'sanctity' of the United Nations Convention on the Law of the Sea 1982 (UNCLOS) in its refusal to enter into arbitration with the Philippines in respect of disputes over the delimitation of maritime boundaries in the South China Sea.[26] In other words, China's reference to the UNCLOS indicates that its defence of the Philippines' claims is based on its respect for the expressed treaty obligations, into which it entered into in good faith and which must therefore be complied with on the basis of *pacta sunt servanda*.

China's adherence to *pacta sunt servanda* might be seen in its relations with some of its neighbours such as Myanmar, as well.[27] The PRC and Myanmar entered into a revised border treaty in 1961 which allowed the pair to demarcate their borders on their own terms rather than on the basis of historical colonialist settlement, and this has been a boundary which the PRC has assiduously respected ever since.[28] As will be seen, a distinction must be drawn then between those treaties into which the country has legitimately and freely entered and those which, in the PRC's understanding, are impacted negatively by a lack of true consent resulting from the unequal nature of the treaty.

This approach is largely built on a distinction between historical, unequal treaties and others which are not seen in the framework of such historical treaty obligations. It highlights an important aspect of the PRC's approach to *pacta sunt servanda*, which it interprets as including exceptional circumstances which give rise to treaties being no longer binding or effective on the basis of being unequal.

24 Luke T Lee, 'Treaty Relations of the People's Republic of China: A Study of Compliance' (1967) 116 UPLR 244, 245.

25 David Salem, 'The People's Republic of China, International Law and Arms Control' (1983) 6 Occasional Papers/Reprint Series in Contemporary Asian Studies 1, 16.

26 Ministry of Foreign Affairs of the People's Republic of China: 'People's Daily: China is Observing International Law in the True *Sense' (Foreign Ministry Website of PRC,* 2015) <www.fmprc.gov.cn/mfa_eng/topics_665678/nhwt/t1326344.shtml> accessed 4 June 2021.

27 Burma-China Boundary Treaty 1961 United Nations New York No 14847 <https://treaties.un.org/doc/Publication/UNTS/Volume%201010/volume-1010-I-14847-English.pdf> accessed 2 May 2022.

28 Maung Maung, 'The Burma – China Boundary Settlement' (1961) 1 AS 38.

In conclusion, it can be said that China adopts a rather unique approach towards international law and *pacta sunt servanda* by incorporating an understanding of unequal treaties into them.[29]

The PRC's approach to its international law obligations is reflected in its renunciation of so-called 'unequal treaties', which are treaties into which a country has entered as a result of coercion or which are not reciprocal in their terms.[30] For example, as a result of the imposition of the Treaty of Nanking by the British in the colonial era, China ceded Hong Kong to the British, and under two subsequent Conventions of Peking, China perpetually leased Kowloon and leased for a period of 99 years the New Territories and some other areas to Britain. These treaties are regarded in Chinese history as unequal, forced, and, hence, morally and legally illegitimate.[31] Under the principle of *rebus sic stantibus*, contracting parties are entitled to alteration or termination of a treaty in the event of a fundamental change of circumstances.[32] According to Li, China historically relied on this doctrine sixteen times to nullify treaties before the VCLT 'era', including the Twenty-One Demands, which it signed with Japan in 1915, and the 1865 Sino-Belgian Treaty.[33]

Another example of the PRC's reluctance to acknowledge obligations set out in unequal treaties is its attempt to revise its historical border treaties with the Soviet Union in modern times.[34] In the exchanges between both countries, the Soviet Union wished to maintain an emphasis on *pacta sunt servanda*, while the PRC argued that these historical treaties were not binding as a result of being 'unequal'. More interestingly, the PRC appears to have seen this negotiation as an attempt to set a historical legal precedent, as the outcome of the dispute does not appear as important as the principle. As Robinson notes, China was quite prepared to maintain the status quo after a renegotiation with the Soviet Union, in terms of the boundary delimitation itself, but wished to do so after an acceptance by the Soviet Union that the older treaties were 'unequal' and therefore not binding.[35] In the end, no real agreement was reached on this issue.[36]

In what might be termed 'orthodox' Western interpretations of international law and *pacta sunt servanda*, the question of 'unequal treaties' has only ever received rather limited treatment.[37] Nevertheless, von Wolff already acknowledged in the 18th century that –

29 Pan (n 20) 71.
30 Greenberg (n 1) 534.
31 ibid.
32 JW Garner, 'The Doctrine of *Rebus Sic Stantibus* and the Termination of Treaties (1967) 61 AJIL 509, 515.
33 Li (n 3) 489.
34 Robinson (n 23) 271.
35 ibid.
36 ibid, 277.
37 Jesse A Finkelstein, 'An Examination of the Treaties Governing the Far-Eastern Sino-Soviet Border in Light of the Unequal Treaties Doctrine' (1979) 2 BCICLR 445, 449.

> treaties are unequal in which the same things or equivalents are not promised by each of the contracting parties . . . therefore moreover, it follows that the condition of one of the contracting parties is made worse by the treaty, or the conditions of those entering into an unequal treaty are not equal.[38]

In other words, in the Western tradition, an unequal treaty could be defined as a treaty in which the obligations of the parties were not equal or as one in which one of the parties is unduly favoured. Nevertheless, there is nothing in the traditionally accepted Western understanding of *pacta sunt servanda* which appears to allow a treaty to be considered non-binding or unenforceable as a result. Von Wolff's definition of an unequal treaty is just that – a definition. Nor does any clause in VCLT suggest that treaties falling under this definition could be considered void. However, the second sentence in Von Wolff's definition suggests that an unequal treaty is one which might also be constituted by the unequal 'conditions' of those who entered into it. This might obliquely refer to a situation in which a party was coerced by force, or threat of force, to accept a treaty or treaty condition. This situation would now seem to fall within the scope of treaties procured by the threat or use of force under article 52 of the VCLT.[39]

However, there is something of a lacuna in Western understandings of international law as far as the notion of unequal treaties goes.[40] Western scholars such as Malawer argue that there is nothing inherently unlawful about unequal treaties *per se* (subject to the prohibition on treaties imposed by or under threat of force contained in article 52 of the VCLT).[41] However, in general, as Craven notes, 'the phenomenon of unequal treaties has largely evaporated as an issue from the domain of international law' with international lawyers displaying 'an unwillingness to engage effectively with the problem of equality'.[42] The doctrine of unequal treaties is therefore maintained largely only in the Chinese understanding of international law,[43] although it ought also to be noted here that Li[44] and others such as Nozari[45] argue that the theory of unequal treaties is one which some such as Craven,[46] Peters[47] or Tseng[48] have sought to promote more widely to help remedy historical injustice in international law.

38 Christian von Wolff, *Jus Gentium Methodo Scientifica Pertractatum* (Joseph H Drake tr, Clarendon Press, 1934) 206.
39 VCLT (n 9) art 52.
40 Alice de Jonge, 'From Unequal Treaties to Differential Treatment: Is there a Role for Equity in Treaty Relations?' (2014) 4 Asian Journal of International Law 125, 125.
41 Stuart Malawer, *Imposed Treaties and International Law* (William S Hein & Co, 1977) 5.
42 Craven (n 2) 336.
43 Dong Wang, *China's Unequal Treaties: Narrating National History* (Lexington Books, 2005) 3.
44 Li (n 3) 467.
45 Fariborz Nozari, *Unequal Treaties in International Law* (S Bryan Sundt & Co, 1971) 112.
46 Craven (n 2) 336.
47 Anne Peters, 'Unequal' in Wolfram (ed), *Max Planck Encyclopaedia of Public International Law* (OUP, 2012) 38.
48 Yu-Hao Tseng, *The Termination of Unequal Treaties in International Law* (Commercial Press, 1931) 9.

However, it is clear that the PRC's commitment to renegotiation of, and non-adherence to, historical unequal treaties remains. In other words, the PRC sees the issue of unequal treaties as one of the legal limits to the application of *pacta sunt servanda*. However, one area where it is more difficult to apply this exception is in respect of some non-historical treaties which the PRC has been accused of failing to uphold. These will now be examined.

Revisionism over non-historical treaties

The PRC can be said to have generally a good record of adherence to *pacta sunt servanda* in respect of treaties which do not come under the doctrine of unequal treaties. However, some situations do not appear to fit this pattern. As China's economic strength has grown in the past few decades to rival that of the United States as the dominant economic global power, the PRC has become increasingly assertive.[49] According to Kumar, this has created a spectre of the state seeking to 'recast the regional order in East Asia, South East Asia, and South Asia' in a manner which threatens the territorial integrity or national security of some neighbouring states.[50] Pan has ascribed this notion of pragmatism to the PRC's general approach to international law of being willing to uphold *pacta sunt servanda* when treaties are useful and declaring treaties to be 'unequal' when they are not.[51] The PRC's doctrine of unequal treaties is internally regarded as consistent with its own stated commitments to treaties into which it has entered as expressions of free will and consent, unlike historical treaties. China's perception of the doctrine and its approaches to treaty obligations with some of its neighbours, such as the Philippines as regards the *South China Sea* dispute, discussed at length below,[52] are contrary to *pacta sunt servanda*.

The PRC cites its approach to the UNCLOS as an example of its commitment to *pacta sunt servanda*. The PRC freely entered into the UNCLOS and ratified it, holding it up as a treaty obligation with which it is required to comply.[53] One of the key principles embodied in the UNCLOS is the establishment of sovereignty over the 'territorial sea', which can extend up to a limit of 12 nautical miles from the baseline determined in accordance with the Convention.[54] Also, each state is recognised as being able to exert its rights under the Convention over a range

49 Li Zhaojie, 'China' in Simon Chesterman and others (eds), *The Oxford Handbook of International Law in Asia and the Pacific* (OUP, 2019) 313.

50 Suneel Kumar, 'China's Revisionism Versus India's Status Quoism: Strategies and Counter-strategies of Rivals in Doklam Standoff' (2020) 24 JJIR 73.

51 Pan (n 20) 71.

52 Permanent Court of Arbitration, *The Republic of the Philippines v The People's Republic of China (PCA Case No 2013–19)* award of 12 July 2016.

53 Ministry of Foreign Affairs of the People's Republic of China: 'People's Daily: China is Observing International Law in the True Sense' (Foreign Ministry Website of PRC, 2015) <www.fmprc.gov.cn/mfa_eng/topics_665678/nhwt/t1326344.shtml> accessed 4 June 2021.

54 United Nations Convention on the Law of the Sea (Montego Bay, 10 December 1982) 1833 UNTS 3, entered into force 16 November 1994, art 3.

of 200 nautical miles from the baseline on which the territorial sea is measured through its exclusive economic zone (or EEZ).[55] Despite this, the PRC has long claimed that its EEZ includes a vast swathe of the South China Sea on the basis of what it terms the 'nine-dash-line'.[56] The territory within this nine-dash-line (the origins of which are themselves unclear) exceeds the 200 miles stipulated by China's EEZ, and infringes upon the EEZs of some other states in the region such as Vietnam, the Philippines, Thailand, Indonesia, Brunei, Malaysia, and the contested territory of Taiwan.[57] A number of stand-offs have arisen over the years as a result, particularly caused by the PRC's attempts to create artificial islands and after the United States began to assert a more strident policy towards China that is felt by some in the country as the 'containment' of the PRC.[58] Nevertheless, it is difficult to reconcile China's commitment to the obligations of the UNCLOS with the claims made under the nine-dash line.

The Philippines-PRC arbitration and the India/China border dispute

In 2016, the Philippines claimed China's actions in the South China Sea, such as the building of artificial reefs and islands outside Chinese territorial waters, constituted a breach of the UNCLOS. The Philippines initiated arbitration proceedings against China before the Permanent Court of Arbitration.[59] China's case was that the work took place within its own sovereign territory, set out on the basis of the so-called nine-dash line, which represented historical claims to Chinese territory in the area. The Philippines' counterargument was that China's territorial waters, and the EEZ, were to be measured according to provisions in the UNCLOS. The Permanent Court of Arbitration rendered an award in favour of the Philippines, rejecting China's claim to its territory asserted under the 'nine-dash-line', which it stated 'had no legal basis'.[60] Thus, China's non-compliance with its obligations under the UNCLOS, a treaty that has not been denounced by the PRC and cannot be classified under China's doctrine of unequal treaties, does not appear to be in line with its understanding of either the doctrine of *pacta sunt servanda* or the doctrine of unequal treaties. It is, instead, an anomalous situation that proves the pragmatism in the PRC's more general approach towards international law.

55 ibid art 57.

56 Lowell Bautista and Aries A Arugay, 'Philippines v. China: The South China Sea Arbitral Award: Implications for Policy and Practice' (2017) 9 APP 122.

57 Mingjiang Li, 'China Debates the South China Sea Dispute' in Ian Storey and Lin Cheng-yi (eds), *South China Sea Dispute: Navigating Diplomatic and Strategic Tensions* (ISEAS – Yusof Ishak Institute, 2017) 45.

58 ibid.

59 Hung Pham, 'Case: *Philippines v China: The South China Sea Finally Meets International Law* (2016) 16 C-KJICL 3, 4.

60 Permanent Court of Arbitration, *The Republic of the Philippines v The People's Republic of China (PCA Case No 2013–19)*, award of 12 July 2016.

Also, Kumar states that the PRC's approach towards resolving border disputes with India and Nepal cannot be said to fall strictly within the established framework of unequal treaties.[61] The PRC does not acknowledge any of the treaties signed by India and China at a time when India was governed by the British Empire.[62]

The PRC signed a number of treaties with India and Nepal, such as the Sino-Indian Panchsheel Treaty 1954 and the Sino-Nepalese Treaty of Peace and Friendship 1960.[63] Although these agreements have aimed to maintain the status quo on border issues between India and Nepal, on the one hand, and the PRC, on the other, Indian scholars, such as Kumar, have accused the PRC of violating these treaty obligations.[64] They assert that the PRC's claim to some 5,000 square miles of land to the south of the McMahon Line which it designates as 'Southern Tibet', and ongoing border clashes between the troops of both states, are the result of Chinese 'revisionism' quite at odds with both the accepted understanding of unequal treaties and with the orthodox understanding of *pacta sunt servanda*. However, this dispute is, instead, an example of the PRC's pragmatism in respect of these doctrines.

Additionally, the PRC rejects India's position that the so-called McMahon Line marks its boundary with the PRC, as it was established under the Simla Accord of 1914. The PRC argues that the treaty was a colonialist imposition and that Tibet, one of the signatories, is an integral part of China and does not have the legal competence to accede to the treaty obligations in the first place.[65] This reflects the understanding of the PRC's approach to unequal treaties, which it will seek to renege on by reference to the doctrine of *rebus sic stantibus*.[66]

The British-Sino Joint Declaration

Another example of the PRC's attitude towards revisionism of treaties is the Sino-British Joint Declaration of 1984,[67] the treaty regulating the UK's 1997 handover of Hong Kong to the PRC. One of the provisions in the Joint Declaration was to

61 Kumar (n 50) 73.

62 ibid.

63 Agreement on Trade and Intercourse between the Tibet Region of China and India, signed 29 April 1954, 299 UNTS 57; Sino-Nepalese Treaty of Peace and Friendship, signed 28 April 1960 <https://indiamadhesi.files.wordpress.com/2008/11/sino-nepal-treaties-1960.pdf> accessed 2 May 2022

64 Kumar (n 50) 80.

65 Dmitry Sudakov, 'China has Territorial Claims to Nearly 20 Countries' *Pravda* (Moscow, 17 July 2012) <https://english.pravda.ru/world/121658-china_territorial_claims/> accessed 4 June 2021.

66 Prabhakar Singh, 'Sino-Indian Attitude to International Law of Nations, States, and Colonial Hangovers' (2015) 3 CJCL 1, 4.

67 Joint Declaration of China and the United Kingdom of Great Britain and Northern Ireland on the question of Hong Kong (Beijing, 19 December 1984), 1399 UNTS 3 (entered into force 27 May 1985).

establish conditions under which the legal system of Hong Kong would operate. Annex I of the Agreement, for example, provided that the constitutional position of Hong Kong would allow the region to have its own legislature and retain its capitalist system and way of life for a period of 50 years,[68] as part of a 'one-country two-systems' model to the Hong Kong Special Administrative Region (HKSAR). Recent incidents in Hong Kong, in which elected legislators in the HKSAR's legislature were vetoed by the Standing Committee of the National People's Congress, in favour of a Committee which was established to allow the appointment of more Council Members in a non-democratic manner were declared by the UK's Foreign Ministry to be a 'clear' and 'ongoing' breach of the treaty.[69] The PRC's attitude towards the Joint Declaration appears to be quite contrary to its understanding of *pacta sunt servanda*, with the Foreign Ministry declaring the treaty in 2017 to be a mere 'historical document' which 'no longer binds China'.[70] The Joint Declaration is quite unlike the earlier 'Treaty of Nanking' because the latter was previously denounced by China as an unequal treaty. The Declaration was a bilateral treaty which the UK and the PRC entered in good faith. Therefore, the basis on which China might argue that *pacta sunt servanda* does not apply to this treaty is unclear. Gordon suggests that the reason is simply due to China's approach to 'good faith', taking into account the nature of the historical and contemporary challenges posed by the unique *sui generis* nature of the HKSAR.[71]

Material breach

Another situation in which international law allows for treaty obligations to be avoided is a material, or fundamental, breach. This exception to the general rule of *pacta sunt servanda* is specifically provided under article 60(1) of the VCLT, which reads:

> A material breach of a bilateral treaty by one of the parties entitles the other to invoke the breach as a ground for terminating the treaty or suspending its operation in whole or in part.[72]

A similar provision is also established in respect of the breaches of multilateral treaties under article 60(2), which allows non-breaching parties to suspend the

68 ibid Annex I.

69 UK Government, Foreign Ministry, 'Foreign Secretary Declares Breach of Sino-British Joint Declaration' (UK Foreign Ministry Website, 2020) Press Release, <www.gov.uk/government/news/foreign-secretary-declares-breach-of-sino-british-joint-declaration> accessed 4 June 2021.

70 Reuters Staff, 'China Says Sino-British Joint Declaration on Hong Kong No Longer Has Meaning' *Reuters* (30 June 2017) <www.reuters.com/article/us-hongkong-anniversary-china-idUSKBN19L1J1> accessed 4 June 2021.

71 Gordon (n 5) 349.

72 VCLT (n 9) art 60(1).

whole or parts of the treaty either in relation to all the members of the treaty, or just as between the defaulting state and the rest of the members.[73]

The overall effect of article 60(1) and (2) is similar to the provision in the contract laws of many different states, which allow for the termination of all existing and future contractual obligations if a party commits a fundamental breach, such as the provisions in the Vienna Convention on Contracts for the International Sale of Goods 1980.[74] Such provisions aim to recognise that agreements, be they treaties or contracts into which the parties entered in good faith, should no longer be binding if there is such a material breach as to undermine the purpose of the treaty itself. However, there is a high threshold for a breach to be considered 'material'. As provided for by article 60(3)(a) and (b), this threshold is satisfied only if there is a repudiation by one of the parties in a manner not sanctioned by the Convention, or where there is a violation of the provision essential to the accomplishment of the object or purpose of the treaty itself.[75]

The rule of material breach appears to be accepted as part of the Chinese approach to treaty law and does not pose too many difficulties here. Given the PRC's declarations in respect of the Sino-British Joint Declaration to the effect that it no longer binds China, scholars in recent times to assess whether China might, possibly, be able to rely on article 60 of the VCLT.[76] However, this does not seem possible, as there is no basis for an argument that the UK has repudiated or otherwise been in material breach of the Declaration. Instead, scholars such as Gordon point to a more 'elastic' understanding of *pacta sunt servanda* to perform obligations in 'good faith'.[77] It seems that international law cannot easily reconcile the Chinese and Western understandings of *pacta sunt servanda*.[78] The reasons for differences of opinion in the approach to *pacta sunt servanda* are likely to be political in nature. China, a great power in the modern and historical world, had a period of weakness in the 18th and 19th centuries and feels a degree of resentment at the fact that it had treaties imposed upon it which were not in its best interests and which were, to one degree or other, unequal. Now that the state has recovered its power and standing on the international stage, these treaties operate as continual reminders of a national humiliation and are thought of as being required to be erased from operation one way or another. This does not lie particularly well with the way in which *pacta sunt servanda* has traditionally been understood by Western nations, and it is therefore understandable that an alternative understanding of the rule of *pacta sunt servanda*, allowing for revisionism in the event of unequal treaties, has been put forward by China.

73 ibid art 60(2)(a)(b).

74 United Nations Convention on Contracts for the International Sale of Goods (Vienna, 11 April 1980) 1489 UNTS 3, entered into force 1 Jan. 1988, art 25.

75 VCLT (n 9) art 60(3)(a)(b).

76 Gordon (n 5) 346; see also Alvin HY Cheung, 'Road to Nowhere: Hong Kong's Democratization and China's Obligations under Public International Law' (2015) 40 BJIL 467, 510.

77 Gordon (n 5) 388.

78 ibid.

Conclusion

In conclusion, China has upheld and maintained *pacta sunt servanda*. However, the PRC's relations with its neighbours remain troubled at times as a result of China's understanding of international law and *pacta sunt servanda* in particular. This understanding emphasises the importance of unequal treaties being void or voidable, of *rebus sic stantibus*, and the fact that treaties can be avoided in the event of material breach. All these lead to ongoing disagreements on the way in which the PRC gives effect to *pacta sunt servanda*.

However, some situations appear as outliers here, most notably China's attitude towards the provisions in the UNCLOS and the South China Sea, which are difficult to be reconciled even with the Chinese understanding of the doctrine. China has been accused of failing to respect *pacta sunt servanda* in its disputes with India and Nepal or with the Soviet Union in years gone by. This can largely be explained by the application of the doctrine of unequal treaties, which plays an integral part in China's understanding of the treaty law.

PRC's border disputes with India and Nepal must be seen in the light of its refusal to accept the binding application of the McMahon Line, or the Treaty of Simla, as both of these were established by colonial Britain, with the predecessor states of India, Nepal and China today.[79] Though a Western tradition might consider that the law of state succession leaves no space for a doctrine of 'unequal treaties' unless there was coercion through the threat or use of force, as under article 52 of the VCLT, this is not so under the Chinese understanding of international law.

As has been noted throughout, this chapter did not aim to determine whether or not China complies with *pacta sunt servanda* from merely one perspective, but whether China does so according to its own understanding of international law. Though China appears to believe that its understanding of *pacta sunt servanda* is consistent with international law, it is certainly the case that many of its neighbours do not see things in quite the same way.

79 Utkarsh Pandey, 'The India-China Border Question: An Analysis of International Law and State Practice' (2020) ORF Occasional Papers No 290 <www.orfonline.org/research/the-india-china-border-question/> accessed 4 June 2021.

14 *Pacta sunt servanda*

Comfort letters in an age of instability and strategic rivalry

Joel Slawotsky

I Introduction

In the context of debt, comfort letters (or keep-well agreements) provide written assurances or 'comfort' to a creditor relating to re-payment.[1] However, in contrast to formal contracts, comfort letters do not contain any express guarantees or promises of payment nor do they generally reference any specific debt details such as an amount or a payment schedule. Instead, comfort letters usually consist of a nebulously worded intent to ensure sufficient liquidity to the debtor and/or to maintain the debtor's solvency.[2] The purpose of these enigmatic 'gentlemen's agreements' is dual-functional from the issuer's perspective; inducing lenders to provide capital but simultaneously avoiding contractual obligation. Vested with plausible deniability, enforceability of comfort letters is intrinsically challenging.[3]

Extensively employed in the offshore Chinese debt market, a staggering amount of debt, '[a]bout [US]$119 billion of Chinese offshore bonds outstanding', is backed by comfort letters.[4] Chinese onshore borrowers seeking to attract capital are incentivised to 'go offshore', primarily in the Hong Kong Special Administrative Region ('HKSAR'), to legally evade the Mainland's law and regulations forbidding onshore parent entities from expressly guaranteeing the offshore debt of subsidiaries.[5] Typically, the capital is borrowed via a Special Purpose Vehicle

1 See Leon Trakman and Robert Walters, *Contemporary Issues in Finance and Insolvency Law – Volume 2* (Routledge, 2022) ch 4 (comfort letters have a variety of purposes in corporate law).

2 Bloomberg News, 'China Record $30B Bond Defaults Seen Rising This Year', *Bloomberg* (12 January 2021) <www.bloomberg.com/news/articles/2021-01-11/china-s-record-30-billion-bond-defaults-seen-rising-this-year> ('The keepwell provision often involves a Chinese company's pledge to keep an offshore subsidiary that is issuing the bonds solvent – but without any guarantee of payment to the bondholders.')

3 Reuters Staff, 'Administrator for China's PUFG rejects keepwell deed for $300 mln bond' (23 August 2020) <www.reuters.com/article/china-bond-keepwell-idUKL4N2FP01J> (Administrator disclaims responsibility for debt as no guarantee was provided in the comfort letter).

4 Bloomberg News, 'What "Keepwell" Means With Bonds Like Evergrande's', *Bloomberg* (20 May 2020) <www.bloomberg.com/news/articles/2020-05-14/how-a-keepwell-clause-protects-china-bonds-or-not-quicktake>.

5 HKTDC Research, 'Foreign Exchange Administration Framework', *HKTDC Research* (29 August 2018) <https://research.hktdc.com/en/article/NDM0NzIwMTQw> (China's regulatory strictures lifted in the offshore capital raising context).

DOI: 10.4324/9781003358305-17

(‘SPV’) which receives a comfort letter from the onshore People’s Republic of China (‘PRC’) corporate parent memorialising the parent’s intent with respect to maintaining the liquidity of the SPV borrowing the capital.

Generally, scant attention is given to the enforceability of comfort letters when financial stability reigns and debt payments continue unimpeded. However, given the unprecedented global environment of astonishingly high indebtedness, capital markets are increasingly at risk of substantial losses.[6] Indeed, over a decade of extraordinary low interest rates encouraged excessive risk-taking and market bubbles.[7] Specifically with respect to China, excessive debt levels (and in particular debt fuelling housing speculation) have led to anxieties over uber-leverage some opine is even higher than expected.[8] Indeed, emerging indications in China point to a potential wave of restructurings and defaults in both the private and state-linked sectors.[9] The exemplar of asset managing company, Huarong, which was ostensibly profitable with no indication of debt problems is indicative of potential enormous hidden debt problems.[10] Further exemplifying the potential scope of the debt problem are the financial challenges at Evergrande Group (‘Evergrande’), a large Chinese property developer.[11] Evergrande’s massive US-$300 billion debt and financial problems amid lacklustre property sales highlight the risks in China’s housing sector.[12]

6 Jeremy Grantham, ‘Waiting for the Last Dance’ (5 January 2021) <www.gmo.com/asia/research-library/waiting-for-the-last-dance/> (global markets are in an ‘epic bubble’).

7 International Monetary Fund, ‘Global Financial Stability Report: Lower for Longer’ (IMF, October 2019) <www.imf.org/en/Publications/GFSR/Issues/2019/10/01/global-financial-stability-report-october-2019>.

8 Shen Wei, ‘Shadow Banking System in China – Origin, Uniqueness and Governmental Responses’ (2013) 1 Journal of International Banking Law & Regulation 20, 21: ‘Shadow banking in China also involves the use of off-balance-sheets. Local governments’ huge and opaque debt has been seen as one of the big risks looming over the Chinese economy.’; Qizheng Mao, ‘Measuring the off-balance-sheet wealth management business of commercial banks: The case in China’ in: Proceedings of the Sixth IFC Conference on ‘Statistical issues and activities in a changing environment’, Basel, 28–29 August 2012 <www.bis.org/ifc/publ/ifcb36d.pdf> (banks might be carrying substantially higher debt levels).

9 Morgan Davis, ‘It’s crunch time for Chinese SOE bonds’ *Global Capital Asia* (20 April 2021) <www.globalcapital.com/article/b1rh29j3r7fwq5/its-crunch-time-for-chinese-soe-bonds> (recent debt problems highlight the risks of acquiring Chinese state-owned corporate debt).

10 Edward White, Thomas Hale and Sun Yu ‘China investigates senior bad debt official for corruption’ <www.ft.com/content/3d33d458-1442-48ef-a652-d2af13a98479> *The Financial Times* (9 June 2021) (noting corruption at Huarong whose Board Chairman was executed as well as investigations over corruption at other Chinese state-linked businesses).

11 See n 4 (describing the potential risk in comfort letter backed debts).

12 China Evergrande and Its Units Suspend Trading in Hong Kong (21 March 2022) <https://news.bloomberglaw.com/bankruptcy-law/china-evergrande-and-its-units-suspend-trading-in-hong-kong> (‘Embattled Chinese real estate developer China Evergrande Group along with its other units suspended trading in Hong Kong’); ‘Weizhen Tan, ‘China’s embattled developer Evergrande is on the brink of default’ CNBC (16 September 2021) <www.cnbc.com/2021/09/17/china-developer-evergrande-debt-crisis-bond-default-and-investor-risks.html> (discussing the debt problems of Evergrande).

Litigation over comfort letters is a likely outcome of future Chinese debt defaults and the judicial proceedings with respect to CEFC Shanghai International ('CEFC') serve to highlight this likelihood.[13] CEFC, an onshore Chinese entity, issued comfort letters in support of a subsidiary's offshore debt and the subsidiary defaulted. Creditors filed claims in the HKSAR (the locus of dispute resolution) against CEFC. Evidently CEFC did not defend and the HKSAR court entered a default judgment, which CEFC never paid. Creditors subsequently filed an enforcement suit in the Shanghai Financial Court ('SFC')[14] for recognition of the HKSAR default judgement pursuant to the Arrangement on Reciprocal Recognition and Enforcement of Judgments between Mainland China and Hong Kong SAR ('Reciprocity Agreement')[15] between the PRC and HKSAR to mutually enforce judgements.

Pursuant to the Reciprocity Agreement, Mainland courts are empowered (and likely required) to refuse to enforce a HKSAR judgement failing to comport with the PRC's social and public interests,[16] the SFC recognised the default judgement.[17] While not directly opining on the enforceability of comfort letters,[18] the

13 Another litigation is related to Peking University Founder Group wherein an onshore Mainland administrator reportedly declined to honour a comfort letter. See Fitch Ratings, 'PUFG Decision Challenges Enforceability of China Offshore Debt's Keepwell Structure' *Fitch Ratings* (27 August 2020) <www.fitchratings.com/research/corporate-finance/pufg-decision-challenges-enforceability-of-china-offshore-debt-keepwell-structure-27-08-2020>. At the time of writing this chapter, there was no available information with respect to any ruling or whether an appeal has been filed.

14 The court was established in 2018 and designed to help establish China as a financial centre. See Susan Finder, 'Some Quick Thoughts on Shanghai's Financial Court' *Supreme People's Court Monitor* (29 April 2018) <https://supremepeoplescourtmonitor.com/2018/04/29/some-quick-thoughts-on-shanghais-financial-court/>.

15 Arrangement on Reciprocal Recognition and Enforcement of Judgments in Civil and Commercial Matters by the Courts of the Mainland and of the Hong Kong Special Administrative Region, <www.doj.gov.hk/en/mainland_and_macao/pdf/Doc3_477379e.pdf>.

16 ibid art 12: 'Where a people's court of the Mainland considers that the recognition and enforcement of a judgment given by a court of the HKSAR is manifestly contrary to the basic principles of the law of the Mainland or the social and public interests of the Mainland, . . . the judgment shall not be recognised or enforced.'

17 Wang Shan Zheng Qian, 'The first case in the country! The Shanghai Financial Court concluded a case involving the application for recognition and enforcement of a court judgment of the Hong Kong Special Administrative Region involving a "keepwell agreement"' *Shanghai Financial Court* (16 November 2020) <https://mp.weixin.qq.com/s/vzsaooPIZcpQ8ql2jfVEQw> (Defendant letter issuer CEFC claimed the Hong Kong default judgment failed to comport with the PRC's social and public interest – which is a legitimate basis (and arguably a directive) for declining recognition and enforcement under the Arrangement. The Shanghai Financial Court held enforcement of the judgment did not impinge on public interests and ruled to recognise and enforce the HKSAR default judgment.)

18 Research has not uncovered any formal ruling by mainland Chinese courts on the enforceability of comfort letters.

ruling was noteworthy inasmuch as the court did not decline enforcement of the HKSAR default judgement.[19]

In the future, if Chinese corporate offshore debt will not be paid,[20] foreign investors may seek the enforcement in either Mainland or HKSAR courts of comfort letters which are 'only starting to be tested in court'.[21] Depending upon the action of the Chinese government and/or PRC courts, foreign investors might subsequently file arbitration claims pursuant to an investment treaty for losses caused by governmental conduct. The interplay between an investment treaty and the possibility of using the national or essential security exception found in such treaties to override the agreement is intriguing and directly raises the *pacta sunt servanda* principle – 'agreements must be observed'.[22] The principle is well-recognised in China's Civil Code on contracts.[23] In the international dispute context, China has invoked *pacta sunt servanda* in.[24]

19 Moreover, in addition to the power conferred by the Reciprocity Agreement with respect to judgment enforcement, a PRC court is empowered to refuse to enforce the comfort letter itself since defending core interests overrides other interests. See Civil Code of the People's Republic of China (2021), art. 1: 'This Law is formulated in accordance with the Constitution of the People's Republic of China for the purposes of protecting the lawful rights and interests of the persons of the civil law, regulating civil-law relations, *maintaining social and economic order*, meet the needs for developing socialism with Chinese characteristics, *and carrying forward the core socialist values*.' (emphasis added); art 132: 'No person of the civil law shall abuse his civil-law rights and harm the interests of the state, the public interests, or the lawful rights and interests of others'. See also art 534: 'Where the parties take advantage of the contract to commit an act that endangers the State's interests and public interests, the market regulatory authority and other relevant administrative authorities shall be responsible for supervising and handling it in accordance with the provisions of laws and administrative regulations'.

20 Eric Ng, 'Fantasia, another debt-laden Chinese property developer, defaults on US$205 million bond, as Evergrande crisis rolls on' *South China Morning Post* (5 October 2021) <www.scmp.com/business/article/3151197/fantasia-another-debt-laden-chinese-property-developer-defaults-us205> (payment problems at Fantasia Holdings Group leading to increasing concerns of future defaults in housing sector).

21 Above n 4. Most comfort letters in the Chinese offshore corporate debt provide that dispute resolution will be in the courts of the HKSAR.

22 Gerhard Von Glahn and James Larry Tolbee, *Law Among Nations: An Introduction to Public International Law* 498 (4th ed, Routledge, 1981): *Pacta Sunt Servanda* is '[o]ne of the oldest principles in international law'.

23 See PRC Civil Code (n 19) art: 509: 'The parties shall fully perform their respective obligations as contracted. The parties shall comply with the principle of good faith'. See also art 7: 'When conducting a civil activity, a person of the civil law shall, in compliance with the principle of good faith, uphold honesty and honor commitments'. The Civil Code discusses the context of statements that might be relied upon by another party which is precisely the context of comfort letters: see Article 142 'Where an expression of intent is made to another person, the meaning of the expression shall be interpreted according to the words and sentences used, with reference to the relevant terms, the nature and purpose of the civil juristic act, the custom, and the principle of good faith.'

24 China is observing international law in the true sense (23 December 2015) <http://in.china-embassy.gov.cn/eng/xwfb/201512/t20151222_2223159.htm> (China criticising the Philippines for allegedly failing to comply with *pacta sunt servanda*).

This Chapter aims to discuss a legal issue that is likely to surface in coming years as comfort letters are relied upon to obtain recovery on defaulted debt. The chapter begins in Part II with a basic overview of comfort letters. Following this, Part III discusses how Chinese domestic courts have viewed comfort letters in the context of enforcement. Part IV raises the possibility of foreign investors filing an arbitration claim based on the comfort letter and how panels might evaluate such claims. Overall, the chapter finds that good faith is the elixir although applying the principle will be inherently difficult. The chapter also suggests an approach based on a US Federal court ruling which lists several controlling factors a court should examine in determining whether to enforce comfort letters.

II Comfort letters – a brief primer

A General overview

Comfort letters are statements given by a third party intended to incentivise a transaction between two other parties one of which is related to the letter issuer.[25] The overarching characteristic of comfort letters is the refusal to formally guarantee payment[26] *while simultaneously intimating at a guarantee, or arguably implying so*, thus inducing a transaction.[27] In deciding whether to find an 'enforceable contract' based upon a comfort letter, courts examine the parties' intentions. However, given vague terminology, establishing the parties' intent might be extraordinarily difficult.

Moreover, ascertaining intent is difficult since the motivations of both parties may in fact evince both 'good' and 'bad' reasons. Legitimate reasons for using a comfort letter do exist such as tax considerations; avoiding the necessity of including contingent liabilities in disclosures; or a number of other business reasons. Chinese corporations may resort to comfort letters to bypass overly-restrictive regulations and tap the offshore US dollar bond market, which lowers borrowing costs and supports governmental efforts to manage China's foreign reserves.[28] Yet motivations might also be nefarious such as inducing a creditor notwithstanding the letter issuer's foreknowledge of future debt problems.[29] Arguably, the opaque

25 Herbert Bernstein and Joachim Zekoll, 'The Gentleman's Agreement in Legal Theory and in Modern Practice: United States' (1998) 46 American Journal of Comparative Law 87, 99: '[A] comfort letter of this type is aimed at being something more than a letter of introduction, but something less than a guaranty or suretyship commitment.'

26 Larry DiMatteo, 'The CISG and the Presumption of Enforceability: Unintended Contractual Liability in International Business Dealings' (1997) 22 Yale Journal of International Law 111, 114.

27 In an express guarantee, the guarantor warrants to the creditor that, in the event of default, the guarantor will pay the creditor, and generally has the right to collect from the debtor through subrogation.

28 George Calhoun, 'Beijing Embraces "Moral Hazard" – The Huarong Bailout Was The Right Move' *Forbes* (23 August 2021) <www.forbes.com/sites/georgecalhoun/2021/08/23/beijing-embraces-moral-hazard – the-huarong-bailout-was-the-right-move/?sh=5b494b044fd6>.

29 Another illustration of bad faith is the possibility of collusion between debtor and letter issuer to loot the capital out of the borrower's control to an unreachable location under the control of the parent or some other third party.

representations negligently, recklessly or intentionally *lead the creditor to make the untoward presumption* that the letter issuer will ensure ultimate payment.

B Enforcing comfort letters based on estoppel

Despite a lack of express written language, a holistic view of the transaction may, depending upon the facts, allow for enforceability based upon a theory of promissory estoppel.[30] Under estoppel, statements provided to a party which could be reasonably expected to induce reliance, which in fact caused good-faith detrimental reliance,[31] may act to remove the technical strictures of a contract and transform the letter into an enforceable statement.[32] The estoppel argument relies on a duty to prevent a promisee's detrimental reliance implicating notions of tortious conduct.[33]

Estoppel might be particularly relevant in the context of disputes over comfort letters issued by state-linked entities since such letters presumably carry the authority of sovereign backing. Reliance on a governmental promise *might conceivably* carry more weight than a purely private promise, perhaps leading to an enhanced duty to preclude a detrimental reliance – implicating the principle of good faith very strongly. The status of the promisee – the debt-holder – may also be a factor as courts generally understand that sophisticated parties are well-aware of the obligation to perform due diligence and the bar to demonstrate reasonable reliance on statements is higher as opposed to ordinary public investors.[34]

C The importance of good faith

To interpret the written statements of parties, courts reviewing the performance of contractual obligations will utilize good faith.[35] However, there is no bright line

30 See *Lasalle Bank National Association v Citicorp Real Estate Inc.*, [2003] WL 21671812 (SDNY 2003) at 7 ('*Lasalle*'): '[A]lthough comfort letters in general do not give rise to legally binding obligations, courts will enforce them on a contract or promissory estoppel theory depending on the specific circumstances.')

31 Eric Mills Holmes, 'Restatement of Promissory Estoppel' (1996) 32 Willamette Law Review 263, 515–16.

32 For a comprehensive overview of developments in promissory estoppel which has taken root in US jurisprudence, see Charles L Knapp, 'Rescuing Reliance: The Perils of Promissory Estoppel' (1998) 49 Hastings Law Journal 1191. The theory has become accepted in the United States and other common law jurisdictions. The relevance to Chinese offshore debt is clear; the locus of dispute resolution will often be Hong Kong, a common law jurisdiction.

33 Eric Mills Holmes, '*The Four Phases of Promissory Estoppel*' (1996) 20 Seattle University Law Review 45 (noting that some scholars opine promissory estoppel is really a tort-based claim).

34 See *Landesbank Baden-Württemberg v. Goldman, Sachs & Co.*, 821 F. Supp. 2d 616, 624 (SDNY 2011): 'Indeed, "as a matter of law, a sophisticated plaintiff cannot establish that it entered into an arm's length transaction in justifiable reliance on alleged misrepresentations if that plaintiff failed to make use of the means of verification that were available to it, such as reviewing the files of the other parties"' (citation omitted).

35 In conceptualising good faith in our context, we are referring to good faith in the performance of an agreement as opposed to good faith of negotiating an agreement.

test and contours of good faith are often unclear and based upon the perspectives of the parties' history, self-interest and perceptions.[36]

> It is undisputed that good faith has a subjective component that requires a party at least to make an honest judgment. An honest judgment in one's own self-interest is sufficient to meet this subjective component.[37]

Good faith is ultimately linked to honesty and fairness – a sense that fairness is the overarching goal. To a degree, this is conveyed in the slogan 'honour among thieves' that even criminals who will enthusiastically commit other crimes value honesty and will in fact refuse to lie to achieve their goals.[38]

Several factors underscore the particular importance of good faith in the context of enforcement of comfort letters.[39] One, the language used is often plausibly deniable and good faith is particularly important in discerning contestable intentions. Two, good faith may be especially relevant when a state-linked entity provides the letter as such assurances might be understood as conveying a sense of being more 'solid'. Three, with respect to estoppel, evidence of the overall relationship is inextricably linked to good faith.[40] Four, good faith is a critical core principle of international law and investment-treaty arbitration,[41] and particularly relevant to the application of the essential security exception.[42]

III Enforcement of comfort letters and *pacta sunt servanda*

A The enigmatic context of good faith and investor sophistication

In response to a debt default, the creditor may, depending upon the terms and locus of dispute resolution, initiate legal proceedings in domestic courts to

36 Agasha Mugasha, 'A Conceptual-Functional Approach to Multi-Bank Financing' (1995) 6 Journal of Banking & Finance 5, 23–24.

37 E Allan Farnsworth, 'Good Faith in Contract Performance' in J Beatson and D Friedmann (eds), *Good Faith and Fault in Contract Law* (Clarendon Press, 1995) ch 6, 163.

38 John Grisham, *The Summons* (Randome House, 2002) 316 (Patton French, the King of Torts, proclaims to Ray Atlee, 'I don't lie. I cheat and bribe, but I don't lie.')

39 Arthur Rosett, 'Critical Reflections on the United Nations Convention on Contracts for the International Sale of Goods' (1984) 45 Ohio State Law Journal 265, 287: 'No written contract is ever complete; even the most carefully drafted document rests on volumes of assumptions that cannot be explicitly expressed

40 Bernstein and Zekoll (n 25) 94–95. Within the ambit of good faith, distinctions between common law and civil law jurisdictions exist. For an overview of good faith in common law and civil law jurisdictions, see Leon E Trakman and Kunal Sharma, 'The Binding Force of Agreements to Negotiate in Good Faith' (2014) 73 CLJ 598–628 (comparing notions of good faith in various jurisdictions noting the inconsistencies and tracing the doctrinal basis).

41 See Steven Reinhold, 'Good Faith in International Law' (2013) 2 UCLJLJ 40.

42 Chao Wang, 'Invocation of National Security Exceptions under GATT Article XXI: Jurisdiction to Review and Standard of Review' (2019) 18 Chinese Journal of International Law 710 (States are limited to good-faith invocation of the security exception).

enforce the comfort letter. However, ambiguous wording relating to 'maintaining solvency' or 'liquidity' or more tenuous statements alluding to using 'best efforts' (or merely 'efforts') to maintain the solvency or liquidity of the borrower can render establishing express obligations an extremely challenging, perhaps an even insurmountable task.[43] Unsurprisingly, in the absence of a specific promise or guarantee, and given the wide range of potential language employed, courts in various jurisdictions have not uniformly ruled on whether such comfort letters are enforceable.

Analysing the enforceability of a comfort letter within the framework of keeping one's word – *pacta sunt servanda* – is crucial.[44] Pursuant to promissory estoppel, a court might find the letter issuer knew or should have reasonably known that the lender would rely on the letter even in the absence of a formal contract or written guarantee. Given that the likelihood of enforcement proceedings being filed in a common law jurisdiction, the doctrine of promissory estoppel is a potential avenue for creditors to pursue.[45] In the United States, although not automatically applied in all contexts,[46] estoppel is used to prevent detrimental reliance.[47] While in some common-law jurisdictions, such as Hong Kong[48] and the UK,[49] the use of estoppel has until recently been more defensive, estoppel is becoming more pronounced in these jurisdictions.[50]

43 For a discussion of 'best efforts' to maintain the debtor's liquidity, see Jessica Young, 'An Endeavour to Understand Endevaours Undertakings' (2014) 44 Hong Kong Law Journal 95.

44 While *pacta sunt servanda* is a core tenet of international law, it is relevant to interpreting domestic contracts as well. See Hans Wehberg, 'Pacta Sunt Servanda' (1959) 53 American Journal of International Law 775.

45 Civil law jurisdictions do not generally embrace estoppel although alternative theories often lead to similar outcomes. See Mohamed Yehia Mattar, 'Promissory Estoppel: Common Law Wine in Civil Law Bottles' (1988) 4 Tulane European and Civil Law Forum 71, 73–74: 'in the civil law [there is] no counterpart to the doctrine of promissory estoppel'. An exemplar is the German legal doctrine of culpa in contrahendo. See also ibid, 108–16.

46 See, e.g. *Stone v Commonwealth Fin. Corp.* (127 Misc 368, 370 [Sup Ct, NY County 1924] (dismissing breach of contract claim based upon letter assuring 'full cooperation and support, and are ready to place our resources behind this project to the extent that may be necessary to insure its complete success.' *affd* 215 AD 704 [1st Dept 1925], *affd* 243 NY 528 [1926]). Compare *Robert Plan Corp. v Perot Sys. Corp.* 278 AD2d 119 [1st Dept 2000]) (comfort letter confirmed the commitment 'to make available to [the corporate defendant] the capital necessary for it to fully perform its [contractual] obligations to [the plaintiff]').

47 See American Law Institute, *Restatement of the Law, Second: Contracts* (American Law Institute, 1964), § 90: 'A promise which the promisor should reasonably expect to induce action or forbearance on the part of the promisee or a third person and which does induce such action or forbearance is binding if injustice can be avoided only by enforcement of the promise. The remedy granted for breach may be limited as justice requires'.

48 See *Luo Xing Juan v Estate of Hui Shui See* (2009) 12 HKCFAR 1.

49 Charles Calleros, 'Cause, Consideration, Promissory Estoppel, and Promises Under Deed: What Our Students Should Know About Enforcement of Promises in a Historical and International Context' (2013) 13 Chicago-Kent Journal of International and Comparative Law 83.

50 Lang Thai, 'Comfort Letters – A Fresh Look?' (2006) 17 Journal of Banking & Finance 15 (comparing comfort letters and estoppel within the United States, United Kingdom and Australia).

For estoppel, good faith reliance is essential and the absence of reliance militates against enforcement.[51] If the text of the letter has been purposely drafted with an intent to obfuscate (and perhaps even if the opaqueness is not intentional) and good faith reliance exists, estoppel is a potentially valid avenue. Enforcing a comfort letter based upon a consideration of these factors comports with conceptualising statements more holistically, reducing strict emphasis on requiring a formalistic contractual framework.[52] Therefore, if the creditor can demonstrate good faith reliance on the letter – and that such reliance was reasonable *based upon the totality of the circumstances* – the letter might be enforceable as an implied contract based upon promissory estoppel.

In the context of offshore debt, several factors impact the good faith inquiry. Since peaking in the early 1980s, interest rates in the United States and many Western nations commenced a multi-decade bear market. Therefore, was the creditor aware of the risks but simply decided to take the risk based on the ultra-low interest rate environment? Alternatively, was the creditor a sophisticated buyer with knowledge of likely debt problems seeking to opportunistically re-sell the risky debt to unsophisticated investors hungry for yield? Did the creditor (or secondary investor) engage in a form of predatory lending extracting high interest rates opportunistically and knowingly presuming risks?[53]

Another factor is specifically related to Chinese offshore debt given China's state-centric governance and prevalence of state-linked letter issuers. The expectation of implicit State support may blur the normal due diligence framework as presumably a State will act to ensure 'too big too fail' strategic entities do not collapse and cause economic problems. If the borrower or letter issuer is a state-linked entity does that make reliance on a comfort letter more justifiable particularly if past practice demonstrates a willingness to bail out such entities? Yet such borrowers might be incentivised to play 'fast and loose' and engage in excessive risk-taking believing that ultimately the government will rescue any malevolent investment or corruption-induced losses such as with Huarong, which had corruption problems. If so, was the creditor willing to take risks based upon the implicit-guarantee of a government bailout – and if so is this reliance reasonable? Conversely, did the investor – in a hunt for yield – truly rely upon the letter or is it a self-serving rationale of a sophisticated purchaser perhaps even with

51 In *Lasalle* (n 30), the Court found the plaintiff's reliance on the letter was unreasonable as claimant was a large global financial institution and sufficiently knowledgeable that no express guarantee was intended.

52 Lutz-Christian Wolff, 'The relationship between contract law and property law' (2020) 19 Common L World Rev 31, 33: 'Contracts are seen as relationships consisting of promises which are enforceable by law'. Noting the view that contracts are a 'cluster concept' and a 'promise will constitute a contract where it (i) is reciprocated by a requested act of performance; or (ii) is reciprocated by a promise; or (iii) is intended to, and does, *induce reasonable reliance or expectation*' (emphasis added) (citation omitted).

53 Renae Merle, 'How One Hedge Fund Made $2 Billion from Argentina's Economic Collapse' (29 March 2016) <www.washingtonpost.com/news/business/wp/2016/03/29/how-one-hedge-fund-made-2-billion-from-argentinas-economic-collapse/>.

foreknowledge based on due diligence of heightened risks that the debt might not be repaid?

The potential impact on good faith and reliance based upon the 'sophistication' of the parties is illustrated by an example arising from the sub-prime crisis.[54] The Senate Hearing regarding Goldman Sachs' ('GS') aggressive marketing of a large amount of Collateralised Debt Obligations ('CDOs') revealed that GS internally believed the CDOs would not be fully repaid.[55] Despite full awareness of the likelihood of default, the top priority of GS was to sell the CDOs to its customers. In response to Senator Levin's incredulity that GS would purposely sell these securities to customers, GS executives responded that GS did nothing wrong because it sold securities based upon 'the market price', i.e. what buyers were willing to pay,[56] conceding GS awareness of the CDO risks and opining investors must undertake independent due-diligence.[57] Hypothetically, in terms of good faith, should GS be able to enforce comfort letters if it knew Timberwolf CDOs when it initially acquired the debt?

B Judicial perspectives on comfort letters

In light of the above-referenced complexities, evaluating good faith in the context of offshore debt is not an easy task. Some courts find comfort letters create legal obligations; other rulings hold that mere statements of intent such as keeping a subsidiary solvent but not containing an express guarantee are not enforceable. In *Kleinwort*, the parent issued a comfort letter because it was not willing to guarantee the indebtedness of its wholly-owned subsidiary.[58] The English High Court found in favour of enforcement finding that the 'comfort letters came into existence as part and parcel of a commercial banking transaction, [and] the plaintiffs clearly acted in reliance'.[59] But the English Court of Appeal reversed this decision because the language merely noted the present intent of the parent entity as opposed to anything further *and the refusal to provide an express guarantee underscored the lack of the intent to provide one*.[60] Under this construct, comfort letters are almost inherently unenforceable as the statements prove the absence of intent to provide a real guarantee. In other words, as the creditor is free not to enter

54 US Senate Permanent Subcommittee on Investigations, *Hearing Wall Street and the Financial Crisis: The Role of Investment Banks* <www.youtube.com/watch?v=whlzFWwVv98> (Senator Carl Levin examining Goldman Sachs over internal knowledge that the securities were in effect 'suckers bets' that Goldman sold to clients).

55 ibid.

56 ibid.

57 ibid. GS was sued and settled at least one case where an investor claimed losses exceeding $1B. See Narayanan Somasundaram and Jonathan Stempel, 'Goldman sued for $1.07 billion over Timberwolf CDO' *Reuters* (28 October 2011) <www.reuters.com/article/us-goldmansachs-lawsuit-idUSTRE79R4JE20111028>.

58 *Kleinwort Benson Ltd. v Malaysia Mining Corpn Berhad* [1989] 1 WLR 379 ('*Kleinwort*').

59 *Kleinwort Benson Ltd. v Malaysia Mining Corpn Berhad* [1988] 1 WLR 799, 808, 811.

60 *Kleinwort* (n 58) 393–94.

into the transaction backed by a comfort letter, it is taken to knowingly accept the risk if it does decide to engage in the transaction.

In another example, an Indian court refused to compel a parent entity to honour a comfort letter issued in support of its subsidiary. The creditor, in arguing for enforcement, claimed that the comfort letter constituted an unequivocal commitment and formed an integral part of the loan. The letter issuer parent countered that there was no wording of guarantee and an imprecise commitment is no substitute for an actual assurance or guarantee. The court agreed with the letter issuer finding the lack of an express guarantee the controlling factor and held that the parent had no liability.[61]

In contrast, according to the decision in *Lasalle Bank National Association v Citicorp Real Estate Inc.*,[62] even if no formal express guarantees exist, the letter *might* constitute an enforceable implied contract and liability could ensue.[63] The *Lasalle* court examined whether reasonable reliance existed pursuant to an estoppel theory.[64] The court ruled that if the plaintiff could demonstrate reliance on the letter – and that such reliance was reasonable based upon the totality of the circumstances – the letter might be enforceable on grounds of promissory estoppel.[65] To resolve whether an implied contract existed under an estoppel theory, the court suggested an array of useful factors to inform a judicial decision: the wording of the letter; the overall context in which the letter was provided; the sophistication of the parties; prior transactions and relationships; the understanding of such letters in the specific business area; whether attorneys were involved; unwritten representations if any; whether the creditor was reasonable in relying upon the letter under an implied contract, promissory estoppel or detrimental reliance theory.

Based upon *Lasalle*, in the context of Chinese offshore debt, specific considerations impacting resolving the question of good faith might include: the history of bailouts in the specific business sector and whether corporations were previously rescued; whether domestic debt holders are treated more favourably than foreign US dollar offshore debt holders; if the debtor is state-linked; what statements, if any, did Chinese governmental officials provide regarding government support for the debtor, letter issuer, or state-linked entities generally; whether the investor made statements to the effect it is aware of the risks or conversely if it relied on implicit state-backing; what role (if knowable) do governmental authorities play in terms of directing the letter issuer's conduct; the sophistication of the creditors; whether due diligence was conducted and the creditor misled or not conducted at

61 Rohit Jain, 'Zee vs Yes Bank: Letter of Comfort Not A Guarantee, Bombay High Court Says' *Bloomberg Quint* (19 August 2020) <www.bloombergquint.com/law-and-policy/zee-vs-yes-bank-letter-of-comfort-not-a-guarantee-bombay-high-court-says>.

62 *Lasalle* (n 30).

63 Bernstein and Zekoll (n 25) 100: 'The parent company, however, may find itself held liable as a guarantor when a court considers the letter in the context of the whole relationship among the three parties and finds it to be part of an implied contract'.

64 *Lasalle* (n 30) 5–7.

65 ibid.

all; the motivation of the creditor in investing; and whether Chinese government is selectively rescuing specific entities or treats all financially troubled businesses equally. China's unique political-economic governance and the fact that it practices state-centric capitalism will inherently raise perceptions that will impact the good faith issue.

IV Comfort letters and international arbitration

A Foreign investors and the potential role of international arbitration

Foreign investors in defaulted Chinese offshore debt might claim governmental action damaged their economic interests triggering an applicable investment treaty violation based on several potential scenarios.[66] One, presuming *arguendo* that a direct claim could be made to domestic PRC courts, the variety of language in comfort letters and the fact that the Supreme People's Court has not ruled that comfort letters are automatically enforceable likely means at least some (if not most) Chinese rulings will probably reject investor claims.[67] Two, even if some PRC courts held comfort letters to be enforceable (either in domestic claims or enforcing a foreign court judgment), courts will decline enforcement if doing so would harm Chinese security and stability interests;[68] violate the Anti-Foreign Sanctions Law;[69] or contravene the 'Blocking Statute'.[70] Three, alternatively, if investors file a claim in a foreign court, investors might succeed and obtain a favourable ruling, but enforcement in PRC courts might be difficult. For example, in recent years, most comfort letters provide for the statements to be controlled by English law and/or for jurisdiction to be vested in HKSAR courts. As discussed above, while the Reciprocity Agreement between the PRC and HKSAR provides for mutual recognition of judgments,[71] even if the HKSAR grants a favourable

66 China has an extensive network of investment agreements where arbitration is the dispute resolution mechanism. See https://investmentpolicy.unctad.org/international-investment-agreements/countries/42/china.

67 Research has been unable to uncover any formal ruling on the enforceability of comfort letters as of this paper's writing.

68 See n 19.

69 See Article 3 (as translated by China Law Translate <www.chinalawtranslate.com/en/counteringforeignsanctions/>): 'If any foreign country violates international law and the basic principles of international relations, contains or suppresses China based on various pretexts or its own laws, takes discriminatory restrictive measures against Chinese citizens or organisations, or interferes with China's internal affairs, China is entitled to take corresponding countermeasures.'

70 PRC Ministry of Commerce, Order No. 1 of 2021 on Rules on Counteracting Unjustified Extraterritorial Application of Foreign Legislation and Other Measures (English translation at <http://english.mofcom.gov.cn/article/policyrelease/questions/202101/20210103029708.shtml>. While the primary aim of the Blocking Statute is to block sanctions, an overseas sanction adversely affecting a Chinese entity might conceivably encompass a foreign legal judgment: see Beibei Zhang, 'A Critical Evaluation of China's New Blocking Statue against Unfair Extraterritoriality' (2021) 52 Hong Kong Law Journal 775.

71 See nn 15–19 and accompanying text.

judgment PRC courts are empowered at a minimum and perhaps required to decline enforcement under the Reciprocity Agreement if it is contrary to the social and public interests of the PRC.[72]

B Invoking the essential security exception

In response to investor arbitration claims based on an investment agreement, China could argue that its conduct was necessary to defend essential security interests, i.e. 'the security exception' commonly found in investment treaties. Pursuant to the essential security exception, the sovereign is able to override treaty protections to defend national or essential security. Interpreted relatively infrequently,[73] the security exception has been classically conceptualised as physical defence of the national bastion.[74] Based upon this understanding, a sovereign would only be justified in refusing to honour the comfort letter if the nation was somehow in fear of military attack or at risk of territorial infringement.[75]

The conceptualisation of essential security limited to physical defence is exemplified in rulings arising from claims arising from the Indian's government's annulment of contracts.[76] In defending the decision to annul the contracts, the Indian government argued its conduct was necessary 'for national needs, including the needs of defence, para-military forces *and other public utility services as well as for societal needs*.'[77] While the arbitrators agreed that India was empowered to annul the contract to protect 'essential security interests', the ruling limited the government's justification to protecting military or paramilitary use. However, with respect to protecting utilities, railroads, communication and other 'societal needs', such interests did not relate to essential security.[78] The arbitrators' failure

72 Kai-hong Patrick Yung, 'Credit-Enhancement Mechanisms for Dim Sum Bonds: Structures and Risks' (2015) 10 Capital Markets Law Journal 295 (noting that the term 'social and public interests' is undefined).

73 Julien Chaisse, 'Demystifying Public Security Exception and Limitations on Capital Movement' (2015) 37 U Penn J Intl L 583, 601 (noting a dearth of rulings on the exception).

74 See Jürgen Kurtz, 'Adjudging the Exceptional at International Investment Law: Security, Public Order and Financial Crisis' (2010) 59 ICLQ 338.

75 But see Joel Slawotsky, 'The Fusion of Ideology, Technology and Economic Power: Implications of the Emerging New United States National Security Conceptualization' (2021) 20 Chinese Journal of International Law 3 (historical interpretation limited to military attack and territorial defence but emerging technologies and other factors militate strongly towards re-conceptualising national security).

76 See CC/Devas Award on Jurisdiction and Merits, CC/Devas v. India, PCA Case No. 2013–09, Award on Jurisdiction and Merits (Perm. Ct. Arb., 25 July 2016) (*Devas*); Deutsche Telekom AG v. India, PCA Case No. 2014–10, Interim Award (Perm. Ct. Arb., 13 December 2017) (*Deutsche Telekom*).

77 *Devas* (ibid) [332] (emphasis added); accord *Deutsche Telekom* (ibid), [265]. For an overview of these two rulings, see Prabhash Ranjan, 'Essential Security Interests in International Investment Law: A Tale of Two ISDS Claims Against India' in: Julien Chaisse, Leila D Choukroune and Sufian Jusoh (eds.), *Handbook of International Investment Law and Policy* (Springer, 2020), ch 23.

78 *Devas* (n 76) [354]–[356]; *Deutsche Telekom* (n 76) [281].

to extend security beyond military defence corroborated the traditional conceptualisation of essential security.[79]

C The essential security exception in a changing world

Two transformational developments are driving the re-conceptualisation of security: (a) emerging threats are increasingly 'virtual' or stem from dual-use technology and the linkage with the -China rivalry; and (b) a growing belief that 'essential security' is interconnected with the well-being and health of a population – 'human security' – analogous to an emphasis on ESG in corporate governance.

(1) Re-conceptualising essential security in light of emerging technology and the hegemonic rivalry

Initially conceptualised as defence from military attack or damage to territorial integrity, the understanding of essential security has broadened substantially in recent years driven by the China-US hegemonic rivalry. The radical transformation in the conceptualisation of national security to encompass economic, technological and ideological threats was discernible in speeches made during the summer of 2020 by the highest US Government officials as well as various policy documents in recent years alleging China poses a dire threat to the United States. Illustrating this new conceptualisation, US Presidential Executive Orders have targeted social media platforms such as WeChat although social media lies beyond the historic understanding of security. Further examples of this new conceptualisation can be found in the November 2021 Report to Congress by the US-China Economic and Security Review Commission which identifies China's technological achievements; ideology (political-economic governance); and global capital market integration, as national security threats.[80]

> China's tightened integration with global financial markets poses distinct economic risks to U.S. investors and national security risks to the United States.[81]

Furthermore, the prospect of a digital Yuan being accepted globally is also viewed as a longer-term national security threat.

> China's digital RMB does not present an immediate challenge to the U.S.-led global financial system, but in the long term it could undermine the status of the U.S. dollar and efficacy of U.S. financial sanctions.[82]

79 See J Benton Heath, 'The New National Security Challenge to the Economic Order' (2020) 129 Yale Law Journal 1044.

80 US-China Economic and Security Review Commission, *2021 Report to Congress of the US-China Economic and Security Review Commission* <https://www.uscc.gov/annual-report/2021-annual-report-congress>.

81 ibid, 11.

82 ibid, 166.

China has also expanded its notions of 'national security' beyond the historical conceptualisation of 'security' as constituting defence of territorial integrity. National interests include the following non-military markers of national security: political and economic stability, public order and defending data.[83] As such, cars equipped with emerging technologies can collect data and are therefore within the rubric of potential security threats.[84] A focus on data is exemplified by regulation of businesses (online content and cross-border data flows); concerns over US audits of listed entities, and the pressure on DiDi to de-list in New York.

To be sure, some expansion is sensible as emerging technologies permit a nation to seriously degrade an adversary without resort to the classic violation of national borders. Election hacking, computer viruses to destroy infrastructure, and perhaps even Central Bank Digital Currencies exemplify how nations can cause harm to an adversary without military attack. An exemplar is the potential for China's digital Yuan to erode the sanctions power of the United States. However, re-conceptualising security is a slippery slope as the exception can swallow the rule. For example, are all data transfer points truly bona fide security threats? Expanding the conceptualisation is necessary but must be reasonable to avoid the 'security exception' employed as a cover for protectionism or competition-driven degradation of adversaries/competitors.

(2) Human security and the health and well-being of the population as bulwarks of security

There is an increasing recognition that states legitimately adopt? a more broad-minded understanding of security not limited solely to physical defence. Security would encompass defending the health and well-being of its citizens – an obligation to defend 'human security'. Economic and societal stability would therefore constitute an integral aspect of 'human security'.[85]

83 Yan Luo and Zhijing Yu, 'China Issued the Draft Data Security Law Inside Privacy' (3 July 2020) (www.insideprivacy.com/data-security/china-issued-the-draft-data-security-law/) (Data Security law defining 'data security' as data that may affect China's national security, economic security, social stability and public order). See also PRC Export Control Law, art 1 (English translation at <www.cov.com/-/media/files/corporate/publications/file_repository/prc_export_control_law_2020_10_cn_en_covington.pdf>.

84 Keith Zhai and Yoko Kubota, 'China to Restrict Tesla Use by Military and State Employees' *The Wall Street Journal* (19 March 2021) <www.wsj.com/articles/china-to-restrict-tesla-usage-by-military-and-state-personnel-11616155643> ('concerns that data the cars gather could be a source of national-security leaks').

85 United Nations Trust Fund for Human Security, 'Human Security in Theory and Practice: Application of the Human Security Concept and the United Nations Trust Fund for Human Security' (September 2009) <www.unocha.org/sites/dms/HSU/Publications%20and%20Products/Human%20Security%20Tools/Human%20Security%20in%20Theory%20and%20Practice%20English.pdf>.

> Human security recognizes the interlinkages between peace, development and human rights, and equally considers civil, political, economic, social and cultural rights.[86]

For example, defending citizens against a severe health emergency probably qualifies as an 'essential interest' that must be safeguarded in order to defend essential security.[87] Illustrative is *Philip Morris v Uruguay*,[88] which held that a plain packaging requirement for tobacco products did not violate international law as the measure was taken by the State to protect public health. The tribunal cited a decision by the Claims Commission in the *Bischoff Case* dismissing a claim for damages arising from measures taken against an outbreak of smallpox stating: '[c] ertainly during an epidemic of an infectious disease there can be no liability for the reasonable exercise of police powers'.[89]

The question of whether defending human security is a legitimate 'fit' with the security exception will likely become more important going forward given various transformational concerns such as climate change, poverty alleviation and sustainability. The link between financial crisis and threats to human security is manifestly clear, potentially providing compelling reasons for arbitrators to broaden the scope of the essential security exception to encompass crucial aspects of human security.

However, expanding conceptualisations of security is a slippery slope. How do you measure economic crisis or health? Moreover, what if China argued overriding the comfort letter was necessary to avoid economic crisis?[90] China wields the second largest economy and would be hard-pressed to claim its economy is poor. Yet, could avoidance of financial contagion and serious economic or social upheaval constitute justification for invoking the security exception? Defending public order is an interesting possible argument if economic failure would cause severe damage to Chinese citizens endangering social and political stability.[91]

86 United Nations General Assembly, 'Resolution adopted by the General Assembly on 10 September 2012' (A/RES/66/290), Preamble 1 (c) <https://undocs.org/A/RES/66/290>.

87 For example, the tribunals in the *Suez I, Suez II* and *Impregilo* cases held that water and sewage services are essential to the health and well-being of humans and therefore an essential interest. *Suez, Sociedad General de Aguas de Barcelona S.A., and InterAguas Servicios Integrales del Agua S.A. v The Argentine Republic* (ICSID Case No. ARB/03/17), Decision on Liability, 30 July 2010, [238]; *Suez, Sociedad General de Aguas de Barcelona, S.A. and Vivendi Universal, S.A. v Argentine Republic* (ICSID Case No. ARB/03/19), Decision on Liability, 30 July 2010, [260], and *Impregilo S.p.A. v Argentine Republic* (ICSID Case No. ARB/07/17), Award, 21 June 2011, [346].

88 *Philip Morris Brand Sàrl (Switzerland), Philip Morris Products S.A.* (Switzerland) and *Abal Hermanos S.A. (Uruguay) v Oriental Republic of Uruguay* (ICSID Case No. ARB/10/7).

89 *Germany – Venezuela Mixed Claims Commission, Bischoff Case* (1903) 10 RIAA 420.

90 Rulings stemming from the Argentine economic crisis declined to extent routine economic crisis as justifying the defence of essential security. But see *Continental* (n 91).

91 See *Continental Casualty Company v Argentine Republic*, ICSID Case no. ARB/03/9, Sept. 5, 2008, [174] (serious and extensive public rioting and looting coupled with governmental breakdown *might* fall within the ambit of defending 'public order'.)

Of course, recognising disruption to 'public order' in the framework of serious public financial losses is an extremely slippery slope and might incentivise nations into an overly zealous invocation of the security exception.

D Good faith and the essential security exception

Sovereigns 'may not invoke the provisions of its internal law as justification for its failure to perform'[92] and thus cannot easily invoke the security exception to override treaty obligations such as guarantees to foreign investors to be treated fairly and equally. Balancing the tension between national interests and international law is therefore not simple and given the transformational challenges and emerging technology, some degree of flexibility in treaty interpretation (i.e. conceptualising essential security more broadly), is sensible.[93]

While the precise contours of the security exception are unresolved, there is agreement that nations can only invoke the exception in good faith.[94] In interpreting national security clauses and, the ICJ has consistently analysed such language within the parameters of good faith. In all ICJ jurisprudence, *good faith acts as a background constraint on the ability of states to interpret treaties as they wish.*[95]

Limiting invocation of the security exception to good faith comports with *pacta sunt servanda*[96] as good faith forms a crucial tenet of international law.[97] As exemplified in the VCLT, good faith is a primary rule of international law and treaty interpretation – widely perceived as black-letter law.[98] Therefore, good faith is the ultimate 'elixir' in evaluating disputes; *pacta sunt servanda* as embedded in the VCLT obligates nations to execute obligations (including the invocation of any treaty exceptions) in good faith.[99] Accordingly, arbitrators should examine the reliance on the security exception within the framework of *pacta sunt servanda* to

92 Vienna Convention on the Law of Treaties (Vienna, 23 May 1969) 1155 UNTS 331, entered into force 27 January 1980 ('VCLT') art 27.

93 VCLT (ibid) art 62. See also VCLT art 31(3)(c) (treaty interpretation should take into account 'any relevant rules of international law relevant in the relations between the parties').

94 See VCLT (n 92) arts 26, 31(1) (good faith essential). See also Chao (n 42) (States are limited to good faith invocation of the security exception).

95 Susan Rose-Ackerman and Benjamin Billa, 'Treaties and National Security' (2013) 40 New York University Journal of International Law and Politics 437, 461 (emphasis added).

96 VCLT (n 92) art 26.

97 *Nuclear Tests Case (Australia v France)* (Merits) [1974] ICJ Rep 253 [46]: 'One of the basic principles governing the creation and performance of legal obligations . . . is good faith. Trust and confidence are inherent in international cooperation, in particular in an age when this cooperation in many fields is becoming increasingly essential. Just as the very rule of pacta sunt servanda in the law of treaties is based on good faith, so also is the binding character of an international obligation.')

98 See VCLT (n 92) art 26. See also Daniel Davison-Vecchione, 'Beyond the Forms of Faith: Pacta Sunt Servanda and Loyalty' (2015) 16 German Law Journal 1165 (the principle has not been challenged in courts it is understood to be non-derogable).

99 Davison-Vecchione, ibid, 1166.

balance the tension inherent between domestic considerations versus international obligations.

E Chinese political-economic governance, moral hazards and good faith

(1) Chinese political-economic governance and good faith

In contrast to the United States and other Western nations which endeavour to separate political interests from economic interests,[100] in China the State has a dominant role in the management of economic activity and markets.[101] Economic-political governance is defined by the single-party ruler of China, the Chinese Communist Party (CCP), which establishes *the balance between political and economic interests* inherently impacting economic and judicial affairs. For example, recent crackdowns on large corporations as well as the mantra of 'Shared Prosperity' demonstrate that *economic interests serve political interests.*[102]

In addition, investors question the 'role the Chinese Communist party may be playing behind the scenes' influencing PRC court decisions.[103] Questions surrounding a potential lack of judicial independence are enhanced by remarks of officials such as the 2017 instructions of Chief Justice and President of China's Supreme People's Court to PRC judges to '[b]are your swords towards false western ideals like judicial independence' and directing courts to be cognisant that the CCP cannot be separated from court decisions.[104] In contrast, US courts have a

100 Larry Backer, 'CPE Working Group on Empire: US-China Trade Talks, Encircling the United States, and the Belt and Road Initiative – Looking to a Critical Gloss on Xi Jinping's Speeches to the BRI Conference' (12 May 2019) <https://lcbackerblog.blogspot.com/2019/05/cpe-working-group-on-empire-us-china.html> (economic governance in China translates into a larger role for national objectives in the construction and management of economic markets.)

101 Li-Wen Lin and Curtis J Milhaupt, 'Bonded to the State: A Network Perspective on China's Corporate Debt Market' (2017) 3 Journal of Financial Regulation 1 (Party-state networking is the distinguishing feature of China's economy.)

102 Orange Wang and Su-Lin Tan, 'China's 'common prosperity' goal to evenly distribute wealth as Xi Jinping sets out stall for development' *South China Morning Post* (18 August 2021) <www.scmp.com/economy/china-economy/article/3145439/chinas-wealthy-urged-xi-jinping-give-back-society-ensure>: 'China must pursue a goal of so-called common prosperity where people share in the opportunity to be wealthy as the main objective for the next stage of its development, while stressing the need for an airtight economy which allows for that smoothing out of wealth.'); Mike O'Sullivan, 'Where Is Jack Ma? Alibaba And China Go Head To Head' *Forbes* (1 January 2021) <www.forbes.com/sites/mikeosullivan/2021/01/01/the-mystery-of-the-missing-billionairesalibaba-under-pressure/>: 'Beijing has a complicated relationship with the private enterprises that it has nurtured with limited foreign competition and red tape, and often regards high-profile entrepreneurs who might present a challenge to its hold on society with suspicion'.

103 Edward White, 'Foreign investors face critical legal test for $82bn in China bonds' *The Financial Times* (8 April 2021) <www.ft.com/content/8a30b7b8-864d-4478-a130-aeabd51863da>.

104 Lucy Hornby, 'China's top judge denounces judicial independence' *The Financial Times* (17 January 2017) <www.ft.com/content/60dddd46-dc74-11e6-9d7c-be108f1c1dce>. See also Shen Wei, *Conceptualizing the Regulatory Thicket: China's Financial Markets after the Global*

strong reputation for judicial independence as exemplified in the *Ralls* litigation wherein a US appeals court found in favour of a Chinese investor challenging an anti-Chinese CFIUS order.[105]

Of course, perceptions do not inherently translate into bad faith. Indeed, bad faith dishonouring of comfort letters or conduct to harm foreign investors may damage China's longer-term interests as it seeks to open up its capital markets, internationalise the Yuan and establish the framework for a Yuan-centric order. China's political leadership understands that courts must be perceived as fair for a nation to become a global capital markets leader. Indeed, the fundamental capitalist nature of China's governance was underscored by the fact that President Xi personally announced plans for the new Beijing stock exchange.[106]

Yet a scenario where debt denominated in Yuan and held mostly by domestic investors is repaid while foreign holders of offshore US Dollar bonds suffer losses is a potential outcome. China's governmental decisions are ensconced in a unique context since the economic serves the political. The CCP clearly envisions China as a major global power and financial centre, and the rule of law including judicial independence is crucial in achieving these goals. Ultimately however, opaque State interests *Über Alles* is the rule. Accordingly, arbitrators will need to incorporate an understanding of China's unique political-economic governance in applying good faith.

(2) Good faith and moral hazard

Furthermore, the implicit assurance of a State bailout raises the moral-hazard problem in state-centric governance. A presumption of governmental bail-outs adds a dimension of complexity if a state-linked entity is ostensibly backing the debt. However, increasing moral hazard and allowing bad debt to be pushed down the road risks future longer-term instability and crisis. Chinese Vice-Premier Liu He is purportedly against bailouts and is evidently considering allowing markets

---

Financial Crisis (Routledge 2020) ch 4 (lack of independence might also arise since judges rely on the government for appointment.)

105 See generally *Ralls Corp. v. Comm. on Foreign Inv. in U.S.*, 758 F.3d 296 (D.C. Cir. 2014) (D.C. Circuit rejects CFIUS recommendation based on due process concerns despite compelling national security argument). See also Gerry Shih, 'In China, many are impressed that, yes, you can sue the U.S. government', *The Washington Post* (8 March 2019) <www.washingtonpost.com/world/2019/03/08/china-many-are-impressed-that-yes-you-can-sue-us-government/>: 'The idea that a foreign company can take on the government in its own courts is all but moot in today's China . . . [Chinese] marveled that the legal case was being waged at all. As in: you can really sue the American government – in America?'; Jeanne Whalen, 'Federal court issues preliminary injunction halting administration's ban of Chinese app WeChat' *The Washington Post* (21 September 2020) <www.washingtonpost.com/technology/2020/09/20/wechat-ban-blocked-trump/> (Despite US-China hegemonic rivalry, US judicial independence demonstrated by granting of preliminary injunction stopping ban of Chinese app WeChat).

106 Laura He, 'China will create a stock exchange in Beijing' *CNN* (3 September 2021) <https://edition.cnn.com/2021/09/03/tech/china-beijing-stock-exchange-intl-hnk/index.html>.

to impose stricter discipline upon both investors and borrowers.[107] By allowing state-linked entities to fail, it could be argued that the 'bargain' between foreign investors and China is violated since until, relatively recently, investors could rely upon China helping out a struggling state-linked entity. From the perspective of the creditor, the refusal to comport with 'past practice' of ensuring the 'implicit guarantee' might demonstrate a lack of good faith. Yet from China's viewpoint, an argument could be made that to further its national development and avoid an even bigger financial problem, enforcement of comfort letters will serve to degrade China's long-term economic and security interests. In sum, good faith in the context of China's state-linked entities is manifestly complex.

V Conclusion

The current uber-leverage in capital markets and willingness of investors to ignore market risks will at some point lead to problems of debt defaults likely implicating comfort letters. Will investors succeed in seeking payment from letter issuers? The legal and financial questions are inextricably linked and bring to the forefront the inherent tension between sovereign discretion, accountability to citizens and the nation's obligations under international law. With respect to China, the political-economic landscape plays an outsized and perhaps opaque role. State interests trump economic considerations which might impact court rulings but developing capital markets is an important goal towards building a de-dollarised financial architecture. The balancing of rights between Chinese letter issuers and investors therefore implicates a dynamic mix of issues: protection of a sovereign; stability in markets; moral hazard; legal certainty in international economic relations; and of course good faith. Ultimately, the issue of comfort letters in the context of offshore Chinese debt will need to be confronted. The role of good faith may prove essential in ascertaining whether enforcement is justified. In both domestic and international contexts, evaluating comfort letters within the framework of *pacta sunt servanda* and good faith is not merely eminently sensible but in fact absolutely vital.

107 Tom Hancock, 'Huarong's Fate May Rest With Xi Confidant Who Loathes Bailouts' *Bloomberg Law* (6 May 2021) <https://news.bloomberglaw.com/capital-markets/huarongs-fate-may-rest-with-xi-confidant-who-loathes-bailouts>.

Part D

Conclusion

15 *Pacta sunt servanda* – a maxim and its exceptions in comparative perspective

Normann Witzleb

Times of great stress are times of truth. The coronavirus disease 19 (COVID-19) pandemic has revealed many truths. It has tested the ingenuity of medical science, the wisdom of our leaders, the capacity of national health systems, the resilience of economies, the cohesion of our communities, and the strength of families and individuals. The expectation on the legal system has been that it would enable robust and swift measures in the fight against the pandemic, yet protect the rights of more vulnerable members of society from abuse and neglect. Given the centrality of the state in the pandemic response, it was primarily public law that needed to be adapted quickly and responsibly. However, private law has also had a major role in managing the disruption the virus has caused to many economic relationships. The unforeseen consequences of the pandemic have thwarted in many cases commercial expectations and required the review of contractual commitments. Where parties could not agree on how the terms of their obligations should be adapted in face of significant hardship, the question arose of whether the binding force of contract could be unilaterally loosened.

On 25 June 2021, the Obligations Lab Asia of the Chinese University of Hong Kong (CUHK) organised an online conference on 'Pacta Sunt Servanda in changing times' to canvass how the tension between contractual certainty and flexibility should be addressed during and following COVID-19. *Pacta sunt servanda*, the principle that contractual commitments need to be honoured, is recognised as an axiom of contract law throughout the world. Yet, like other legal maxims, it is not absolute and allows for exceptions where justice and fairness so require. The conference brought together a diverse range of speakers, from academia and legal practice in Asia and beyond, to discuss the application and strength of the *pacta sunt servanda* principle in different legal fields and jurisdictions. In his opening remarks the Dean of the Law Faculty of CUHK, Lutz-Christian Wolff, explored how COVID-19, and earlier the Global Financial Crisis of 2008–9 have disrupted our lives and challenged the regular execution of contracts. The pandemic affected communities the world over, yet with significant regional variations. Countries with recent experience of large-scale outbreaks of unknown deadly virus, and those which through geographical isolation were better able to close their borders, tended to respond with anti-pandemic measures more swiftly and more rigorously. Countries with greater financial resources tended to employ these to cushion the

DOI: 10.4324/9781003358305-19

blow of anti-pandemic measures to the economy and individual livelihoods. Regional variations can also be discerned in the impact of COVID-19 on contract law, as the comparative examination of the significance of *pacta sunt servanda* in international and domestic laws during the CUHK conference revealed.

Selected papers of the conference are now presented in revised form in this book. Some additional papers have been commissioned to round out the collection.* The authors assembled for this project examine the status and versatility of the *pacta* principle under different perspectives. Each being written by an expert in their chosen field, the chapters examine a diverse range of contexts in which contracts are fundamental. The fields under consideration include rental agreements, cryptocurrency deals, non-compete agreements, consumer contracts, property management contracts and more. It is the purpose of this conclusory chapter to highlight themes that are emerging from the chapters collated in this book and to identify potential avenues for future research and development.

The book begins with Stephen Hall's chapter on 'Pacta sunt servanda, the common law and Hong Kong'. This chapter delves deeply into the history of the maxim, including its Roman origins in the Codex civile. Hall understands the maxim as expressing a 'general legal principle of "simple consensualism"' according to which legally valid agreements are binding without need of formalities, or performance by any of the parties. Hall traces the wording of the *pacta* maxim back to Samuel von Pufendorf's major treatise 'De jure naturae et gentium' (On the law of nature and nations) of 1672, where it appeared in a section heading. From this influential work, the maxim found its way into international law, where it has been widely accepted as fundamental for state relations. It now makes its most prominent modern appearance as the heading of article 26 of the Vienna Convention on the Law of Treaties. The reach of this foundational principle is further explored in another chapter by Hanh Hong Pham and Huong Thi Thu Phung, in which they explore when COVID-19 can be invoked to suspend or terminate the operation of a treaty, as further discussed below.

When considering the status of *pacta sunt servanda* in the legal tradition of the English-speaking world, Hall makes the important finding that

> the common law courts very seldom invoke the familiar *pacta* maxim, and when they do it is little more than a rhetorical flourish in support of the anodyne proposition that parties should be held to their agreements. There is certainly no analysis of the maxim's sources, justification, or implications as to formalities.

Of course, this is not to suggest that the common law does not expect that contractual promises should be performed, or that it fails to provide enforcement mechanisms in cases of non-performance. The reasons for the common law's reluctance to rely on the maxim is merely that contract laws in the English tradition generally insist on the formality of a deed or require proof of a bargain, as established through the provision of consideration. Looking further into the position in Hong

* I thank Prof. Lutz-Christian Wolff, Prof. sparse but establishes and Dr. Dini Sejko for their support during the editing process.

Kong, Hall explores the reach of the principle that obligations entered in good faith must be performed. His observation that, occasionally, also informal agreements are actionable, is established with reference to the decision of the Court of Final Appeal in *Luo Xing Juan Angela v Estate of Hui Shui See, Willy Deceased*,[1] which recognised the principle of promissory estoppel in the context of financial contributions made by one party to a cohabitating relationship to the mortgage of another. The court held that a promissory estoppel may arise where a party conveys a clear and unequivocal promise to the other that the promisor will not enforce or exercise some of their rights or powers arising from the parties' relationship; and where in reasonable reliance upon that promise, the promisee alters their position so that it would be inequitable or unconscionable for the promisor to act inconsistently with the promise.

While not explored in the Hall chapter, we can add that the binding force of agreements has also been maintained during the pandemic. In line with the law in other common law jurisdictions, Hong Kong law affords protections, albeit limited in nature, to contracting parties who have been severely affected by the coronavirus outbreak or containment measures. Force majeure clauses can provide relief where they are included in contract. However, the Court of Final Appeal has made clear in *Goldlion Properties Ltd v Regent National Enterprises Ltd*[2] that it will adopt a strict approach to their construction. Bokhary and Chan PJJ stated that:

> since contracts are made to be performed, clauses invoked to remove or modify obligations of performance ought at least in general to receive a strict construction. Such a construction means that any ambiguity would be resolved against the party seeking to rely on the clause. But that is not to say that such clauses, made within the freedom of contract, are to be viewed with hostility. It is not for the courts to encourage or discourage such clauses.[3]

After COVID-19 broke out in Hong Kong in January 2020, the Government's measures to prevent the spread of the virus included requirements for lengthy hotel quarantine upon arrival in Hong Kong applying to most travellers and measures to reduce social gathering, both of which severely affected the hospitality and the retail sectors. However, a force majeure clause that provided for rent abatement in the case of 'any calamity or causes beyond the control of the Lessor' was held by a Hong Kong court not to include COVID-19, as the pandemic and its countermeasures were not circumstances that rendered the premises 'unfit for commercial use or inaccessible', as provided for in the force majeure clause.[4]

If *force majeure* is unavailable, the common law doctrine of frustration may be relied upon where an unforeseen event so significantly changes a party's

1 [2008] HKCFA 48, (2009) 12 HKCFAR 1.
2 [2009] HKCFA 58, (2009) 12 HKCFAR 512.
3 ibid, 6.
4 *Holdwin Ltd v Prince Jewellery and Watch Co Ltd (Formerly Known as Success Light Investments Ltd)* [2021] HKCFI 2735.

contractual obligations that it would be unjust to hold it to their agreed bargain. Case law arising from the SARS epidemic in the early 2000s demonstrated that frustration has a narrow scope of application, even in times of a deadly epidemic.[5] In particular, the doctrine is not available where performance has become merely more onerous or expensive, or where the difficulty of performance is part of the contractual risk accepted by the party affected. More recent decisions arising from COVID-19 such as *The Center (76) Limited v Victory Serviced Office (HK) Limited* confirm this restrictive stance.[6] In this case, the Hong Kong Court of First Instance rejected a tenant's argument that its lease was frustrated due to the COVID-19 pandemic and the earlier disruption resulting from democracy protests. The Court held that the tenant had failed to establish that the difficulties of operating the business under these unforeseen conditions 'fundamentally or radically changed the nature of the parties' obligations' so as to render contractual performance 'physically or commercially impossible'.[7]

While a mere downturn in business, even if severe, may not be sufficient to invoke force majeure or frustration, different considerations may arise where government regulation require the lengthy shuttering of commercial venues. In the English case of *Bank of New York Mellon (International) Ltd v Cine-UK Ltd*,[8] mandatory closure via COVID regulations to limit the spread of the disease made it impossible for claimants to operate their respective businesses from March 2020 to April 2021. As COVID-19 and COVID Regulations required in that case the complete closure of the tenant's business or limited their operation to such extent that operating would not be commercially feasible, the Court considered whether these could be regarded as a 'supervening event'. The relevant question is whether 'the situation has become so radically different that the present situation is outside what was the reasonable contemplation of the parties so as it to render it unjust for the contract to continue?'[9] In light of the original term of each lease, the predicted period of the disruption and the remaining duration of the leases post-disruption, the situation was held in the specific case not to be so outside of the reasonable contemplation of the parties as to render it unjust for the contract to continue. In a detailed and carefully reasoned summary judgment, the court also rejected the tenants' submission that the lease was frustrated during the periods of lockdown so that temporarily no rent was payable. The court affirmed that the law does not recognise a concept of 'temporary frustration' because frustration ends a contract, rather than suspend it for some time.

5 *Li Ching Wing v. Xuan Yi Xiong* [2004] 1 HKLRD 754.

6 [2020] HKCFI 2881.

7 Other cases in which commercial tenants affected by COVID-19 downturns of business remained unsuccessful in invoking the frustration doctrine include: *Vember Lord Ltd v The Swatch Group (Hong Kong) Ltd* [2022] HKCFI 279; *Holdwin Limited v Prince Jewellery and Watch Company Limited* [2021] HKCFI 2735 at §§33–35; and *Sunbroad Holdings Limited v A80 Paris HK Limited* [2022] HKCFI 142251.

8 [2021] EWHC 1013.

9 ibid, 209.

Frustration as a ground that ends contractual obligations is also discussed in detail in Wayne Courtney's chapter on the law of Singapore. Singapore has adopted the English 'radical change in obligation' test, which was identified in *Davis Contractors Ltd v Fareham Urban District Council*[10] and continues to be the starting point for a frustration analysis. In *Alliance Concrete Singapore Pte Ltd v Sato Kogyo (S) Pte Ltd*, the Singapore Court of Appeal affirmed the requirement of 'a *supervening event* that has occurred *after* the formation of the contract [and] renders a contractual obligation *radically or fundamentally different* from what has been agreed in the contract'.[11] As Courtney points out, a pandemic as such tends not to be a sufficient ground for arguing frustration. It always depends on how the pandemic affects the performance of the contract in question. Given the dearth of relevant decisions from courts in Singapore and England, Courtney also includes US case law in his analysis, which however proved likewise inconclusive. Mostly, these authorities related to the Spanish flu of over a century ago and adopted approaches that are 'hard to square with the current Anglo-Singaporean understanding of the law of contract'.

Of the emerging case law on COVID-19, the *Dathena Science Pte Ltd v Justco (Singapore) Pte Ltd*[12] stands out as the first Singaporean higher court decision that deals with frustration during the pandemic. The case concerned a plaintiff who rented from the defendant commercial premises for a data centre, making clear to the defendant that it needed to move its existing operations by the agreed date because the lease on its existing premises would come to an end. As it turned out, the defendant was unable to fit out the premises by the specified date, because Singapore's 'circuit breaker' measures led to labour shortages and slowed down the works. Negotiations between the parties to defer the start of the lease or to switch to different premises owned by the defendant remained unsuccessful. The court concluded that the lease was frustrated but, in a detailed critical assessment, Courtney takes issues with much of the legal analysis proffered in the decision.

The chapter also considers the various legislative measures enacted in Singapore to manage the impact of COVID-19 on commercial dealings. The COVID-19 (Temporary Measures) Act 2020, and accompanying regulations, provided temporary relief for inability to perform specified types of contract; introduced rental relief and rental waivers for small-to-medium enterprises and not-for-profit organisations; created a mechanism to amend the terms of contracts affected by delays in the performance or breaches of construction contracts or supply contracts; and rights to seek the renegotiation of specified lease, hire or license agreement, or supply contracts gravely affected by the pandemic. Courtney has a positive view of these legislative measures, despite their potentially far-reaching effect on existing contracts, because they proved to be effective, targeted and time-limited and,

10 [1956] AC 696.

11 *Alliance Concrete Singapore Pte Ltd v Sato Kogyo (S) Pte Ltd* [2014] SGCA 35, [2014] 3 SLR 857, [33] (italics in original).

12 [2021] SGHC 219.

most importantly, they provided incentives to parties to renegotiate the terms of their contract in light of the urgency and demands of the pandemic situation.

Another jurisdiction which relied on legislation to address the effect of the pandemic was Macau, a Chinese region located opposite Hong Kong on the Pearl River Delta. In their chapter 'In a Bubble by the Sea: COVID-19, Time and Contract Law in the Macau S.A.R.', Célia F. Matias and Monica Chan describe Macau's way through the pandemic and how it affected contractual agreements. Adopting a policy of isolation from other parts of the world, Macau was successful in avoiding large outbreaks within its borders. However, this strategy caused considerable strain on residents and businesses in an economy that is heavily dependent on gambling, tourism and associated services. The chapter begins with a valuable overview of Macau contract law, which is now contained in the Macau Civil Code of 1999 and follows the Portuguese tradition. Matias and Chan detail the circumstances in which the basic principle of *pacta sunt servanda*, which pervades the Code, has been softened to increase fairness between the parties.

Of primary importance in that respect is the modification or termination of the contract due to change of circumstances, as set out in articles 431–433 of the Civil Code. There is consensus that modification is only available in a narrow set or circumstances. Case law on these provisions is sparse but establishes the need for abnormal circumstances that lead to drastic changes of the contractual bargain and are outside the normal risks of the commercial activity accepted by the party affected. The authors' research has found no visible increase in litigation based on a change of circumstances, despite the difficulties experienced by many operators. Another potential avenue to absolve a party from its contractual obligations are force majeure clauses, but these are relevant for COVID-19 only where they are contained in contractual agreements and cover pandemic risks.

In a hypothetical case study on Macau's rental market, the authors investigate how these adaptation mechanisms operate in the context of long-term commercial tenancies that are affected by the unpredictable downturn of business and tourism. The authors confirm that the principles of good faith and a desire to protect contractual balance create some legal avenues for relief in case of abnormal changes of circumstances but Matias and Chan also observe that these mechanisms are interpreted strictly. As the law provides only some limited coping mechanisms, it is unsurprising that the authors observe that COVID-19-related legal disputes are yet to reach the courts in significant numbers. The authors surmise that 'informal adjustments of contractual commitments, together with governmental measures aimed at supporting the local economy' have taken the heat out of many conflicts. Government measures have included fiscal stimuli for local consumption as well as tax waivers and deductions, waiver of business licence fees and short-term rent reductions for government-owned properties, which have provided some important relief for the local economy. The authors conclude that the combination of legal avenues of redress, governmental support and party-negotiated relief managed to address the worst effects of the pandemic. Yet, they raise the important point that all these mechanisms can operate only temporarily, and come under increasing stress as pandemic restrictions are extended and the opening up of the economy in Macau remains an uncertain prospect.

The present collection also assembles some important contribution on the significance of the *pacta sunt servanda* principle in the new Chinese Civil Code, which has been in force since 2020 and replaced a number of older private law enactments. The ground for the discussion of more specific issues is prepared by Lin Siyi's chapter. It considers 'Exceptions to *pacta sunt servanda* in the Chinese Civil Code', focusing on *force majeure* and the doctrine of changed circumstances. After a historical overview, the chapter carefully examines the current understanding of the *force majeure* and changed circumstances doctrines, and the complex and uncertain interrelationship between these two doctrines. Lin explains that both doctrines can provide assistance when unforeseen events occur after contract formation, but that the *force majeure* doctrine has a longer history than that of changed circumstances in Chinese contract law.

Both doctrines have now been codified in the Chinese Civil Code. In article 180, *force majeure* is defined as 'unforeseeable, inevitable and insurmountable objective circumstances' and provides an excuse for non-performance. In contrast, a change of material circumstances gives a right to seek negotiation or, failing that, rescission of the contract. Pursuant to article 533, it requires a

> material change in the basic conditions of a contract . . . which is unforeseeable by the parties at the time of contracting and falls outside the realm of commercial risk, rendering the continuation of the performance of the contract obviously unfair for either party.

While these two doctrines are now overlapping,[13] it is important to note that *force majeure* is based on impossibility, whereas the changed circumstances doctrine requires only unfairness as a result of continuous obligations to perform. In Guiding Opinions, the Supreme People's Court issued guidance on how these two doctrines should be applied by courts when disputes arise around the performance of a contract that is affected the pandemic or the strict preventive measures that the Chinese Government has put in place to minimise the spread of SARS-Co-V-2.

Guiding Opinions I provides that, where the pandemic or counter measures lead to impossibility, the contract is affected by *force majeure* and the parties shall be exempted from liability, either wholly or partly depending on the impact of pandemic or preventive measures. Where these circumstances make the continuous performance obviously unfair to one party, the court shall upon request by a party consider modifications to the performance period, performance method or price, as best suits the actual circumstances of the case. Following the same general approach, *Guiding Opinions II* determines that the recission of contracts affected by the pandemic or pandemic preventive measures shall only be supported where

13 Under the law prior to the enactment of the Civil Code, *force majeure* events were excluded from events causing changed circumstances.

continuous performance can no longer realise the purpose of the contract, but not where there is only an increase in the cost of performance or a delay in performance. Both *Guiding Opinions* instruct courts to adopt a conservative approach to the application of *force majeure* and changed circumstances doctrines in cases involving the COVID-19 pandemic. These two judicial interpretations specify factors to be considered when deciding the possibility to perform contracts, the modification of contract terms and exemption of liabilities in different types of contracts.[14] Given the potential impact of the pandemic on many contractual arrangements, Lin's chapter concludes that contractual disputes arising out of the COVID-19 pandemic offer a 'litmus test for the viability of *force majeure* and changed circumstances doctrines in the *PRC Civil Code* and SPC's judicial interpretations'. While the *PRC Civil Code* brought some more clarity to the complex relationship between both doctrines, there remain many unresolved issues that Lin calls on the legislature to provide further guidance on.

Chao Xi's chapter on '*Pacta Sunt Servanda* in the Age of Cryptocurrency: The Case of China' considers the binding force of contracts from a very different perspective. His chapter focuses on illegality, which he regards as a limit to *pacta sunt servanda* because the PRC Civil Code provides that a contract that is illegal or contrary to public policy is null and void. Xi examines how the legal ambiguity resulting from China's shifting regulatory positions on cryptocurrencies have challenged the Chinese courts in their approaches to the validity and enforceability of crypto investments and transactions. The chapter traverses the development of China's approach to cryptocurrencies, which developed from initially 'broadly tolerative' to an effective ban crypto asset exchanges and platforms from 2017 onwards and to an outright 'war against cryptocurrencies' in 2021. The 2021 joint regulatory notice has removed any remaining ambiguity over the legality of crypto asset activities by declaring all crypto asset businesses and services, including crypto mining, to be unlawful.

Xi's analysis focuses on the interim period between 2017 and 2021, where the legal status of cryptocurrencies and related business activities had to be determined by reference to a 2017 Circular, which declared that cryptocurrencies did 'not enjoy the same legal status as fiat currencies' and 'should not and cannot be used or circulated in the markets as currencies'.[15] The Circular maintained the existing prohibitions that barred PRC financial institutions and non-bank payment agencies from engaging in any crypto asset business. It also cracked down on crypto asset exchanges yet stopped short of declaring crypto asset transactions *per se* illegal. There is an emerging body of case law in which contract parties have invoked illegality as a limit to the *pacta sunt servanda* in cases involving cryptocurrency transactions during this period. Xi concludes from his case study that controversial new technologies can create legal ambiguity that thrusts the principle of *pacta sunt servanda* principle into a state of uncertainty. As his

14 See III. B. above.
15 2017 Circular, Provision 1(2).

careful analysis shows, contract law can come under strain when regulatory decisions, such as those regarding the legality of particular transactions, leave room for argument.

A further possible exception to *pacta sunt servanda* under the Chinese Civil Code is discussed by Jianbo Lou and Yimeng Ye. In their comparative study, Lou and Ye examine the extent to which the property management service (PMS) contract on the Chinese mainland has only 'soft' binding force. The authors support their view of the exceptional nature of the PMS contract with a number of its specific characteristics, including (1) the long-term and trust-based nature of PMS contracts; (2) the 'one-to-many' relationship between PMS companies and owners, and weak homeowners' associations; (3) PMS companies' limited ability to pursue PMS fee arrears; and (4) the comprehensive and quasi-public-product nature of PMS. These characteristics of the PMS contract under the Chinese Civil Code are at best partially replicated in similar service agreements in Hong Kong, Taiwan, the UK and the US. The authors conclude that *pacta sunt servanda* is important under the Chinese Civil Code, as it is in other jurisdictions, because it provides stability, certainty and predictability. However, the PMS is presented as an example of an agreement in which countervailing social factors are given greater prominence. These factors, which include maintaining social stability, in particular protecting the rights and interests of homeowners, have prompted the legislator, as well as the courts, to adopt 'a more nuanced conception of flexibility'. As the principle of *pacta sunt servanda* is never absolute, and calls for exceptions where appropriate, the authors argue that the soft binding force PMS contracts remains compatible with the rule of law.

As Tomohiro Yoshimasa underlines in his chapter 'The principle of *pacta sunt servanda* and its exceptions under Japanese contract law', the binding force of contracts is also a basic tenet of the Japanese Civil Code. After explaining how binding contracts are entered into under the reformed Civil Code and what remedies are available for breach of contract in Japanese law, the chapter explores the circumstances in which contracting parties are able to invalidate a contract at their own will and when a party's non-performance is excused under Japanese contract law. It also examines when and how the pandemic of COVID-19 may affect the obligations of the parties. While it lies in the Japanese legal consciousness to avoid litigation, Yoshimasa is sceptical about arguments that the *pacta sunt servanda* principle has less significance in Japanese society.

In relation to liability for non-performance, the revised article 415(1) of the Japanese Civil Code provides that non-performance does not trigger an obligation to pay damages if it is due to 'grounds not attributable to the obligor in light of the contract or other sources of obligation and the common sense in the transaction'. Yoshimasa criticises this provision as an 'unsophisticated compromise' between the previous law, which provided for liability where non-performance was due to 'grounds attributable to the obligor', and an emerging school of thought that prefers to direct the focus on a 'breach of an obligation arising from the contract' rather than fault more generally.

Following the outbreak of COVID-19, the issue has arisen of when non-performance caused by the pandemic may be excused under article 415 of the Japanese Civil Code. Yoshimasa explains that the 'answer to the question depends upon the content of the contract and the direct cause of the non-performance'. Important criteria are the contractual risk allocation and whether the pandemic made performance merely more difficult, or impossible. Mere added difficulty in sourcing, or increased cost of, raw materials is unlikely to be grounds to relieve a seller, because the seller will commonly have assumed such risks – whereas non-performance in pursuit of recommended or mandatory public health measures will generally be excused. While Japanese legislation does not adopt the concept of *force majeure*, such clauses are, just as in many other jurisdictions, often contained in standard form contracts. Yoshimasa makes the interesting observation that an exemption from liability for non-performance under *force majeure* clauses should be regarded as 'not an exception to the principle of *pacta sunt servanda*, but a consequence thereof'. Where COVID-19 is an instance of *force majeure* in the circumstances of the case, it becomes necessary to determine by way of contractual interpretation whether the *force majeure* affects the contractual obligation, as defined in article 415.

The doctrine of change of circumstances is also accepted by Japanese courts and academia, however, it is rarely held to apply. Yoshimasa explains the absence of reported decisions on change of circumstances following COVID-19 with the reluctance of Japanese courts to allow exceptions to the principle of *pacta sunt servanda*. Unlike some other jurisdictions, Japan has not legislated for any dedicated rent relief measures as part of pandemic response packages. Statutory mechanisms for adaptation apply for long-term leases under special legislation; applicable to all leases, article 611 of the Code also contains a right to rent reduction if a rental object is wholly or partially unable to be used. This provision has been suggested to support claims for rent reduction where premises in a large commercial facility were closed upon the official request or order under public health legislation. In other cases, where a loss of custom or profits was merely the result of changes to customer behaviour, rent reductions are only available through negotiations with the landlord.

Many of the observations made by Yoshimasa are mirrored in Boeun Chang's chapter on 'Change of circumstances in Korean contract law: An exception to *pacta sunt servanda*'. Korean law likewise considers the binding force of contract as a fundamental principle from which exceptions should be made only in a very narrow set of situations. With a tighter focus on the principle of change of circumstances, this chapter explores the importance of the parties' intention. Where the parties allocated the risk of an unforeseen event, the contract must be fulfilled even if there has been some material change that makes performance more onerous. While the Korean Supreme Court has expressly recognised for some time that the doctrine of change of circumstances is a potential exception to contractual obligations that are dramatically affected by subsequent events, the courts have erected high hurdles to the modification or rescission of a contract on that basis. The case law has identified as the relevant threshold that there must be a 'significant change in circumstances that a party to the contract could not have foreseen at the time of contract formation and when such change in circumstances occurs due to a reason for which the party with the right to rescind is not responsible'. In the absence of statutory recognition of the doctrine, which has been unsuccessfully attempted on two occasions, its application is doctrinally anchored in the principle of good faith. The uncertainty regarding the scope of this exception has in recent years been reduced because there are now a small number of decisions in which the doctrine has not only been recognised as available but actually been applied in favour of debtors. However, there is as yet no case law regarding COVID-19, which makes the analysis in the chapter, including some worked hypothetical examples in which contracts are affected by the pandemic and countermeasures, all the more valuable.

Against this background of emerging jurisprudence and its likely application in the context of COVID-19, Chang identifies issues that require further consideration and makes proposals for their resolution. One area of uncertainty concerns the relationship of changed circumstances with impossibility. It is clear that reliance on a change of circumstances is excluded, where performance becomes impossible – however, it may be unclear when performance becomes impossible, especially in situations of economic hardship or temporary impossibility. Another question is the relationship between termination and modification of contracts affected by a material change of circumstances. In line with other chapters in this collection, Chang identifies the potential role of the change of circumstances doctrine in responding to the disruption caused by the pandemic, but also calls for greater guidance and refinements by the courts.

In common with the codes of Japan and Korea, the principle of *pacta sunt servanda* is not explicitly mentioned in the Taiwanese Civil Code. Nonetheless, it pervades Taiwanese contract law and is firmly established by jurisprudence of the Taiwan Supreme Court. In her chapter 'Post-employment non-compete agreements under the Taiwan Labour Standards Act and *pacta sunt servanda*', Yalun Yen examines the Taiwanese law on non-compete agreements in labour contracts. Under such agreements, employees and company officers are prevented to work or seek employment in similar businesses during, or for a certain period after, their current employment or mandate. These agreements often protect legitimate business interests, such as trade secrets or competitive advantage, yet they curtail the freedom of employees or officers to seek new positions and make gainful use of their abilities. In its jurisprudence, the Taiwan Supreme Court moved over time from a largely permissive attitude to a position where it required a valid non-compete agreement to be reasonable. In using reasonableness as a touchstone, it adopted criteria developed by lower courts and relied upon Taiwan Civil Code article 247-1, which prohibits the use of unfair standard terms.

A watershed moment in this field of law was the enactment in 2015 of Taiwan Labour Standards Act (TLSA) article 9-1, which stipulates a set of specific criteria for assessing the validity of non-compete agreements. These criteria built on, and clarified, the earlier jurisprudence but their mandatory character, and associated Enforcement Rules, have reduced the discretion of Taiwan's courts significantly.

Yen provides detailed analysis of the judicial review process under TLSA article 9-1. She identifies some difficulties with the courts' approaches towards identifying a business's legitimate interests and the provision of reasonable compensation as preconditions of valid non-compete agreements. Her chapter concludes that an overly stringent content control may unnecessarily weaken the *pacta sunt servanda* rule and submits that reading down unreasonable agreements, rather than declaring them entirely invalid, may be preferable in light of the legitimate function of non-compete agreements.

In the chapter 'Contract enforcement during the Global Financial Crisis: Lessons for the coming Tsunami', financial restructuring lawyer Kingsley Ong draws on his experience of previous financial crises and shares his insights for contract enforcement during a severe financial crisis. His lessons are:

1. Financial contracts are complicated, mistakes can be very costly
2. Be prepared for radical changes that impact contract enforcement during a financial crisis
3. Get the basics right
4. Attention to detail is critical
5. 'Market practice' or 'market standard' does not necessarily reflect the law
6. Don't assume 'similar' contracts will achieve identical end results
7. Practical considerations

Each of these lessons is supported with learning from concrete examples and demonstrates that the strength of contractual entitlements is not only determined by substantive law, but also by practical considerations relating to performance and enforcement. Contract lawyers in practice need to be mindful of the particular challenges that arise for their clients in times of crisis, remain alert and responsive at all times, and be prepared for the unexpected.

Geraint Howells' chapter on '*Pacta sunt servanda* and the consumer's right of withdrawal' explores the extent to which rights of withdrawal, as they are commonplace in European consumer laws, challenge the principle of *pacta sunt servanda*. Howells argues that while such rights indeed undermine the binding power of contracts this is justified on consumer policy grounds. This argument echoes Lou and Ye's finding on the 'soft' binding force of PMS in mainland China, because in both contexts, it is the protection of the weaker party that allows them to withdraw from a contractual arrangement at will, provided the statutory conditions are met. Howells recommends that Asian jurisdictions consider adopting rights of withdrawal more extensively than in the past. While empirical data on the use, and potential abuse, of such rights remains scant, the European experience suggests that they can play a useful role in protecting vulnerable consumers and promoting engagement with unknown products, suppliers or markets. Howells suggests that rights of withdrawal are particularly suitable in relation to e-commerce, a distribution channel that is highly developed in many Asian jurisdictions. Their adoption in sectors such as these may therefore be good a testing ground before they are rolled out in other contexts. Howells acknowledges the concern that consumers may not all want, or need, such rights and that their mandatory imposition may therefore be problematic. However, the complexities that would arise if consumer law was 'personalised', and the fact that many consumers have difficulty of protecting their interests effectively, suggest that mandatory laws reflect 'a consensus on what the best rules are for society in general'. Another concern relating to withdrawal rights is that they encourage consumption and lead to waste, such as when consumers order goods without much thinking and then return them at significant cost to suppliers and the environment. Howells, however, regards these concerns, while real, as a largely unavoidable quid-pro-quo for enhancing consumer welfare.

The last three chapters of the collection examine the operation of the principle of *pacta sunt servanda* in the field of public international law, rather than domestic contract law. As Hall pointed out in the opening chapter, international law is the area of the law in which the maxim, and its specific Latin expression, originated. Indeed, Article 26 of the 1969 Vienna Convention on the Law of Treaties is entitled *pacta sunt servanda* and provides that '[e]very treaty in force is binding upon the parties to it and must be performed by them in good faith.'[16] In their chapter 'Invoking COVID-19 to suspend or terminate the operation of a treaty', Hanh Hong Pham and Huong Thi Thu Phung examine the doctrine of fundamental change of circumstances at international law. Recognised in article 62 of the Vienna Convention, it creates – as it does in domestic law – a recognised exception to *pacta sunt servanda*. The particular concern of that chapter is the possibility of invoking COVID-19 as a fundamental change of the situation. The authors conclude that the operation of the doctrine is tightly circumscribed and limited to situations in which COVID-19 has the effect of radically transforming the extent of obligations to be performed under a treaty as compared to the burden of implementation that the parties initially envisaged. Notwithstanding this demanding test, the chapter argues that countries may in suitable cases rely on the effect of COVID-19 and of adopted public health measures as a basis for temporarily suspending the operation of a treaty without violating the *pacta sunt servanda* principle. The authors demonstrate this with the example of travel restrictions and border closures, which were widely imposed during the height of the pandemic to reduce the spread of virus over national boundaries. Pham and Phung argue that the effectiveness of anti-pandemic measures would have been seriously undermined if countries had been bound by international commitments relating to the free movement of non-nationals and had had no way to suspend these obligations temporarily to slow the spread of the pandemic.

In the chapter 'Treaties and *pacta sunt servanda*: A shared concept for the PRC?', Noble Po-kan Lo examines how the People's Republic of China (PRC) conforms with the principle of *pacta sunt servanda* in public international law. Lo highlights the cogent character of this principle as a peremptory and foundational

16 The preambular paragraph 3 of the VCLT also notes that *pacta sunt servanda* rule is universally recognised. See also preamble to the United Nations Charter.

norm of international law. Although the PRC generally adheres to its international obligations, there are some areas in which China's attitude to treaty obligations differs significantly from the way in which other states, particularly in the West, conceive of the rule. Lo's argument is that an unorthodox approach to *pacta sunt servanda* becomes evident in the PRC's response to 'unequal' historical treaties. The PRC considers certain treaties that were entered into by legal predecessors of the Communist government and European colonial powers as not binding under international law. China adopts the position that some of these treaties are 'unequal' because they were imposed on China during a period of weakness in the 19th and 20th century. Yet, the chapter does point out that not all of China's territorial disputes can be explained with reference to its revisionist approach to unequal treaties. As disputes arising from its claims in the South China Sea illustrate, the PRC is using its resurging strength in ways that cause conflict with its neighbours as well as with orthodox understandings of the *pacta sunt servanda* principle.

In the final chapter, Joel Slawotsky assesses the geopolitical implications of the involvement of state-owned enterprises in international contracts. Just as Ong in his earlier chapter, Slawotsky is concerned about the fall-out of another debt crisis, given that multiple serious economic risks are currently converging post-COVID-19. The chapter '*Pacta sunt servanda*: Comfort letters in an age of instability and strategic rivalry' examines the legal issues arising from the practice of Chinese state-owned entities to provide assurance to foreign lenders that have provided capital to Chinese corporate debtors. Given the ostensible non-binding nature of comfort letters, the enforcement of such commitments is difficult although promissory estoppel could be a suitable pathway to some creditors. Promissory estoppel, as was also referred to in Hall's chapter, can provide a basis for holding a party to one's promise even in the absence of a formal agreement, where the other party in reliance on a promise altered their position in good faith. However, the status of that doctrine in Chinese law is at best uncertain.

If domestic Chinese courts were to reject the claims of foreign investors against Chinese state-owned enterprises, investors may also seek protection through international arbitration. This, in turn, raises the possibility of China using the essential security exception in international investment treaties to protect its interests. Slawotsky's chapter explores the potential of relying on this defence in the context of sovereign corporate debt. It is as yet untested in the context of comfort letters whether a serious economic crisis or other national emergency might be claimed by a sovereign as an essential interest that could serve to override obligations under an investment agreement and reject the payment of investors' claims. Slawotsky suggests that transformative changes arising from advances in technology, global health crises and the developing hegemonic struggles may prepare the ground for expanding the notion of essential security to encompass a nation's economic, health and social stability. Yet, such a re-conceptualisation of the security exception would be likely to undermine *pacta sunt servanda* in global financial markets. The chapter concludes that the protection the 'good faith' expectations of contracting parties is likely to be an overriding concern in the resolution of these complex, and high stake, matters.

Taken together, this collection provides a rich array of materials demonstrating the continued vitality and strength of the principle of *pacta sunt servanda*. The basic notion that agreements are binding, and that they must be obeyed and respected, enjoys universal appeal. If legal commitments that have been voluntarily incurred could be renounced or abandoned at will, promises would be devalued and lose their meaning. Yet, it is also clear that there can be circumstances where insistence on performance and execution of an agreement can cause hardship and unfairness. This applies most clearly when circumstances change after contract formation to such an extent that the parties' expected contractual bargain has become illusory and insistence on performance would be incompatible with good faith. The doctrine of change of circumstances, which enjoys widespread support in domestic and international laws, has an important role to play, yet it cannot be relied upon too readily, or else contractual risk allocations are undermined.

One recurring theme of the chapters in this collection has been that the limits of the *pacta sunt servanda* principle are not immutable. These limits should be determined by taking into account the circumstances not only as they exist between the parties, but also in light of changing community expectations. The untold hardship created by the COVID-19 pandemic has raised new challenges for the notion of the binding force of contracts. So far courts in the jurisdictions under consideration have resisted the temptation of softening the requirements to alleviate the burden on affected parties, leaving it mainly to self-directed party negotiations and state support to address some of the arising imbalances and disparities. Yet a number of authors have suggested that, as more litigation makes its way through the court systems, further judicial guidance may arise. It would be a fruitful field for further research to scrutinise these future developments in the case law, and to contrast and evaluate the approaches in cross-jurisdictional work. With its diverse perspectives, the present collection provides an important springboard for such further analysis.

Index

Note: Page numbers in **bold** indicate tables.